D1141490

THE VISUAL ENCYCLOPEDIA OF

THE VISUAL ENCYCLOPEDIA OF
SERIAL
KILLERS

NIGEL BLUNDELL & SUSAN BLACKHALL

GREENWICH
EDITIONS

Published by Greenwich Editions
The Chrysalis Building
Bramley Road, London W10 6SP
An imprint of Chrysalis Books Group

This edition produced 2004 by
PRC Publishing Limited
The Chrysalis Building
Bramley Road, London W10 6SP
An imprint of Chrysalis Books Group

© 2004 PRC Publishing Limited

All rights reserved. No part of this publication may
be reproduced, stored in a retrieval system, or transmitted
in any form or by any means, electronic, mechanical,
photocopying, recording, or otherwise, without the prior
written permission of the Publisher and copyright holders.

ISBN 0 86288 661 9

Printed and bound in China

Photographic Acknowledgements

The publisher wishes to thank the organizations listed below
for their kind permission to reproduce the photographs in this
book. Every effort has been made to acknowledge the pictures,
however we apologize if there are any unintentional omissions.

B = bottom; L= left; R = right; T = top.

Associated Press/54, 62, 65, 87, 108, 116, 355, 356, 371,
373.

British Library Collection/119, 120, 123, 124, 125, 126, 127,
202, 252, 316, 335, 336, 338, 339, 409, 412.

Corbis/Annie Griffiths Belt 111./Bettmann 35, 36, 37, 39TL,
39TR, 40, 43, 53, 67, 73, 78, 154, 159, 161, 162, 163, 164,
165L, 165R, 171, 173, 179, 181, 182, 183, 185, 187, 239,
241, 242, 246, 251, 254, 269, 270, 279, 289, 291, 292, 293,
294, 314, 319, 359, 361, 390, 391, 392, 427, 428, 429./Carl
& Ann Purcell 276, 277./El Tiempo/Sygma 175, 176./E.O.
Hoppe 84./Hulton-Deutsch Collection 351./M.
McLoughlin/N.Y Post/Sygma 405./Matthew Mcvay 364, 366,
369./Michael Boys 220./Shepard Sherbell/Saba
273./Viennareport Agency/Sygma 415.

**Courtesy of the Boston Public Library, Print
Department**/148, 149, 150, 353.

Getty Images/Hulton 253, 255, 343, 345, 346, 348, 395.

**Historical Society of Pennsylvania/The Philadelphia
Record Morgue**/59, 60.

Katz/167, 263, 265, 283.

Mary Evans Picture Library/337.

Mirrorpix/199, 200, 204, 206, 211, 212, 233, 234, 236, 297,
298, 299, 300, 301, 303, 325, 378, 384, 386, 387, 388, 400.

Newspix/48.

Author's Private Collection/24, 26-27, 28, 29, 30T, 30B,
32, 33, 69, 70, 74, 75, 76-77, 79, 81, 83, 90, 92, 95, 97,
107, 135, 136, 137, 138, 146, 168, 198, 201, 207, 209T,
209B, 214, 223, 224, 227R, 259, 260, 264, 281, 282, 286,
288, 296, 317, 321, 323, 324, 330, 375, 397, 398, 399, 402,
403, 417L, 417R, 418, 420, 421, 423, 437, 438, 439, 440,
442, 443.

PA Photos/45.

Courtesy The National Archives/98, 99, 100-101, 102T,
102B, 103, 129, 131, 132TL, 132TR, 132B, 133, 225, 226,
227L, 228, 229, 230.

Reuters/20, 307, 310, 312, 425./Allen Fredrickson 141, 142,
144./Anthony Bolante 363./Fred Prouser 18./Gleb Garanich
332./HO 368, 377, 380, 381, 382./Joe Skipper 435, 436. /
Mohsin Raza 216./Pool 365.

Rex Features/Action Press (ACT) 192, 194-195,
196./Austral Int. (AUS) 309, 313./David Benett 326./David
Muscroft 401./Edwin Walter 14./MGG 433. / Nils Jorgensen
(NJ) 327, 328./NWI 221./Photonews Service Ltd (PNS)
218./PNS 156./PPH 17./Sipa Press (SIPA) 96, 360,
441./South West News Service (SWS) 419.

The Sumter Item/178

Topham Picturepoint/The British Library/411.

CONTENTS

From top: Ted Bundy; pages 68-79
John Christie; pages 97-103
Dennis Nilsen; pages 322-331
Graham Young; pages 437-440

INTRODUCTION

Murder most foul, as in the best it is;

But this most foul, strange and unnatural

—*Hamlet*

Whether we like to acknowledge it or not, murder is a subject that fascinates us all. The frailty of life and the finality of death are as enduring themes throughout history as the notion of good and evil. And when evil and death are conjoined, we have murder.

The ease, simplicity, and swiftness with which the breath of life can be snatched away is probably why the crime of murder consumes us most. Chillingly, no one finds the subject more fascinating than the murderers themselves—especially when they become as addicted to the thrill as an addict to the hardest drug.

From this addiction evolves a unique breed of cunning killer. It is what makes, not just a murderer, but a serial killer. A single slaying, even a bloody, brutal slaughter, can never sufficiently satisfy. He (or sometimes she) must strike again and again. It is a compulsion and it leads to deeds so vile that they are almost beyond the bounds of comprehension and invariably beyond the power of forgiveness.

So what is a serial killer? And what makes him or her? An answer to the first question was attempted by the Federal Bureau of Investigations and, although it is far from a conclusive description, it is not wide of the mark. The FBI defines a serial killer as someone who has murdered a min-imum of three to four people over a period of time. A series of killings that happen at the same time or within hours of each other creates a "mass murderer" or a "spree killer," whereas a serial killer strikes in sequence, with a cooling off period between killings. Quite simply, one act of murder is insufficient, and each that follows is performed with equal satisfaction.

The second question—what makes a serial killer?—is even more difficult to answer. Serial killers can be male or female, young or old, working singly, in pairs, or in a team. They can be from any walk of life. He or she could be your next-door neighbor. They can be of any nationality or ethnic background. Although, strangely, there are "hot spots" of serial killing, including places and times which we would prefer to think of as being the most advanced—the United States and the present day, for example.

The FBI's Behavior Science Unit created a profile of the "typical" serial killer to help them and other agencies identify the potential multiple murderer. He turned out to be a caucasian male between the ages of 18 and 32 who suffered abuse as a child. In return, he probably abused animals and, for some reason, had a history of arson. He tended to be a loner—another reason why he is often so difficult to detect.

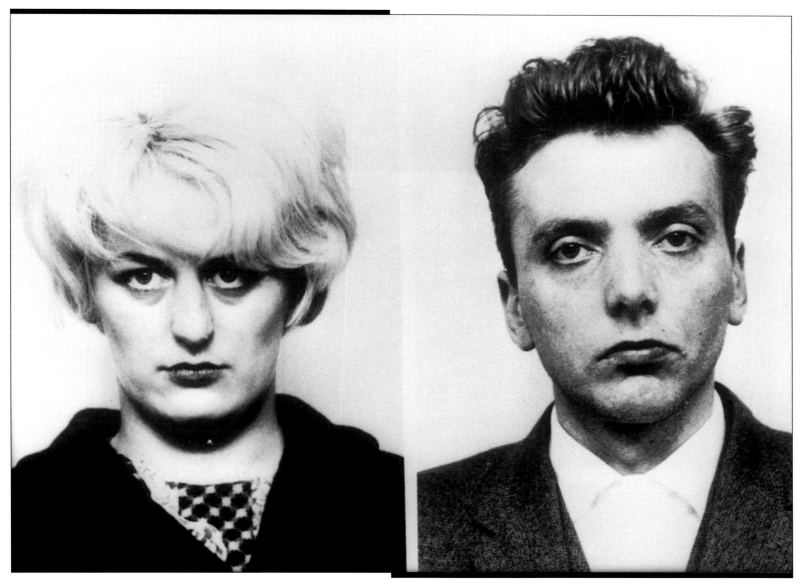

Myra Hindley and Ian Brady, also known as the Moors Murderers, were convicted of murdering children in 1966. Their crimes have never been forgotten.

In this category are murderers like Jack the Ripper of Victorian England, who could never have known that he would one day be classified in the chronicles of crime as a "serial killer," a phrase unheard of at the time. Nor Hermann Mudgett, creator of Chicago's "Torture Castle" of the 1890s, who is often recorded as the first serial killer to be brought to justice in America.

These two raise another question: when did serial killing begin? That too is difficult to answer because it is obvious that there have always been villains who murdered in sequence. A fourteenth-century Scottish brigand named Sawney Beane and his bloodthirsty family claimed anything up to 1,000 victims before being hacked to death in front of an Edinburgh mob. The so-called "Werewolf of Chalons" was a French monster who slaughtered dozens in an orgy of cannibalism that ended with his burning at the stake in 1598. At about the same time, Hungarian countess Elizabeth Bathory

Charles Manson was a notorious serial killer of the
1960s who masterminded the murdering sprees undertaken
by his followers, known as the Family.

was slaying dozens of young girls to provide her daily bath in virgin's blood until she too met her end, walled up in her own castle.

These people, however, lived in an age when life was held to be cheaper than in latter times. So, for the purpose of this book, the starting point for the study of sequential slaying is the beginning of the nineteenth century. The infamous Bender family of Kansas, "Black Widow" Belle Gunness of Indiana, France's poisoning peasant Helene Jegado, and the Scottish bodysnatchers Burke and Hare thereby fall into this category.

So too, of course, do the aforementioned Hermann Mudgett and Jack the Ripper. This highlights another contradiction in that Mudgett slew as many as 200 and the Ripper only five. Yet the scalpel-slashing Jack is possibly the best-known multiple murderer of all time, his nickname synonymous with serial killer—and his notoriety secured by the fact that he was never caught. The number of victims of a serial killer is not necessarily a qualification for the highest echelons of infamy, but can depend on how much attention the killings receive at the time and the level of intrigue involved.

It is also the drive by the perpetrators, once having abandoned any notions of simple decency, to test how far they can stretch the bounds of morality. Some of the most manic, murdering monsters the world has ever known are catalogued in these pages. Many have mutilated the bodies of their victims. Some have resorted to cannibalism. Others, to satisfy their perverted sexual desires, have snuffed out the lives of children.

England's "Moors Murderers" are a case in point. They killed five innocents in the 1960s and, by the standards of later multiple murders, one would have thought their crimes would have faded from public consciousness. Yet the names of Myra Hindley and her lover Ian Brady are still the most reviled in British criminal history, she being portrayed as the incarnation of evil. The fact that a woman could tape-record a child being sexually tortured to death almost ended an age of innocence in that country. Myra Hindley is dead but tough policemen can still be brought to tears by the memory of that little girl's screams. That is the true horror of the serial killer: the perpetrator can end a life in the most obscene manner then go on to kill again.

America has particularly become known for breeding serial killers. In one especially bad year, 1983, serial killers accounted for the deaths of 5,000 Americans. One estimate claimed as many as 35 of the maniacs were on the loose at any one time. If the US was in danger of becoming a nation that bred multiple murderers, then Southern California was the capital. The region produced a full ten per cent of the world's identified serial killers in the later half of the twentieth century. In true Californian style, their nicknames tended to

> **"In one particularly bad year, 1983, serial killers accounted for the deaths of 5,000 Americans. One estimate claimed as many as 35 of the maniacs were on the loose at any one time"**

glamorize their sick trade. There was the "Hillside Strangler," the "Trailside Killer," the "Trash Bag Killer," the "Co-Ed Killer," the "Scorecard Killer," the "I-5 Killer," the "Sunset Strip Slayers," the "Night Stalker," and the rest.

According to Interpol, the European-based police organization, this is an astonishingly high count of serial murders compared with elsewhere in the world. Yet these deadly epidemics are not a phenomenon unique to the US. Germany saw a similar rash of sequential slayings between World Wars I and II. The hunts for the "Vampire of Dusseldorf" and the "Butcher of Hanover" were impeded by an overlapping rash of killings, so that no police force had a clue as to who was murdering whom. No one can explain these phenomena. If California suffered a peak of killings in the 1970s because it was rich, how come Germany suffered in the 1930s when it was poor?

There is no logic to this type of crime. Serial killers act without reason, only an innate evil instinct. That is why they are difficult to analyze, quantify, and, of course, catch. Even in a book of this size, it is impossible to record the deeds of every person who has killed habitually. Indeed, it is only in the last century or so that society has been in a position to record them comprehensively. In addition, the distinction between serial killer and mass murderer, spree killer or thrill killer is a difficult one to make. That is why this encyclopedia attempts to take as wide a cross section of killers and as broad a spectrum of types of crime as possible.

At their coolest, calmest, and perhaps most elusive, a serial killer can be in a venerated position of trust: a doctor, for instance, like Michael Swango who preyed on the sick in North America

Number 25, Cromwell Street was just an ordinary house in an ordinary street. Little did the neighbors know about what went on inside the home of murderers Fred and Rosemary West.
- - - - - - - - - - - -

and Africa, or Harold Shipman who dispatched between 200 and 300 of his patients in England. Another type of serial killer murders to fulfil his greedy ambitions, like "Acid Bath Murderer" John Haigh or voodoo zealot Adolfo de Jesus Constanzo. He may have a hatred of prostitutes, like Jack the Ripper and his latter-day namesake Jack the Stripper, usually indicating feelings of inadequacy. Or, similarly, he may prey on homosexuals, like

John Wayne Gacy or the aptly named Michael Lupo.

Then, plumbing further depths of depravity, there is the unholy breed of sex-driven psychopaths, the reapers of lives whose deeds are more revolting in their reality than could ever be created in the most shocking horror fiction. These are the butchers whose crimes are so sickeningly evil that it is hard to accept that the perpetrators could share any place at all among humans beings in a supposedly civilized world. Add to their personality, a peculiar cunning and a twisted track of thinking that even psychologists cannot unravel, and you have the most odious type of serial killer of all.

Take Albert Fish, the "Moon Maniac," who has to be one of the most loathed murderers in American criminal history. His speciality was molesting, torturing, and castrating children, occasionally eating his dozens of victims. Or Edward Gein, who cut up his victims and wore their skin over his own. Henry Lee Lucas who confessed to between 150 and 600 murders across the southern US, accompanied by rape, torture, and mutilation. When arrested in 1983, Lucas's reasoning for his crimes was as revealing as any quote from the mouth of a serial killer: "I was bitter at the world. I had nothing but pure hatred." He might have been echoing the sentiments of an earlier multiple murderer, Carl Panzram, who, as he went to the gallows in 1930, spat out the words: "I wish the whole world had but a single throat and I had my hands around it."

The true accounts of such monsters might prompt readers of this encyclopedia to attempt what has often been tried and failed by scientists, sociologists, psychologists, and policemen: to get into the mind of a serial killer. We must return to those initial, tantalizing questions—what is and what makes a serial killer? They remain unanswered. And the reason for this enigma is clear, for if you met a serial killer in the street then you would not recognize him or her. They have no distinguishing marks.

Serial killers can be loners, like brooding cannibal Jeffrey Dahmer; they can be a couple, like devil-may-care David and Catherine Birnie; they may work as a deadly duo, like the sinister "Hillside Stranglers" Kenneth Bianci and Angelo Buono; or they can work as a team, like the crazed Manson Family. They can be as mad as Russia's "Rostov Ripper" Andrei Chikatilo or as sane as Britain's Archibald Hall. They can be as frighteningly ugly as "Gorilla Murderer" Earle Nelson or as suave and intelligent as that infamous multiple murderer with film-star looks, Ted Bundy.

All those we have mentioned above are serial killers who have been caught. This book tells the stories of these most infamous and prolific killers. But there are many others out there who have evaded capture so far. So read on. But take care...

ANGELS OF DEATH

It was every hospital's nightmare: elderly patients in remission from terminal illness were inexplicably found dead in their beds.

But this was no hand of fate or God deciding their mortality. It was the hand of evil. And as many as 60 or more old folk died at the decree of someone who had once taken an oath to care for the sick. Their murderer bragged that he might have killed up to 100. It was no wonder that nurse Efren

Saldivar became known as the "Angel of Death"— a chilling title that has been applied to the other nurses in this section, all of whom used their medical position to prey on the sick, the weak, and the vulnerable.

To his colleagues, Efren Saldivar was a competent nurse working the "graveyard shift" at the Glendale Adventist Medical Centre near the Ventura Freeway in Los Angeles in 1996. His main role was as a respiratory therapist, putting tubes down patients' throats if they were unable to breathe properly on their own. He was also qualified enough to use a stethoscope, insert needles into arteries, put patients onto ventilators, and he had a good knowledge of drugs. Being on the 11pm to 7am shift suited Saldivar because hardly anyone was around. If there were suspicions about one or even several deaths on his shifts, Saldivar always seemed to be in the clear. He was even called on to help out at other medical centers and hospitals.

Even when, in April 1997, fellow respiratory therapist Bob Baker suggested to his head of department, John Bechthold, that some deaths seemed mysterious, checks on Saldivar's night log showed nothing to give cause for concern. The fact that more patients seemed to die when Saldivar was around than at any other time was attributed to the hospital authorities as pure coincidence.

But slowly the rumours grew about Saldivar having a "magic syringe." There was also talk that

FACT FILE.

Name: Efren Saldivar, Donald Harvey and others, aka "Angels of Death"

Born: Saldivar born September 30, 1969; others various

Location of killings: Various

Killed: between 60 and 100 attributed to Saldivar; 40 to 100 to Harvey; others various

Modus operandi: lethal injections and suffocation, among others

Justice: life sentences where convicted

he had actually discussed whether certain patients should live or die. Acting on a tip-off, John Bechthold found phials of muscle relaxant in Saldivar's locker. Action was swift and the 32-year-old nurse was whisked away to the local police station, where he at first acted confused and demanded to know why he had been removed from the hospital. Then he confessed all—and it was a terrifying story he told.

Saldivar said he had killed his first patient in 1988 when he was 19 and fresh out of his training at the College of Medical and Dental Careers in North Hollywood. The victim was an elderly female patient who was on a life-support system. She was terminally ill with cancer and her relatives had already agreed no more should be done to save her. Saldivar said he felt sorry for the woman and suffocated her. He later claimed another victim by dripping a lethal drug into her intravenous drip tube. His first lethal injection was in 1997. After that, he injected more and more elderly patients because he simply felt they should no longer live.

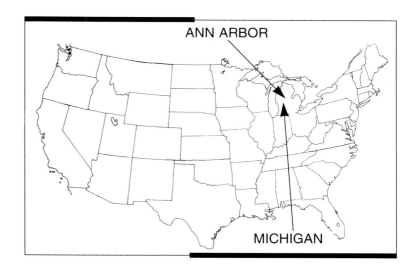

"They were ready to die"

The investigation took an even more damning turn when Saldivar suggested that what he had done was common practice at the medical center. As a result, 37 other members of staff in the respiratory department were suspended pending investigations. Saldivar told police that he only picked patients who were under a "Do not resuscitate" order, adding: "They were ready to die." The drugs he used were Succinylcholine and Pavulon, the latter causing the throat to close up and "conscious paralysis" to take effect. Death would not

be merciful. The two drugs are hard to detect in the body unless specific tests are carried out. Police searched Saldivar's home and although they found piles of pornographic magazines, they did not discover any incriminating drugs.

The case against Saldivar seemed fated when he suddenly withdrew his confession, claiming mental illness. He told police he had made everything up. To convict Saldivar now meant exhuming bodies. That was no mean feat when it was realized that around 1,000 people had died during his eight years' employment at the Glendale Adventist Medical Center. It was agreed that 20 of the most recent deaths were the ones to focus on. While the exhumations and investigations were going on, Saldivar was allowed to walk free but was barred from all medical work.

Brian Andreson, of California's Lawrence Livermore Forensic Science Center, was put in charge of the pathology reports. It was his job to prove that although Pavulon was a synthetic muscle relaxant sometimes given in low doses to

Stefanija Meyer, Irene Leidolf, Maria Gruber, and Waltraud
Wagner, nurses accused of the mass murder of patients in their
care, appeared in a Viennese courtroom in 1991.

- - - - - - - - - - - -

patients on respirators, any abnormal quantities
of it present in a body meant foul play. Andreson
found six patients whose bodies contained large
amounts of the drug, allowing police to arrest
Saldivar on six counts of murder.

This time Saldivar was ready to confess all. He
said he had killed the patients because there were
too many of them and his department was under-
staffed. He told police that sometimes he looked at
the names of the elderly in his care and wondered
to himself: "Who do we have to get rid of?" Saldivar

admitted he had killed patients at other hospitals
too. There could be up 60 victims he said—or
maybe more than 100. "You don't plan this sort of
thing," he said. "But after that, you don't think
about it for the rest of the day—or ever."

Saldivar's court hearing was dramatic. A fellow
respiratory therapist, Ursula Anderson, got immunity in exchange for testifying that she had given
Saldivar the Pavulon and knew what he was doing
with it. One witness, Jean Coyle, a former patient
of Saldivar's at Glendale, told how on February 26,
1997, she had pressed her emergency bell for help
and Saldivar had attended her. Mrs. Coyle said she
recalled blacking out, coming round only some
hours later. She had thought nothing of it at the

time but realized how close she had been to death when Saldivar was arrested.

During the trial, Saldivar's background was revealed. He had not entered the nursing profession out of any sense of commitment. Born in 1969 of Mexican immigrants, Saldivar had been a failure at school, preferring to idle his days away with local gangs rather than concentrate on his studies. When he left school, he went to work in a supermarket. But the job was boring, he said, and when he saw a friend wearing the uniform of the College of Medical and Dental Careers, he was sufficiently impressed to enrol at the same college. Saldivar qualified just a year later, in 1989. He had the uniform, the training and he was just 19. There were several part-time positions before he started at Glendale. By the time he started working there he had perfected his fatal bedside manner.

In March 2002, Saldivar pleaded guilty to six murder charges, having been told that he would escape the death penalty if he confessed. He was given six consecutive life sentences and 15 more years for the attempted murder of Jean Coyle. He later issued a belated apology to the families whose elderly members he had killed: "I know there is nothing I can say that can soothe their anger or bring relief to their anxiety. I want to say I am truly sorry and I ask forgiveness although I don't expect to get any."

It would have been a dark irony had Saldivar been sentenced to death instead of life imprison-

> ❛❛ The same drugs he used to dispatch his patients would have been used to end his life ❜❜

ment. For the same drugs he used to dispatch his patients would have been used to end his life too.

Another male nurse who should never have been allowed near the sick or the vulnerable was Donald Harvey, who in 1987 confessed to killing about 100 patients—which, if true, would have broken John Wayne Gacy's record body count at the time. Harvey's mental state, however, made it difficult to sift fact from fiction.

Don Harvey was born in 1952 and raised in Booneville, Kentucky, a small town in the Appalachian Mountains, where he enjoyed a normal childhood. In his teens, however, he realized that he had homosexual leanings and grew increasingly reserved, becoming a student of the occult. In 1972 he joined the US Air Force but was discharged less than a year later on grounds that were never specified. He was subsequently committed to the Veterans' Administration Medical Center in Lexington where attempts were made to cure his mental disorders by the application of electroshock therapy. Although this patently failed, it did not deter him from entering hospitals again, with tragic results.

Harvey had held a string of minor jobs but gravitated toward the medical profession ever since taking his first part-time post in 1970 as an 18-year-old junior orderly at Marymount Hospital in London, Kentucky. There, he was later to confess, he killed 12 patients in ten months by suffocation or removing their oxygen supply in order "to ease their suffering."

Three years later, disguising his own recent medical history, he secured a part-time job as a nursing assistant at two Lexington hospitals and then as a clerk at a hospital in Fort Thomas. It appears that he had no opportunities to murder patients at these medical centers—but the killings started anew when he moved to Ohio in 1975. For the next ten years, he worked at the Cincinnati Veterans Association Medical Center in various jobs ranging from nursing aide to laboratory technician to mortuary assistant.

Again, Harvey demonstrated that an obvious criminal bent is no impediment to securing work in a hospital. In July 1985 he was searched by security guards as he finished his shift and was found to be carrying hypodermic needles, cocaine-snorting equipment and a .38 caliber pistol. He was fined $50 and sacked—yet within seven months he had picked up a new post as a nurse's aide at the city's Drake Memorial Hospital. Patients were dying at Harvey's hands throughout his year in the job until, at long last, an autopsy on one of them revealed the presence of cyanide. Harvey was the obvious suspect—particularly since his colleagues had by now begun calling him "Angel of Death" because so many patients died on his shifts.

Harvey was arrested in April 1987 and was found to have kept a diary of his crimes. It revealed that during his ten years at the Cincinnati Veterans Association Medical Center, he had mur-

dered 15 patients. He had also attempted to murder his lover, Carl Hoeweler, after they had fallen out. Hoeweler ended up in hospital but survived. So did Hoeweler's mother. His father was also admitted to hospital but died in May 1983 after Harvey had visited him and sprinkled poison on his food.

In his 13 months at the Drake Memorial Hospital, Harvey murdered another 23 patients. The methods he had used over the years included: injecting air into patients' veins, sprinkling rat poison onto their desserts, adding arsenic to fruit juice, injecting cyanide into the buttocks, disconnecting life support machines, and suffocation with plastic bags and wet towels.

As Harvey's trial date loomed, the killer began a spate of plea bargaining to avoid Ohio's death penalty. He also played the insanity card. He confessed to 33 murders, then made it 50-plus, then 80-plus. The Cincinnati prosecutor's office rebutted questions about his mental state by saying: "This man is sane and competent but is a compulsive killer. He builds up tension in his body, so he kills people."

In court on August 18, 1987, Harvey pleaded guilty to 24 counts of murder, four of attempted murder and one of assault. He added a further guilty plea to murder as the case ensued. The Cincinnati court handed down a total of four consecutive 20-years-to-life sentences. In November his further trial opened in Kentucky, where he pleaded guilty to 12 murders at the Marymount

> **During his ten years at the Cincinnati Veterans Association Medical Center, he had murdered 15 patients**

Hospital and was sentenced to eight life terms plus 20 years. Back in Cincinnati in February 1988, he pleaded guilty to three further murders and three attempted murders, drawing three further life sentences plus three terms of seven to 25 years. That made a total of 40 murders but few doubt the true figure is more than double.

Few lessons seem to have been learned over the years about the early identification of serial killers who operate under the guise of nurses seeking to "put patients out of their misery." In December 2003, former nurse Charles Cullen, 43, appeared in court in New Jersey after telling prosecutors that he killed 30 to 40 hospital patients. Cullen, from Bethlehem in Pennsylvania, was charged with one count of murdering a Roman Catholic priest, who died of a heart attack after being given a lethal dose of the heart drug digoxin, but investigators were looking into his other self-confessed crimes. Under questioning, Cullen said he had killed many others at several hospitals in New Jersey and Pennsylvania during his 16-year career as a nurse. He described them as "mercy killings" of terminally-ill patients.

By their own nature, it is notoriously difficult to apportion blame in the case of hospital killings. Leading forensic scientist Henry Lee, speaking in Los Angeles after the Efren Saldivar case, said murders by nursing staff were the most difficult serial killings to detect and on which to obtain a conviction. "You have to figure out who the victims were long after they were buried," he said. "Then you have to link to the suspect. Prepare to fail."

That is exactly what happened In the case of a spate of mysterious deaths at the Ann Arbor Veterans' Administration Hospital, Michigan. In just six weeks of 1975, no fewer than 56 patients

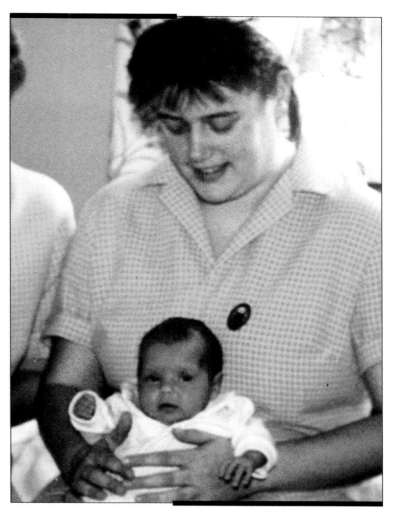

Nurse Beverley Allitt on a Children's ward where she was alleged to have killed four children.
- - - - - - - - - - - - - -

died. There were eight deaths on one night alone in only three hours. A muscle relaxant drug called Pavulon, derived from a South American poison, was revealed as the cause, and it was likely that large doses had been given intravenously, causing patients to cease breathing. The FBI were called in but the deaths of yet another eight patients, while investigations were taking place, virtually closed the hospital. Suspicions fell upon two Filipino nurses, 30-year-old Filipina Narcissco and 31-year-old Leonora Perez. Both had always been on duty when the deaths occurred.

Efren Saldivar, a former respiratory therapist at the
Adventist Medical Center in Glendale, known as the "Angel of
Death" for killing up to 50 patients, was arrested in 2001.

Despite concerns about another hospital worker who committed suicide in 1976, Narcissco and Perez went on trial the following year charged with eight murders, poisoning, and conspiracy. The case collapsed when it was revealed that although patients had stopped dying in large numbers once the nurses had been removed from duty, no one had actually seen them adding anything to the intravenous drips. Perez was discharged on instructions of the judge and Narcissco was found not guilty of murder. Both were convicted of poisoning and conspiracy, but those convictions were also set aside when an appeal was lodged. Awaiting a retrial, the two women underwent psychiatric testing but were pronounced sane and normal. All charges against them were dismissed at a second trial in February 1978. What exactly happened at the Ann Arbor Veterans' Administration Hospital was to remain a mystery.

Another mysterious spate of hospital deaths occurred half a world away, in Vienna, Austria, in the 1980s. Nursing aides at the city's Lainz Geberal Hospital were overheard laughing and joking in a bar about speeding the death of one of their patients. A horrified doctor at an adjoining table reported the conversation to police and an investigation was launched that, at one stage, put the total body count at an astonishing 300 elderly people.

The ringleader, Waultrad Wagner, had been 23 when she claimed her first victim in 1983. When finally arrested in 1989, she initially confessed to 39 killings. She said: "The ones who got on my nerves were dispatched to a free bed with the good Lord. They sometimes resisted but we were stronger. We could decide whether the old fools lived or died. Their ticket to God was long overdue anyway."

Wagner later withdrew her confession and admitted only ten cases of "mercy killing to ease their pain." In March 1991, she was sentenced to life for 15 murders and 17 attempted murders. Her accomplices were also imprisoned: Irene Leidolf receiving life for five murders, Stefanija Meyer getting 15 years for one manslaughter and seven attempted murders, and Maria Gruber getting 15 years for two attempted murders. Politicians and media were outraged at what they saw as the failure of the police and courts to reveal the full scale of the murders, which were described as "the most gruesome and brutal crime in Austria's history."

The difficulty in weeding out hospital employees who are a danger to patients was illustrated with tragic consequences in the British case of nurse Beverley Allitt, whose unremarkable appearance and manner belied a personality disorder that led her to the murder, not of elderly patients on this occasion, but of the young. It is the fact that she killed innocent children, rather than the number of her victims, that has made her one of the most frightening cases in British criminal history. It is also the reason why she has been the subject of several studies into the mind of a serial killer.

Beverley Allitt was a plain, overweight, even

> ❝ **The ones who got on my nerves were dispatched to a free bed with the good Lord** ❞

Efran Saldivar worked at the Adventist Medical Center for eight years, possibly killing up to 50 patients before he was arrested and charged with murder.

- - - - - - - - - - - - - - -

frumpy little girl of whom nobody at home or school took much notice but who was always relied on to be sensible, caring, and diligent. It was a role into which she drifted easily. Hers was a happy enough home and what quickly struck her parents and friends was her eagerness, even as a child herself, to play the role of nanny and carer for the younger village children. Very early on in life, Beverley Allitt told everyone she wanted to be a nurse.

In June 1985 Allitt left school at Corby Glen, Lincolnshire, with disappointing exam passes but, to her joy, was immediately accepted on a pre-nursing course at Grantham College. She was 17, determined to walk the wards and on her way to

becoming an "Angel of Mercy." After a two-year course and an ill-fated fling with her first serious boyfriend, Allitt got her first posting at the Grantham and Kesteven General Hospital, Lincolnshire, as a trainee nurse on the paediatric ward, looking after sick children just as she had always longed to do.

Student nurse Allitt remained unremarkable. But the hospital's own medical records should have rung alarm bells. For Allitt was suffering from the rare condition Munchausen's Disease By Proxy and had visited doctors no fewer than 50 times with phantom ailments, including pregnancy, a stomach ulcer and a brain tumour. Allitt's freak condition can also cause a much more dangerous side effect: sufferers will actually hurt others delib-erately, so they can make them better later.

It was this undiscovered syndrome which led Allitt to become a hospital serial killer. On May 17, 1993, she also entered criminal history as the worst British female serial killer of modern times when she was found guilty at Nottingham Crown Court of murdering four children and attacking nine others in hospital. All of Allitt's little victims suffered at her hand on Ward Four at Grantham and Kesteven, one of them, 11-year-old Timothy Hardwick, within three hours of being admitted. For the families of victims, the jury's verdict ended two years of torture. A lengthy police and medical investigation had at first failed to find the cause of a series of mystery deaths of children on Ward Four. Then, slowly, they had begun to discover the agonizing truth.

In 58 insane days, Allitt committed her dreadful crimes. Eight-week-old Liam Taylor was her first murder victim. He died on February 23, 1991, just two days after being admitted to Ward Four with a chest infection. As his distraught parents slept in a nearby room, after keeping vigil for hours on end by their infant's bedside, Liam suffered a massive heart attack which was too much for his tiny frame to bear. He died within hours. Ten days later, young Timothy Hardwick, a terribly mentally and physically handicapped child, died after being treated by Allitt for an epileptic fit. The following month, five-week-old Becky Phillips died after suffering convulsions at home hours after being released from hospital. She too had been under the care of Nurse Allitt on Ward Four. Finally, Claire Peck, aged 15 months, died on April 22 after supposedly routine treatment for asthma.

Tiny Claire was the last of Allitt's victims to die, although nine other children's conditions had become dramatically life-threatening during the period. After Claire's death, police were called for the first time to investigate what horrors lay behind the recurrent nightmare of Ward Four. Initial inquiries centered on one of the survivors, five-month-old Paul Crampton, who was found to have had abnormal levels of insulin in his blood. In fact, there was only one recorded higher reading that was in the body of a doctor who had deliberately injected himself with a massive overdose of insulin to commit suicide.

It was clear that Paul had been injected with the drug while in hospital and, after blood tests were conducted on other victims, it quickly became apparent that the common factor was Allitt. She had cold bloodedly administered lethal and near-lethal overdoses of both insulin and potassium chloride to her pathetic victims—some of whom, it emerged, she had also tried to suffocate. At her trial at Nottingham Crown Court in May 1993, as a jury heard how she believed she was doing no wrong in murdering without mercy, Allitt showed not a shred of emotion. She was sentenced to serve life, four times over, in a prison for the criminally insane.

So why does an "Angel of Mercy" become an "Angel of Death?" In an interview at the Warren Correctional Institution in Lebanon, Ohio, in 1991, former male nurse Donald Harvey, serving several life sentences for murdering dozens of his patients, gave a brief insight: "People controlled me for 18 years, and then I controlled my own destiny. I controlled other people's lives, whether they lived or died. I had that power to control. After I didn't get caught for the first 15, I thought it was my right. I appointed myself judge, prosecutor, and jury. So I played God."

BENDER FAMILY

The Bender Family were a thoroughly unsavory lot. There was old man Bender, a 60-year-old surly East European immigrant, his shrewish wife aged 50, a half-witted son in his mid-twenties, and an ugly, unmarried daughter who claimed psychic powers.

Together they ran one of the least palatial hostelries in nineteenth-century America. As owners of the decrepit, dingy Wayside Inn, beside a dusty Kansas trail, the villainous Benders were always on the lookout for travelers desperate enough to stay the night—and just wealthy enough to be worth robbing.

Such guests would be treated with great care at the dinner table, their hosts always ensuring that they were seated with their backs to a

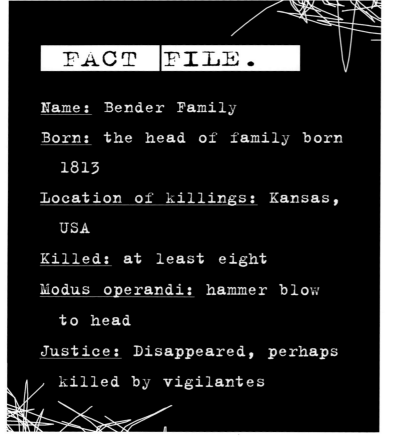

FACT FILE.

Name: Bender Family

Born: the head of family born 1813

Location of killings: Kansas, USA

Killed: at least eight

Modus operandi: hammer blow to head

Justice: Disappeared, perhaps killed by vigilantes

curtained-off sleeping area. One of the family would be waiting behind the curtain to smash the victim's skull with a heavy hammer and finish him or her off with a knife to the throat. After searching the victim for valuables, the body would be dropped through a trapdoor into the cellar below. Then after nightfall, it would be buried in a shallow grave.

The murderous trade carried on by this loathsome clan came to an end only after the family of one of their victims determined to solve the mystery of his disappearance. Dr. William York had left his brother's house at Fort Scott, Kansas, on March 9, 1873, to ride home to the town of Independence. He did not arrive. The doctor's brother organized groups to search the area between Independence and Fort Scott but there was no trace of him. After several weeks without news, the brother, a colonel in the US Cavalry, set out to scour the trail. His search brought him to the Wayside Inn, a dirty, fly-swept, 16ft by 20ft cabin surrounded by farmland on the outskirts of the hamlet of Cherryvale, where the Benders offered him food and shelter. The colonel knew his brother had intended breaking his journey there, and that night he too got to know the unsavory family.

Locals knew little about the Benders, except that they spoke in thick, guttural accents. But there had been strange stories about them. One suggested the family had something to do with the body of a man found with his skull smashed under the ice of a frozen creek. A Mr. Wetzell recalled visiting the inn after seeing a newspaper advertisement offering mystic healing by Professor Miss Kate Bender, who also gave impromptu seances at traveling shows. Wetzell called at the Wayside Inn with a friend and was greeted by the buxom daughter of the house who assured Wetzell that her skills as a spiritualist and psychic healer would soon cure his facial neuralgia. The guests were invited to stay for supper—but as they sat down, could not help but notice the girl's father and brother disappear behind the curtain. Something worried Wetzell and his companion enough to make them eat their dinner standing up. This enraged Kate who became abusive and the two startled guests quickly left.

Now it was Colonel York's turn to encounter the sinister household. The Benders all denied any knowledge of Dr. York, blaming bandits or Indians for the brother's disappearance. They even offered to help with the search by dredging the nearby river for any trace of a corpse. They obviously convinced the colonel because he rode on to search further down the trail. A few days later another search party arrived to make inquiries at the inn. Again the Benders denied that they had ever seen the missing doctor, and again the searchers were satisfied and rode away.

The Benders, however, panicked and, hurriedly packing their meager belongings onto a cart, they fled. On May 9 another search party on the trail of Dr. York found the Wayside Inn abandoned. Hearing sounds of distress coming from cattle at the back of the inn, the searchers found many of

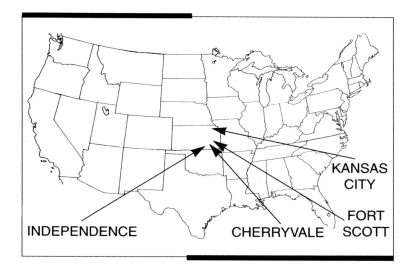

INDEPENDENCE CHERRYVALE KANSAS CITY FORT SCOTT

the creatures, together with a small flock of sheep, were either dead or dying from obvious hunger and thirst. The next thing that struck the group was the smell of decomposition coming from within the house.

Then one of the party noticed that the dry half-acre of orchard to the right of the house looked strange. The topsoil had been ploughed between the trees and recent rains had exposed a freshly dug grave. A few minutes' spadework revealed the body of Dr. York. His skull was smashed and his throat had been cut from ear to ear. Before darkness fell, further digging had revealed the remains of no fewer than seven other victims. All of them had been killed in the same way apart from a small girl. Judging from her position, it was apparent she had been thrown into the shallow grave while still alive.

The following morning when digging resumed, another child's body was unearthed. It was later discovered to be that of a girl of eight years old or thereabouts. The poor little corpse was so badly decomposed any identification at all was almost impossible. The child's right knee had been disconnected and her breastbone driven in.

As owners of the Wayside Inn, the Bender family were able to murder guests without detection for many years. Here relatives arrive to see if their loved ones are among the victims.

Meanwhile, other members of the search party were investigating the source of a foul smell that permeated the cabin. Beneath a trapdoor in the floor they found a roughly-dug pit, its floor and walls stained with blood.

Following these grisly discoveries, posses were formed to hunt down the Benders—an added lure being the belief that they were carrying about $10,000 stolen from their victims. The family were distinctive, both because of their appearance and because one of the wheels on their cart had a fault that left a zig-zag trail, but the official records state that they were never discovered. However, a man named Brockman, who had been a business partner of the Benders and who was suspected of being an accomplice in their crimes, was captured and

brought in by the vigilantes. In an attempt to force him to reveal the Benders' escape route, the unfortunate Brockman was hanged from a tree until seconds from death. Whether or not a confession was ever squeezed out of him is in unknown—but it is possible. For it is believed that one of the several vigilante patrols did indeed track down the fleeing family.

An enduring rumor was that one of the posses caught the Benders, tortured them to try to discover where their money was hidden, then burned them alive. A local sheriff strongly hinted to an official search party that it would be unnecessary for anyone to seek further for them. Another lawman reported that a wagon with a badly skewed wheel had been found riddled with bullets. Whatever the fate of the vile family, their only legacy was a plaque erected by the State of Kansas commemorating "The Bloody Benders."

DAVID BERKOWITZ

In a twisted irony, quiet post office worker David Berkowitz could be described as a man of letters.

He may even have personally overseen, through New York's mail system, the chilling notes he wrote and sent giving tantalizing clues to his identity— as one of America's most publicized serial killers. By day, Berkowitz was a soft-spoken employee of the US Mail, and no one who worked alongside him ever guessed at the deadly double-life he was leading. By night, he was a stalker of young women, prowling the streets of New York's Bronx and Queens seeking his prey. The plump, angel-faced bachelor brought fear to the streets for a year, from July 29, 1976, to August 1, 1977, killing six women and viciously wounding another seven. And throughout his reign of terror, he taunted police with a series of letters, bragging about his deeds.

As pressure grew on the police to capture the gun-toting killer, Berkowitz noted with glee their failure to find him. He would retire to his tiny suburban apartment to pen letters bragging about his murders. "I'll be back—I love to hunt," he wrote to police after one vile killing. Determined to achieve the most notoriety, curly-haired Berkowitz also penned notes to the *New York Post* and the *New York Daily News*. And he gave himself an eerie nickname: "Son of Sam."

Berkowitz's first victim was Donna Lauria, a pretty 18-year-old who, keeping a promise to her father not to be too late home, was closing her car door and saying goodnight to her friend Jody Valente when the killer struck in the early hours of July 29, 1976. Berkowitz had obviously been watching as the two girls sat and chatted outside the neat Bronx apartment of Donna's parents. He then ran from the shadows, stood on the footpath to Donna's home, pulled his .44 caliber gun from a paper bag, crouched down and fired three shots. Donna died and Jody was wounded.

As far as the cops were concerned, it was just another randomly crazy crime in a city whose

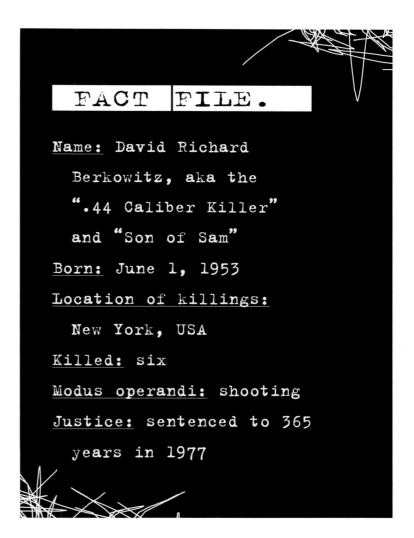

FACT FILE.

Name: David Richard
Berkowitz, aka the
".44 Caliber Killer"
and "Son of Sam"
Born: June 1, 1953
Location of killings:
New York, USA
Killed: six
Modus operandi: shooting
Justice: sentenced to 365
years in 1977

murder rate stood at 30 a week. Donna's parents were left to grieve as their daughter's death became yesterday's news. But police were forced to reopen the murder file again on October 23. Again, the tar-

❝ I am the monster— Beelzebub ❞

gets were two hapless young people in a parked car, this time at Flushing, Queens. Detective's daughter Rosemary Keenan, 18, escaped the bullets but her friend Carl Denaro, 20, had his plans to enlist the following week in the US Air Force shattered when he was critically wounded in the head. Incredibly, he survived the attack. Even then, no one yet contemplated that New York was in the grip of a serial killer.

A month later, however, Berkowitz struck again. Two young women were sitting on the steps of their home in Floral Park, Queens, when a gunman walked up and shot them both. Joanne Lomino was wounded and recovered but Donna DeMasi, with a bullet in her spine, was permanently paralyzed. In January 1977, John Diel and girlfriend Christine Freund were sitting in their parked car in the Ridgewood district when two bullets shattered the passenger window. Christine was unhurt but her date was killed instantly.

Visiting Bulgarian student Virginia Voske-

David Berkowitz addresses the media after calling a news conference at the Attica Correctional Facility during his trial in 1977.

- - - - - - - - - - - - -

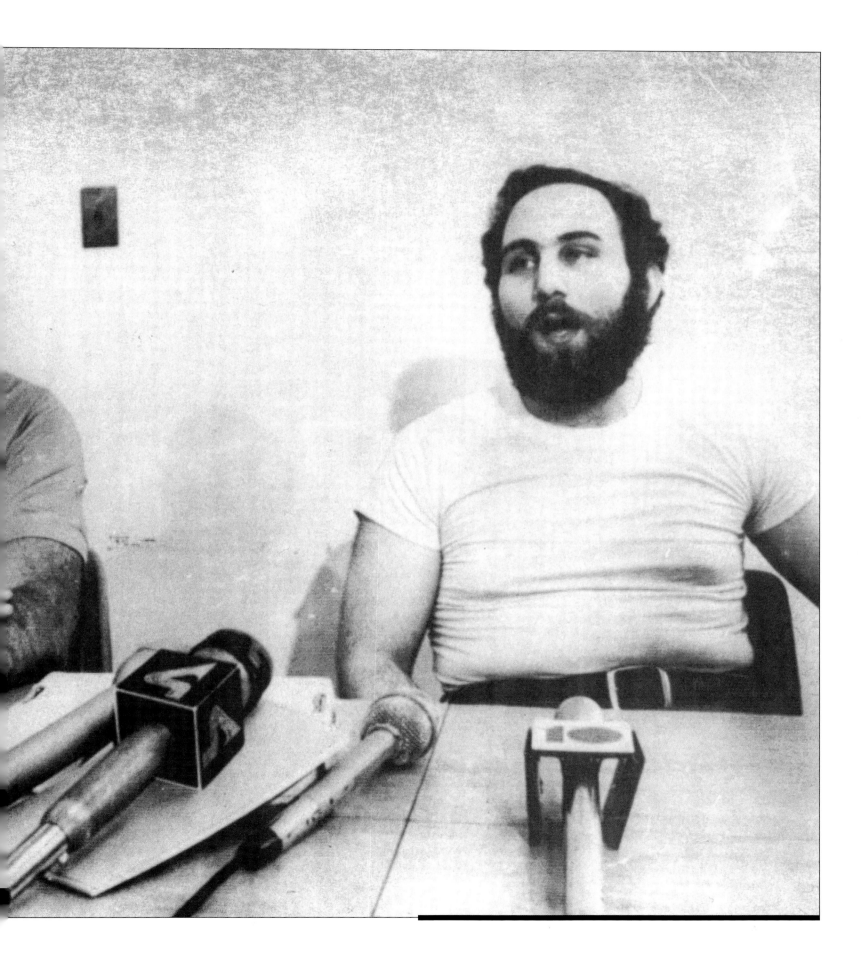

David Berkowitz was a soft-spoken employee of the US Mail, and no one who worked alongside him ever guessed at the deadly double-life he was leading.

- - - - - - - - - - - - -

richian was the next victim, shot in the face as she approached her home in Forest Hills one evening in March. The bullet that killed her was found to be from the same .44 Caliber pistol as had been used in the previous shootings. Following this discovery, a ".44 Killer" Task Force was organized, although for a long time the 300-strong squad found themselves working in the dark. No motive for the shootings could be deduced. The same gun was being used but the victims were totally random.

It was in April 1977 that detectives realized they were dealing with a particularly unusual breed of killer. Examining the bodies of student Valentina Suriani and boyfriend Alexander Esau, shot as they sat in their car in the Bronx, police found that their assassin had left more than death in his wake. Berkowitz had planted the first of a series of callously teasing letters.

He complained he was "deeply hurt" that newspapers were calling him a woman-hater. "I am not," wrote Berkowitz. "But I am a monster. I am the Son of Sam. I am a little brat. Sam loves to drink blood. 'Go out and kill' commands father Sam... I am on a different wavelength to everybody else—programmed to kill. However, to stop me you must kill me. Attention all police: Shoot me first— shoot to kill or else. Keep out of my way or you will die! I am the monster—Beelzebub, the Chubby Behemoth. I love to hunt. Prowling the streets looking for fair game—tasty meat. I live for the hunt—my life. I don't belong on earth. I'll be back! I'll be back! Yours in murder—Mr. Monster."

But who was "Mr. Monster?" David Berkowitz was born illegitimately in Brooklyn on June 1, 1953. His name at birth was Richard David Falco, his 39-year-old mother Betty being an ex-chorus girl who had once performed with the famous Ziegfeld Follies. Betty had been deserted by her husband 13 years before David was born and was having a long-term affair with a Long Island businessman at the time. He ordered her to get rid of the child and she did.

Although the young David knew little or nothing of his real mother and father, he was fortunate enough to be raised by caring, adoptive parents Nathan and Pearl Berkowitz, who ran a hardware store in the Bronx. He was to be their only child. Of above-average intelligence, David was reasonably popular at school and was good at sport but he was a habitual truant, feigning sickness to stay at home with his doting mother. He was deeply affected when Pearl Berkowitz died in his early teens. He complained that her death was "part of a masterplan to break me down," adding: "It was no accident that she got cancer. Evil forces put something in her food." He once wrote of his self-pitying teenage days: "I begged God for death. I used to sit on the fire escape and thought of throwing myself down, wanting to jump. When I thought about dying, I thought about being transported into a world of bliss and happiness."

When he was 18, his adoptive father remarried and the disapproving David left home. He enlisted in the Army, serving in Korea, and, before leaving three years later, converted from Judaism to fundamentalist Christianity. Off duty, he would preach from street-corners in Louisville, Kentucky, where he was stationed, warning of "the burning fires of Hell that lie in wait for all sinners." In the spring of 1974 he returned to New York and rented an apartment in the Bronx. After a spell as a security guard, he joined the US Mail, sorting letters. In this role, Berkowitz may well have handled the mailbags that contained his own letters as Son of Sam.

As he sorted the mail, Berkowitz's warped fantasies grew—until he put them into bloody practice in the summer of 1976. As his crimes became recognized as the work of a serial killer, the chubby mailman craved even greater recognition. After first taunting the New York Police Department, he extended his letter writing by sending notes to the *New York Post* and the *New York Daily News*. Soon the newspapers and the police came to dread the psychopathic scrawl that was dropping through their mailboxes. It meant that Son of Sam had

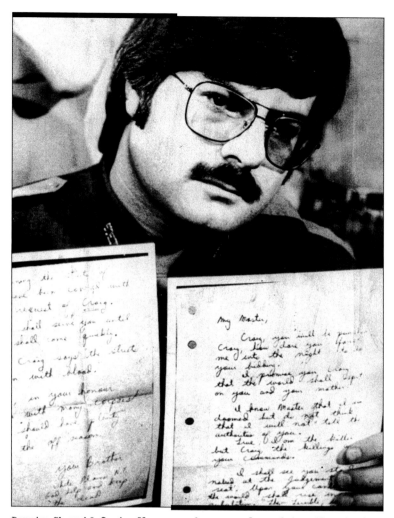

Deputy Sherrif Craig Glassman shows samples of two threatening letters he received, which were very similar in style to the "Son of Sam" notes.

killed ... and was planning his next murder. *New York Daily News* columnist Jimmy Breslin began writing letters back to Son of Sam in his column. It was a controversially dangerous tactic. But, though horrified that a murdering psychopath was in their midst, New Yorkers could not help but be fascinated by the bizarre communications between Breslin and Son of Sam.

Written on May 30, 1977, one letter to the columnist read: "Hello from the gutters of N.Y.C. which are filled with dog manure, vomit, stale wine, urine, and blood. Hello from the sewers of

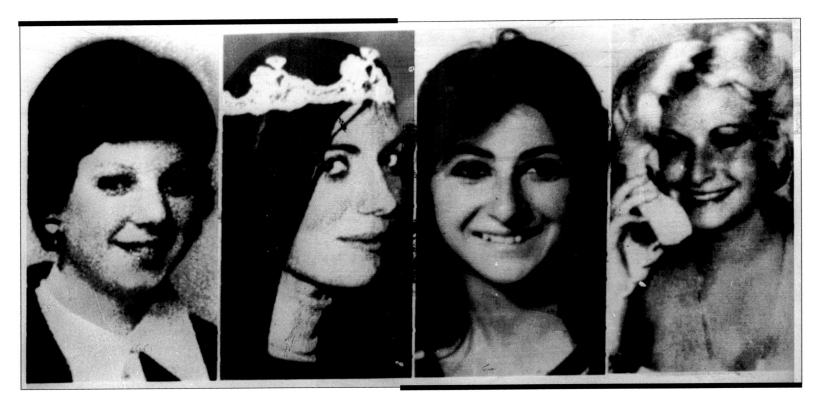

Four of the six victims killed by Berkowitz before he was finally caught in 1977.

Berkowitz when he was first arrested on suspicion of committing six murders.

N.Y.C. which swallow up these delicacies when they are washed away by the sweeper trucks. Hello from the cracks in the sidewalks of N.Y.C. and from the ants that dwell in these cracks and feed on the dried blood of the dead that has seeped into these cracks." Breslin was warned by the killer that he was by no means finished. "Mr. Breslin, sir, don't think that because you haven't heard from (me) for a while that I went to sleep. No, rather, I am still here. Like a spirit roaming the night. Thirsty, hungry, seldom stopping to rest." It was, Breslin thought, a letter from Hell.

"Will you kill again?" Breslin wrote to Son of Sam a year after the first murder. Berkowitz refused to be drawn. He was still sorting mail on July 29, 1977, the anniversary of his first attack, and the date passed uneventfully. Instead, Berkowitz chose the very next night to strike, shooting Stacy Moskowitz and her date, Robert

Violante, as they sat in their car in a Brooklyn street. Stacy, 20, died in hospital and her boyfriend was blinded.

New York was now a city under siege. Hysteria set in among those living on Berkowitz's killing beats. It seemed that the murderer had a penchant for brunettes, five of his victims having been dark-haired, and this sparked off panic-buying of blonde wigs by women in a desperate bid to stay alive on New York's streets. The reign of terror of Son of Sam was drawing to an end, however—in the most extraordinary manner.

In the days following the Moskowitz murder, Detective James Justus, a veteran member of NYPD recently recruited into the Task Force, telephoned the owners of several cars which had been given parking tickets around the vicinity of the latest death scene, hoping someone might have seen something suspicious. It was a boring, routine part of police work, and no one expected anything dramatic to come of it. But Justus was doggedly persistent, especially in his attempts to contact the owner of a 1970 four-door Galaxie which had been ticketed for parking too close to a fire hydrant just 30 minutes before the most recent murder. When Justus found that his repeated telephone calls to the owner went unanswered, he rang the local Yonkers police force to ask them to call on the man, a David Berkowitz.

Justus spoke with Yonkers switchboard operator Wheat Carr—an incredible coincidence given her family's association with the killer, which suddenly came to light. When Justus mentioned

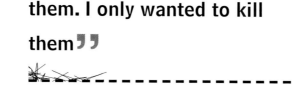

❝ I didn't want to hurt them. I only wanted to kill them❞

Berkowitz's name, Carr told him: "He is the guy that I think is responsible." She went on to describe several bizarre incidents involving Berkowitz, including claims that he had shot her with a .44-caliber gun and had been sending threatening notes to her father, whose name happened to be Sam. An excited Justus immediately reported this conversation to his superiors.

The following day, detectives Ed Zigo and John Longo were sent to Berkowitz's address, an apartment building in suburban Yonkers. As they approached the Pine Street apartments, the detectives noticed the cream Galaxie, licence plate 561XLB, parked outside. Through the windows, they saw a rifle butt protruding from a duffel bag in the back seat. They broke into the car and, in the glove box, found an envelope addressed to Timothy Dowd, a deputy inspector leading the Son of Sam Task Force. Zigo opened it and read the enclosed letter, which Berkowitz had intended leaving at the scene of his next shooting. It promised more attacks, including a planned massacre at a Long Island nightclub where Berkowitz planned to "go out in a blaze of glory."

A call was made for a search warrant to allow the detectives to enter Berkowitz's apartment. It was not needed, for at 10pm the night stalker himself, dressed in jeans, brown boots, and a white short-sleeved shirt, walked out of the building. In his hand was a brown paper bag, and inside was a .44-caliber gun. Berkowitz sauntered casually to his car, so confident that he didn't bother to look

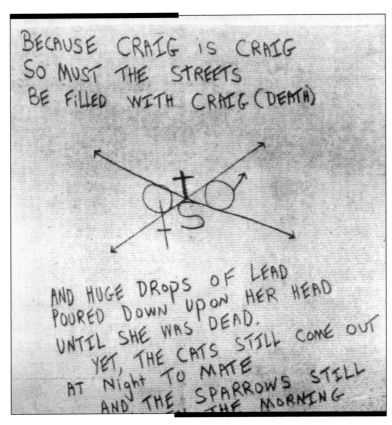

BECAUSE CRAIG IS CRAIG
SO MUST THE STREETS
BE FILLED WITH CRAIG (DEATH)

AND HUGE DROPS OF LEAD
POURED DOWN UPON HER HEAD
UNTIL SHE WAS DEAD.
YET, THE CATS STILL COME OUT
AT Night TO MATE
AND THE SPARROWS STILL
THE MORNING

This note was found by police in the car owned by David Berkowitz when they arrested him. It was a vital clue as it was written in the style of the other notes that he left.

- - - - - - - - - - - -

around. He switched on the ignition but got no further. The barrels of 15 guns were suddenly leveled through the car windows directly at his head. Berkowitz merely smiled. "Okay," he said, "you've got me. What took you so long?" Back at HQ, the suspect was grilled for two hours, confessing to all of Son of Sam's crimes.

When he was arraigned at a Brooklyn courthouse the following morning, the press and public expected to see a chained, wild-eyed monster. Instead they encountered a meek, smiling David Berkowitz. He looked as dangerous as a lamb. Nevertheless, a mob of several hundred angry citizens chanted "Kill him! Kill him! Kill him!" and there were numerous telephoned death threats to

the switchboard at the Kings County Hospital where he was taken for psychiatric evaluation. It was during his enforced stay at the heavily-guarded hospital that Berkowitz responded to a letter smuggled to him from Steve Dunleavy, a columnist with the *New York Post*. The reply to Dunleavy was chilling. It spoke of Sam as "one of the devils of Satan, a force beyond the wildest imaginations of people. He is not human." It continued: "When I killed, I really saved many lives. You will understand later. People want my blood but they don't want to listen to what I have to say. There are other Sons out there. God help the world."

Berkowitz underwent many days of psychiatric tests to delve into the mind of this self-confessed monster. The killer had long been uncomfortable in female company and believed that women avoided him and thought him ugly. "There is a force to turn people away from me," he once wrote. "Somebody wants me destroyed, makes people dislike me and makes girls be not attracted to me in any way. If I had close friends or girlfriends, I would be able to resist the force." Still a virgin when arrested, he revealed that he had tried to kill two women in random knife attacks in 1975, a full year before his first shooting. His would-be victims had saved themselves by screaming as they fought him off. Tellingly, Berkowitz said later: "I didn't want to hurt them. I only wanted to kill them."

Berkowitz told a criminal psychiatrist: "The tension, the desire to kill a woman had built up in me to such explosive proportions that when I finally pulled the trigger, all the pressures, all the tensions, hatred, had just vanished, disappeared." He added that after killing one young woman, "I was literally singing to myself on the way home."

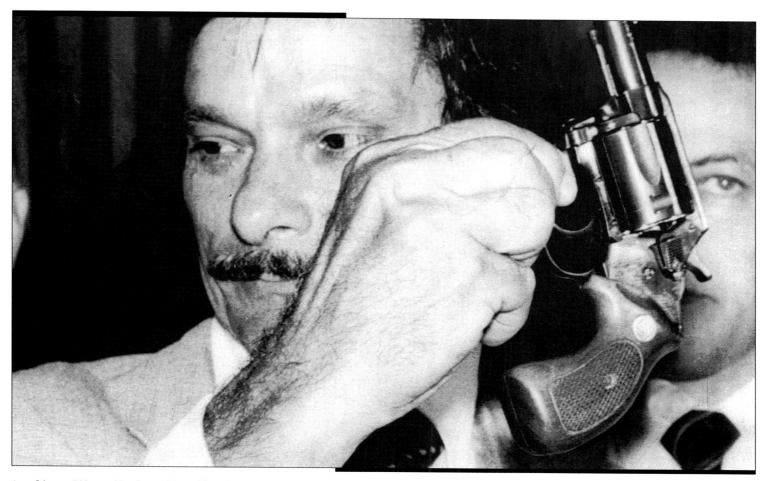

A police officer displays the .44 caliber gun used by Berkowitz to murder his victims. Police found the gun in Berkowitz's apartment and were able to identify him as the killer "Son of Sam."

- - - - - - - - - - - -

Psychiatrist Dr. David Abrahamsen, who examined Berkowitz and judged him sane, said of him: "He found sexual gratification in killing women. He could not approach a woman as a man would do and date her or have sex with her. That was not for him. I think he developed a great deal of contempt for women. He is very dangerous."

But why "Son of Sam?" Weirdly, the explanation seemed to be that Sam was a neighbor, Sam Carr, whose dog kept him awake at night with its barking. The dog, a black labrador, would howl as Berkowitz lay in bed in his squalid apartment,

dreaming of the occult and listening to "voices" that ordered him to kill. Berkowitz said he had tried to kill the dog in 1977 but demons deflected his bullet and the wounded animal recovered. He had only managed to increase the volume of the animals' nightly barking. Police who searched the apartment found the walls covered with scrawled slogans, the most common being: "Kill for my master."

All this would have tended to serve a defence plea of insanity. But Berkowitz forestalled any such attempt by pleading guilty to all charges. On August 23, 1977, he was sentenced to 365 years, to be served at the Attica Correctional Facility. There, in July 1979, Son of Sam almost died after a fellow inmate slashed his throat with a razor, the wound requiring 56 stitches. The chubby mailman doggedly refused to name his attacker.

KENNETH BIANCHI AND ANGELO BUONO

It was just the break Californian police had been waiting for: a name that could be seriously linked with the disappearance of 12 girls.

And the fact that two victims were found dead after telling friends who they were going to meet clinched it. After a two-year-reign of terror, police had finally caught up with the "Hillside Stranglers."

At first the disappearance of young women and girls did not cause a ripple in the manic city that is Los Angeles. People disappear all the time, many unnoticed, many considered to be human debris that will not be missed. But for one man, a single week changed all that. Instead of enjoying Thanksgiving in 1977, Detective Bob Grogan had to deal with the discovery of five female bodies in the Glendale-Highland Park area of the city. What shocked Grogan most was that this was no gang-land killing or the work of a prostitute-hating pervert. The victims were young, one only 12 years old, another only 14. They were all someone's children, kids from nice homes who had been abducted from their middle-class neighborhoods.

A city, once indifferent to its daily murders, became gripped with fear. Parents refused to let their children out after dark or to walk around alone. The sale of guns rocketed and locks on doors were strengthened. Later on, there would be talk that two men, not one, was responsible for the sickening series of murders.

Those two were Kenneth Bianchi and his cousin Angelo Buono, who had set out on their murder spree simply to satisfy their curiosity about what it would be like to kill someone. Bianchi, born in 1951, was raised by foster parents, Frances Bianchi and her husband, in Rochester, New York State. His real mother was an alcoholic prostitute who gave him up at birth. It was said that as soon as he learned to talk, Bianchi also learned to lie. When he was five years old, he worried Frances with his lapses into trance-like daydreaming. Bianchi was also prone to temper.

FACT FILE.

Name: Kenneth Bianchi and Angelo Buono, aka the "Hillside Stranglers"

Born: May 22, 1951 (Bianchi), October 5, 1934 (Buono)

Location of killings: Los Angeles and Washington, USA

Killed: 12

Modus operandi: raped, bound, and strangled

Justice: both sentenced to life in 1980

Doctors said his behavior had come about because of his dependency on his mother.

After her husband's death, Frances went out to work while her son attended High School. Bianchi married as soon as he graduated in 1971

❛❛ Deep down, he had a loathing for women and a desire to humiliate and injure them❜❜

but the marriage only lasted eight months. This was the second time a woman had left him and betrayed him. Bianchi went to college but soon dropped out and eventually drifted into a job as a security guard, which provided him with valuable opportunities to steal. Some of the stolen property went to Bianchi's girlfriends as he attempted to buy their loyalty. This penchant for petty crime meant Bianchi had constantly to be on the move before finally arriving in Los Angeles in 1977. Bianchi then teamed up and shared an apartment with his cousin Buono, who was 16 years his senior but intellectually challenged.

Angelo Buono was an ugly man both physically and mentally. He was coarse, ignorant, and sadistic. Incredibly, he was also very popular with women and gave himself the nickname "Italian Stallion." Born in Rochester, New York, in 1934, he moved to Glendale, California, in 1939 with his mother Jenny and his older sister Cecilia. Now

Angelo Buono, one of the "Hillside Stranglers" pleaded innocent on all charges against him in 1979. He was accused of 25 felonies including ten murders and several sex offenses.

divorced, Jenny supported the family by doing part-time work in a shoe factory. Buono was brought up as a Catholic, but neither his religion nor his public education shaped him into a worthy human being. He had a desperate need for sex, alternating between being kind to a good woman to get it or being violent to a woman when sex was paid for. Deep down, he had a loathing for women and a desire to humiliate them. At 14, he boasted to friends about raping and sodomizing girls.

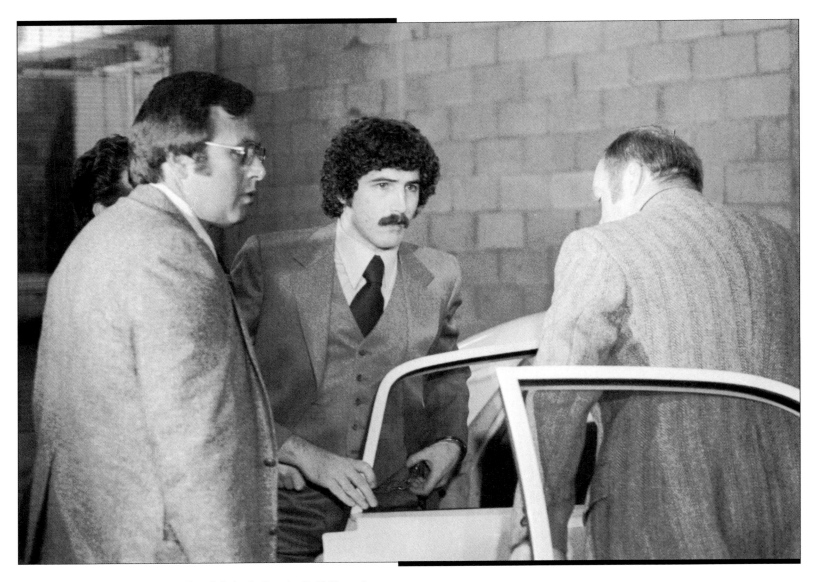

Kenneth Bianchi arriving at the Criminal Courts Building where he was charged with murdering five women in the Los Angeles area late in 1977 and early 1978.

Buono's life of petty crime ensured he was sent to the Paso Robles School for Boys after he was convicted for auto theft. After making his girlfriend Geraldine Vinal pregnant, he married her, only to walk out a week later. Geraldine gave birth to Michael Lee Buono in 1956 when the baby's father was again in jail for car theft.

At the end of 1956, Angelo had another son, Angelo Anthony Buono III. In 1957, he married the mother, Mary Castillo, who then gave birth every year or two: Peter Buono in 1957, Danny Buono in 1958, Louis Buono in 1960, and Grace Buono in 1962. In 1964, Mary filed for divorce because of his violence and perverse sexual needs. Mary went on welfare to feed the children and when, desperate for money, she went to see Angelo about reconciliation, he handcuffed her, put a gun to her stomach, and threatened to kill her. Other relationships followed. So did several other children.

By 1975, Buono had built himself a reasonable reputation as an auto upholsterer. He bought a house at 703 East Colorado Street to use as both

Kenneth Bianchi testified in a courtroom against his
accomplice Angelo Buono.

his home and business. The building also provided the privacy he needed. Despite his total
disrespect for women, Buono held some sort of
magnetism. The women who flocked to his door
must have been naive about sex or did not think
that Buono's demands were abnormal. On one visit
by Bianchi, he found his cousin with dyed black
hair, gold chains around his neck, a large gaudy
turquoise ring on his finger, red silk underwear,

and a virtual harem of "jailbait" girls. Both men
became regular users of prostitutes at Buono's
home. It would be these girls who would become
the first victims of the evil duo. Hollywood hooker
Elissa Kastin, aged 21, died at the hands of
Bianchi and Buono and her body was found on a
hillside on Chevy Chase Drive on October 6, 1977.
She had been violently raped before death.

Their second victim was 19-year-old Yolanda
Washington whose body was found dumped near
the Forest Lawn Cemetery on October 18. Great
care had been taken to clean the corpse, which still
bore marks where rope had bound the necks,

wrists, and ankles. Again, the victim had been viciously raped before being strangled. Her body had been left naked and spread-eagled. But it was the discovery of a third body that made police realize innocent girls were also prey to what, until that time, they assumed to be a single killer. On October 31, Judith Miller, just 15 years of age, was found dead on a hillside in Glendale. Her murder bore all the trademarks of the earlier two—except that from sperm samples, police knew that two men had been involved. This was information they kept secret, however, and they allowed the nickname "Hillside Strangler" to be applied to the case.

As other bodies turned up, a pattern emerged. The girls were mainly part-time prostitutes who had been stripped naked, raped, and sometimes sodomized. They had been carefully cleaned by the killers so as to leave no clues. They had finally been dumped by roadsides where they were certain to be discovered. Some of the bodies bore the marks of crude experimentation with hypodermic syringes, suggesting Bianchi and Buono had tried out new ways in which to torture their victims.

Often the bodies were displayed in lascivious postures. And, to the fury of the detectives on the case, the corpses were generally found near to police stations. It was if the killers were taunting them. In fact, Bianchi had applied for a job with the Los Angeles Police Department—and had actually been taken for several rides with officers while the Hillside Strangler was being sought.

The killers' method of trapping their victims

> **" Some of the bodies bore the marks of crude experimentation with hypodermic syringes "**

was to cruise Los Angeles in Buono's car, using fake badges to persuade girls that they were undercover cops. Ordered into the "unmarked police car," the girls were driven to Buono's home, where they were tortured. After being abused by both men, the girls were strangled. Other methods of killing, such as lethal injection, had been tried by the murderers but rejected.

In one single week in November 1977, five bodies of murdered girls were discovered. One was 12-year-old Dolores Cepeda, whose body was found along with that of 14-year-old Sonja Johnson in Elysian Park. Both girls had been missing for a week from St. Ignatius School. They had last been seen getting off a bus and going over to a large two-tone sedan car. Two men had been seen inside the vehicle.

The body of 20-year-old Kristina Weckler was found on a hillside in Highland Park the same night. A quiet honors student at the Pasadena Art Center of Design, Kristina's death caused investigating officer Bob Grogan to weep. As he searched her apartment, it was obvious from the girl's diaries that she was a hard-working student with everything to look forward to in life. When Kristina's parents arrived to pick up their dead daughter's belongings, Grogan vowed to them that he would find the man responsible.

On November 28, the day before Thanksgiving, another young woman's body was found, badly decomposed and covered in maggots. It was that of Jane King, 28, who had been dumped in the most visible location: the exit ramp of the Golden

Kenneth Bianchi, shown here in 1979, pleaded guilty to five murders in the L.A. area whereas Buono, his accomplice, maintained that he was innocent of all charges against him.

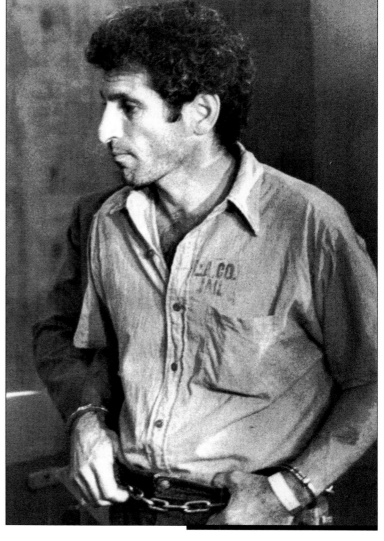

Angelo Buono cruised the Los Angeles' area in his car with Bianchi, using fake badges to dupe girls into thinking they were undercover cops.

State Freeway. Jane had been a stunning girl with model looks and figure and once again Detective Grogan wept with anger and frustration.

The fifth body, found the next day, was Lauren Wagner, an 18-year-old student who lived with her parents in the San Fernando Valley. Lauren had been abducted from her car as she drove into her parent's driveway. Seeing his daughter's car obviously abandoned with its door open, Lauren's

father started questioning his neighbors to see if they had witnessed anything. One, Beulah Stofer, said she had seen Lauren arrive home around 9pm that night. Two men had then pulled up in a car alongside. Lauren appeared to have been arguing with them. The activity outside in the street was enough to cause Mrs. Stofer's Doberman dog to bark furiously.

Detective Grogan hurried around to Mrs.

Angelo Buono is seen talking to a girl in front of his uphol-
stery shop. Buono was Bianchi's cousin and close associate and
they lived together for a time.

- - - - - - - - - - - -

Stofer's home. The woman was in a highly anxious
state. She had just had a phone call from a man
with a New York accent. "You the lady with the
dog?" he had asked her. When Mrs. Stofer said that
she had a dog, he told her to keep her mouth shut
about what she had witnessed or he would kill her.
Mrs. Stofer did not realize that Lauren had been
abducted. She thought that she had just witnessed
a quarrel. She described the assailants' car as a
large and dark with a white top. One of the men

had dragged Lauren from her car into his. She had
heard Lauren cry out, "You won't get away with
this!"

Mrs. Stofer was so terrified by the incident that
she did not even tell her husband who had been
home the whole time. The horror of the whole thing
had thrown her into a violent asthma attack. But
she managed to give Bob Grogan a very good
description of the two kidnappers. One was tall
and young with acne scars; the other one was
Latin-looking, older and shorter with bushy hair.
Most important of all, Mrs. Stofer was certain that
she would recognize them again. Grogan was sure
that this valuable witness was not being com-

pletely truthful about where she had been when she saw the abduction. The detail she gave was too vivid from someone claiming to have just caught a glimpse from a window. Det Grogan was convinced that Mrs. Stofer had been in the street very, very close to where Lauren was abducted. He assumed total fear was the reason she wanted to distance herself.

With the abduction of Lauren Wagner, the killers saw the whole city as their cruising ground. Nowhere was safe. At least when the crimes were confined to Hollywood and Glendale, police could intensify their efforts in those areas. Now, nobody knew where the stranglers would strike next.

On December 14, police found the naked body of Kimberly Martin. The pace of the killings then briefly slackened. But on February 17, 1978, the naked body of Cindy Hudspeth was found in the trunk of a car. L.A.P.D. believed that at last there must be a breakthrough. But the body had been immaculately cleaned and, despite a public outcry at their inability to hunt down the Hillside Strangler, the special police squad were no nearer to making an arrest. Then the killings stopped...

The L.A.P.D. were baffled. But the reason for the cessation of the serial murders could not have been simpler—Bianchi had become sickened because of the filthy conditions in Buono's home. He had left his cousin and moved to Bellingham, Washington State, where he took a job as a security guard while again applying for a post with the local police force. Police were later stunned to

‟ He didn't think he himself was involved in any of the killings ”

discover that instead of being a loner, Bianchi lived with his long-term girlfriend Kelli Boyd and had a baby son.

Back in Los Angeles, the special murder squad had been disbanded. In Washington, however, the nightmare was to begin again. In January 1979, the bodies of two girl students were found in the back of a car in Bellingham. Police were able to piece together the events leading up to the death of Diane Wilder and Karen Mandic. They had told friends they had been hired by a young man from a security firm to house-sit a luxury residence in Bellingham. The name of that man was Bianchi. He was immediately arrested. Forensic evidence proved him to be the killer. A number of blood-stained items of clothing were found hidden at his home. The man leading the murder investigation, Chief Mangan, now recalled similar killings in Los Angeles and Bianchi was grilled over these too.

Bianchi played mind games with the police. He tried to fool psychiatrists that he had split personalities; that he was a Jekyll and Hyde figure who had committed murder only after blacking out and assuming a temporarily bestial role. When a hypnotist was called in, Bianchi even faked a trance, in which his several other identities became apparent. In fact, the killer had studied psychiatry himself and had long planned this form of defence in anticipation of the day he would be caught.

On July 6, 1981, Bianchi gave an unbelievable courtroom performance. To convince the judge that they could not use his testimony against Buono, he said that he might have faked the multiple personality disorder but he didn't know whether he was telling the truth or not when he said that his cousin Angelo was involved in the murders. In fact, he didn't think he himself was involved in any of the killings either.

Bianchi did, however, manage to persuade six Washington State psychiatrists into labeling him insane. This saved him from the death penalty in Washington, where he would have faced hanging for the two murders. Instead he did a deal with police prosecutors to plead guilty in return for a life sentence and removal to California. There, he pledged, he would nail his accomplice Buono.

Back in Los Angeles, however, the ruling of the six Washington psychiatrists that Bianchi was insane prevented his evidence against Buono from being used in a trial. Arrested in 1979, following Bianchi's conviction, it was not until November 1981 that Buono's trial began. It was to last nearly two years.

During the trial, involving more than a thousand exhibits and 400 witnesses, the prosecutors got an excellent break. One of the most important of those witnesses was 27-year-old Catherine Lorre, daughter of actor Peter Lorre. She identified Bianchi and Buono as two men who had stopped her on a Hollywood street claiming to be police

> **" Angelo Buono and Kenneth Bianchi subjected various of their murder victims to the administration of lethal gas, electrocution, strangulation by rope, and lethal hypodermic injection "**

officers. She had shown them her identification, including a photograph of herself as a child alongside her famous father. That photo saved her life. It transpired that the killers had decided not to abduct Catherine for fear that murdering a celebrity's daughter would heighten the manhunt for them.

A second vital witness was a woman whom Buono had terrorized in a Hollywood library while he was waiting for Bianchi the night they killed Kimberly Martin. Her testimony tied Buono to the pay phone that had been used to summon Kimberly to her death.

Buono himself denied all charges and blamed the slayings on his cousin. Indeed the forensic evidence against him was slim, so immaculately had he cleaned his home to remove all traces of the murdered girls' visits. Detectives failed to find a single fingerprint of the victims, nor even one of Buono himself. However, fibers from one of the bodies was matched to a chair in Buono's home. And a single eyelash from one of the girls was found in the house.

The jury gave their verdict on October 31, 1983—at least on the murder of Lauren Wagner. Buono was found guilty. On November 3, the jury voted that Buono was not guilty of the murder of Yolanda Washington. A few days later, he was found guilty of Judy Miller's murder. Under California law, as a multiple murderer, Buono

Kenneth Bianchi grimaced as he begun to cry during legal proceedings in Bellingham, Washington, where he admitted to killing two college students.

faced either the death penalty or life in prison without possibility of parole. Buono then took the stand to show his contempt for the legal process. He said: "My moral and constitutional rights have been broken."

After deliberating for an hour, the jury surprisingly sentenced Buono to life in prison rather than condemning him to a death sentence. Judge Ronald George was not happy. He told the court: "Angelo Buono and Kenneth Bianchi subjected various of their murder victims to the administration of lethal gas, electrocution, strangulation by rope, and lethal hypodermic injection. Yet the two defendants are destined to spend their lives in prison, housed, fed, and clothed at taxpayer expense, better cared for than some of the destitute law-abiding members of our community."

Angelo Buono was first sent to Folsom Prison, where in 1986 he went through a jail marriage to Christine Kizuka, a mother of three and supervisor at the Los Angeles office of the state Employment Development Department. He was later transferred to Calipatria State Prison where, at the age of 67, he was found dead on September 21, 2002. Cause of death was suspected to be from a heart condition.

Kenneth Bianchi was sent to Walla Walla prison in Washington, where no doubt the last words he heard from Judge Ronald George remained with him. Said the judge: "I am sure, Mr. Buono and Mr. Bianchi, that you will only get your thrills by reliving over and over the tortures and murders of your victims, being incapable as I believe you to be of ever feeling any remorse."

43

BIBLE JOHN

The hunt for the mysterious killer Bible John petered out in a wintry Scottish cemetery.

It had been hoped that DNA testing might have provided a rock-solid identification of the suspected strangler of three young women in the 1960s. But it was not to be.

Bible John, believed to have been a twisted religious fanatic, haunted Glasgow's Barrowland Dance Hall, where he pinpointed his first victim, 29-year-old Patricia Docker, whom he strangled with her own tights on February 23, 1968. On August 16, 1969, Jemima McDonald, 32, was found dead in derelict flats. Two months later,

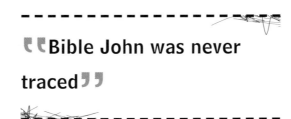

"Bible John was never traced"

Helen Puttock, 29, was murdered on October 30 and her body dumped at a bus stop. Each murder bore remarkable similarities. All the women were of a similar age, all had been strangled, all had their handbags stolen, and all were menstruating at the time of their deaths.

Helen Puttock's sister, Jeannie Williams, gave a full description of the man Helen had danced with on the night she died. She recalled him quoting from the Bible and condemning adultery—and the killer was given the nickname "Bible John." Other

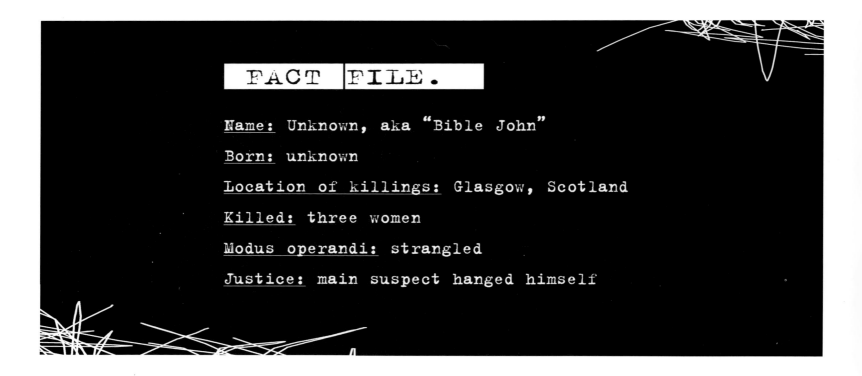

FACT FILE.

Name: Unknown, aka "Bible John"

Born: unknown

Location of killings: Glasgow, Scotland

Killed: three women

Modus operandi: strangled

Justice: main suspect hanged himself

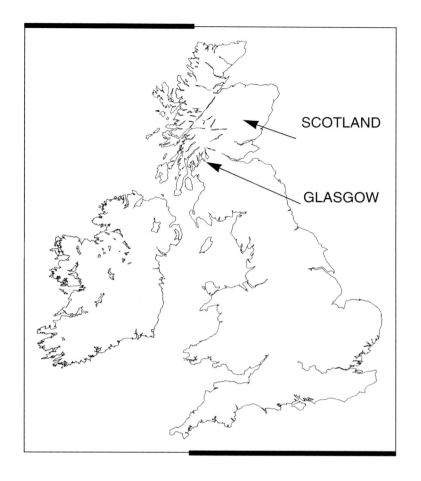

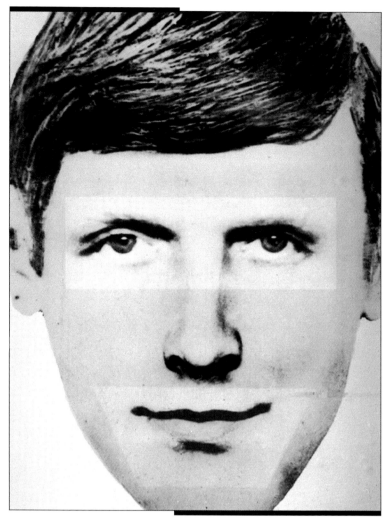

Police photofit of 1960s killer Bible John who was never caught. A police forensic team exhumed the remains of John Irvine McInnes in October 2000 believing him to be the killer.

witnesses who saw him chatting to Helen had also overheard him quoting Biblical texts but added that he seemed to be "a nice guy." But despite a massive police hunt, the interviewing of 5,000 people, a televized documentary about the crime, and a good response from the public, Bible John was never traced.

In February 1996, 28 years after the death of Bible John's first victim, detectives gathered in a frozen cemetery to resume the hunt for the killer.

They exhumed the body of Former Scots Guard John Irvine McInnes from a family grave at Stonehouse Cemetery, Lanarkshire, where he was buried after committing suicide in 1980 at the age of 41. In the years since his death, genetic fingerprinting has become commonplace and DNA taken from the remains of McInnes were thought by scientists to link him with fluid found on the tights used to strangle Helen Puttock. The results were, however, inconclusive.

DAVID AND CATHERINE BIRNIE

They had two things in common—deprived childhoods and latent urges to kill which became a reality.

David and Catherine Birnie have become known as the Bonnie and Clyde of serial killers. The evil couple, from Western Australia, first met when they were 15 and became lovers. Their lives had been anything but settled. David was the eldest of five children and ended up in care after his parents' marriage broke up when he was ten. He never had contact with his mother and father again and quickly realized he had to look after himself. He took his first job when he was 15, working at a horse-racing stable. His odd sexuality was already

becoming apparent and he was sacked after approaching a young female member while naked except for a stocking over his head.

Catherine's mother died when she was small and her father took her to South Africa. There, he found the child a burden and dispatched her back to Australia. Catherine lived with her grandparents and was isolated from other children of her age. It was the sight of her grandmother having an epileptic fit in the street that gave Catherine her first truly traumatic experience. She became so difficult that her grandparents handed her over to an uncle and aunt. Catherine was living with them when she first met the slim, weak-looking David Birnie.

They sought solace in each other, feeling that life had wronged them both. Even when Catherine was pregnant with her first child, they continued their life of crime. Together they carried out a series of burglaries that led to a short spell in a detention center. When released, they went their separate ways, both marrying and leading new lives. Catherine's husband was the son of the household for whom she worked as a domestic help. Five more children came out of the relationship but, like her first, they were to be taken away from her. Fate was to deal a particularly wicked hand when both Catherine's and David's marriages ran into trouble and they met up once more.

Catherine readily gave in to Birnie's voracious sexual demands. He demanded intercourse up to six times a day but Catherine's willingness to

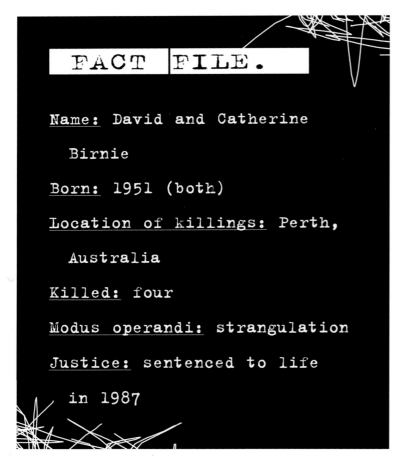

FACT FILE.

Name: David and Catherine
  Birnie

Born: 1951 (both)

Location of killings: Perth,
  Australia

Killed: four

Modus operandi: strangulation

Justice: sentenced to life
  in 1987

comply did not inspire affection from her partner. On one occasion Birnie had sex with his brother James. He also allowed his brother to bed Catherine as a 21st birthday present.

Birnie and Catherine, who adopted her lover's surname, decided to take their perverted sexual tendencies fatally further. They coldly discussed snatching and raping young girls—but their first victim happened by chance. On October 6, 1986, 22-year-old student Mary Neilson knocked on the door of 3 Moorhouse Street, Willagee, a shabby bungalow on the outskirts of Perth, which was to become notorious. Mary had come to buy cheap tyres that Birnie managed to secure through his job at a car wreckers yard. Something snapped inside the Birnies when they realized their opportunity. Within moments of her arrival, Mary was frogmarched into a bedroom at knifepoint and raped by Birnie as Catherine watched. This did not satisfy the two sadists. They drove Mary to nearby Glen Eagle State Forest where Birnie raped her again. She begged for her life as he tied a nylon cord around her neck. After mutilating the body, the Birnies buried it in a shallow grave.

Satisfying such urges now seemed simple. Two weeks after killing Mary Neilson, they picked up 15-year-old hitchhiker Susannah Candy and kept her prisoner for several days. The teenager was repeatedly raped by Birnie. She was also forced to write letters home telling her parents she was safe and well but just wanted some space to herself. This time it was Catherine who did the strangling because, police later believed, her twisted mind turned to jealousy when she thought Birnie was giving Susannah too much attention. The girl was buried alongside Mary Neilson.

The next victim was known to the Birnies. An

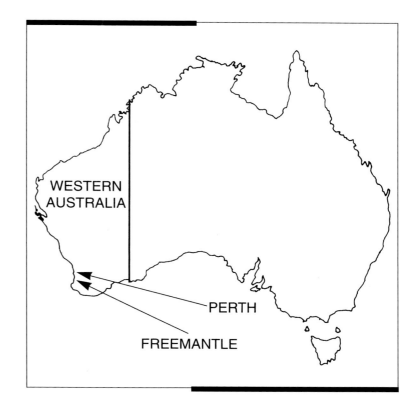

air hostess, 31-year-old Noelene Patterson, considered the two her friends after they helped her decorate her home. So when they drew up alongside after her car ran out of petrol, Noelene was more than grateful to see them. Noelene was abducted and raped over a period of three days. Again, Catherine became jealous as what she saw as sexual favoritism and demanded Birnie murder Noelene. He must have had some sort of conscience about killing someone he knew, because he strangled her only after a large dose of sleeping tablets had taken effect.

Denise Brown, a 21-year-old computer operator, was snatched by the two on November 4, 1986, raped at their home and forced to telephone a girlfriend to say all was well. She was then taken to a pine plantation, raped again, and suffered unspeakable pain as Birnie's first attempts to stab her to death failed. He only succeeded when Catherine handed him a bigger knife.

David Birnie was sentenced to 30 years imprisonment for the murders of Denise Brown, Susannah Candy, Mary Neilson and Noeline Patterson.

— — — — — — — — — — — —

The girls' disappearances were causing concern with local police, for they were not drifters but all came from good backgrounds and had no reason to leave home. On the case was Detective Sergeant Paul Ferguson who, unconvinced by the fact that two of the victims had made contact after disappearing, came to the shocked conclusion that he was now dealing with a serial killer. But Ferguson was lucky enough to have the mystery swiftly solved, ending the Birnies' five-week sex and slaughter spree.

The detective was notified that a 17-year-old girl had run naked and weeping into a supermarket in Fremantle. She told police she had been dragged into a car as she walked through the affluent Perth suburb of Nedlands. Her abductors, a man and a woman, then drove her to their home where she was chained to a bed and raped. The girl only managed to escape when the man had left for work and the woman made the mistake of freeing her from the chains.

Though deeply distressed, the girl gave clear details of her kidnappers and where they lived. She had noted David Birnie's dark hair and particularly striking long nose and described Catherine as a small, hard-faced woman with high cheekbones and a tight mouth. It was Catherine Birnie who opened the door to the police. Within the hour, she and David were being interrogated. The two had known that with their last victim's escape, their time was up and they confessed to the four rape-murders.

Their arrest almost certainly prevented further murders. While searching the Birnies' seedy, white-painted brick bungalow, police found a newspaper with an advert ringed in red ink. It read: "URGENT. Looking for a lonely person. Prefer female 18 to 24 years, share single room flat."

The couple did not resist police demands to be taken to where their victims' bodies lay. The police convoy traveled along Wanneroo Road and through the pine forests, with Birnie chatting in a relaxed fashion. It was now dark and he had trouble locating the first grave, that of Denise Brown, buried on the edge of the Gnangara pine plantation. They then traveled on to the Glen Eagle picnic area on the Albany Highway near Armadale where Birnie guided police up a narrow track and to the body of Susannah Candy.

Catherine insisted she take police to where Noelene Patterson was buried. She was proud that she needed no help to find it. Once there, she spat on the grave, saying she never had liked the poor girl. Catherine later admitted she had been so anxious about Birnie's affection for Noelene that she had actually attempted to commit suicide by stabbing herself. But with further questioning, police dismissed any thoughts that Catherine had been an unwilling partner in the crimes. She had played an active part and even taken photographs as Birnie raped her victims. It was clear that, while insanely jealous of other women, she actually enjoyed helping David have sex with them.

Even hardened detectives and psychiatrists were disturbed by Catherine Birnie's obsession with her lover, an obsession that had her prepared to do anything to help him satisfy his deranged lust. Her whole life was one of total dedication to this man. During their first killing, Catherine said she had just wanted to know "if the girl could make

"She spat on the grave, saying she never had liked the poor girl"

David excited." She later signed a detailed statement admitting direct involvement in the murders.

Birnie himself thought that pretending to show remorse would aid his case. He said he wanted to plead guilty to spare his victims' families. None of this impressed the inmates of the prison where he was awaiting trial. A group of them attacked him and he needed hospital treatment.

On March 3, 1987, Catherine and David Birnie pleaded guilty to the charges of rape and murder. The judge, Mr. Justice Wallace said: "These horrible crimes were premeditated, planned and carried out cruelly and relentlessly over a comparatively short period." The couple were each sentenced to life imprisonment, although technically eligible for parole after serving a minimum of 20 years. But Mr. Justice Wallace decreed that David Birnie "should not be let out of prison—ever."

David and Catherine Birnie were finally separated. She was sent to serve her time in Bandyup prison, northern Perth, and he at Fremantle prison where he was regularly at the center of violent frays. Neither ever made any appeal against their sentence and it was expected that the scheduled parole hearings starting from 2007 would pass with the barest of acknowledgments.

LAWRENCE BITTAKER

When Hollywood actor Glenn Scott was allowed access to the confession tapes of serial killer Lawrence Bittaker to prepare for a screen role, he was reduced to tears.

The actor felt he would be able to handle what he heard in a bid to acquaint himself with the work of a FBI profiler, the role he was due to play in *The Silence of the Lambs*. Instead, he left the office of real life profiler John Douglas in tears—and no longer against the death penalty but in favor of it. Indeed, all of America felt that the gas chamber was no less than Bittaker deserved for his callous kidnapping and killing of young girls.

Lawrence Sigmond Bittaker was born in Pittsburgh on September 27, 1940, and was given his name by Mr. and Mrs. George Bittaker who adopted him as baby. The family were constantly on the move as Mr. Bittaker's work in aircraft factories saw him employed at sites in Pennsylvania and then in Florida, Ohio, and California. The continual moving had an affect on the young Bittaker and a feeling of restlessness and rootlessness set in. This led to several brushes with the law and young offenders' offices, with Bittaker finally dropping out of school when he was 17. With delinquent behavior now the norm, he was arrested for stealing a car, causing a hit-and-run accident and trying to avoid arrest, crimes which resulted in him being detained at the Californian Youth Authority for two years.

There seemed no way out of Bittaker's criminal existence. Within days of his release in August 1959, he was arrested again for car theft and sentenced to another 18 months at a reform center in Oklahoma. Within weeks of winning his freedom again, he was once more in prison for a robbery in Los Angeles. His indeterminate sentence of one to 15 years was accompanied by obligatory sessions with prison doctors. One of them in 1961 found Bittaker to have "superior intelligence" but also to be "manipulative and having considerable

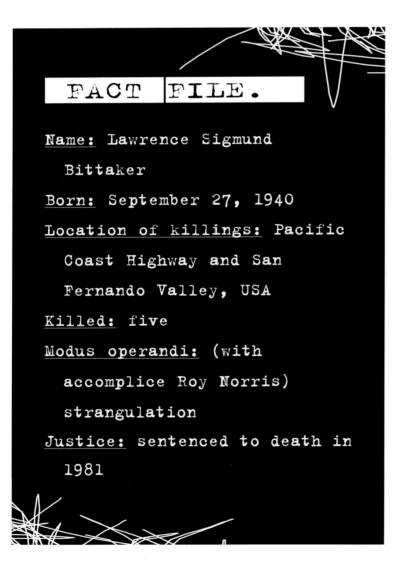

FACT FILE.

Name: Lawrence Sigmund Bittaker

Born: September 27, 1940

Location of killings: Pacific Coast Highway and San Fernando Valley, USA

Killed: five

Modus operandi: (with accomplice Roy Norris) strangulation

Justice: sentenced to death in 1981

concealed hostility." A hint of the violence that would later erupt came in other psychologists' reports that Bittaker was a "borderline psychotic," "basically paranoid," and had a tendency toward "poor control of impulsive behavior." Nevertheless, he won parole in 1963.

But being fortunate enough to have served barely a sixth of his possible prison sentence did not mean Bittaker would change his ways. Two months later, he was in prison again for violating his parole conditions and on suspicion of robbery. A further parole violation saw him in jail in October 1964. Prison doctors listened as Bittaker told them that stealing and other crime made him feel important. More disturbingly, they noted his belief that what happened was beyond his control and not his fault. Another note was made about his psychotic mental state but his crime sprees continued. There were further parole violations, more thefts, more car crimes and another hit-and-run offence, with Bittaker in and out of prison serving sentences of between six months and three years.

In 1974, Bittaker stabbed a shop assistant who was trying to stop him shoplifting. He went back behind bars but incredibly was out on the streets again four years later. This was despite warning signs again reported by medical experts of Bittaker's increasingly dangerous mental state. One psychiatrist, Dr. Robert Markman, banded Bittaker a "classic sociopath who is incapable of learning to play by the rules." Dr. Markman's further assessment gave even more of a hint of the killer in the making when he wrote: "Bittaker is a highly dangerous man with no internal controls over his impulses, a man who could kill without hesitation or remorse."

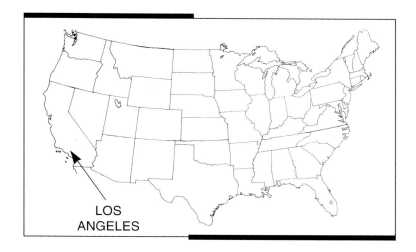

LOS ANGELES

Even when yet another doctor examined Bittaker during his prison term and labeled him "a sophisticated psychopath," his words went unheeded and Bittaker was released in November 1978—having made a very special friend in prison. Roy Lewis Norris was later to say that Bittaker had twice saved his life in jail and such a bond was to tie them together forever. Bittaker, in turn, began to share Norris's fascination with domination, rape, and torture. Both men were to win themselves a place in the sickening history of serial slaughter.

Norris was born in Greeley, Colorado, in 1948. Like Bittaker, he was a school drop-out and destined for a life of crime. By 1969, Norris had already attempted to rape a woman motorist and attacked another woman in her own home. In the next few years, he stalked other women, including a college student and a girl walking home alone.

Fate could not have provided a more sickening opportunity. Two months after Bittaker left prison, Norris was released too. The men arranged to meet at a seedy hotel in downtown Los Angeles where they rekindled their fantasies and made plans to grab girls off the streets and subject them to unspeakable horrors.

Bittaker bought a silver 1977 GMC cargo van which had no side windows but a large sliding door on the passenger side—handy, Bittaker reckoned, "for us to pull up close and not have to open the doors all the way when we see someone." He called the vehicle "Murder Mack" and the two men installed a bed in the back. From February through to June 1979, he and Norris cruised up and down the Pacific Coast Highway, stopping at beaches and practicing their rather crude art of flirting with the girls who hung out there. The two men found the girls were happy enough to pose for photographs not realizing they were being earmarked as potential murder victims. Police were later to count over 500 photographs of the smiling females, many of whom were never identified.

As well as identifying possible rape and torture targets, Norris, and Bittaker toured the coast tracking down some of the remotest areas where they could take their prey. The ideal spot, they decided, was an isolated emergency vehicle road in the San Gabriel Mountains overlooking Glendora. After smashing through a padlocked gate, Bittaker and Norris realized they had found the perfect hideaway; now the time was right to find the perfect victim too.

Bittaker spent the night before his first killing in Murder Mack, which was parked outside the trailer home where Norris now lived with his mother. When they awoke, the two men checked that a body could easily be concealed beneath the bed in

Murder Mack. Around midmorning, they started driving around the area.

It was a Sunday and plenty of people were out on the beaches. One who was not was 16-year-old Cindy Schaeffer, who was walking to her grandmother's house after attending a Christian Youth meeting at the St. Andrew's Presbyterian Church. Cindy declined the offer of a lift by the two men she did not know but was bundled into the van when Norris jumped out further along the way and blocked her escape. Inside Murder Mack, Cindy was bound by the wrists and ankles. Her cries for help were first drowned out by the van's loud radio and then stopped with tape bound tightly around her mouth. A single shoe left on the pavement was the only evidence of her fate.

Bittaker was late to recall that "throughout the whole experience, Cindy displayed a magnificent state of self-control and composed acceptance of the conditions and facts over which she had no control. She shed no tears, offered no resistance and expressed no great concern for her safety. I guess she knew what was coming."

Cindy was driven to the remote road. The two men smoked dope and asked the terrified girl about her family. Finally they ordered her to strip and Bittaker left the van for an hour to allow Norris time to rape her. When he returned he did the same. Norris was later to say that on his arrival back at Murder Mack, Bittaker was bungling his attempts at strangling the teenage girl. "Her body

> **"Her cries for help were first drowned out by the van's loud radio and then stopped with tape bound tightly around her mouth"**

was still jerking and alive to some degree because she was breathing or trying to breathe," said Norris, who said he finished the job with a wire coat hanger made into a makeshift garrote. Cindy's body was then tossed into a deep canyon.

It was another sunny Sunday when Bittaker and Norris killed again. They picked up hitchhiker Andrea Hall on July 8, 1979, as the 18-year-old thumbed a lift along Pacific Coast Highway. Andrea accepted the lift because there was only one occupant in the van and she gratefully accepted the offer of a cold drink. But as soon as she got into the vehicle, Norris leaped out from under the bed where he was hiding. Andrea was bound just like Cindy and taken to the same remote spot where Norris and Bittaker took turns raping her. Bittaker then dragged the girl outside and took photographs capturing her terror. He stabbed her twice with an ice pick and hurled her body off a cliff.

Less than two months later, on America's Labor Day on September 9, Norris and Bittaker committed a double killing. The two girls, 15-year-old Jackie Gilliam and 13-year-old Leah Lamp, were sitting on a bench with no particular plans for the day. They eagerly accepted an offer from the men to join them in smoking a joint on the beach but became agitated when they realized they were not being driven toward the shore. They were overpowered and subdued before being taken to the secret mountain site. Leah and Jackie were kept alive for two days during which Norris and Bittaker videotaped their rape and torture ordeal. The tape caught Norris raping Jackie as he demanded she role-play the part of his cousin, a girl at the center of some of Norris's sexual fantasies. Jackie was finally attacked with the ice pick and then strangled. Leah was strangled and clubbed with a

Lawrence Bittaker attempted to discredit the testimony of his accomplice, Ray Norris, who pleaded guilty to the murders of five teenage girls to avoid the death penalty.

sledgehammer. Both girls were thrown off the cliff. The ice pick was still in Jackie's skull.

That same month, on September 30, the evil pair pounced on 16-year-old Shirley Sanders on a visit to her father in Manhattan Beach. When Shirley refused a lift, Norris sprayed her in the face with chemical mace and dragged her in the van. She was raped by both men but incredibly she managed to escape. Shirley reported the attack to the police but was in such a distressed state she

Laurence Bittaker is shown in 1981 after hearing the jury's recommendation that he be sentenced to death. It was the first murder trial in California to be televized.

- - - - - - - - - - - -

could recall few details. Without any identification of the car or Shirley's assailants, detectives found the case difficult to pursue.

Bittaker and Norris did not know this, however. They felt their time was nearly up and that Shirley would have supplied enough information to have them caught. Getting nervous as the weeks went on, they planned one last sickening murder.

It was October 31, Halloween Night, and an occasion that appealed to Norris and Bittaker's twisted sense of humor. As real-life spooks, they decided against their regular beach haunts and instead joined in the Halloween revelers along the streets of the Sunland and Tijunga district of the San Fernando Valley. Among them was 16-year-old Lynette Ledford who was hitching a lift. She happily got into the van and within moments was thrown to the floor and tied up. This time, Norris and Bittaker did not drive to their mountain hideaway but tortured and raped Lynette as they drove around. After strangling her, they dumped her body on a front lawn where it was discovered early the next morning.

The discovery baffled police who believed that the recent arrest of another Californian serial killer, Angelo Buono, nicknamed "The Hillside Strangler," would end the mystery of the disappearing girls. In fact, Norris solved the mystery for them by bragging of his killings to a former prison mate. The friend, Jimmy Dalton, was so horrified that he called his lawyer and the two men went to Los Angeles Police Department to tell what they knew. A chance remark about Norris and Bittaker's silver van turned out to be crucial, for it was one of the few details Shirley Sanders had been able to supply. After thumbing through hundreds of photographs, Shirley picked out Norris and Bittaker and police launched an undercover watch on the two.

Police got an excuse to take Norris in when they witnessed him selling drugs, after which they also arrested Bittaker on charges relating to Shirley Sanders. It was Norris who broke first, initially saying Bittaker made him commit murder, but then confessing to his part in all five killings. Both men were charged with five counts of first-degree murder, kidnapping, robbery, rape, deviant sexual assault, and criminal conspiracy. Announcing the charges, Los Angeles County

Sheriff Peter Pitchess said that Bittaker and Norris might be linked to the disappearance of 30 or 40 other victims. A stack of 500 photographs of women found in their van included 19 missing persons, none of whom were ever traced.

In February 1980 Norris led Deputy District Attorney Steve Kay on a grisly tour of their murder locations. They found the bodies of Leah Lamp and Jackie Gilliam, an ice pick still embedded in her skull, but there was no trace of Andrea Hall or Cindy Schaeffer. To ensure a conviction, Steve Kay reluctantly agreed to waive the death sentence for Norris if he testified against Bittaker. But even while awaiting trial, Bittaker was intent on murder; he was charged with soliciting two other inmates to kill Shirley Sanders.

The trial made chilling listening. Norris was described as "compulsive in his need and desire to inflict pain and torture upon women." Talking about the killing of Andrea Hall, Norris said: "Lawrence told me he was going to kill her. He wanted to see what her argument would be for staying alive."

During the three-week trial, Steve Kay broke down in tears several times at the defendants' seeming enjoyment of relating what they had done. The court heard of the pickaxe still embedded in Jackie Gilliam's body and jurors visibly flinched when they heard the tape recording made of Lynette Ledford's last moments. Bittaker was heard slapping Lynette and hitting her with a hammer, all the while shouting: "Say something girl! Go ahead and scream or I'll make you scream." Norris turned state's evidence against his friend and in return for his cooperation received a sentence of 45 years to life, with parole possible after 30 years.

Bittaker denied everything but was sentenced to death on March 24, 1981, after the court was told that if ever released, "there is little doubt that he would return to a life of crime and possible violence." The judge imposed an alternate sentence of 199 years, to take effect in the event that Bittaker's death sentence is ever commuted to life imprisonment. Bittaker was subsequently allowed to launch several appeals, including one after his execution date was fixed for December 29, 1989. On June 11, 1990, the California Supreme Court refused to hear his case again. Bittaker used his time on San Quentin's death row to bait the system by filing strange claims against the authorities, such as suffering "cruel punishment" when his lunchtime biscuit arrived broken. He continued to sign all correspondence "Pliers," the self-penned nickname referring to how he used pliers to tighten wire coat hangers around his victims' necks.

> **❝Norris was described as compulsive in his need and desire to inflict pain and torture upon women❞**

WAYNE BODEN

A sexual sadist, Wayne Boden had a fascination with vampires and an obsession about women's breasts.

He would strangle his victims, rape them, and then bite their breasts to drink their blood. Boden became infamous as Canada's "Vampire Rapist" after his distinctive modus operandi. Stalking his victims, principally in the neighborhood of Montreal, he sparked a two-year reign of terror with attacks that were frenzied and ferocious.

Boden carried out his murders between 1968 and 1971. In only two cases among his five victims were there signs of a struggle. In the others, the girls seemed serene in death—one even having a faint smile on her lips. Detectives speculated that the killer, who was attractive to women, had targeted girls who had masochistic inclinations. They may have agreed to certain sexual experimentation before the fierce urges of the Vampire Rapist caused him to lose control and probably asphyxiate the victims in the height of their lovemaking. He would then bestially abuse their bodies.

Boden's first murder victim was a 21-year-old teacher, Norma Vaillancourt, who was found dead in her Montreal apartment on July 23, 1968. She had been raped and strangled and her breasts were covered with teeth marks but baffled police could detect no sign of a struggle. The pathologist reported that the victim had died with a passive, faint smile on her face. A year elapsed before Boden struck again. The body of Shirley Audette was found dumped behind a Montreal apartment complex. She had been strangled, raped, and there were bite marks on her breasts. Shortly afterward, jewelry store clerk Marielle Archambault was found dead in her apartment with similar bite marks. Jean Way, 24, was killed in her apartment in 1969 and, although she had been strangled and her breasts gnawed, her face looked serene in death.

Then, to the relief of Montreal police, the killings stopped—only to start again 2,500 miles away in Calgary. In May 1971, schoolteacher Elizabeth Porteous failed to turn up to work and was discovered dead in her apartment. Elizabeth

FACT FILE.

Name: Wayne Boden, aka the "Vampire Rapist"

Born: unknown

Location of killings: Montreal and Calgary, Canada

Killed: five

Modus operandi: strangulation

Justice: sentenced to life in 1972

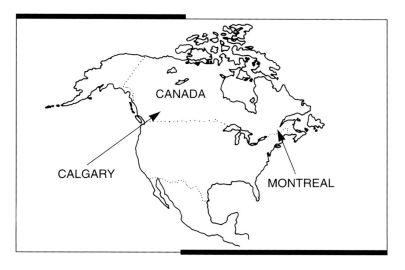

had put up a fierce fight for her life before being raped and strangled. Among the wreckage of her bedroom furniture was a broken cufflink.

Boden was eventually captured when the blue Mercedes in which he and Jean Way had been seen on the day of her murder was tracked down by police. The missing cufflink was his. They also identified him from a crumpled photograph found at Marielle Archambault's apartment. Dental experts matched a cast of Boden's teeth with bite marks found on his victims' bodies.

Boden was sentenced in Calgary to life imprisonment for the murder of Elizabeth Porteous. He was then returned to Montreal to be found guilty of three other murders and receive three further life sentences. Bafflingly, Boden always protested his innocence over the murder of Norma Vaillancourt.

MORRIS BOLBER

Morris Bolber and his gang made a fortune from disposing of poor Italian immigrants to America in the thirties.

Working as a team, they arranged murders in order to claim life insurance payouts. The three men would seduce women and then involve them in plots to kill their husbands and claim on their policies. In all, they are thought to have murdered more than 30 people over five years.

Bolber's early career of crookedness was conducted in a less violent manner. Calling himself Dr. Bolber, although his qualifications were entirely bogus, he was well known in the Italian community of Philadelphia as a provider of medicinal potions, almost all useless. Among the most popular was a mixture of ginger beer and saltpeter

that, he told naive housewives, would curb their husbands' unreasonable sexual urges. It was a visit by a grocer's wife seeking such a potion that turned the charlatan doctor into a killer. He persuaded her to take out life insurance on her ailing husband and then helped him to a "merciful release" by adding poison to his medicine.

Bolber decided there were riches to be had in relieving unhappy wives of their husbands and decided to expand his business by recruiting an Italian tailor, Paul Petrillo, and Petrillo's cousin, spaghetti salesman Herman, to help him in his campaign of seduction, murder, and fraud. In

1933, Bolber also teamed up with the so-called "Philadelphia Witch," Carina Favato, who, having poisoned her own husband, now provided the names of further potential victims through her contacts in the murky world of contract crime.

One of their victims was pushed off a building site roof. Another, a fisherman, was completely unaware that one of the gang had impersonated him to take out a policy on his life, leaving his widow a handsome sum to share with her partners in crime. Bolber and his ever-widening band of villains progressed from contrived "accidents" to

death by "natural means:" dealing victims heavy blows with canvas bags filled with sand to cause cerebral haemorrhages without leaving signs of violence.

> " [He dealt] victims heavy blows with canvas bags filled with sand to cause cerebral haemorrhages without leaving signs of violence "

Bolber's murderous business began to fall apart in February 1939 after Herman Petrillo bragged to an ex-convict friend about his sure-fire insurance scam. Cousin Paul was brought in and seemed to be trying to persuade the police that he was insane by calling himself a "professor of witchcraft" who could communicate with the devil and the spirit world and who could kill "with a powder at the snap of my fingers." Mrs. Favato was arrested, along with another recent widow, Mrs. Stella Alfonsi. The bodies of their spouses as well as those of several other victims were exhumed and found to have traces of arsenic in their systems. Every member of the gang tried to avoid justice by blaming another. But by doing so, they helped police build up a dossier on their entire murderous operation.

The Philadelphia District Attorney at first put

FACT FILE.

Name: Morris Bolber, aka
  "Dr. Bolber" and
  "the Rabbi"
Born: unknown but circa 1890
Location of killings:
  Philadelphia, New Jersey,
  and New York, USA
Killed: with conspirators,
  30-plus
Modus operandi: poisoned or
  hit with sandbag to claim
  insurance
Justice: sentenced to life in
  1939

the number of dead at ten or twelve with the profits of the crimes being estimated at between $50,000 and $100,000. But as further evidence was gathered, the estimates of the dead mounted, with one detective telling newspapers: "This case will make the famous Bluebeard murders in France pale into insignificance."

The sensational court case that followed heard evidence that Herman Petrillo was the "dealer in death powders," who in his hunt for more ingenious methods of murder, had even tried to obtain typhoid germs from a physician. On March 21, 1939, Herman was found guilty of murder for gain in Philadelphia, New Jersey, and New York, Judge Harry McDevitt declaring that the evidence had "only scratched the surface" and that there were "scores and scores more victims" of the insurance ring. He pledged "relentless prosecution for this group of assassins."

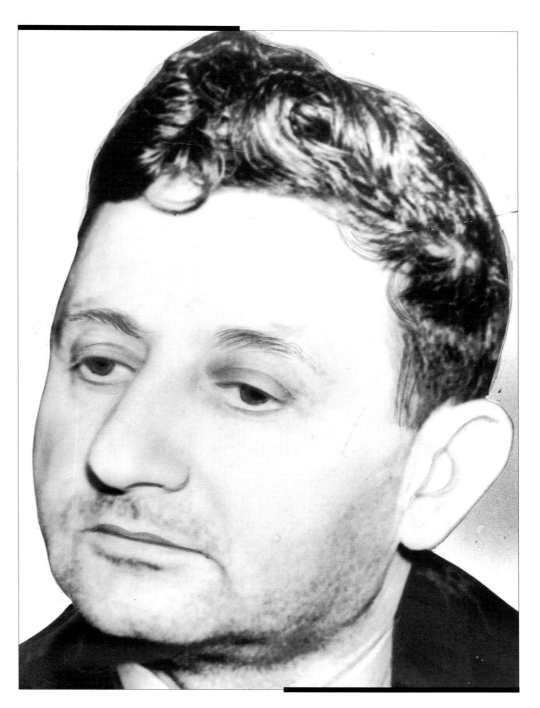

Morris Bolber was well known in the Italian community of Philadelphia in the 1930s. He reputedly killed some 30 people over five years.

As he was being led out of court, Petrillo cursed the jury and took a swing at its foreman. He had nothing to lose, for the verdict against him carried with it an automatic sentence of death by the electric chair. As the other members of the gang were lined up for their trials, police began to exhume the bodies of 70 further suspected victims. The evidence against the gang was overwhelming and, at her trial, Carina Favato grew increasingly agitated as her former friends willingly gave evidence

The bodies of suspected victims were eventually exhumed by police and found to have traces of arsenic in their system.

against her in a bid to save their own skins. Then the middle-aged widow shocked the jury by suddenly halting her own trial and pleading guilty to three counts of murder, including that of her husband and her stepson. "I might just as well get it over with," she said. "Let them send me to the chair. What have I got to live for?"

With Mrs. Favato now freely giving evidence against the syndicate, arrest warrants were issued for Morris Bolber, now known in the criminal fraternity as "the Rabbi," and for his secretary Rose Carina, alias "Rose of Death." She was found to have had five husbands, three of whom were dead.

By the end of 1939, 14 people had been found guilty of varying counts of murder. Of the principal conspirators, the Petrillos met their deaths in the electric chair, while Bolber and Favato escaped the death penalty and were sentenced to life imprisonment.

People for the Ethical Treatment of Animals
www.peta.org.uk

Top Tips
FOR ANIMALS!

1. Spay or neuter your animal companion.

2. Go vegetarian...or even better vegan.

3. Don't wear animals' skins or fur.

4. Always choose cruelty free products.

5. Speak out against cruelty whenever and wherever you see it.

6. Teach children to be kind to animals.

7. Tell your friends not to buy from pet shops.

8. Volunteer at your local animal shelter.

9. Never leave a stray animal in the street.

10. Try to do one nice thing for animals each day.

Visit the website below
for more information
and resources
on how to help animals!

www.peta.org.uk

**PEOPLE FOR THE ETHICAL
TREATMENT OF ANIMALS**
PO Box 36668, London SE1 1WA
E-mail address: info@peta.org.uk

Recycled paper

WILLIAM BONIN

It could have been watching his mother become servile to his violent father or her total dotage to her son that turned William Bonin into a serial sex killer.

Whatever the cause, Bonin was destined to lead a life of sadism and slaughter. His first criminal conviction was when he was only ten and was followed by repeated stays in detention centers. At 22, the truck driver, from Downey, California, was convicted of his first sex crimes: the kidnapping, molestation, and forcible oral copulation of young boys in four separate attacks. He was diagnosed as a mentally disturbed sex offender and sent to Atascadero State Hospital.

Bonin was released in May 1974, with psychiatrists saying he was no longer a danger—but he went on to murder at least 14, mainly homosexual young men. Bonin himself boasted that he raped and murdered four times that many between the years of 1972 and 1980 and was proud to be known as the Californian "Freeway Killer."

The first victim police could positively say had died at the hands of Bonin was 14-year-old

Thomas Lundgren, who was abducted from Reseda on May 28, 1979, and whose body was dumped the same day near Malibu. But many other murders of men and boys before that time—perhaps more than 40—were believed to have been committed by Bonin and accomplices. His principal partner in crime was 22-year-old Vernon Butts who cruised the highways of Los Angeles and Orange counties

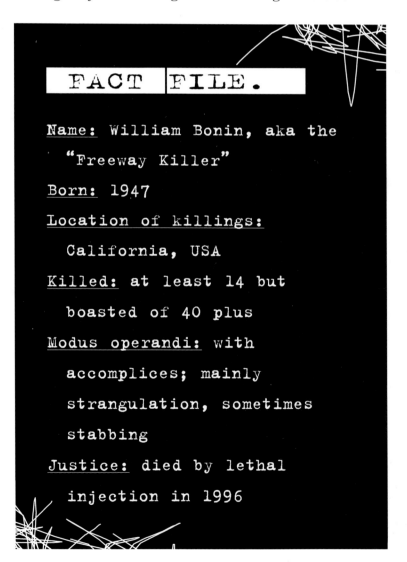

FACT FILE.

Name: William Bonin, aka the "Freeway Killer"

Born: 1947

Location of killings: California, USA

Killed: at least 14 but boasted of 40 plus

Modus operandi: with accomplices; mainly strangulation, sometimes stabbing

Justice: died by lethal injection in 1996

CALIFORNIA

SAN FRANCISCO   LOS ANGELES

with Bonin looking for young homosexuals. The number of victims suddenly rose after the discovery of Thomas Lundgren's body. They included 17-year-old Mark Shelton, Marcus Grabs, 17, Donald Hyden, 15, and David Murillo, 17, whose bodies were found between May and September 1979. Butts, who had fallen under what he would later describe as Bonin's "hypnotic" spell, had gone from being sickened by his first killing to actively enjoying raping, torturing, and murdering. He told police: "After the first one, I couldn't do anything about it. Bonin had a hypnotic way about him."

It was Bonin's attempt to recruit 18-year-old William Pugh into his killing games that led to his arrest. The horrified teenager tipped off police who set up a 24-hour surveillance of Bonin. On the night of June 11, 1980, they caught him in the act of forcibly sodomizing a young victim in the back of his van. Bonin was arrested and while in custody heard that Vernon Butts had also been picked up by police as an accomplice in six of the now infamous "Freeway Murders." Bonin was charged with 14 counts of murder, 11 counts of robbery, and one of sodomy.

In August that year, two mentally deficient

William Bonin, the "Freeway Killer" listening to the jurors after they returned a verdict against him in California, 1983. The total number of murder convictions against him was 14.

men, James Munro and Gregory Miley, both 19 years of age, were also arrested in connection with two of the murders. All three of Bonin's accomplices decided to co-operate with police to avoid the death sentence. They said in their statements that Bonin enjoyed torturing his victims and that he loved "those sounds of screams." In January 1981, Butts hanged himself in his cell. It was the fifth suicide attempt he had made after his arrest.

At Bonin's trial in November 1981, the court was subjected to horrific descriptions of the killings, mainly involving acts of sadism before the bodies were "thrown like garbage along the streets and freeways." Miley and Munro testified against Bonin, saying he had urged them to start "going around and grabbing anyone off the street and killing them." Bonin himself said he simply couldn't stop killing, adding: "It got easier with each one we did." Convicted on 14 murder counts, Bonin was sentenced to death by Judge William Keene on January 5, 1982, but it was to be another 14 years before the execution was carried out at San Quentin Prison.

Now aged 49, Bonin was taken out of death row for the last time on February 23, 1996. There were no last words of remorse or pleas for forgiveness.

❝Doped on Valium, he was led to the room that had previously been used as a gas chamber and was strapped down while the first of three chemicals was pumped into him❞

He told his warders that he thought the death penalty was unfair. By way of moral guidance, he said: "I would suggest that when a person has a thought of doing anything serious against the law, that before they did they should go to a quiet place and think about it seriously." However, moments before the lethal concoction of drugs took Bonin's life he had to confess: "If I had not been arrested I would still be killing. I couldn't stop killing."

Bonin was the first person to be executed by lethal injection in California. Doped on Valium, he was led to the room that had previously been used as a gas chamber and was strapped down while the first of three chemicals was pumped into him. Sodium pentathol, which rendered him immediately unconscious, was followed by pancuronium bromide, which paralyzed him and prevented his breathing. Finally, potassium chloride stopped his heart. Three minutes after the first injection, he was declared dead. No relatives were present at William Bonin's execution and none came forward to claim his body. He was cremated and his ashes scattered across the Pacific Ocean, a more pleasant location than the littered freeways where his victims' mortal remains were dumped.

WERNER BOOST

In a period during the early 1950s, lovers' lanes and shadowy lay-bys throughout Düsseldorf, West Germany, were no longer frequented by those seeking clandestine pleasures.

The threat of being murdered by a madman was too high a price to pay. That maniac was Werner Boost, later to be known as the "Doubles Killer," who preyed on courting couples as they sat in their cars.

Born in 1928, Werner earned a living after World War II transporting refugees across the East German border. He moved to Düsseldorf in 1950. Three years later he committed his first murder, taking along with him an accomplice, Franz Lorbach. Unwittingly, the two men chose as a

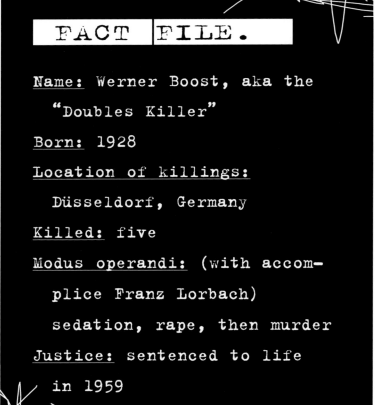

FACT FILE.

<u>Name:</u> Werner Boost, aka the
  "Doubles Killer"

<u>Born:</u> 1928

<u>Location of killings:</u>
  Düsseldorf, Germany

<u>Killed:</u> five

<u>Modus operandi:</u> (with accom-
  plice Franz Lorbach)
  sedation, rape, then murder

<u>Justice:</u> sentenced to life
  in 1959

victim someone who would make it a very high profile killing.

On January 7, 1953, distinguished lawyer Dr. Lotha Serve was in the back seat of his parked car close to the Rhine when his attackers crept up alongside. Suddenly, the car doors were pulled open and Serve was faced with two men wearing handkerchiefs over their faces. He was beaten, shot in the head, and robbed. But the lawyer had not been alone. He was in the back seat with his male lover, 19-year-old student Adolf Hullecremer, who pleaded to be spared. The two assailants beat and robbed the young man but then, shaken by the enormity of the crime, Lorbach struck a whispered deal with him: that Hullecremer should play dead after allowing Lorbach to beat him over the head with a pistol. The terrified student was more than willing to comply and save himself. Though knocked unconscious, he came round shortly afterward and fled the scene.

Stumbling through the snow-covered streets and shaking in the bitter cold, Hullecremer eventually found his way to a police station, where he gave a garbled account of what had happened. By the time police got to the scene of the attack, fresh snow had fallen and all signs of escaping car tracks had been obliterated. No fingerprints had been left on the car and, since the dead lawyer's wallet was missing, the natural assumption by police was that they were looking for a couple of local armed robbers.

That conclusion had to be re-examined three weeks later when a tramp handed in a .32 pistol that he had found in the woods nearby. Tests showed it to be the murder weapon, and markings on the bullets it fired proved unique. Circulated to all police stations, photographs of the bullets jogged the memory of detectives in Magdeburg, in former East Germany, who said the gun had been used some years earlier to shoot two refugees fleeing to the West. There were no further clues and the trail went cold.

Two years later, Düsseldorf police realized the murderous duo were still on their patch. A baker named Friedhelm Behre and his fiancée Thear Kurmann left a restaurant in the early hours of November 1, 1955, and vanished. They were reported missing by relatives but were not found until the Christmas holiday when their car was spotted in a water-filled gravel pit outside of the city. Behre had been shot through the head and his 23-year-old fiancée had been raped then garrotted. Both of their skulls had then been inexplicably crushed.

Now labeled the "Doubles Killer," Boost carried out his final double killing five weeks later. The charred bodies of chauffeur Peter Falkenberg and his girlfriend, 23-year-old Hildegard Wassing, were discovered in a smoldering haystack near the village of Lankilverich on February 8, 1956. He had been shot through the head and she had been raped before being strangled, the charred remains of a rope still around her neck. A missing Mercedes belonging to Falkenberg's employer was found with its interior spattered with blood.

Boost was caught on June 10, 1956, as he was about to pounce on a couple parked in woods on the outskirts of Düsseldorf. He was obviously

Werner Boost covered his face when he was taken from the court in Düsseldorf after being found guilty of the murder of a trade union official. He was sentenced to life imprisonment.

guilty but he denied the murders. When his younger apprentice, 23-year-old Lorbach, was picked up, police realized he was a drug addict and locked him up until his withdrawal symptoms made him plead to be allowed to tell all. He described Boost as a "monster" whose method was to sedate the couples, then rape the women before killing them. He said he had been hypnotized into helping with the crimes.

Boost, aged 31, was sentenced to life on December 14, 1959, for the murder of Dr. Serve. Lorbach was jailed for six years. Evidence linking the two men to the other murders could not be proved. The fact that, while awaiting trial, another couple had been murdered in a car near Cologne was a defense argument that seemed to have swayed the jury.

JERRY BRUDOS

Since childhood, Jerry Brudos had an irresistible fetish for women's clothes in general and shoes in particular.

His mother rebuked him for playing with her shoes when he was just five years old. As an adolescent he was fixated by black stiletto heels. And as a freckle-faced teenager he would steal out at night to remove women's clothes from washing lines. At 16, he dug a tunnel in a hillside with the aim of luring a girl there and attacking her. His obsessive behavior finally brought him to the notice of police when, at the age of 17, he forced a woman to pose for naked pictures at knifepoint. He was confined to a mental hospital for nine months with a personality disorder.

After his release, Brudos continued to increase his collection of stolen underwear. Unknown to

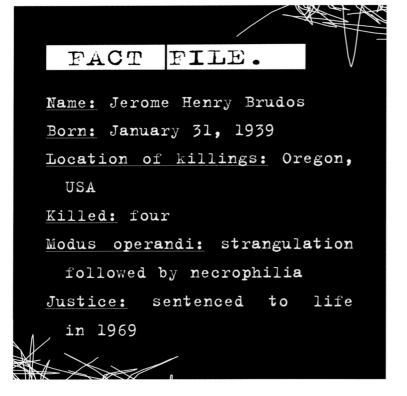

FACT FILE.

Name: Jerome Henry Brudos

Born: January 31, 1939

Location of killings: Oregon, USA

Killed: four

Modus operandi: strangulation followed by necrophilia

Justice: sentenced to life in 1969

members of his family, he had begun to stalk women, knocking them down and fleeing with their shoes. Despite his weird behavior, Brudos managed to find himself a wife, a 17-year-old whom he had made pregnant. A second child came along and the family moved from California to settle in Portland, Oregon, where Brudos worked as an electrician.

Then, on January 26, 1968, the seemingly normal 28-year-old family man committed his first murder. The victim was salesgirl Linda Slawson, aged 19, who happened to knock on the door of the Brudos home in Portland's Salem district to try to interest him in a set of encyclopedias. With his family upstairs, Brudos knocked the young woman unconscious then strangled her. Then he abused the corpse, dressing it with clothes from his collection and photographing his handiwork. Finally, he chopped off the left foot and, with a newly fitted shoe, put it in his refrigerator. The body was finally bound to an old engine block and disposed of in the nearby Willamette River.

Three other murders followed. In November 1968, Brudos spotted 23-year-old Jan Whitney standing beside her broken down car and inveigled her to his home to collect a toolbox. There, he strangled her, sodomizing her corpse before dressing the body and photographing it. He left it hanging on a hook in his locked garage for several days, returning to abuse it again and again. His final savage act was to amputate one of her breasts, which he kept "as a paperweight," the rest of her body being dumped in the Willamette.

In March 1969, student Karen Sprinkler, 19, was raped before and after being strangled. When her body was found, both her breasts were missing. Linda Salee, 22, was raped and murdered a month later, her body attached to cables to see whether it would react to electric shocks after death. All the victims had been photographed shortly after death.

After quizzing fellow students of Karen Sprinkler at Oregon State University, police discovered several girls had received phone calls from a man asking to meet them. He had claimed to be a Vietnam veteran with psychic powers and most of the students he had phoned had wisely turned him down. However, one foolhardy student who had taken up his offer reported that he was fat, freckled, and very odd. He had referred to "those two poor girls whose bodies were found in the river" and agreed she was wise in declining his offer of a drive in his car because, as he put it, "How do you know I wouldn't take you to the river and strangle you?" When Brudos called the girl for a further date, she rang the police and a trap was set.

They questioned Brudos but released him for lack of evidence. Only when they dug into his past was an arrest warrant issued and the killer was captured hiding under a blanket in the back of his car while his wife drove. When they got him to the police station, they discovered that he was wearing women's underwear. His home was raided and drawers of carefully sorted women's clothes and shoes were uncovered. They found that his electrician's wiring exactly matched that used to bind the corpses. They found a woman's breast, hardened with varnish, in full view on the mantelpiece.

Mrs. Ralphene Brudos leaving the court after pleading innocent to a charge of murder. She was charged with aiding her husband to smother and strangle Karen Sprinkler.

But the most damning evidence was a photograph of Jan Whitney's abused body hanging from a hook in his garage. At the victim's feet was a mirror— showing a reflection of the man taking the gruesome snapshot. It was clearly Brudos.

Police at first could not believe that Brudos's wife Darcy could be unaware of her husband's crimes. She was finally cleared of a charge of abetting the murder of Karen Sprinkler. Brudos himself was charged with three of the four murders. He pleaded insanity but psychiatric reports declared him sane and he was sentenced to life imprisonment at Oregon State Penitentiary.

TED BUNDY

Theodore Bundy, the all-American boy who seemed to have everything going for him, finally ran out of luck on January 24, 1989, when he was executed in Florida's electric chair.

He took with him to his ignominious end a number of mysteries. One was whether he had committed the nine murders with which he was officially attributed or the 20 to 30 to which he had confessed or the 100-plus with which some investigators credit him. But the greatest mystery of all is what made Ted Bundy tick. What, within seconds, could turn this charming chancer into a vile and vicious killer?

If there is such a thing as an "average" serial killer, Bundy was never it. He was as far from our idea of a homicidal maniac as it is possible to be. Handsome, charming, witty, and well educated, he was every mother's ideal son, every young male's ideal buddy, every girl's ideal date. As a youngster, Theodore had been a Boy Scout, did a paper-round, and started his own lawn-mowing business. A high school athlete and then a graduate of the University of Washington, he was never short of a pretty girl on his arm. He was a campaign worker both for the Republican Party and for the Crime Commission in Washington State. According to experts who have studied the man, he could have ended up a leading lawyer, a top politician, perhaps even a Senator. Yet this was Ted Bundy, one of the most feared serial killers in American history. And what follows are some of the things of which he was capable.

Lynda Ann Healy, a 21-year-old law student at the University of Washington State, in Seattle, set her alarm for 7am on the morning of January 31, 1974. It went off as planned. Two hours later it was still ringing. At 9am her roommate walked in to find her gone with a one-inch bloodstain on the pillow, the only evidence that she had been there the previous night. Six weeks later, on March 12,

FACT FILE.

Name: Theodore Robert Bundy, birth name Cowell

Born: November 24, 1946

Location of killings: Seattle, Utah, Colorado, Florida, Idaho, California, Michigan, Pennsylvania, and Vermont, USA

Killed: at least 19, probably 30 or more

Modus operandi: mainly strangulation

Justice: executed in electric chair on 1989

student Donna Gail Manson, aged 19, walked from her dormitory and headed across the Evergreen State College Campus to a student faculty music recital and was never seen again. On April 17, Susan Rancourt, aged 18, left a meeting at the university campus to walk to a movie theater 400 yards away. She too vanished, as did 22-year-old Roberta Parks who failed to return from a late-night walk on May 6. On June 1, 22-year-old Brenda Ball walked out of a Seattle bar with an unknown man and was never seen again. Georgeann Hawkins, aged 18, left her boyfriend's apartment on June 11 heading for her sorority house; she never made it.

On July 14, with temperatures in the 90s, a crowd of 40,000 were swimming and sunbathing at Lake Sammamish State Park, near Seattle. One of the sunseekers was Janice Graham, a 22-year-old office worker, who came within seconds of dying at the hands of the killer and who was able to give a perfect description of Bundy. As she told police later, she was standing near the park's bandstand when a man in his mid-twenties approached her. She noticed that he was wearing jeans and a white T-shirt and his left arm was in a sling and plaster cast. He asked: "Say, could you help me a minute? Would you help me put my sailboat on top of my car?" She agreed and he led her to a Volkswagen Beetle in the nearby parking lot. There was no sign of a sailboat, however, and Bundy explained: "I forgot to say, it's at my folks' house just up the hill." Janice Graham nodded in agreement then suddenly hesitated. "I have to meet my husband," she said, "and I'm running late." Afterward, she recollected that the stranger was so charming that she had almost changed her mind again and went with him: "He was really friendly,

Ted Bundy is shown in July 1978 after his arrest. He was one of the most feared serial killers in American history and evaded capture for years.

very polite at all times, very sincere, easy to talk to. He had a nice smile."

If she had stepped into Bundy's car she would never have been seen alive again. As it happened, she walked back to the bandstand and watched fascinated as Bundy, having chatted up another girl, wandered with her toward his car. "A fast worker," she thought. Bundy's second target was also named Janice, a 23-year-old probation office

Bundy was adept at disguises and he took on many identities to escape prosecution. The photographs range in time from 1975 (top left) to 1978 (bottom right), taken after his arrest.
- - - - - - - -

worker named Janice Ott, who had been approached as she sunbathed. Witnesses who overheard their conversation recalled that a young man with his arm in a sling had introduced himself as "Ted" and asked for help with his sailboat. Janice had smiled, stood up, and wheeled her bicycle to where his car was. She was never seen alive again.

That same day, Denise Naslund, an 18-year-old secretary, wandered with a party of friends to a nearby stream that ran into the lake. They swam together until late afternoon, when Denise left the water to walk to public restrooms. She became victim number eight. Two months later, on September 7, a team of grouse beaters found the remains of both Denise and Janice under a copse of trees. They had both been murdered in a sexual frenzy. Their bodies had also been stripped bare and their jewelry stolen.

The body of a third woman found nearby could not be identified. The bodies of two more women were found by another hunter in the same area on October 12. One of them was identified as Carol Valenzuela, aged 20, who had vanished on the Washington-Oregon border two months earlier. The other was never identified.

When detectives began their murder hunt following the discovery of the first three bodies, they found that several women who had been approached at Lake Sammamish that same day by a handsome young man with his arm in a sling.

> **"He handcuffed her and dragged her into his Volkswagen but she escaped by rolling out of the vehicle as it slowed at a bend"**

He had told them all: "Hi, I'm Ted." Ted Bundy, then 28 years of age, had become sufficiently emboldened to operate in daylight and even to give his own name. The accurate descriptions of the killer and his car allowed the Kings County Major Crimes Unit to issue a public appeal, with drawings of their quarry. More than 3,000 callers telephoned the police hotline, one of them naming as a suspect a young law student named Ted Bundy. If he was ever checked out, he must have been considered too squeaky clean to warrant further investigation. Meanwhile, their "Most Wanted" man was about to move on to his next killing fields.

On August 30, Bundy quit his job at the Washington State Office of Emergency Services—putting on his resignation letter: "The World Needs Me"—and moved to Utah, where he enrolled at the University of Utah Law School in Salt Lake City. Two months later the killings began again. On October 2, Nancy Wilcox, aged 16, disappeared in Salt Lake City. On October 18, Melissa Smith, aged 18, was raped and murdered. On October 31, 17-year-old Laura Aime was battered and strangled. Debbie Kent, aged 17, died on November 8. That same day, an attempt on the life of Carol Da Ronch, aged 18, failed after Bundy approached her, posing as a police officer and saying: "Hi, I'm Ted." He handcuffed her and dragged her into his Volkswagen but she escaped by rolling out of the vehicle as it slowed at a bend.

The slaughter spread from Utah to Colorado. Between January and April 1975, at least five Colorado women went missing: Caryn Campbell, 23, on January 12; Julie Cunningham, 26, on March 15; Denise Oliverson, 25, on April 6; Melanie Cooley, 18, on April 16; and Shelly Robertson, 24, on July 1. But police still had no clues as to the identity of their abductor. They knew only that he was a methodical killer who traveled from state to state, seeming to have no fixed abode.

> **"He was polite, well-spoken, and utterly convincing"**

Then police got a lucky break. On the evening of August 16, 1975, Highway Patrolman Robert Hayward was answering a routine call in his hometown of Granger, Utah, when he saw a Volkswagen pull away from the kerbside in front of him at speed with no lights on. He forgot about the callout and instead chased the car, his siren wailing. Ted Bundy stopped and Officer Hayward ran over to the Volkswagen, gun in hand. He questioned Bundy and asked him what he had inside his car. The killer replied: "Just some junk." The "junk" turned out to be a pair of handcuffs, a crowbar, a ski mask, and a nylon stocking.

Incredibly, despite discovering what must have appeared to have been the tools of a burglar's or rapist's trade, Bundy was booked only for failing to stop for police—and he was released on bail. It was not until the following day that he was arrested in his apartment at 565 First Avenue, Salt Lake City, and charged with possessing tools for burglary. The charge was a minor one but the net was closing in. Carol Da Ronch, the girl who had escaped from Bundy's car when it slowed down, was reinterviewed. She told police that the vehicle she was snatched in resembled Bundy's Volkswagen and identified her assailant from pictures on his driving license. Bundy, still out on bail, was put in an identification parade and was immediately picked out by Da Ronch.

Police were still utterly frustrated to find there was no evidence to link Bundy to the murders. Again, he was bailed on a charge of kidnapping and of possessing tools for burglary. The mass-murderer headed back to Seattle to await his trial, for which he returned to Utah on February 23, 1976.

Ted Bundy, then aged 29, made a great impression in court. It was hard to believe that this graduate of the University of Washington, who had worked as a campaigner for the Crime Commission in Seattle, could be charged with anything but a surfeit of charm. He was polite, well-spoken, and utterly convincing. The jury obviously wondered why such a man needed to kidnap a girl when he could date the prettiest.

So who was this man who could entrance hardened lawyers and, thus far, literally get away with murder? Bundy was born to 19-year-old Louise Cowell in a home for unwed mothers in Burlington, Vermont. The identity of his father remains a mystery but is believed to have been a member of the armed forces whom she dated briefly. Having confessed her predicament to her parents Sam and Eleanor, both strict Methodists, they agreed that she should leave her Philadelphia

Ted Bundy waved to a TV camera at his indictment for the murders of Lisa Levy and Margaret Bowman. The court forbade him from speaking to journalists.

– – – – – – – – – – –

home and arrange the birth out-of-state to avoid scandal. Afterward Louise traveled back to Philadelphia alone while the question of adoption was discussed.

Two months later, the decision was made to keep the baby, but to pretend that it was the adopted son of Sam and Eleanor. It was a fairly transparent deception and neighbors saw through

it immediately but the plan was put into operation and Louise returned to Vermont to collect her child. Although the Cowell family's subterfuge did not work for the neighbors, it certainly did for young Theodore. He adored his grandfather, a landscape gardener, and later spoke of a wonderfully adventurous childhood filled with trips to the coast, fishing in rivers, or camping in the countryside. He had differing memories of his grandmother, however. Eleanor suffered from depression and agoraphobia and ended up as a virtual recluse in the home.

Another relative, Ted's Aunt Julia, experienced a disturbing incident with little Ted when he was just three. Julia, then 15, awoke one night to find that Ted had lifted the blankets and was placing butchers knives beside her body in the bed. "He just stood there and grinned," she recalled. "I shooed him out of the room and took the knives back to the kitchen. I told my mother about it but remember thinking at the time that I was the only one who thought it was strange. Nobody else did anything."

In 1950, Louise took her son across America to Tacoma, Washington, where she met and married hospital cook Johnnie Bundy. He adopted Ted as his own son and the couple went on to have four more children. Young Bundy grew up with them in apparent domestic harmony and became the all-American boy. He had a paper round, joined the Boy Scouts, and went from house to house doing lawn-mowing jobs for pocket money. He got good grades at school, although reports warned of his explosive temper. He was a high school athlete and then a student at the University of Washington. With his film-star good looks, he was never short of a date. But his girlfriends, while praising his charm, recalled him as a sadistic bedfellow who acted out bondage and sado-masochistic fantasies. Bundy became a campaigner for the Republicans in Washington State. And in 1971, in a supreme twist of irony, he became a counsellor at a Seattle rape crisis center after being screened for "maturity and balance."

This then was the face that Ted Bundy presented to the court in Utah when facing the charge of kidnapping in February 1976. Why would such an innocent-looking young man need to kidnap a girl? Surely he could pick the prettiest without

Bundy leaving Leon County Court in 1978.
- - - - - - - - - - - - - -

resorting to violence? As he himself once boasted: "Why should I want to attack women? I had all the female companionship I wanted. I must have slept with a dozen women in that first year in Utah and all of them went to bed with me willingly." The case almost went Bundy's way. But after months of legal arguments, he was found guilty of kidnapping and sentenced to between one and 15 years. Relieved, police then moved their prisoner from Utah to Colorado to stand trial for the murder of 23-year-old student Caryn Campbell, abducted from a ski resort where Bundy had been prowling on the night of January 12, 1975.

Sadly, security was not as tight in Colorado. During a break in a court session in Aspen, Bundy leaped from a courtroom window. He was recaptured eight days later. Then, on December 30,

❝During a break in a court session in Aspen, Bundy leaped from a courtroom window.❞

using a stack of books as a stepladder, Bundy cut through a ceiling panel of his Colorado Springs cell with a hacksaw blade. He stole a police car and headed first for Chicago, then south to Florida.

Wherever he stopped, Bundy took on a different identity. The killer was on the top of the list of America's most wanted criminals, yet he went unrecognized. When he rented a room near the University of Florida, Tallahassee, no one suspecting that he was anything but a polite, intelligent, courteous visitor to the capital. The mass murderer was free to kill again.

On January 15, 1978, he crept into the Chi Omega sorority house, a female dormitory at the university, where the sleeping students had just returned from their Christmas vacation. Bundy was carrying a heavy wooden club. His first victim was 21-year-old Margaret Bowman. He beat her mercilessly and strangled her with her own tights before taking bites out of her buttocks. In the same way, he murdered Lisa Levy, aged 20. He savagely beat two others, Karen Chandler and Kathy

Keiner, scarring both of them for life, before fleeing. Bundy's next monstrous attack was in Lake City, Florida, on February 8. There he killed his youngest known victim, 12-year-old Kimberly Leach. He strangled her, sexually violated her and left her body decomposing in a shed used for keeping pigs.

Luck ran out for Bundy a week later when, in the early hours of February 15, a Pensacola policeman checked the number plate of a Volkswagen in a restaurant car park and found that it had been

Bundy shown in 1978 during his trial for killing a 12-year-old girl.

stolen. The driver identified himself as Ken Misner—just one of 21 identities that Bundy had assumed, complete with credit cards, check books, passports, and company IDs. When questioned further, Bundy attacked Patrolman David Lee and tried to escape. The officer was swifter than the killer, however, and he tackled him and clubbed him unconscious. When Bundy came round, he told Lee: "I wish you would have killed me."

The mass murderer was charged with the single murder of 12-year-old Kimberly. At his trial, jurors were shocked by evidence that confirmed that bite marks on the child's body could only have been made by his teeth. Nevertheless, Bundy received messages of support and even proposals of marriage. Found guilty and sentenced to the electric chair, he got sackfuls of mail from adoring women who could not believe that such a devastatingly handsome man could be responsible for such hideous crimes.

Bundy lived in the shadow of the electric chair for almost ten years, still protesting his innocence. He stalled his execution with numerous appeals which went as far as the US Supreme Court. Then, when he saw there was no way out, he broke down and confessed to almost 40 murders and admitted: "I deserve to die for them." He had killed girls in Idaho, California, Michigan, Pennsylvania, and Vermont. Some were committed as "day trips" with Bundy jetting into a city, selecting his victim, killing her, and flying out again.

Bundy's repeated appeals cost the American

Ted Bundy showed no emotion as he was found guilty of first degree murder on July 24, 1979. He was convicted of killing a 12-year-old girl and was to live in the shadow of the electric chair for another ten years.

- - - - - - - - - - - - - -

The public gather to see Ted Bundy being escorted from the Leon County Courthouse in 1978.

- - - - - - - - - - - - -

taxpayer an estimated four million dollars during the years he spent on death row. But time finally ran out for the serial killer at Starke Prison in Florida in February 1989. Religious broadcaster James Dobson spent the final night with him in his cell. Bundy refused his condemned man's last meal and wept openly as he told Dobson of his perverted crusade of death. Dobson later wrote: "Ted Bundy said society had a right to be protected from him. He said that after he killed the first woman

he went through a period of great distress for six months. He was extremely guilty, he didn't believe he could have done something like that. But that gradually subsided and the sexual frenzy which he would go through occurred again and he killed another to sate it. Each time became a little easier to cope with and he did that so many times that he got to the point where he could not feel any more."

Ted Bundy finally fried in Florida's electric chair in 1989 and there were no tears for him. The last thing he felt was the cold metal of Old Sparkey's electrodes clamped to his leg in the

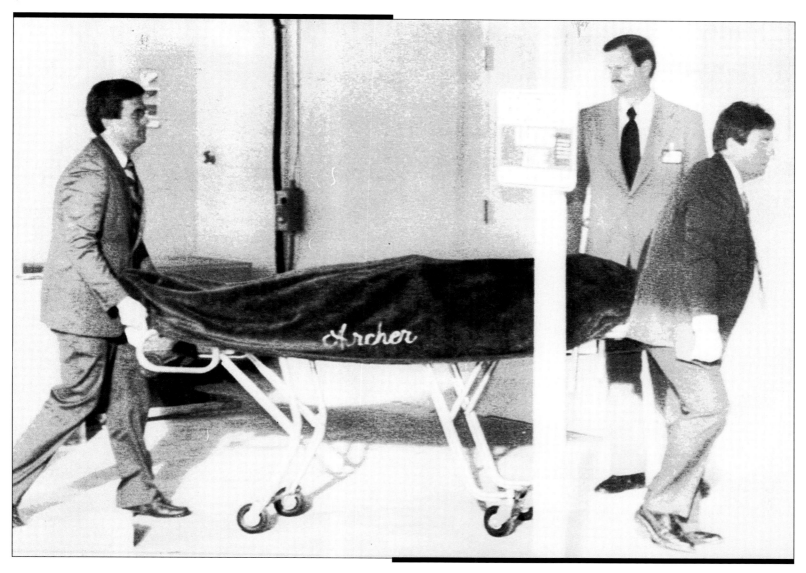

The body of Ted Bundy is taken away after his execution on
January 24, 1989.

death chamber. His epitaph was the chant: "On top of Old Sparkey, all loaded with juice, goodbye to old Bundy, no more on the loose!" A local DJ told listeners near the state jail: "Turn down your coffee makers folks because they're gonna need all the juice they can get there today." As 3,000 volts of electricity, costing the Florida taxpayer precisely three dollars, coursed through the killer's body, revelers outside the prison whooped: "Burn Bundy burn."

WILLIAM BURKE AND WILLIAM HARE

By day, Surgeons' Square in Edinburgh appeared the perfect model of respectability—a place where the frontiers of medicine were daily pushed back, where young men of intelligence were schooled by the world's best doctors, where exploration of the human body was advancing at an inexorable rate.

Yet to further these altruistic aims there was a darker side. In the early eighteenth century, it was practically unheard of for people to donate their bodies to science. How were the surgeons of the future to learn their craft if not through first-hand experience at the dissecting table? There was only one answer. A supply of corpses had to be provided, and the fresher the better.

Word had long since spread around the Scottish capital that doctors at the college would pay good money for a "corp." So it was on a night shortly before Christmas 1827 that two furtive strangers presented themselves at No. 10, Surgeons' Square, the establishment of the brilliant anatomist Dr. Robert Knox. The doorman knew enough of the kind of tradesmen with whom his master and the other doctors there did business, and asked them inside. The strangers had

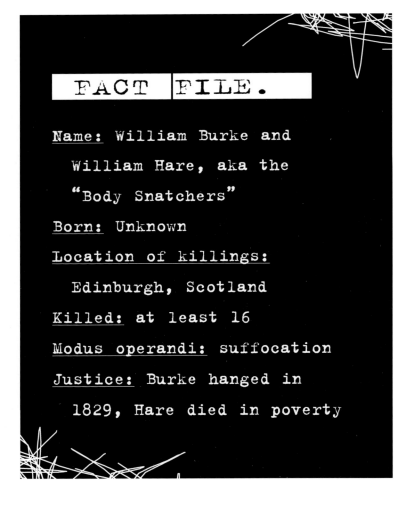

FACT FILE.

Name: William Burke and
William Hare, aka the
"Body Snatchers"

Born: Unknown

Location of killings:
Edinburgh, Scotland

Killed: at least 16

Modus operandi: suffocation

Justice: Burke hanged in
1829, Hare died in poverty

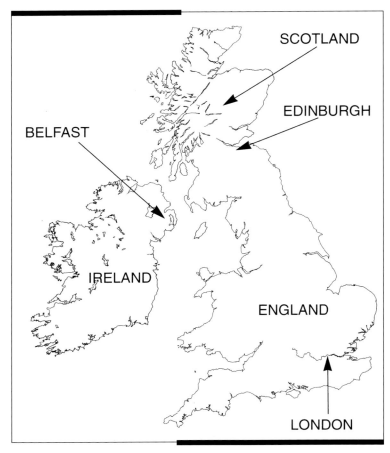

something to sell, merchandise that was good and fresh, and delivery could be guaranteed that night. The men were told to return close to midnight.

They arrived with the goods in a sack that Dr. Knox himself inspected and pronounced acceptable. The price was struck at seven pounds and ten shillings, and the pair were sent on their way with the words of one of the good doctors ringing in their ears: "We'll be glad to see you again, gentlemen, when you have another to dispose of." William Burke and his accomplice William Hare had just sold their first corpse. It was the opening chapter in the case of Scotland's most celebrated and gruesome serial murderers.

Burke and Hare came together when the former, who had deserted his wife and young family in Ireland, knocked on the door of Hare's cheap lodging house in 1827. Burke, who was accompanied by a girlfriend, Helen M'Dougal, whom he had acquired in his travels, found he had much in common with his landlord. William Hare was also Irish born and had just moved in with a widow who had inherited the threepence-a-night tramp hostel on the sudden death of her husband.

The couple were greedy landlords, however, and took exception to their tenants falling behind with their rent. So when an elderly Army pensioner known as Old Donald finally succumbed to a long illness, Hare was sorely grieved. The man owed him £4 and there seemed no chance of recovering the debt. Then Hare hit upon a plan. Why not sell the corpse to the doctors at Surgeons' Square? All he needed was an accomplice, and his countryman and fellow whisky-lover Burke fitted the bill perfectly.

The pair talked and plotted over large quantities of drink and decided to swap the body that lay

William Hare was said to have died in poverty in London. He escaped conviction by giving evidence against William Burke.

in a coffin in their backyard for a bag of tanner's bark. The undertaker left with a casket suitably weighted while Old Donald's cadaver, now showing signs of rigor mortis, was tumbled into a bed and covered with a sheet. That same night Burke and Hare made their fateful visit to Dr. Knox.

In the following days it struck this unholy alliance that selling bodies was the perfect business partnership. The only problem was in maintaining a steady supply. Hare's lodging house might have been an unhealthy, stinking cesspit but dead tenants were still a rarity. They could raid graveyards, of course, but these were now well guarded at night because of previous raids by grave robbers and many tombs even had iron bars around them. The only solution was to make corpses to sell to their distinguished customer at No. 10.

The first of 16 victims was an old man called Joe the Mumper, who fell ill with a high fever and was too weak to offer resistance as Burke and Hare laid a pillow over his face and held him down until he suffocated. His body fetched £10 at Surgeons' Square. The second victim was dispatched in what became the hallmark of Burke and Hare's murder technique. A lodger, whose name they did not even know, was confined to his bed with jaundice. While the man was asleep, his landlord, together with Burke, held his mouth and nose until there was no sign of breathing. Third to die was an old woman tramp, whom Hare and his wife met in a city bar, lured to their lodging house and suffocated. In the spring of 1828 the killers saw off two more lodgers, both destitute women.

Then came the murder of a prostitute, Mary Paterson, a voluptuous girl on whom both Burke and Hare had designs. Whether they succeeded was never made clear; what is known is that Burke was discovered by his wife lying on a bed with the inebriated, semiconscious Mary at his side and another prostitute, Janet Brown, sitting next to him. A drunken fight ensued. Burke's wife didn't mind her man's murderous habits but she took exception to him sleeping with the goods first. Mary was finally done away with and her corpse

❝The sight of her naked body, barely six hours into death, aroused great excitement among the medical students, one of whom claimed to recognize her❞

sold for the usual £10. The sight of her naked body, barely six hours into death, aroused great excitement among the medical students, one of whom claimed to recognize her. Mary's shapely figure and good looks were even remarked upon in the popular newspapers. Dr. Knox gladly reveled in the publicity for his research efforts. Rather than take the body straight onto the dissecting table, he had it preserved in whisky for three months, allowing it to become a macabre tourist attraction.

His junior assistant, a Dr. Lonsdale, later wrote: "The body of the girl Paterson could not fail to attract attention by its voluptuous form and beauty; students crowded around the table on which she lay and artists came to study a model worthy of the best Greek painters. Here was publicity beyond the professional walk."

Burke and Hare, meanwhile, were already back at their business, becoming increasingly audacious. On one occasion, Burke encountered a drunken woman being escorted along the street by a policeman. He intervened, convinced the officer that he was a "Good Samaritan"—and the hapless wretch was released into Burke's care. She was delivered to Surgeons' Square that very night.

In June 1828, the partners committed their vilest crime. An Irishwoman, who was leading a deaf and dumb boy by the hand, stopped Burke in the street. She said she had come to Edinburgh to seek a relative, and asked Burke for directions. He told her he knew the person she was looking for, then led her to his home where she was murdered in the usual way. Burke and Hare were unsure what to do with the boy, however. They considered turning him out onto the streets, in the hope that he could tell no tales against them. Instead, Burke took the boy over his knee and, as he later told police, "broke his back" while the terrified youngster stared piteously into his face. The two victims were then stuffed into a barrel and sold for £16 the pair.

It was shortly after this piece of butchery that some tensions among the body-traders began to surface. Firstly, Hare's wife tried to persuade Burke to convert Helen Burke into "merchandise"—on the grounds that, as a Scotswoman, she could not be trusted. He seems to have resisted the idea and apparently put forward the name of one of her cousins, Ann M'Dougal, as an alternative target. Then a new, more serious quarrel broke out after Burke discovered from a source at Surgeons' Square that Hare had been trading on his own account, selling the body of a woman for £8. The pair fought bitterly but their joint vow to dissolve the partnership and never work together again was soon forgotten. Within months they were back in business, with poor cousin Ann, invited to the city from her home in Falkirk, the chosen victim following the usual all-day session with a whisky bottle.

Next to be stifled was a charwoman, Mrs. Hostler, whose body Burke hid in the coal cellar pending removal to the doctors' quarters. This was quickly followed by the murder of prostitute Mary Haldane—easily identifiable to her clients by virtue of the single, large tooth that became visible when she smiled—and her daughter Peggy.

William Burke was hanged on January 28, 1829 bringing an end to his serial killing that lasted from 1827 to 1828.

- - - - - - - - - - - - -

As the gruesome trade continued, Dr. Knox never once questioned the source of these fresh bodies. By the time of the fifteenth murder, a hapless idiot well known to the folk of Edinburgh as "Daft Jamie," Knox must surely have had the gravest suspicion, yet said nothing.

In the end, Burke and Hare were trapped by the enemies of all serial murderers: over-confidence and carelessness. On October 31, 1828, a female lodger, her suspicions aroused about the alcohol-fueled carousing of the night before, lifted the corner of a straw mattress and was horrified to discover the body of a naked old woman, her face horribly bloodstained. The lodger and her husband

Graveyards, such as the cemetary beneath Edinburgh Castle, were well guarded at night because of raids by grave robbers. Many tombs had iron bars around them.

- - - - - - - - - - - -

packed their few pieces of luggage and prepared to leave, but not before they had confronted Helen Burke with what they had seen. She begged them to stay silent, promising it would be worth £10 per week to them but they refused her offer and headed straight for the police station.

Burke and Hare, along with their women, were arrested. Because all of them denied murder, and because medical evidence was insubstantial, charges could not immediately be brought. After weeks of unsuccessful interrogation, William Hare was given an opportunity to turn King's Evidence and thereby obtain immunity. He immediately denounced his former partner.

The trial began on the morning of Christmas Eve 1828 and continued without pause until the last guilty verdict was returned against Burke at 9.20am on Christmas morning. Incredibly, the jury found the charges against M'Dougal not proven and her husband, standing alongside her in the dock, was the first to congratulate her. "Nellie," he ventured, "you are out of the scrape."

Not so Burke. The chief judge, Lord Meadowbank, informed him that the court's only unresolved question was whether or not his body should be hung in chains after he was executed. In the end, the court's decision was a piece of poetic justice. Burke would be hanged and his body would be used for medical science—to be publicly dissected by the anatomists.

As he waited for the execution date, Burke seemed to be attempting a religious conversion. Yet he still showed little sign of remorse. On one occasion, speaking to a welfare visitor, he insisted: "I think I am entitled, and ought to get, that £5 from Dr. Knox which is still unpaid on the body of the woman Docherty." His visitor asked him why, since "Dr. Knox lost by the transaction as the body was taken from him." Burke replied acidly: "That was none of my business. I delivered the subject and he ought to have kept it. I have got a tolerable pair of trousers and since I am to appear before the public I should like to be respectable. I have not got a coat and waistcoat that I can appear in and if I got the £5, I could buy them."

What of the other players in this vile pantomime? Hare was freed but lived out a miserable existence, dying a poverty-stricken blind beggar in London. Helen Burke was a victim of mob hate wherever she went, though she later found anonymity in the West Country. Mrs. Hare fled to Belfast, where her fate is unknown.

❝Burke's the murderer, Hare's the thief, and Knox the boy who buys the beef❞

The infamous Dr. Knox found his career in ruins. He died in disgrace on December 20, 1862. The few mourners at his funeral would have recalled the rhyme chanted the length of mid-nineteenth century Britain: "Burke's the murderer, Hare's the thief, and Knox the boy who buys the beef."

As for William Burke, he had the life choked out of him on the gallows on January 28, 1829, watched by a crowd of around 25,000, the largest then seen in the city. Among them was the poet Sir Walter Scott, having rented one of the prime seats. When the corpse was cut down, the mob dived forward, fighting in the pouring rain to grab fragments of the rope as a ghoulish souvenir. The body was then removed to the medical rooms, where guests were admitted to watch it being dissected. The day degenerated into farce when hundreds of students, who also wanted a look, fought outside with police. Eventually Monro calmed the situation by allowing them entry in batches of 50 at a time to see the body. The following day, the general public was admitted, 30,000 people filing past Burke's remains. His body was then salted and put into barrels for use in future experiments.

DAVID CARPENTER

David Carpenter was a major suspect in California's infamous Zodiac murder case of the late 1960s.

At the time, he was between stints in prison for violent offences against women and was therefore one of the names that was automatically investigated by the Zodiac squad, hunting a gunman who was bragging about his murders in letters to newspapers. Carpenter was ultimately cleared of any involvement—but a decade later he was claiming lives of his own. He was responsible for a series of murders known as the "Trailside Killings" in the San Francisco Bay area between 1979 and 1980.

Carpenter, noted for his awkward stutter and

```
FACT FILE.

Name: David Carpenter, aka
  the "Trailside Killer"
Born: 1927
Location of killings: San
  Francisco Bay, USA
Killed: ten
Modus operandi: Shot in head
  following rape
Justice: sentenced to death
  in 1988
```

voracious sexual appetite, had first showed his dangerously violent nature in 1960 when, at the age of 33, he was sentenced to 14 years for attacking a woman with a knife and hammer. He served little more than half of that before being released, only to be sent back inside in 1970 for kidnapping. He attempted a jailbreak with three other convicts but was recaptured. In 1977 he was out again, legitimately this time, and was ready to graduate to murder.

His first murder victim may have been a girl whose death was not attributed to the Trailside Killer until after Carpenter's eventual apprehension. Anna Menjivar disappeared from her home in late 1979 and was found dead in Mount Tamalpais Park, near San Francisco. Ominously, this was to be the scene of Carpenter's next three murders.

The first of these subsequent deaths was certainly down to him. In August 1979, the body of a hiker, 44-year-old Edda Kane, was found in Mount Tamalpais park. She had been raped and then shot through the back of the head. The bullet had entered her skull while she was bent in a kneeling position, so the killer had probably made her crouch down and beg for mercy before firing the fatal shot. Seven months later, 23-year-old Barbara Schwartz was found stabbed to death through the chest. She had also been on her knees when murdered. Then came 26-year-old Anne Alderson, found dead in the park in October 1980 with three bullets in her head. She, too, had been in the kneeling position at the time of her death. Police now got sidetracked in their hunt for the Trailside Killer. When a mother and son were found dead at their home on Mount Tamalpais, detectives believed they were close to catching their man. But when the killer was apprehended hiding in surrounding woods, it was realized that he was a member of the same family and that the murders had been a case of domestic violence. Proof that the real serial killer was still on the loose came soon afterward with a horrific burst of killing.

On November 29, 1980, 25-year-old Shawna May's body was found in a shallow grave in Point Reyes Park. Shawna, who had a bullet hole in her head, had gone missing two days earlier while on a hiking expedition. Alongside her body was that of a second victim, 22-year-old Diane O'Connell, who had disappeared in the park a full month before. She had also been shot through the head. Later the same day, as police searchers swept the park, two more bodies, in a greater state of decomposition, were uncovered from shallow graves. Cynthia Moreland, aged 18 and 19-year-old Richard Towers had been killed the previous month—the same October weekend that Anne Alderson had met her fate in Mount Tamalpais Park.

The discovery of four bodies in one day created public panic and a media frenzy, with intense pressure on the police to end the murderous rampage. The killer did not show his hand again, however, until the following March. Hitchhikers Gene Blake and Ellen Hansen were confronted at gunpoint by Carpenter in a park at Santa Cruz. Ellen was threatened with rape and, when she resisted, the gunman shot her dead. Her companion was also shot but he managed to crawl for help,

David Carpenter, the "Trailside Killer," was convicted of the murders of two hikers in Santa Cruz County and for five murders in Marin County. He was given the death sentence.
- - - - - - - - - - - -

bleeding heavily from wounds to his face and neck. From his hospital bed, Gene Blake was able to give police a useful description of the killer, one of whose more repulsive features was his yellow, crooked teeth. Evidence from other visitors to the park helped identify the killer as the owner of a small red car seen parked close to the murder spot.

At this point, detectives might well have checked back through their files on all sex attackers from the San Francisco Bay area. If they had gone back ten years, they would have turned up the name of David Carpenter, a suspect in the "Zodiac Killings." He had been hauled in for questioning in the late 1960s when a serial killer began sending taunting letters, some emblazoned with supposed zodiac symbols, to San Francisco newspapers. Carpenter had been eliminated as a suspect through fingerprint and handwriting comparisons but his propensity for sexual excess and violence was all too evident and remained well documented in police and prison files.

However, the connection was never made and Carpenter remained free long enough to commit one further murder, that of 20-year-old Heather Scaggs on May 1, 1981. Now, at last, his luck was running out. Heather had worked in the same print shop as the killer, who was trying to date her and was on the way to his home when she disappeared. It was the police who now knocked on Carpenter's door—and they immediately noticed a resemblance to a recently issued photofit, based on the description given by shooting survivor Gene Blake. They also noticed a red Fiat in the driveway. The police had at last identified the Trailside Killer but, as yet, had insufficient evidence to arrest him. Carpenter was kept under surveillance until, after Heather's body turned up in Big Basin State Park, they finally pounced.

The case against Carpenter appeared watertight. He had a history of sex crimes. A friend admitted selling him one of the guns used in the killings. A witness said he had bought another of the murder weapons from him. Bullets used to kill Heather Scaggs matched those fired at Gene Blake and Ellen Hansen. It was also revealed that his first probable victim, Anna Menjivar, had been an acquaintance of Carpenter.

Charged with the murders of Heather Scaggs and Ellen Hansen, Carpenter's trial opened on July 6, 1984, in Los Angeles, after being switched from San Francisco because his lawyers claimed he would not get a fair trial in that terrorized city. After the jury returned a guilty verdict, the judge offered Carpenter a pithy character reading. "Your life," he said. "has been a continuous expression of violence and force almost beyond exception. I must conclude with the prosecution that if ever there was a case appropriate for the death penalty, this is it." He then sentenced Carpenter to be executed in the gas chamber of San Quentin. At a second trial, he was convicted of five more murders and two rapes and again sentenced to death. Carpenter launched appeals on technicalities but the reign of terror of the stuttering Trailside Killer was finally over.

ANDREI CHIKATILO

To his family and friends, he was a mild-mannered former schoolteacher, a contented husband, and proud father of two children.

And despite the rumors that life behind the front door of his untidy flat was not all it seemed—there was gossip that he was constantly belittled by his wife and had the bizarre habit of sleeping on the bathroom floor—there was no real reason to think that Andrei Chikatilo was to be exposed as one of the most dangerous and terrifying killers in history. Yet even those who arrested him and brought him to justice were so touched by his evil that they could barely look at him.

In court, Chikatilo's presence caused ripples of fear. In a specially constructed cage stood the raging and crazed monster who tortured, murdered, mutilated, and ate as many as 53 victims throughout southern Russia. Among them were a large number of children.

Yet Chikatilo's educated background made him an unlikely serial murderer. A university graduate and loyal member of the Communist Party from his days of military service, Chikatilo was 27 when he met Fayina, the woman who would

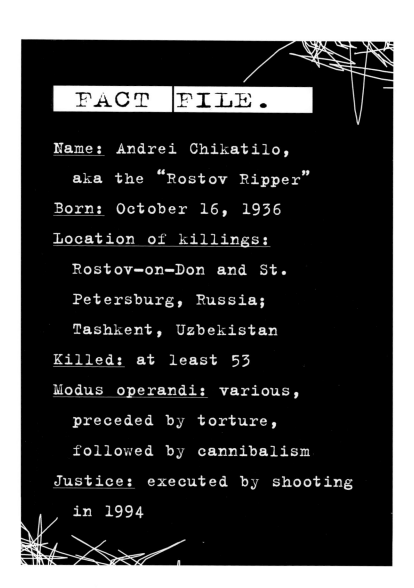

FACT FILE.

Name: Andrei Chikatilo, aka the "Rostov Ripper"

Born: October 16, 1936

Location of killings: Rostov-on-Don and St. Petersburg, Russia; Tashkent, Uzbekistan

Killed: at least 53

Modus operandi: various, preceded by torture, followed by cannibalism

Justice: executed by shooting in 1994

ST PETERSBURG

ROSTOV

MOSCOW

Andrei Chikatilo first
killed in December 1978,
when he persuaded Lena
Zakatnova to go with him to
an isolated house.

become his wife. A pit worker's daughter from the mining town of Novoshakhtinsk, she was introduced to Chikatilo in 1963 and they married that same year. They went on to have two children: Lyudmila in 1965 and Yuri in 1969. But Fayina later told friends: "We were never really in love, not even when we got married. I only married him because he was shy and didn't smoke or drink."

Chikatilo proved himself a studious husband. After years of home study, he won a degree in Russian literature and in 1971 got a post as a teacher. He seemed well settled in the job but ten years later he suddenly gave it up. His decision baffled both colleagues and family, especially when he then started work as a humble supply clerk. Little did anyone suspect that Chikatilo was already a killer. His new job involved a lot of travel and gave him greater scope for his perverted murders. He went on to kill and violate people in St. Petersburg in the north-west and Tashkent in Uzbekistan, as well as closer to home where he would hang around bus stops and railway stations, stalking possible victims. Sometimes he simply targeted them on the streets or out walking.

Chikatilo first killed on December 22, 1978, when he was 42. Pretty nine-year-old Lena Zakatnova had needed to use the toilet and, after chatting to the man who reminded her of her grandpa, allowed herself to be taken to an isolated rundown house near Rostov-on-Don. The child could not have known that Chikatilo had bought

"He would hang around bus stops and railway stations, stalking possible victims"

the shack especially for the purpose of bringing back drunks and prostitutes for sex. Once he had Lena inside, Chikatilo tried to rape her but failed and it was this frustration that tipped him over the edge. He repeatedly stabbed Lena and then dropped her body into a river. Her corpse was discovered under a bridge on Christmas Eve.

The effect that the experience with little Lena Zakatnova had on him was to be a telling trademark of Chikatilo's serial slayings. He could not rape his terrified victims and that infuriated him. He would become enraged at his impotence and sexual intercourse was only possible when he had worked himself into a frenzy as he stabbed and mutilated his victims. Chikatilo could only rape the dead. Fayina was later to admit that her husband was unable to make love to her properly.

A further insight into his twisted inadequacies was revealed when he talked about the time in May 1983 when he was still a schoolteacher and had gone swimming in the river with some of his pupils. He had swum over to a 15-year-old girl and grabbed her. Recalling this incident to the police, Chikatilo said that when the girl screamed he realized her fear gave him tremendous pleasure. It was also later revealed that when they were children, Chikatilo and his sister were repeatedly told how their older brother Stephan was kidnapped and eaten during the 1934 Ukrainian famine. The image and thought of this was forever to pray on Chikatilo's mind.

Chikatilo was a chilling sight in the courtroom as he swung his head, rolled his eyes, and waved pornographic magazines at his audience.

Chikatilo's second victim was 17-year-old Larisa Tkchenko, who was at her job of cutting glass in Rostov when the killer approached. Perhaps it was the promise of money that encouraged the impoverished girl to accompany him to the woods for sex. When she laughed at his failure to perform, Chikatilo strangled her, gnawed at her throat, and abused her with a stick. Now, there was no turning back for the beast who both craved and failed at sexual intercourse and who would never be able to satisfy his blood lust. The victims he chose were mostly runaways or prostitutes and were happy to go off with him on the promise of small gifts such as chewing gum or to watch a video or to take up the offer of a meal. They believed no harm could come their way from this kindly soul who spoke about his family life.

But Chikatilo was later to tell police: "I often used to spend time at railway stations, in trains, and on buses. There were a lot of tramps there. The questions arose of whether these degenerate elements had the right to exist. It is not difficult to become acquainted with these people. They crawl into your soul demanding money, food, vodka, and offering themselves for sex. As soon as I saw a lonely person I would have to drag them off to the woods. I paid no attention to age or sex. We would walk for a couple of miles or so through the woods and then I would be possessed by a terrible shaking sensation."

Chikatilo's youngest victim was seven-year-old Igor Gudkov and his oldest was 44-year-old prostitute Marta Ryabyenko. There was also a mother and daughter—Tanya Petrosyan, 32, and her 11-year-old daughter who were invited by Chikatilo to a picnic and never seen again. Nearly all his victims were raped and mutilated, sometimes disembowelled, and had organs cut out or bitten off. Chikatilo would also remove the eyes, fearing the lifeless gaze as he set about his mutilation. Sometimes he bit off nipples in a sexual frenzy. There were stories of how he ate wombs taken fresh from the bodies of his victims. Eleven bodies were found in 1984 alone. Chikatilo did not see children as innocents. Instead he believed their simple walks through the forest would turn them into the "rootless elements" he so despised.

Lieutenant-colonel Vikto Burakov, who led the murder hunt, said: "In our search for the criminal, we just couldn't imagine what sort of person we were dealing with. This was the height of sadism, the like of which we had never seen."

Chikatilo was free to continue his horrific stalking and killing of victims by a series of

> **❝Nearly all his victims were raped and mutilated, sometimes disembowelled, and had organs cut out or bitten off❞**

blunders. Incredibly, he was arrested and questioned several times during the 12-year hunt for the so-called "Rostov Ripper" and each time was allowed to go free. The first time was after Lena Zakatnova's death, when neighbors reported a light had been on at the shack that night, and Chikatilo was interviewed no less than nine times. Strangely, enquiries then switched to another suspect living nearby. Even more bizarre was the fact that the man confessed to the horrific crime—and was found guilty and executed.

On a second occasion, on September 13, 1984, a police inspector arrested Chikatilo after watching him make his way across the city, attempting to pick up women. The bag he was carrying contained lengths of rope and some knives. Chikatilo was kept in jail for ten days pending further investigations. Even when it was discovered that he had been questioned before by police and his description matched that of a man seen with a murder victim, Chikatilo was not considered to be the Rostov Ripper—particularly after his blood samples did not match up with the type police wrongly believed to be the killer's.

Chikatilo was sent to prison, however, but only on an old charge of stealing linoleum. No one seemed to realize that the killings stopped during the three months Chikatilo was not around. He quickly caught up with what he saw as lost opportunity and slaughtered eight people in a single month after his release.

There was yet another time that Chikatilo could have been stopped. After he was released and at the height of the murders, police kept regular surveillance in woods around Rostov. Chikatilo was stopped near the scene of one murder carrying an attaché case containing a knife. That day, November 7, 1990, Sergeant Ivor Rybakov saw Chikatilo leave the woods and wash his hands. There was also the tell-tale bloodstain smeared across his face. But amazingly Chikatilo talked his way out of suspicion. The Rostov Ripper was free once more to continue his violent and perverted killing.

It seems incredible that Chikatilo could have carried out his vile attacks for so long. But the search for the serial killer was fated. As well as failing to see Chikatilo as the killer he was, the police were overwhelmed by the sheer number of people they questioned. Around half a million were interviewed, producing reams of paperwork for the already overworked squad. There was also the problem of many victims disappearing but no reports being made to the police.

One aspect of the hunt was deadly accurate, however. Local psychiatrist Dr. Alexander Bukhanovsky compiled a profile of the man he believed responsible for what was to become known as the sickest series of killings in history. Dr. Bukhanovsky said the man was a middle-aged, self-pitying misfit, heterosexual but impotent and

If I had known what my husband was doing all those years, then of course I would have done something to stop him. In a way, I feel I am to blame

probably worked as a supplies supervisor at a factory. Said the doctor: "This man's internal world is a thousand times richer than the surface expression of that world." He said the man they were seeking had a fetish for the immature body of either sex and had a brain that was the playground for the most depraved perversions. At the same time, it was blessed with an exceptional memory. In fact, Chikatilo had memorized the lives and biographies of every American president, as well as the exact circumstances of each of his murders years after he had committed them. Chikatilo was so impressed with this profile of himself that he asked Dr. Bukhanovsky to be present when he was executed.

In the end, however, it was simple, down-to-earth police work and crucial witnesses that led to the arrest of the Rostov Ripper.

After the body of Chikatilo's final victim, a young boy, was discovered, police gathered evidence from the site of the murder and painstakingly cross-checked it against an index of around 25,000 possible suspects. Witnesses had also reported seeing a middle-aged man hanging around as the boy bought a rail ticket. Police attention now centered on the railway station and 600 men were deployed on the forest path along the rail line. Chikatilo was finally arrested outside a cafe on November 20, 1990, as he tried to lure a potential teenage victim.

When she learned of his arrest and the sickening truth about her 56-year-old husband, Fayina went into hiding, taking Lyudmila and Yuri with her. She later faced death threats from the victims' relatives and was give a police guard for her protection. She always denied knowing anything of Chikatilo's sickening secret life but admitted: "I had noticed blood on my husband's clothing but he explained it away saying he had cut himself when he helped the drivers load cargo at work. I just washed the stains out of his clothes. He used to blame the fact that he often didn't come home at nights on problems at work. He would also say that he had missed the last train home and had to spend the night at the station. I believed him. If I had known what my husband was doing all those years, then of course I would have done something to stop him. In a way, I feel I am to blame."

Chikatilo admitted murdering 11 boys and 42 girls during his reign of terror but there may have been many more. Fayina told friends: "How was I to know? I could never imagine my husband being able to murder one person let alone 53. He was always so quiet. He could never hurt anyone."

Chikatilo himself admitted: "My case is an exceptional one. I am ready to give evidence of the crimes that I have committed, but please do not torment me with the details because my psyche could not cope. Everything I have done makes me tremble." He told police: "I have discovered sex and this is how I enjoy it. I get a great sense of sexual excitement from this way of killing and have achieved orgasms during my efforts. The eating of my victim is the ultimate sacrifice they can make for me. They are literally giving themselves to me."

When the monster went on trial in Rostov, he

When Chikatilo went on trial, he did so chained in an iron cage that stood in the courtroom.

did so chained in an iron cage that stood in the courtroom. Relatives of his victims bayed for justice, and on the first day of the trial, proceedings were delayed for half an hour as the hysterical crowd demanded Chikatilo be handed to them as a human sacrifice. Ambulancemen gave spectators sedatives. Chikatilo cut a chilling figure as from within the cage he rolled his eyes, swung his head, and waved pornographic magazines at his audience. He greeted the judges' bench with a mocking, "Good morning gentlemen."

Chikatilo's trial started on April 14, 1992. On October 15 that year, he was found guilty. Judge Leonid Akubzhanov was fiercely critical of the

Andrei Chikatilo was kept behind bars during his trial for murder in 1992.

- - - - - - - - - - - -

police, saying: "If they had done their job in 1978 after the first killing, 51 lives could have been saved. Or if they had not released him after questioning in 1984, at least 20 people would not have died." Judge Akubzhanov described Chikatilo as an "animal" adding, "He enjoyed the feeling of total control over his victims. He deliberately prolonged their suffering with terrible cruelty so he could get as much pleasure as possible." Fayina paid one

last visit to her husband in jail. Referring to sexual failing in their marriage, he said to her: "If only I had followed your advice and got treatment."

Andrei Chikatilo was sentenced to die with a bullet in the back of the neck. He was held on death row at Novocherkassk high-security prison, where one of the wardens was the father of a Chikatilo victim. Labeled by the press as "the world's most sadistic and perverted killer," he was finally shot dead in prison on February 14, 1994, after President Boris Yeltsin rejected an appeal for clemency.

JOHN CHRISTIE

Quiet, fussy, bespectacled, balding, gaunt, respectable, and boring— they were all descriptions given by neighbours of John Reginald Halliday Christie.

John Christie was a smartly dressed man that few would suspect of murderig and raping several victims over more than a decade.

Yet unbeknown to them, over a period of 13 years, this dapper little man raped, killed, and committed necrophilia in a quiet residential London street without arousing the least suspicion. The house where the murders took place, 10 Rillington Place, is still one of the most enduringly chilling addresses in English criminal history. There is another enduring aspect to this case. When Christie was hanged in 1953, he left behind a mystery—over how he had allowed another man to go to the gallows before him for murders that he himself probably committed.

So who was this monster in disguise, this repressed sex killer who could achieve satisfaction

FACT FILE.

Name: John Reginald Halliday Christie

Born: April 8, 1898

Location of killings: London, England

Killed: eight

Modus operandi: strangulation

Justice: hanged in 1953

only through embracing the bodies of his victims? John Christie, known as Reg, was one of seven children born in Halifax, Yorkshire, to a respectable carpet designer and an amateur actress. The insipid child, who preferred to scamper in cemeteries instead of local playgrounds, was a choirboy and later a Scout master, but remained aloof, unpopular, and unpleasant. Later in life, he claimed that, as an eight-year-old, the sight of his dead grandfather, waxy and impassive, had had a vital influence on him.

Christie enlisted in the British Army to fight in the World War I, but his service came to an abrupt

A body was found hidden in the kitchen. The discovery of the human remains elsewhere in the house led to the police manhunt of Christie, who was arrested and brought to trial.

end when a mustard gas shell exploded and injured his eyes and larynx. He was demobbed in 1919 with a small disability pension. Back home in Halifax, he took a job in the main post office and

> **"Who was this monster in disguise, this repressed sex killer who could achieve satisfaction only through embracing the bodies of his victims?"**

began dating Ethel Waddington, a local girl he had known for years. They married when they were 22 but if Ethel thought she was in for a cosy, routine marriage, she was sorely mistaken. Christie was consorting with prostitutes, a habit he had taken up in his army days, and he showed no sign of giving up his sexual adventures for domestic bliss with Ethel. Also, he was a thief but not a very good one, it appears. He was caught stealing postal orders from his employer and was sent to jail, the first of several spells behind bars for petty crimes.

Following a series of rows, job-hopping Christie eventually left Yorkshire and moved to London alone. There followed more crimes and a conviction for violence against a prostitute. Pondering his predicament in a prison cell, Christie wrote to his typist wife for the first time in nine years to ask for a reconciliation. She agreed and on his release they set up home together,

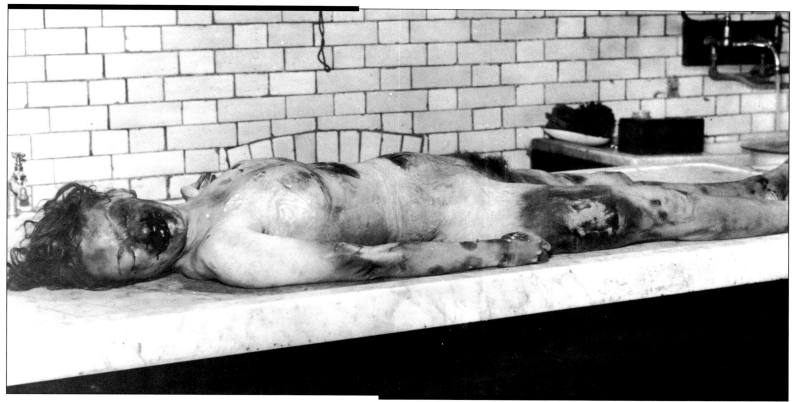

Christie denied all sexual aspects of the murders. The killings were all accidental, he claimed, despite evidence to the contrary.

choosing the then seedy West London area of Notting Hill. In 1938 they moved to the ground floor of 10 Rillington Place, one of three apartments in a rundown house with a tiny garden and a communal lavatory.

Astonishingly, when the World War II broke out in 1939, Christie was accepted as a special constable in the War Reserve Police, no checks having been made for previous convictions. Soon after, while Ethel was away visiting relatives in Yorkshire, Christie, dapper in his uniform, picked up 17-year-old Ruth Fuerst, an Austrian refugee and ex-nurse who was also probably a part-time prostitute. Back at 10 Rillington Place, Christie took a rope and strangled her. He first hid the body beneath the floorboards. Then he dragged it into the toilet, concealed it behind some rubbish and dug a grave in his garden, in full view of the neighbours. Finally, under cover of darkness, he buried Ruth's body, where it lay undisturbed for a decade.

Before the end of the war, Christie was sacked from the police and went to work in a radio factory where he met attractive 31-year-old Muriel Eady. Although she already had a regular boyfriend, Muriel was enticed back to Christie's home when he knew his wife was out. Reclining in an armchair, she was tricked into inhaling coal-gas fumes. As she slipped into unconsciousness, he raped her and strangled her with a stocking. In his confession, Christie said, "I gazed down at her body and felt a quiet, peaceful thrill. I had no regrets." He buried her alongside his first victim.

In 1948 Christie had a new neighbor in the rooms above him. Truck driver Timothy Evans, his wife Beryl, and their baby Geraldine had moved in, and when Beryl found herself pregnant with an unwanted baby, Christie persuaded her to allow him to carry out an abortion. That same day Beryl died, although at whose hands no one can really be certain to this day. Events then took a bizarre turn when Timothy Evans walked into a police station in distant Merthyr Tydfil, South Wales, claiming to have killed his wife and stuffed her down the drains. Police searched the house but failed to find Beryl's body where Evans had told them it would be. They also failed to uncover the bodies buried in the garden. Finally, after several visits, they found Beryl Evans's body stashed in the washroom—next to that of 14-month-old Geraldine.

On hearing that his daughter had also been killed, Evans seemed shocked and dramatically changed his story. He was innocent, he insisted; his neighbour Christie was the killer. Evans, who had an extremely low IQ, said Christie told him that an abortion on his wife had gone wrong and that the baby was being adopted. Christie cut a much finer figure in court than Evans ever could. He convinced the judge and jury that he was an innocent bystander, and his damning words sealed Evans's miserable fate. Evans was convicted and sentenced to the gallows. He was executed on March 9, 1950.

Christie and Ethel continued to live together, although the secret killer's behavior became increasingly odd. He was not at all plagued by guilt but suffered instead a variety of minor ailments including headaches, backache, and amnesia for which he consulted a doctor. The urge to kill came upon Christie again in 1952. This time his victim was the unfortunate Ethel herself. She was strangled in bed and buried

Ethel Christie was strangled in bed and buried under the floorboards. Her dead body was not violated by Christie, unlike the majority of his other victims.

Police found 14-month-old Geraldine stashed in the washroom next to Beryl Evan's body. Timothy Evans was accused of murdering them, but it was in fact Christie.

- - - - - - - - -

It was not until a new tenant moved to 10 Rillington Place that Christie was unmasked. The unbearable stench resulted in the unearthing of all the bodies.

- - - - - - - - - - -

under the floorboards. Her dead body was not violated by Christie, unlike the majority of his other victims.

Now the neurotic killer's existence became even more squalid than before. Work-shy and jobless, he had to sell almost every stick of furniture to raise money. His straightened circumstances did not stop him seeing prostitutes, however, three of whom were gassed or strangled, abused, and stuffed into cupboards. Rita Nelson, aged 25, accosted Christy in the street on January 2, 1953, and was strangled shortly after entering his apartment. Ten days later, another prostitute, Kathleen Maloney, 26, a happy drunk whom he had met in a cafe, was gassed. Christie claimed his last victim, Hectorina MacLennan, 26, on March 6. Then he moved out of Rillington Place, took his mongrel dog to the vet to be destroyed and hit the road.

It was not until a new tenant moved in and noticed the unbearable stench that pervaded the house that Christie was unmasked. Believing a rat may have died under the floorboards, the tenant poked about in a newly-wallpapered alcove and exposed a woman's legs. His frantic call to police resulted in the unearthing of all the bodies. In the yard they found a tobacco tin containing four sets of pubic hair. Christie, who had been paraded by the police as their principal prosecution witness in the trial of his neighbor, was now their most wanted man in one of the biggest manhunts ever. Homeless and alone, he was arrested after being recognized by a policeman as he leaned over Putney Bridge.

Despite a physical and mental breakdown, the glib manner that served him so well did not fail him as he faced interrogation. With suffocating hypocrisy, he referred to the murders as "those regrettable happenings." The killings were all accidental, he claimed, caused by the victims themselves in their struggles. He denied all sexual aspects of his crimes. At his trial at London's Old Bailey, Christie pleaded insanity. But just three days into the case, on June 25, 1953, he was found guilty of four of the murders, including that of Ethel. The judge described the case as "a horrible one and a horrifying one" and sentenced him to death.

While Christie awaited execution, a government tribunal inquired as to whether there had been a miscarriage of justice in the case of Timothy John Evans. The controversial verdict was that it was not a miscarriage of justice. The tribunal decided that Christie had confessed to the murder of Beryl Evans only to help his own case by adding

The home of John Christie, 10 Rillington Place, was demolished after its grizzly contents were discovered and the murderer convicted.

weight to his plea of madness. Many Members of Parliament and the Howard League for Penal Reform refused to accept the findings. Christie himself refused to throw any further light on the case and, the day after the tribunal's findings were announced, he was hanged at Pentonville Prison on July 15, 1953.

Public disquiet about the possible miscarriage of justice rumbled on until 1966 when an inquiry under Mr. Justice Barbin ruled: "It is more probable than not that Evans killed Beryl Evans and it is more probable than not that Evans did not kill Geraldine." It was not satisfactory as far as campaigners were concerned—but it was enough to get Evans a long-overdue posthumous royal pardon. His body was reburied in consecrated ground after being exhumed from Pentonville Prison where it had lain in an unmarked grave close to that of John Christie, the man who had put him there.

DOUGLAS CLARK AND CAROL BUNDY

Douglas Clark claimed he was inspired to murder after reading the book
Ted Bundy: All-American Killer.

By coincidence, Clark's girlfriend was also named Bundy. The pair put their fantasies to the test in the summer of 1980, when Douglas Clark and Carol Bundy would regularly drive along famed Sunset Boulevard in Los Angeles picking up prostitutes. Once a girl had stepped inside the car, she would be driven to a quiet street where Clark would

```
FACT FILE.

Name: Douglas Daniel Clark
   and Carol Bundy, aka the
   "Sunset Strip Slayers"
Born: Clark in 1948, Bundy in
   1943
Location of killings: Los
   Angeles, USA
Killed: Clark convicted of
   six murders, Bundy of one
Modus operandi: shooting of
   prostitutes
Justice: Clark sentenced to
   death in 1983; Bundy sen-
   tenced to life
```

force her to perform oral sex on him while Bundy watched. As he climaxed, Clark would shoot the girl in the head.

The depravity did not end there, however. Clark would engage in further sexual acts with the girl's body. The victim would then be taken to the home he and Bundy shared and, in one case, decapitated. The head was kept in the freezer and regularly taken out, groomed, had make-up applied and, according to Bundy, "played with" as if it was a Barbie Doll.

Douglas Clark, born in 1948, was the son of a former naval admiral who in his new job as an engineer traveled the world with his family before finally settling in southern California. There, in January 1980, handsome Clark met and seduced Bundy, an overweight, mentally disturbed 37-year-old mother of two who worked as a diabetic vocational nurse. He moved into her modest apartment in Burbank and made her his willing sex slave. He brought younger women home for sex while she watched and photographed them. One of the girls was just 11 years old. Apart from the psychological damage to these minors, none of Clark's partners seems to have been physically harmed—until, in June 1980, he went for what he had dreamed of as the ultimate kick.

His first victims were step-sisters, 15-year-old Gina Marano and 16-year-old Cynthia Chandler, whose bodies were found beside the Ventura

Freeway on June 12, each having been shot in the head. The girls had last been seen alive at Huntington Beach where they had been walking out to meet friends. It is probable that Bundy did not have anything to do with this crime, although she listened with rapt attention as her lover described how he had shot the girls after forcing them to perform sex acts on him.

On June 24, two more bodies were found in separate locations in the Burbank area; Exxie Wilson, 20, and Karen Jones, 24, both prostitutes, had been shot with the same gun as the first two victims. Wilson's head was missing. According to Bundy, Clark had taken the head home with him so he could engage in oral sex with it at his leisure. She said that while her two children were out, Clark had produced the head from the freezer, ordered her to comb the hair and apply make-up to it. "We had a lot of fun with her," she told police. "I was making her up like a Barbie." The head turned up three days later in a box in the driveway of a house in Hollywood.

On June 30, the corpse of Sunset Strip hooker Marnette Comer, 17, last seen alive a month earlier, was found near Sylmar in the San Fernando Valley. Two weeks later the dismembered body of a woman who was never identified turned up in Malibu, Clark's last known female victim. The killings were not ended, however. There

"The head was kept in the freezer and regularly taken out, groomed, had make-up applied and, according to Bundy, "played with" as if it was a Barbie Doll"

was one more murder that finally brought police to the killers' door.

During her affair with Clark, Carol Bundy was still seeing a former boyfriend, John Murray, who made the mistake of telling her about his suspicions that Clark could be the Sunset Strip Slayer. Bundy panicked and, after arranging to meet him near the bar where he worked, she murdered him. His headless torso was later discovered in his van. He had been stabbed nine times. His missing skull was never found.

Perhaps Bundy had been trying to prove to Clark that she too could kill with callous indifference. It proved not to be the case, for two days after Murray's body was discovered, she broke down and told a fellow nurse what she had done. The colleague called the police and the Sunset Strip Slayers were arrested on August 11.

The murderous pair at first blamed each other for the murders but Bundy later confessed her involvement in the crimes, pleading guilty to the murder of Murray and becoming a key witness against her sick boyfriend. Clark was found guilty on six counts of murder and on February 11, 1983, was sentenced to death. The Californian Supreme Court affirmed the sentence on June 1992. Bundy received prison terms of 27 years to life and 25 years to life, the terms to run consecutively.

ADOLFO CONSTANZO

Inside a foul hut, a small group of men gathered in a circle round an evil-smelling cauldron, their blood-chilling chants echoing into the night.

Their leader, the high priest, bowed before the cauldron and signaled for silence. All eyes turned to what appeared to be a bundle of rags in a shadowy corner—except that the bundle was now jerking spasmodically and moaning piteously. Two men, their faces hidden behind high-collared outfits, moved to the corner and dragged out a tightly-bound youth, who screaming with terror, was dragged to the cauldron and was forced to bow his head above the evil brew. Suddenly in the dim candlelight there was a flash of steel as a machete sliced through the youth's head, removing in one blow the top half of his skull. Bone, hair, blood and brains tumbled into the cauldron. The boy was a human sacrifice to a savage and vengeful god.

Was this a scene from some ancient Aztec ritual? An act of religious frenzy from the darkest ages in the tribal jungles of Africa? In fact, it took place just a few short miles south of the Texas border in 1987. The sacrificial victim was a middle-class American student and the high priest was Adolfo de Jesus Constanzo, the wealthy leader of a voodoo-like cult called Palo Mayombe. Constanzo believed he was "the chosen one" of this vicious and violent cult that once held sway in the

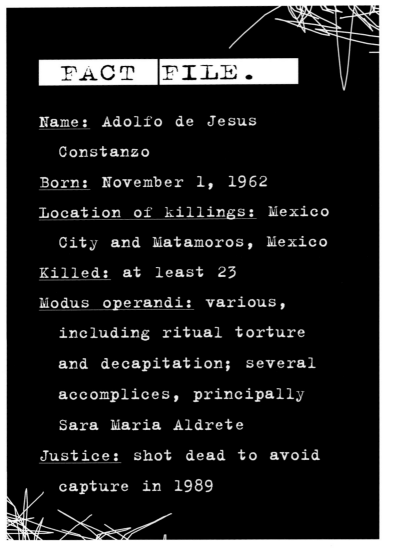

FACT FILE.

Name: Adolfo de Jesus
   Constanzo
Born: November 1, 1962
Location of killings: Mexico
   City and Matamoros, Mexico
Killed: at least 23
Modus operandi: various,
   including ritual torture
   and decapitation; several
   accomplices, principally
   Sara Maria Aldrete
Justice: shot dead to avoid
   capture in 1989

Congo region of Africa and whose followers believed they gained magical powers through cruelty and violent death. Constanzo was a devotee of this strange religion for the power it gave him over others and because it allowed him to satiate his bloodlust with regular torture and human sacrifices. His reign of terror was ended as a direct result of the human sacrifice described above. But his fascination with the black arts that spawned such cruelty had begun in childhood.

Adolfo Jesus de Constanzo was born in 1962 in Miami Beach to a 15-year-old mother of Cuban extraction, who like many of her expatriate peers, followed the Santeria, or Saint's Path. This was a quasi-Christian religion brought to the New World by African slaves and adapted to fit in with the ways of their Catholic masters. Palo Mayombe is the dark sister of the Santeria. If the Santeria, which involves sacrifice of animals, could be likened to white magic, Palo Mayombe is definitely black. The religion accepts no after-life, so an adherent is free to do whatever he wants here on earth. The spirits of the dead exist in a kind of limbo, forced to wander the material plane. Newly dead spirits can be harnessed by a Palo Mayombe priest, if regularly appeased with fresh blood.

The religion centers round a *nganga*, a cauldron kept constantly filled with blood, a goat's head, a roasted turtle, and, most importantly, a human skull—preferably that of a person who has died a violent and painful death. Non-believers, especially Christians, are considered to be animals and are therefore targeted as victims. The more painful and horrific their death, the more potent the spell that the high priest can cast.

Despite his mother's humble beginnings, she provided ably for the young Adolfo. She married a

Adolfo Constanzo was known by his followers as "The Godfather." He offered human sacrifices, according to his own twisted philosophy, to appease Satan.

prosperous businessman who took the family to Puerto Rico. But when his stepfather died in 1973, his mother remarried and moved back to Florida. This marriage was not a success and after rows and quarrels it ended in divorce. At just 12 years of age, Adolfo found himself the man of the household and set about boosting the family income by shoplifting and trading in drugs. He was caught stealing more than once but discovered that a glib tongue and an easy charm could often allow him to talk his way out of trouble. In his teens, this slim, dark, and handsome youth with piercing eyes

Sara Aldrete, companion to Constanzo, spoke with reporters
after her arrest. She was acquitted of Constanzo's murder but
was imprisoned for "criminal association."

- - - - - - - - - - -

discovered something else about himself: that he
was bisexual. Although he was later to have two
children, during his teens he gained his sexual
kicks through frequenting gay bars.

At the age of 21, Constanzo moved to Mexico
City where in 1983 he launched himself as a Palo
Mayombe priest and began wooing wealthy, bored
businessmen and aristocrats, who were turned on
by this charismatic young man and his exciting
occult religion. Telling fortunes with apparently
uncanny accuracy earned him his own fortune. His

fame as a sorcerer spread and his occult abilities
came to the notice of the narcotics cartels. At a
time when US law enforcement agencies were
cracking down on cross-border smuggling, superstitious Mexican drugs "godfathers" turned to
Constanzo for advice and magical protection at an
astonishing $50,000 a spell. As a consequence, his
cauldron needed constant replenishment with
fresh blood and skulls, and decapitated corpses
were regularly fished out of rivers and lakes.

In April 1987, Constanzo approached one of
his principal customers, drugs family godfather
Guillermo Calzada, and demanded that, as his
magic was the source of the family's success, he
should receive half their profits. Calzada refused

and Constanzo left in a rage. A few days later he called Calzada to express regret for his demands and, as a sign of remorse, offered to perform a special ceremony that would give extra protection to the whole cartel. Shortly afterward the drugs baron, his wife, his mother, his partner, his secretary, his maid, and his bodyguard were all dragged from a river. All seven had been dreadfully mutilated before being killed. Their fingers and toes and, in the case of the men, their genitals, had been sliced off. Their heads were also missing—gone to feed the cauldron.

Suddenly Constanzo had his own crime syndicate. He also began believing ever more implicitly in his own voodoo powers. Like the drug leaders he had wiped out, he was hooked on his own mumbo jumbo and needed to perform regularly the ceremonies that would bring him protection.

He decided to move his voodoo circle to the border town of Matamoros, where the drugs cartels were even richer. There he teamed up with an American ex-girlfriend, Sara Maria Aldrete, with whom he had once had an affair and whose parents now lived in Matamoros. Sara, who became the High Priestess of the gang, remained under Constanzo's spell, despite the fact that he lived in a menage-a-trois with two homosexual lovers, Omar Ochos, who played the role of his "wife," and Martin Rodriguez, who played the "husband."

Sara Aldrete was a strange choice as a partner in crime. Until 1988 she had been a respected and popular student at Southmost College in Brownsville, Texas. With her athletic, six-foot

> **"He also began believing ever more implicitly in his own voodoo powers"**

physique, she was a star of the college track team and was expected to graduate with honors in physical education. "I thought I would be famous in sport," she later said. "I wanted to earn a master's degree." All that changed the day she visited Mexico City and fell under the spell of Constanzo, then aged 26, who showed the glitzier sights of town from the bench seat of his white Cadillac. To her, he seemed superhuman. He could even run further and faster than Aldrete, the star athlete. After their brief but torrid affair in Mexico City, Sara was under Constanzo's spell.

When they teamed up again in Matamoros, Sara was able to provide her lover with a valuable introduction to local businessmen, including Elio Hernandez, head of a family drugs empire. The American girl helped lure Hernandez into the Palo Mayombe circle and, sure enough, his business picked up. The Hernandez gang fell totally under the spell of Constanzo's voodoo, and by 1988 the area round Matamoros was thick with dismembered corpses. Between May that year and March 1989, Constanzo tortured and ritually sacrificed at least 13 people. All male, they were were often rival dealers but they also included innocent strangers picked up at random.

One victim was a police undercover agent who had infiltrated the gang but had been discovered, possibly through a tip-off from one of the police officers on Constanzo's payroll. On another occasion, Hernandez himself was ordered to supply the coup-de-grace to a struggling young victim at the bubbling *nganga*. Only after slicing off the youth's head did he recognize the green and white striped football shirt he was wearing. He had killed his own cousin.

Constanzo's normal method of sacrifice was to have the victim soundly beaten, then dragged into the shed containing the sacred cauldron. Here he would cut off the nose, ears, fingers, toes, and genitals of the hapless wretch and partially flay him. Then the others would be ordered out while Constanzo sodomized him. Only then would there be a merciful release through death. It was essential to the success of the ceremony that there should be as much pain as possible and the victim should die screaming. The spirit had to be confused and terrified as it left the body, making it easier to subjugate. It was this particular evil that was to bring about Constanzo's downfall.

In February 1989 the selected victim was a small-time Mexican drugs dealer. Every torture was applied to him but the tough little man would not cry out, even when his upper body was skinned. He endured every torture, even castration, but died silently. Constanzo declared the ceremony a failure and sent his men out to kidnap a softer touch. He was easy to find.

On March 14, 1989, a group of students were celebrating the end of term at their university by crossing the border for a night of cheap alcohol. When one became separated from his colleagues outside a Matamoros saloon, he was lured by a young beauty who was giving him the eye and he strolled into a dark alley to talk to her. As he approached her, he was grabbed from behind by two men, bundled into the back of a truck and driven to Constanzo's remote Santa Elena ranch. His name was Mark Kilroy, a 21-year-old medical student and he must have screamed sufficiently to satisfy Constanzo before his brains were tipped into the cauldron, for the leader declared the ceremony a great success. The gang was now unstoppable. With an American spirit as well as any number of Mexican spirits to protect them, they were not only safe but invisible to the law.

This time, however, the cultists had overreached themselves. Kilroy's parents were devout and loving people who would not rest until they had found out what had happened to their son. They were aided by the boy's uncle, who happened to be a US customs official. The manhunt that ensued stretched across both sides of the border.

Success came swiftly. Mexican police set up a road block near Matamoros. One of the Hernandez brothers, Serafin, was driving a truck when he came upon it but, having been persuaded by Constanzo that he was invisible, he simply ignored it and drove straight through. The stunned police scrambled into their cars and captured him—but only after he had taunted them to shoot him because he was certain the bullets would pass safely through his body. Detectives then rounded up three more of the cultists who, puzzled by the lack of magical protection, confessed all.

> **" He would cut off the nose, ears, fingers, toes, and genitals of the hapless wretch and partially flay him "**

Matamoros, where Constanzo decided to move to with his voodoo circle and team up with Sara Maria Aldrete.

– – – – – – – – – – – – – – –

Police swooped on the ranch but Constanzo, his priestess Aldrete, and the rest of his followers were nowhere to be found. There were drugs and guns, however, plus the revolting cookpot, brimming with blood, bones, deer antlers, a turtle shell, scorpions, a cat, and a human brain. Disgusted police forced the four captured cultists to do the dirty work of digging up the bodies, one of the most recent of which was that of student Mark Kilroy. The grave was marked by a length of wire sticking out of the ground. Subsequent examination revealed that a strip of thin but strong wire had been pushed through the length of the boy's spine. Once the body had decomposed sufficiently, it had been Constanzo's intention to pull out the backbone and add it to the stomach-churning mix in his cauldron.

Constanzo, along with a few of his favored inner circle, had fled to Mexico City but there his magic at last failed him. The apartment he was hiding in was in a poor part of town but the cult leader left his luxury limousine in the street nearby. On May 5, 1989, two policemen spotted it and strolled over to investigate, suspecting it had been stolen. When Constanzo saw them, he assumed the game was up. Suddenly the cops found themselves under fire from a nearby apartment building and radioed for help. A heavily armed riot team was summoned to surround the gang's apartment, where they encountered the bizarre sight of armfuls of cash being thrown out of windows. From other windows cultists sprayed the police with bullets.

After emptying his gun into the street, Constanzo calmly stepped into a walk-in closet with his lover Martin Rodriguez and ordered another gang member, professional hitman Alvaro de Leo Valdez, to shoot them both. When Valdez stared back at him aghast, Constanzo slapped him hard across the face and ordered, "Do it or I'll make things tough for you in hell. Don't worry, I'll be back." They were his last words.

He and his lover died in a final embrace as Valdez pumped lead into them. Sara Aldrete fled the building screaming, "He's dead, he's dead. Don't shoot. They've killed themselves."

Interrogation of the four survivors of the shoot-out and the subsequent round-up of other cult members allowed police to close the files on a number of mystery killings. There had been 15 human sacrifices at the ranch, two at another ranch nearby and several in Mexico City. Added to these were the killings of rival gang members and the savage murders of his own followers who had been slaughtered to maintain discipline.

Back in Matamoros, the police had the *nganga* and the shed in which it was housed exorcized by a white witch and a priest. Then they doused the shed with petrol and burned it to the ground. Constanzo's body was claimed by his mother and taken back to Miami, where it was cremated.

Meanwhile, the cult leader's surviving followers faced long jail terms, as there is no death penalty in Mexico. In the aftermath of the raid, 14 cultists were indicted on various charges, including multiple murder, weapons and narcotics violations, conspiracy, and obstruction of justice. Valdez was given a 30-year sentence for killing Constanzo and Rodriguez. Constanzo's other lover Ochos was convicted of murder but died of AIDS before he could be sentenced. Sentences of up to 67 years were handed out to other killers, including Serafin Hernandez, the drug runner who thought he was invisible.

Facing trial in August 1990, Sara Aldrete proclaimed her innocence and complained bitterly about the tortures she claimed she had suffered at the hands of the police. "They stripped me of my

> **Fourteen cultists were indicted on various charges, including multiple murder, weapons and narcotics violations, conspiracy, and obstruction of justice**

clothes," she said. "They hung me up and they beat me. They covered my head in a plastic bag. They put my head under water. They took me to the morgue and they made me lie next to Constanzo's body. They kept saying, 'Sleep with him and bring him back to life, witch. Eat his heart, because that is what you enjoy.' That's why I signed confessions but they are not true." Aldrete received little sympathy. Cleared of Constanzo's murder, she was jailed for six years for criminal association. At a subsequent hearing in 1994, she was finally tried for murders at the Santa Elena ranch and was sentenced to 62 years without parole.

From her cell, the stunning six-footer tried to explain how she had changed from sports-loving college girl with a golden future ahead of her into a follower of a barbaric cult. "Constanzo loved me, he really loved me," she said. "I had a friendship with him but it was no more than that to me. I cared for him but not in the way he wanted me to care. I could not leave him because he threatened to use witchcraft on my family. I really believed that he could. I am so sorry about everything that has happened but I was not there when it was going on. I knew these people. I knew them but I never really knew the things that they did."

Few believed Aldrete's protestations as she languished in her cramped Mexican jail, where she continues to be known as "Bruja," the Spanish word for a witch.

DEAN CORLL

The story that the long-haired, disheveled young man told police was shocking. But the true horror of his confession came with the discovery of 19 corpses of teenage boys in a boat shed, with even more bodies scattered throughout an area popular with holidaymakers.

Those grim finds were to catapult Dean Corll into the history books as one of America's most prolific serial killers. It was one of Corll's evil accomplices, high school dropout Wayne Henley, who finally alerted police in Houston, Texas, to the sickening string of murders. But by then, 33-year-old Corll was himself dead—shot by Henley after an argument.

No one could have guessed that Dean Arnold Corll, who had looked so dashing in his army uniform during his service in the 1960s, would turn into a sickening sex murderer. But it was at this time that he realized that his sexual urges could only be satisfied through the torture and killing of boys.

Released from the army at the age of 25 in 1964, Corll returned to his job at the confectionery factory owned by his mother. His trade later earned him the title "Candy Man Killer," for Corll initially tried to lure boys by giving them sweets. When their complaints about his sexual advances became public, his mother sacked him from the factory and Corll became even more desperate to satisfy his lust.

He started to pay for sexual services and one of his first willing boyfriends was 12-year-old David Brooks, who later became his accomplice. Three years later, Corll committed his first murder. The victim was university student Jeffrey Konen,

whom police believed was picked up by Corll while hitchhiking.

Operating in the rundown Heights area of Houston, Corll and Brooks had no problem persuading boy drug addicts to go to Corll's apartment

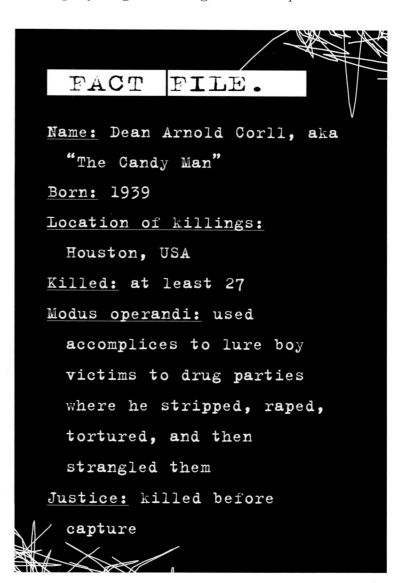

FACT FILE.

__Name:__ Dean Arnold Corll, aka "The Candy Man"

__Born:__ 1939

__Location of killings:__ Houston, USA

__Killed:__ at least 27

__Modus operandi:__ used accomplices to lure boy victims to drug parties where he stripped, raped, tortured, and then strangled them

__Justice:__ killed before capture

Dean Corll (left) had two accomplices. Elmer Henley (right) and David Brooks helped him procure boys to be plied with drugs. Afterward they would be taken to Corll's "torture room."

with the promise of wild parties. Brooks's job was to find the boys that Corll would forcibly have sex with before killing them. "He killed them because he wanted to have sex and they didn't," Brooks later told police.

The sex and strangling spree continued, often with two boys at one time being raped and killed. Soon Wayne Henley, originally earmarked as one of Corll's victims, joined in. He missed death by his willingness to do literally anything as long as it paid well—and that included delivering his best friends into Corll's evil clutches.

With Brooks and Henley cruising the area for victims, as well as helping commit the occasional murder themselves, Corll's tally of victims rose to 27. Despite the anxiety of parents over their missing sons, local police failed to come anywhere close to solving the mystery.

Corll, now working as an electrician for the Houston Lighting and Power Company, suddenly decided to go straight. Although still seeing one of his boyfriends whom he had picked up in a public toilet, he now also had a girlfriend, mother-of-two Betty Hawkins. His double life—in public a pleasant man who gave out sweets and in private a violent sex killer—was taking its toll. Corll was also tiring of changing addresses to avoid detection.

Despite his and Betty's plans to make a new life in Colorado, Corll could not resist one final murder. The victim was to be one of Henley's friends, Tim Kerley, who was more than happy to accept an invitation to a glue sniffing party at Corll's apartment. Things went wrong when Henley arrived with his girlfriend, Rhonda Williams. Corll objected, turned on Henley and handcuffed and bound him. Eventually, after sweet-talking Corll into untying him and letting Rhonda go, Henley knew his only chance of escape was to shoot his captor. Corll died from a spray of bullets from his own pistol. Kerley and Rhonda alerted the police who at first assumed that Henley was a victim too—before he gave the game away with a chance remark over the amount of money he had received for procuring boys for Corll.

Forced to confess, Henley led police first to a boatshed where 17 decomposing bodies of boys lay, then to local tourist spot Lake Sam Rayburn, where more naked corpses were unearthed. The body count came to 27 but police believe there were even more never found, for they had 42 boys listed as missing from the area during Corll's reign of terror between 1970 and 1973.

Wayne Henley and David Brooks were tried at San Antonio in 1974. Henley was found guilty of nine murders and sentenced to 594 years in prison. Brooks got life after being found guilty of one murder. Their pleas of insanity went unheeded.

JUAN CORONA

It was little wonder that Californian police seeking the murders of Mexican migrants had no cause to suspect Juan Vallejo Corona.

For Corona was a Mexican migrant himself. He was also happily married and the father of four daughters. But away from this picture of settled family life, Corona was combining his secret homosexuality with sadistic murder. And not only was he on the lookout for possible victims, he was also busy digging graves in preparation for them.

Born in 1933, Corona plodded through childhood without any secure family base or proper education. He earned cash as an itinerant fruit picker, finally crossing the border from Mexico to California with his wife Gloria in the 1950s. Despite his inadequate schooling, Corona managed to secure several jobs and in the early 1970s was put in charge of hiring migrant workers to pick the fruit crops of California's Yuba City area.

But all was not as it seemed. Corona was suffering various forms of mental illness, eventually leading to him being diagnosed a schizophrenic. The men he hired were easy targets. Housed by Corona in barrack-like buildings on a ranch, the workers were single and many of them were alcoholics, social misfits, or drop-outs. No one would notice them if they simply disappeared.

And they did—at least 25 murdered after being sexual assaulted by Corona. The month of May in 1971 was the peak of Corona's killings, and psychiatrists were later to say that there was something about that time of year with its abundance of sweet-smelling, ripening fruit that acted as a trigger in his deranged mind.

On May 19, a local fruit farmer noticed that a large hole had been dug in his peach orchard. Returning there the next day, he saw that the hole was now a mound of freshly dug earth. Fearful of what he might find, the man alerted the police who began the gruesome task of finding out exactly who or what was buried beneath. They unearthed the body of itinerant Kenneth Whitacre, who had been stabbed to death and his head almost severed with a machete. Tests later showed that he had been sexually assaulted.

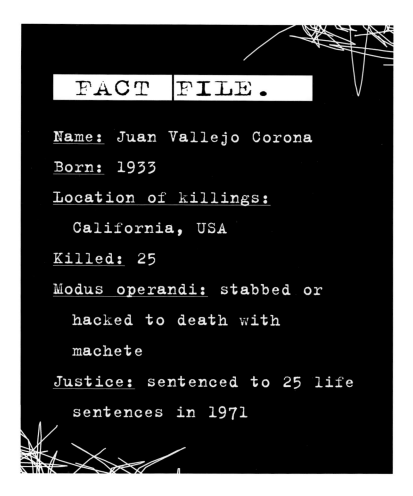

FACT FILE.

Name: Juan Vallejo Corona

Born: 1933

Location of killings:
   California, USA

Killed: 25

Modus operandi: stabbed or
   hacked to death with
   machete

Justice: sentenced to 25 life
   sentences in 1971

Corona first went to the United States as a migrant worker.
Within ten years he built up his own labor-contracting
business. Many who worked for him were to end up dead.

- - - - - - - - - - - - - -

The discovery sparked off the hunt for more
buried bodies. There were indeed plenty, with 25
eventually being found, but police still maintain
there were many more victims of Corona. One
grave alone yielded nine male bodies. All had been
raped before being stabbed and viciously slashed
around the head.

But Corona had left clues which made the
police think he had wanted to be caught. They
found meat market receipts bearing Corona's
name on several of the bodies. Two others carried
bank deposit slips bearing his name.

When police searched Corona's farmhouse
near Feather River they found a machete, a pistol,
two butcher's knives, bloodstained clothes, and a
notebook meticulously recording the names of the
dead men. Despite the police's belief that Corona

must have simply been waiting to be discovered,
he denied all 25 charges of murder.

At his trial in 1973, the evidence was damning, not only that found at his home but the fact
that he had quite obviously dug graves in preparation for his killings. Corona's defense lawyer
made pleas about his client's mental state but he
was found guilty and given 25 life sentences. His
mental illness did, however, allow him to lodge a
subsequent appeal against his sentence. He told a
prison doctor: "Yes, I did it but I'm a sick man and
can't be judged by the standards of other men."
Corona was retried in 1982 and again found guilty.
He returned to Corcoran State Prison where he was
stabbed 32 times by a fellow inmate and blinded
in one eye.

Technically, Corona could apply for parole,
which he did six times up until September 2003,
by which time he was 69. That was also the first
occasion on which Corona revealed his true self.
He told District Attorney Carl Adams: "The victims
were all people who didn't have a family and they
were ready to go to the next world." Reporting to
the parole board, Carl Adams said it was the first
time Corona had acknowledged "knowing something about the murders and revealing he picked
people who didn't have anyone who would worry
about them or know they were missing."

Back behind bars, Corona continued to be visited by psychiatrists and doctors. At one time, he
tried to convince them that another man partnered
him in the serial murders and police actually tried
to track down a second suspect. But no other possible perpetrator of the crimes was found and those
who had got to know the mass killer believed that
the "other man" existed only in Corona's schizophrenic mind.

MARY COTTON

Mothers in the late nineteenth century would threaten their naughty children with the prospect of a visit from Mary Cotton, the "Monster in Human Shape."

Youngsters themselves skipped in the streets to a rhyme: "Mary Ann Cotton, she's dead and she's rotten." A stage play was performed in the theaters of Victorian England titled *The Life And Death of Mary Cotton.* Who was she?

The answer to that question is difficult to give with any certainty even today. Mary Cotton was a mass murderer—but one who fascinated the poverty-stricken population of industrial northern England when her crimes came to light. One of the most enigmatic figures in the annals of crime, she seemed to have evoked revulsion and sympathy in equal measure. She was also unlike most serial killers in another way. She knew her victims, for all of them were members of her immediate family.

No one will ever be sure how many people died at her hands but the candidates include: her mother, two of her three husbands, one bigamous husband, ten of her 12 children, five other children, her best friend, and a lover. The total is 21 but might well be higher. She was certainly Britain's greatest mass murderess.

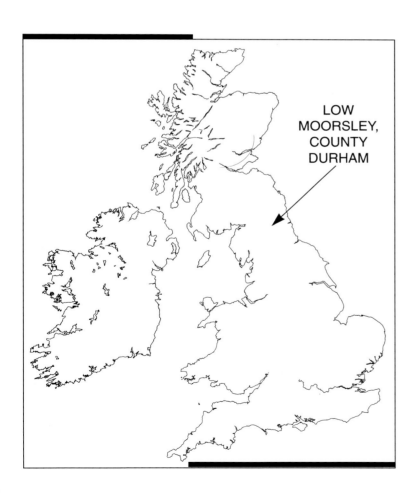

LOW
MOORSLEY,
COUNTY
DURHAM

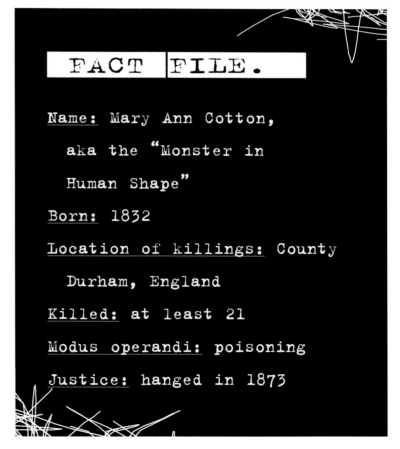

FACT FILE.

Name: Mary Ann Cotton, aka the "Monster in Human Shape"

Born: 1832

Location of killings: County Durham, England

Killed: at least 21

Modus operandi: poisoning

Justice: hanged in 1873

Mary Ann, raised as a strict Methodist in the County Durham mining village of Low Moorsley, was married in 1852 at the age of 20 to William Mowbray. They had eight children. But from this, her first family, only one daughter, Isabella, survived. Isabella was sent to live with her grandmother while those remaining at home—her father, brothers, and sisters—all died of gastric fever. After her husband's death, Mary Ann married George Ward. Yet after only 13 months he too was dead. The merry widow even murdered her own mother, who became ill at the same time as her third husband, James Robinson, asked Mary Ann to marry him. Mary Ann herself became mother to James Robinson's five children, taking with her Isabella, the surviving daughter from her first family. Within a few short months Isabella and four of the Robinson children had died from supposedly natural causes. Robinson left Mary Ann, taking away with him his only surviving child—and in doing so became the only husband to survive Mary Ann.

Even though she was still legally married, Mary Ann next wed Frederick Cotton, who had two children from a previous marriage. His bride soon fell pregnant and had another child. A year into the marriage, Frederick Cotton was also dead. Gastric fever was blamed.

It was at this stage of her killing spree that Mary Ann Cotton met up with a former lover, Joseph Nattrass. The resumed romance was ill-fated, however, as the greedy widow found yet another way of improving her lifestyle. This time

> **" I won't be troubled long. He will go like all the Cotton family "**

her heart was set on a customs officer by the name of Mr. Quick-Manning—and everyone else became no more than millstones around her neck. Mary Ann killed Joseph Nattrass, along with her ten-year-old stepson Frederick and her 14-month-old baby by Cotton, Robert.

That left only her seven-year-old stepson Charles. Cotton tried to place him in a workhouse and when that means of disposal was refused, she told neighbors: "It is hard to keep Charlie when he is not my own. He is stopping me from taking in a respectable lodger. But I won't be troubled long. He will go like all the Cotton family." After sending poor Charlie on an errand for some arsenic and soap to rid the house of bedbugs, the poor boy did indeed go the way of so many of his relations before him, expiring on July 12, 1872.

It was this final murder that doomed Mary Ann Cotton. Little Charlie had been fine one day and dead the next. A doctor who had seen the boy the day before his death pressed for an autopsy. An inquest into his death was held at the Rose and Crown public house next to Mary Ann's terraced stone cottage in the town of Great Auckland. The simple table-top autopsy had revealed no traces of poison and the inquest jury had no alternative to pass a verdict of "death by natural causes" and allow his body to be committed to a pauper's grave. His stepmother was free to pick up a small insurance policy on his life and no doubt believed she

Mary Ann Cotton became infamous as one of Britain's greatest mass-murderers.

Mary Ann Cotton was found guilty of the murder of her step-son Charles Edward in 1873 and subsequently hanged. She had poisoned him and many other members of her family with arsenic.

- - - - - - - - - - - -

had got away with murder once again. However, the doctor had secretly kept back some of Charlie's stomach contents and later subjected them to a more thorough chemical analysis. He found traces of arsenic and informed the police, who began feverishly investigating the strange family history of the Cottons. Suddenly the cause of all the deaths became apparent. Mary Ann was a mass poisoner, using arsenic to kill her victims. She was arrested and police began exhuming the bodies of family members.

The resultant trial at Durham Assizes was the most sensational murder case of the Victorian age. The 40-year-old killer was escorted into the dock on the morning of March 5, 1873, on only one charge: that of murdering her stepson Charles Edward Cotton with arsenic. The motives were twofold: she saw the boy as an impediment to marrying her new lover Quick-Manning and she stood to gain £8 from an insurance policy. Everyone in the crowded courtroom knew this was a sample charge and that many more deaths would be laid at the door of the accused. The newspapers were calling it the worst murder case in history and the publicity had caused the courtroom to be packed to the doors and seats had to be provided alongside the judge so that local dignitaries could be adequately accommodated.

Mary Ann Cotton wore a black and white shawl, black dress, and black bonnet. Her physical features were not particularly striking, yet she had managed to ensnare a series of husbands and lovers. As the region's main newspaper, the *Newcastle Journal*, reported: "Perhaps the most astounding thought of all is that a woman could act thus without becoming horrible and repulsive. Mary Ann Cotton, on the contrary, seems to have possessed the faculty of getting a new husband whenever she wanted one. To her other children and her lodger, even when she was deliberately poisoning them, she is said to have maintained a rather kindly manner." The paper, which had given her the epithet "Monster in Human Shape," concluded its commentary by saying: "Pity cannot be withheld, although it must be mingled with horror."

Cotton's defense lawyer Thomas Foster, who had been appointed only two days before the trial when Cotton failed to raise the money to pay for her own, had an uphill struggle arguing her case against the prosecution's prestigious advocate, Sir Charles Russell, later raised to the peerage as Lord Chief Justice. Foster's defence was that Charles Cotton's death was caused by arsenic in the coloring of some green wallpaper in his bedroom. He argued with the judge, Sir Thomas Archibald, that evidence of earlier deaths in the family should be withheld from the jury as it would prejudice this single case. When the judge overruled this plea, the defense case collapsed.

On the third day of the trial, the jury left the courtroom for an hour to discuss their verdict: guilty. The judge donned his traditional black cap and intoned one of the most sonorous speeches in British legal history. Before sentencing Cotton to death, he said:

"Mary Ann Cotton, you have been convicted, after a careful and patient trial, of the awful crime of murder. You seem to have given way to that delusion, which sometimes takes possession of persons wanting in proper moral and religious sense, that you could carry out your wicked designs without detection. But while murder by poison is the most detestable of all crimes, and one at which human nature shudders, it is one the nature of which, in

> **❝Mary Ann was a mass poisoner, using arsenic to kill her victims❞**

the power of God's providence, always leaves behind it complete and incontestable traces of guilt. Poisoning, in the very act of crime, writes an indelible record of guilt. In these last words I shall address to you, I would earnestly urge you to seek for your soul that only refuge which is left for you—in the mercy of God through the atonement of our Lord Jesus Christ. It only remains for me to pass upon you the sentence of the law..."

Cotton promptly fell into a faint and had to be carried from court by two wardresses. She protested her innocence to the very end. While petitioning for a reprieve, she gave birth to yet another child, a daughter by her lover Quick-Manning. She had a hand in choosing the adoptive parents, a childless married couple. But five days before the date for her execution, when it came time to hand over the child, she clung to the baby, which had to be forced from her arms. Even the tough prison wardresses were in tears, for a moment forgetting that this parent was probably the most dangerous mother in history.

On March 24, 1873, Mary Ann Cotton went to the gallows at Durham Prison. After the trapdoor swung open, her body convulsed at the end of the rope for three full minutes.

THOMAS CREAM

It would take much to make a hangman blanche, but what England's official executioner James Billington heard as he pulled the lever on the gallows at Newgate Prison on November 15, 1892, made him freeze.

For the last words of the hooded convicted killer as he stood with a hood over his head and a noose around his neck were: "I am Jack the..." Then the trap door burst open and the rest of the sentence was cut from him, along with the breath of life.

The hooded figure apparently intent on making a last-minute claim to be the infamous Jack the Ripper was Dr. Thomas Neill Cream, a con-

victed killer of almost equal evil if never the same level of infamy. Cream, tagged the "Lambeth Poisoner," was indeed a suspect in the relentless search for Jack the Ripper, the slaughterer of five women in London at the close of the last century. He certainly had the medical know-how displayed by the Ripper, who savagely disembowelled his victims. Yet at the time the Ripper was in action, Cream was safely in jail in Joliet, Illinois, where between 1881 and 1889 he was imprisoned for murder. So his astonishing last words, silenced by the hangman's noose, was a final flight of fancy by a man who appeared to be rapidly losing his hold on reality.

Cream was born in Glasgow on May 27, 1850, one of eight children of William and Mary Cream. Before he celebrated his sixth birthday, his family had emigrated to Canada, where his father became the manager of a Quebec shipbuilding firm. At first, young Thomas was a shipbuilder's apprentice but his heart was set on a career in the medical profession. He studied at McGill University and emerged with an American MD qualification. This bright, eligible young man became engaged to one Flora Eliza Brooks but before they could be married Flora fell pregnant. Obligingly, Cream carried out an illegal abortion, leaving her seriously ill.

When her parents realized what had occurred, they were furious. Her father confronted Cream and insisted that he marry Flora or face the

---

FACT FILE.

Name: Dr. Thomas Neill Cream,

   aka the "Lambeth Poisoner"

Born: May 27, 1850

Location of killings: London,

   England; Ontario, Canada;

   Chicago, USA

Killed: seven

Modus operandi: poisoning

Justice: hanged at Newgate

   Prison, London, in 1892

consequences. This was to be a genuine shotgun wedding and it duly took place in September 1876. The next day, Cream cynically fled the country. He arrived in England, where he studied at St.

"His astonishing last words, silenced by the hangman's noose, was a final flight of fancy by a man who appeared to be rapidly losing his hold on reality"

Thomas' Hospital, London, and the Royal College of Physicians and Surgeons in Edinburgh.

As far as the records show, Cream lived an orthodox existence throughout this period—apart from one strange incident later recalled by a prominent lawyer of the day. Marshall Hall was asked to defend a man accused of bigamy with a string of women. After advising him to plead guilty, the lawyer was surprised to hear the man declare himself innocent. Not only that, he had an alibi. He was in prison in Australia at the time of the offences, and a cable from the jail confirmed his innocence. When Hall attended the trial of Dr. Cream much later, he recognized the errant doctor as being the same man charged with bigamy. There must have been collusion with a double, Hall concluded, although no one knows how long or to what extent this continued.

With his new qualifications, Cream returned to

Thomas Neill Cream was one of the few genuinely competent medics to turn murderer. He was sentenced to death in 1892 for the murder of Matilda Clover.

Canada—safe from the wrath of his wife, as he was by now a widower—and set up a practice in London, Ontario. Soon afterward the body of chambermaid Kate Gardener was found in the water closet behind his rooms, killed by chloroform. Although it was known she was visiting him for an abortion, no action was taken against the doctor.

Cream next moved to Chicago where another woman seeking an abortion, Julia Faulkener, died in August 1880. This time he was taken into

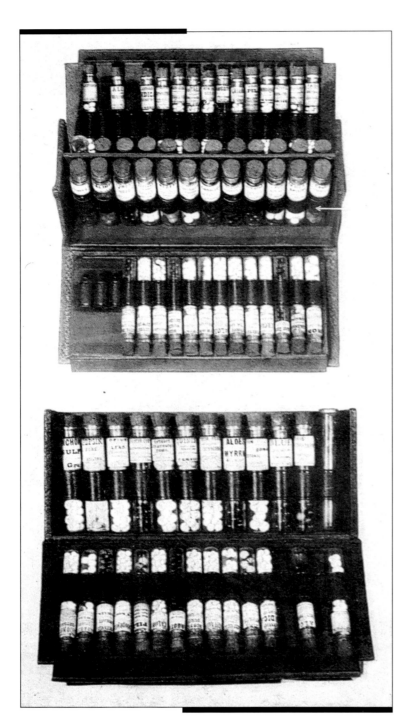

Dr Cream's portable medicine case contained the lethal strychnine pills that he used to poison his victims.

- - - - - - - - - - - -

custody but once again slipped through the net— in time to kill off another woman patient. His luck ran out, however, with his next murderous fling. Cream then took up with an attractive married

woman, Julia Stott. She had visited him to buy a medicine he marketed for epilepsy in the hope it would help her ailing and ageing husband. After eventually taking his medicine from Cream, Daniel Stott died in agony.

The death of his lover's husband would have remained unremarkable if Cream himself had not written an anonymous letter to the coroner and district attorney accusing the chemist of meddling with the medicine. Stott's body was exhumed and the poison strychnine was discovered in his stomach. Cream tried to flee but was brought to book and sentenced to life for murder in November 1881. With remission, he was released only a decade later. He returned to Canada to collect cash left to him by his father and then went on to England. His mind was clearly unbalanced, as companions noticed, possibly addled by an addiction to morphia. His conversation was centered on poisons, pornography, and money.

His next chosen victims were mainly prostitutes. In October 1891, Louisa Harvey picked up a man with a noticeable eye defect and, after spending the night with her, gave her some pills that he said would help clear a rash on her face. Suspicious because of her client's insistence that she swallow them all, Louisa merely pretended to consume them, and in doing so saved herself from the Lambeth Poisoner.

Another prostitute, nineteen-year-old Ellen Donworth, was not so lucky. She was found in the road suffering violent convulsions and, before her death, was able to tell her landlady that she had taken a mystery drink from a cross-eyed stranger who had bushy whiskers and wore a silk hat. The description was that of Cream, who wore a false beard beneath his moustache when he was up to

A portrait of Cream from the *Illustrated Police News*, November 5, 1892.

no good. An inquest found that Ellen had died from strychnine poisoning.

A letter written in Cream's hand found its way to the coroner's office, pledging help in the search for the killer in exchange for a huge sum of cash. It was signed "A. O'Brien, detective." Another letter was sent to Frederick Smith, of the stationery company W. H. Smith, claiming that he knew Ellen Donworth and demanding cash. Cream also printed 500 leaflets claiming that the killer of Ellen was on the staff of the Metropole Hotel. All the residents, he alleged, were in danger. These letters baffled police and have perplexed historians, who are still unable to establish his motives.

Only a week after the death of Ellen Donworth, another prostitute, Matilda Clover, died the same agonizing death. This was put down to alcoholic poisoning but Cream wrote yet another of his crackpot letters, this time trying to blackmail a doctor over the death. Police were alerted but when the blackmail attempt fizzled out, they failed to pursue the case.

London was saved from more of his lunatic behavior when Cream met and fell in love with Laura Sabbatini. The pair became engaged, although their wedding plans were delayed by a business trip Cream made to the United States in 1892.

Nine days after his return, two prostitutes in lodgings woke in the early hours writhing and screaming in pain. Alice Marsh, aged 21, and Emma Shrivell, 18, had spent the evening in the

THE EXECUTION OF DR NEILL CREAM.

CLOSING SCENES IN THE CAREER OF A GREAT CRIMINAL.

The case of Dr. Cream was infamous at the time, attracting much coverage in newspapers, which kept a curious public well informed.

ble for the prostitutes' murders. In the letter, he also mentioned the killing of Matilda Clover, who at that time was still thought to have been a victim of alcohol poisoning. Police at last seriously concerned themselves with the suspicious deaths occurring in the seedy slums of London. Their breakthrough came when PC Cumley again saw Cream and followed him home.

Two undercover men were put on the case: Patrick McIntyre, a police sergeant, and John Haynes, a covert government agent. Cream condemned himself in confidences to them both. His knowledge of the deaths were too detailed to have been gained from newspaper reports. Finally a prostitute who had narrowly escaped being poisoned came forward, and the police persuaded Dr. Harper to press charges for blackmail.

company of a stout man with whiskers, wearing glasses to correct a squint. It was, of course, Cream—although unbeknown to him, he had been spotted leaving them in the early hours by sharp-eyed Police Constable George Cumley.

Cream next tried to extort money from Dr. Joseph Harper, father of a fellow lodger, in a letter which claimed his son Walter had been responsi-

On June 3, 1892, Cream was arrested at his home in London's Lambeth Palace Road. He pompously told the police inspector: "You have got the wrong man, but fire away!"

The body of Matilda Clover was exhumed and strychnine was discovered in her stomach. A jury which sat at the delayed inquest into her death decided she had died of strychnine poisoning at the hand of Thomas Neill Cream.

In the dock at the Old Bailey, Cream was faced with several charges of murder and two counts of blackmail. He pleaded not guilty to all. Finally, the Crown proceeded with the murder of Clover alone. A pharmacist gave evidence that Cream had purchased gelatine capsules and nux vomica from him. Police told the court they had found seven bottles of strychnine in Cream's rooms. Prostitute Louisa Harvey also gave damning evidence of her lucky escape from Dr. Cream's clutches.

Despite all of this, Cream was confident he would be freed. He might have been, too, if Mr. Justice Hawkins had not ruled that he would hear evidence in the other cases, not just that gathered by the police relating to the death of Clover. His barrister's defense was so eloquent and stirring that Cream sang and danced in his cell, sure

The Lambeth poisoning case as it was illustrated at the time in 1892.

that acquittal was only hours away. The judge thought otherwise. His summing-up of the case was damning, and the jury took just ten minutes to decide Cream was guilty. As he strutted out of the dock, Cream muttered defiantly, "They shall never hang me." Less than a month later, he died on the gallows—with his strange final words ringing in the hangman's ears: "I am Jack the..."

GORDON CUMMINS

Gordon Cummins was unpopular with his fellow RAF servicemen because of his constant boastful references to his supposed aristocratic forebears.

He claimed to be the illegitimate son of a member of the House of Lords and, in a cultivated upper-class accent, bragged about his friends in high places and the grand social circle he enjoyed when out of uniform. Because of his pretensions, he was nicknamed "The Duke" and "The Count." But Cummins was more than just a man who made up incredible stories about himself; he also led a dark and secret life during the blackout days of wartime London.

In just one week, Cummins killed four women as he stalked the bomb-blasted streets, bringing even more terror to the city already under siege from Hitler's aircraft. Called up to serve in the RAF in 1941, RAF Aircraftsman 525987 was billeted in St. John's Wood, north London, while awaiting pilot training. He could have become one of the famous fliers of the RAF but instead 27-year-old Cummins went on a killing spree in February 1942. With his good looks and fake cut-glass voice, he had no problems attracting women. But that, coupled with the fact he had a wife at home, did not stop him buying the services of prostitutes.

One of these was 43-year-old Margaret Frances Lowe, who lived in shabby lodgings in Gosfield Street in London's West End. Missing for three days, Margaret's absence did not cause concern among the dubious crowd with which she mixed. It was only the visit of her 14-year-old daughter on February 14 that launched the murder hunt. The teenager found her mother dead and naked, her body cut with a razor blade and a silk stocking still tied tightly around her neck. The policeman in charge of the enquiry, Detective Chief Inspector Greeno of Scotland Yard, described the sight as "like seeing a crudely butchered carcass."

Chief Inspector Greeno now knew he was on the trail of a man who had killed before. For Margaret's murder on February 11 was all too similar to that of prostitute Evelyn Oatley, whose body had been found in her Soho flat on February 10.

FACT FILE.

Name: Gordon Frederick
   Cummins, aka "The Count,"
   "The Duke," and the
   "Blackout Ripper"

Born: 1914

Location of killings: London,
   England

Killed: four

Modus operandi: strangulation

Justice: hanged in 1942

Cummins' murderous activities during 1942 earned him the nick-name of the "Blackout Ripper." He picked up women on the streets, killed them, and mutilated their bodies.

Police discovered that Evelyn worked under the name Nita Ward and had been forced to turn to prostitution to support herself. Near her body was a bloodstained can opener that had been used to slash at her naked torso.

The murder of a woman the day before Evelyn Oatley did baffle police for a while because she was not a prostitute. Evelyn Margaret Hamilton was a respectable, 42-year-old teacher who had been unfortunate to encounter Cummins during her wartime job as a chemist. She had been found dead in an air-raid shelter in Montague Place, in the Marylebone area of London on February 9. She was Cummins' first victim.

Before the subsequent murders, police had believed the motive was robbery as Evelyn Hamilton's handbag and purse containing £80 was missing. In fact, Cummins needed the cash to support his fantasy tales of being a member of the landed gentry. Now they began to believe that a killer rivaling the infamous Jack the Ripper was stalking the streets of London. The fact that the can opener had been used to "rip" Evelyn Oatley's body was ominous. The fact that this was a killing spree condensed over just a few days added to the similarities. Because of wartime paper rationing, the newspapers of the day had less space than usual to highlight the murders but Cummins was nevertheless labeled "The Blackout Ripper."

Cummins' quick-fire killing spree ended on February 14 with the murder of Doris Jounannet who was strangled and mutilated in her flat in

Sussex Gardens, Paddington. Several souvenirs of the murder had been taken, including a fountain pen and comb. Doris was 32 and, with a husband aged 70, she was not averse to picking up soldiers more her own age in Leicester Square public houses. Sometimes she demanded money for her sexual favors. It was her husband who found her body after returning from his job as night manager of the Paddington Hotel. The man had entered the house with trepidation after noting that the milk had not been taken in. Doris had last been seen the night before in the company of a man in uniform. Now her poor husband faced the sickening sight of his young wife dead and terribly mutilated. Her body was still warm when Chief Inspector Greeno arrived.

The police officer was now heading a major murder hunt and set up a special incident room. Chief Inspector Greeno knew that one psychopath was responsible. The murderer obviously hated women and seemed to select his victims randomly. Prostitutes were quizzed and begged to trust the police who were trying to discover who was murdering their friends.

Two more prostitutes were to fall into the hands of Cummins but both had incredible escapes. Margaret Heywood was more than happy to join Cummins for a drink and something to eat at a pub called The Captain's Cabin, her haunt in the Haymarket. Using her working name of Greta, the woman had enough experience to know whether the man she was with was safe.

> **"Her poor husband faced the sickening sight of his young wife dead and terribly mutilated"**

Something about Cummins told her he was not. Walking through the blacked-out streets of London, Margaret tried to disentangle herself from the arm Cummins had thrown roughly across her shoulders. He turned nasty, threw her into a doorway and tried to strangle her. Mustering all her strength, Margaret managed a scream and, luckily, a delivery man came to her rescue. Cummins fled—leaving behind the damning evidence of his gas-mask bearing his service number 525987.

Instead of disappearing into the night, Cummins was arrogant enough to try to kill yet another woman. He picked up working girl Cathleen Mulcahy and the two went to her flat in Southwark Street, Paddington. Calling herself Kate King, the prostitute was getting ready for business when Cummins grabbed her from behind and tried to strangle her. Used to men with violent tendencies, Cathleen knew how to defend herself and kicked and fought so furiously that Cummins was forced to flee. This time he left behind his uniform belt.

It did not take Greeno and his men long to track down Cummins. Although he maintained his innocence, they had a gas-mask and belt both bearing his RAF number. Cummins first said the gas-mask wasn't his, then that his log book would prove that he had been in his billet at the time of the murders and attacks. Police became anxious when the log book did indeed show Cummins had signed in at the billet at the times he said. Then

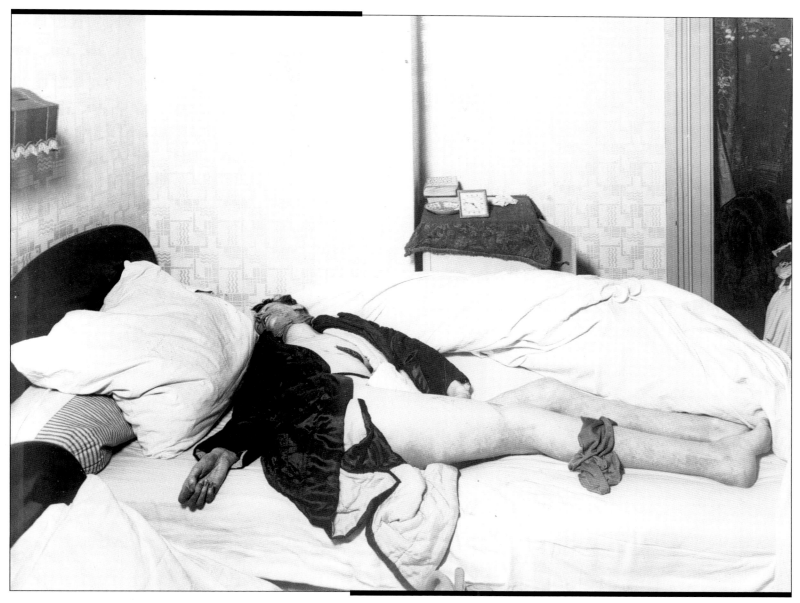

Cummins strangled and then cruelly mutilated his victims with
a tin-opener.

- - - - - - - - - - - - - -

investigations revealed that, for the price of a drink, servicemen would sign in absent colleagues. One fellow airmen even confessed that one night after signing in, he and Cummins had left the billet building by means of a fire escape.

The final proof was the discovery among Cummins' personal possessions of cigarette cases belonging to Margaret Lowe and Evelyn Oatley and a fountain pen owned by Doris Jouannet. Cummins' trial at the Old Bailey lasted just two days and the jury took only half an hour to return a verdict of guilty. The presiding judge, Mr. Justice Asquith, pronounced the death sentence. An appeal launched by Cummins was dismissed by Lord Chief Justice Humphreys who ordered that the murderer must face the gallows. The official hangman, Albert Pierrepoint, performed the execution at Wandsworth Prison on June 25, 1942, to the sound of sirens blasting out during an air raid.

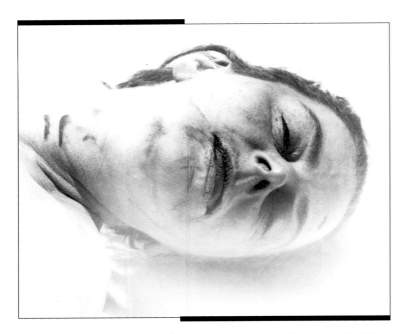

Police found the unmistakable marks of the left-handed Cummins on his victims.

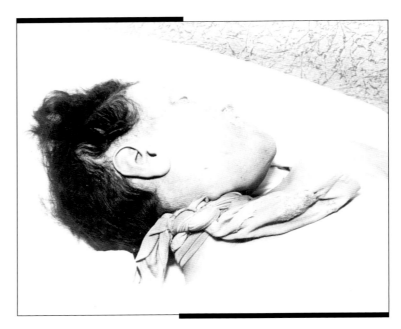

Cummins killed his victim with one of her own silk stockings, which was left still tied tightly around her neck.

The man who had carried out post mortems on the women victims, Sir Bernard Spilsbury, now, as British law decreed, had to carry out one on their killer.

> **Prints taken from the can opener-used to slash Evelyn Oatley's body matched those of Cummins perfectly**

The Cummins case has gone down in criminal history for other reasons than his brief killing spree. His was the first serial murder case in which fingerprinting played a significant part. Detective Superintendent Fred Cherrill, accomplished head of Scotland Yard's Fingerprint Bureau, had devised a means of marking a magnifying glass with rings and using its measurements to record individual fingerprints. All the prints Cummins carelessly left at the murder scenes were meticulously logged. He had no previous record for police to refer to during their investigations but Detective Superintendent Cherrill had an easy job when he was finally arrested. Prints taken from the can opener, used to slash Evelyn Oatley's body, matched those of Cummins perfectly. He was also left-handed, just as the fingerprint expert had said.

The prints would later link Cummins with two

Cummin's first victim, Evelyn Hamilton, was found in an air-raid shelter. Marks on her throat gave a vital clue suggesting the killer was left-handed.

further deaths, those of a Mrs. Church in October, 1941, and of a Mrs. Humphries shortly afterward. Cummins had probably been a killer much earlier than previously thought.

All of Cummin's victims were killed in a similar way and left for dead during the blackout of wartime London.

JEFFREY DAHMER

Even as a child, he was evil: torturing, killing, and mutilating animals for fun.
Aged just 18, he committed his first brutal murder.

Nine years later he began an obsessional killing spree that would shock the world. Everyone knows the name of Jeffrey Dahmer, the monster who held a city in the grip of terror for two long years as he kidnapped, drugged, murdered, sexually molested, and finally ate his victims.

Dahmer cleverly switched between his two personalities, fooling everyone who knew him. By day he was the mild-mannered, helpful, anonymous little man who worked conscientiously in the local chocolate factory.

By night he was a crazed cannibal who kidnapped people off the street to satisfy his perverted cravings. Dahmer was a real-life Hannibal the Cannibal and, like the character made famous in *Silence of the Lambs*, he was not satisfied with merely killing. He was a necrophiliac who ate choice parts of his victims, kept other parts as grotesque and grisly souvenirs, and disposed of the bodies in acid baths, in drains, and sewers.

It was on a warm July night in Milwaukee in 1991 that police finally uncovered the secret life of America's most twisted serial killer. Yet no one had suspected that Number 213 Oxford Apartments had been turned into a slaughterhouse. As detectives and forensic experts began pouring into the

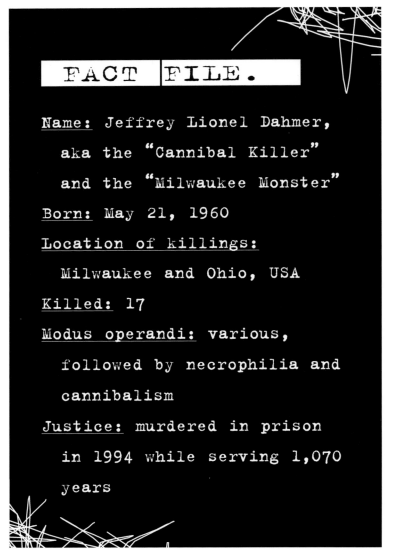

FACT FILE.

Name: Jeffrey Lionel Dahmer,
  aka the "Cannibal Killer"
  and the "Milwaukee Monster"
Born: May 21, 1960
Location of killings:
  Milwaukee and Ohio, USA
Killed: 17
Modus operandi: various,
  followed by necrophilia and
  cannibalism
Justice: murdered in prison
  in 1994 while serving 1,070
  years

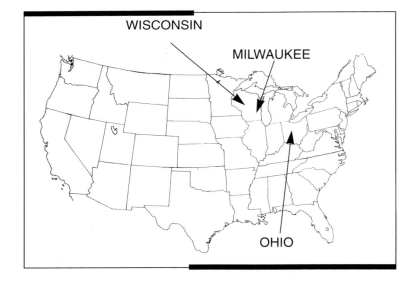

WISCONSIN

MILWAUKEE

OHIO

From as far back as his school days, Dahmer was remembered by his school companions as "one weird dude."

flat, it became apparent that Dahmer had been indulging in an orgy of murder for well over a year. A 47-gallon barrel of acid contained the decomposing remains of at least three dissected human torsos. Decomposed hands and genitals were kept in pots in kitchen cupboards, along with human skulls and rotting hands and fingers. Polaroid pictures showed 15 different victims in various states of undress and, in the words of a forensic report, "in different degrees of surgical excision."

Pictures from gay magazines hung on the bedroom walls and a collection of kinky and pornographic videos littered the living room. The only normal food in the flat was chips, mustard, and beer. Dahmer had not only killed his victims but, after satisfying his lust on their dead bodies, he had eaten their flesh. He later told police that he had fried and eaten one man's biceps. He said that after tenderizing and marinating in steak sauce, the meal tasted "just like beef." Hamburgers made from strips of human flesh and muscle were found in his refrigerator. The evidence was taken away by police in special anti-toxin suits. Film of police and forensic experts carrying vats of acid, decomposing body parts, and bones was broadcast day after day to a sickened American public.

Dahmer had put Milwaukee on the map for something other than beer and football. Yet, unlike most serial killers, he came from a respectable background. His father Lionel, a research chemist in Bath, Ohio, had married his sweetheart, Joyce Flint, in 1959 and Jeffrey was born nine months later. As far as is known, his childhood was not particularly traumatic, though his hobby appeared to be collecting dead animals from the highway and skinning or dissecting them or killing small creatures for the fun of it. Another pastime was drawing chalk outlines of dead bodies on the floor, homicide-style.

He had trouble maintaining relationships as he was considered strange by other people. One of his favorite games was to imitate mentally retarded people. Dave Borsvold, a fellow pupil of Dahmer, recalled, "He was a class clown but not in the wholesome sense. He was only amused by the bizarre. He was definitely a bit different but he didn't seem dangerous." Dahmer's High School guidance counsellor, George Kungle, recalled, "Jeff was never a discipline problem. He was a quiet but not introverted guy. He never let anyone get to

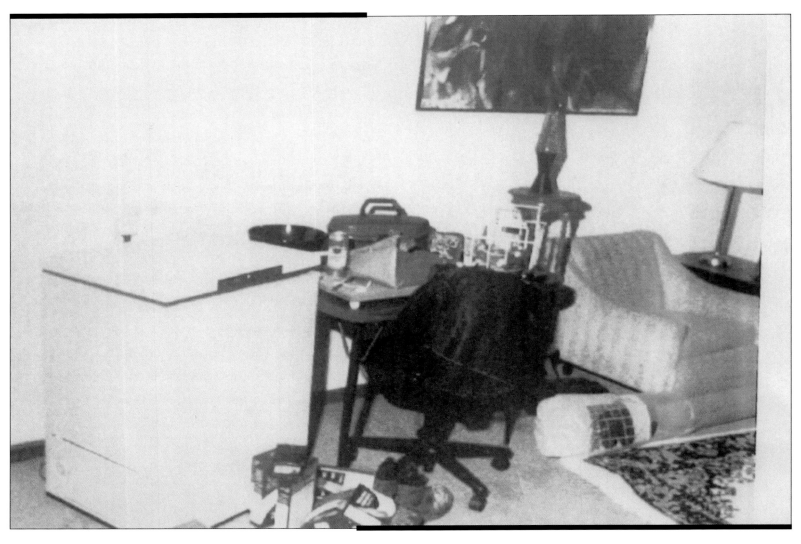

When police entered Dahmer's apartment, what hit them first was the strange nauseating stench. They discovered parts of human remains, including a head.

- - - - - - - - - - - - - -

know him well. I would try to talk to him like you would any kid, hoping to get some insights. He just never said a lot about himself."

When he was 18, Dahmer's mother and father split up and he moved into a motel to fend for himself while his parents fought for custody of his 11-year-old brother. In the bitter divorce battle, Dahmer's father referred to his wife's gross cruelty and neglect and her history of mental illness. No one knows exactly what turns a man into a serial killer but, in Dahmer's case, a family history of mental illness might have been a factor.

One night shortly after his parents' divorce, Dahmer drove out and picked up hitchhiker Stephen Hicks. He bludgeoned and strangled him, smashed his bones with a sledgehammer and scattered them in the woods behind his home. That same month, Dahmer killed Stephen Toumi in a hotel room in Milwaukee. These two killings were later admitted by Dahmer but were not included in the charges against him.

Dahmer then apparently kept his killing urges controlled for nine years. He went from high school to university but dropped out to join the army. He

Dahmer went on trial in 1991. He was later murdered in prison after receiving a life sentence.

had dreams of being a military policeman but instead became a medical orderly. He served in Germany but was finally discharged from the army for alcohol abuse. The rudimentary knowledge of anatomy picked up during his time as a medic was to serve him well. Back in America, Dahmer drifted from job to job, finally returning in 1982 to Milwaukee to live with his grandmother.

He began exposing himself to young children and was charged with the sexual abuse of a 13-year-old boy—whose brother was later to become one of Dahmer's victims. Found guilty, Dahmer wrote a lucid letter to his trial judge asking for clemency. "The world has enough misery in it without my adding more to it," he wrote. "That is why I am asking for a sentence modification, so that I can continue my life as a productive member of society." Dahmer was sentenced to eight years in jail, but was released as a model prisoner after serving just ten months.

He was assigned to social worker Donna Chester, who saw him as just another minor sex offender trying, through counseling and rehabilitation, to find his way back into society. Ms. Chester had another 121 cases on her books and

MILWAUKEE COUNTY

after two years she applied for a waiver that made visits to his home unnecessary. It was a decision that Milwaukee police chief Philip Arreola was to criticize bitterly when Dahmer's dark secret was finally revealed. "We try to put these people away for a long time," he fumed. "Then they get let back on the streets. We can see the tragic results of a system that has ceased to function."

In 1988, Dahmer began his slaughtering in earnest. His victims that year were 15-year-old James Doxtator on New Year's Day and 23-year-old Richard Guerrero on March 2. Both were killed and dismembered at the home of Dahmer's grandmother. The house was also the location for Dahmer's next sick murder in March 1989, that of 24-year-old Anthony Sears. The first person to die in Apartment 213 on Milwaukee's North 25th Street was 30-year-old Raymond Smith in May 1990, followed by 23-year-old Edward Smith, 23-year-old Ernest Miller, 23-year-old David Thomas, 17-year-old Curtis Straughter, 19-year-old Errol Lindsey, and 32-year-old Anthony Hughes.

It was the murder of Dahmer's next victim, Konerak Sinthasomphone, which was to cause the greatest outcry because of a massive police blunder. A 14-year-old refugee from Laos,

> **"Sinthasomphone had been drugged with sleeping tablets, Dahmer's favored way of rendering victims helpless while he strangled them"**

Dahmer was arrested in 1991 and charged with multiple counts of murder while he was still on probation for abusing a 13-year-old boy.

Sinthasomphone ran out of Dahmer's flat naked, apparently drugged and bleeding, in May 1991. Neighbors, most of whom were black, called the police, but allege that when the three officers arrived they were more or less told to "stop bothering the white guy." Yet Sinthasomphone had been drugged with sleeping tablets, Dahmer's favored way of rendering victims helpless while he strangled them. The officers returned Konerak Sinthasomphone to Dahmer, who told them he was a lover with whom he had quarreled. Within hours, Dahmer strangled him, had oral sex with the corpse, and then dismembered it, all the time taking Polaroid snaps.

Sinthasomphone's death would later haunt police chief Philip Arreola, the same man who criticized "the system" so loudly after Dahmer's release from jail. As further details about the botched call-out emerged, it was realized that the three police officers, all of whom were later fired, had actually entered Dahmer's home of horror without realizing anything was wrong. Worse, there were tiny drill marks visible in Sinthasomphone's forehead at the time they returned him to his killer. Dahmer had long fantasized about creating zombie-like lovers who would never leave him and would obey all his bidding as sex slaves. Sinthasomphone was one of those victims with whom he was experimenting by attempting crude lobotomies with a hand-held power drill and acid. One wretched victim lay conscious in his death agonies for a whole day before expiring.

There were to be four more victims of Jeffrey Dahmer in 1991, his last year at large. On June 12, he murdered 21-year-old Matt Turner and put his head in a freezer. Just over a month later, on July 13, the head of 24-year-old Jeremiah Weinberger joined it. The heads of 25-year-old Oliver Lacy, killed on July 14, and 25-year-old Joseph Bradehoft, who died on July 15, were also placed in cold storage.

Dahmer's capture came about by accident. Two patrolmen, Robert Rauth and Rolf Mueller, were sitting in their car when they saw a black man running toward them, a pair of handcuffs dangling from his wrist. The man, Tracy Edwards, spilled out a wild accusation against a resident of the nearby Oxford Apartments. He told the police officers that he had met Dahmer in a shopping mall and had agreed to go back to his flat to drink beer. When he said he wanted to leave, Dahmer threatened him with a knife and snapped on the handcuffs. Edwards said he had been held in Dahmer's lair for several hours, during which time he had lain on Edwards, listening to his heart, which he had threatened to cut out and eat. But then he had got restless, swaying and chanting and seeming to go in and out of a trance. Edwards had seized his chance to escape, thereby narrowly avoiding becoming Dahmer's eighteenth victim.

> **He had been held in Dahmer's lair for several hours, during which time he had lain on Edwards, listening to his heart, which he had threatened to cut out and eat**

The police officers entered the apartment block and knocked on Dahmer's door as the terrified Edwards waited a safe distance away. The door was opened by a slight man with dirty blond hair, wearing a blue T-shirt and jeans. What hit the policemen instantly was the strange, nauseating stench, and pots bubbling on the stove containing an evil-looking goo. In the sink were unwashed dishes with traces of the same substance on them. When the two cops radioed police headquarters to "run a make" on Dahmer, they learned he was still on probation following his release from jail for a sexual assault on a 13-year-old boy. Dahmer was arrested and handcuffed. It was then that Officer Mueller opened the refrigerator—and leapt back in horror. "Oh my God!" he remembered yelling. "There's a goddamn head in here. He's one sick son of a bitch." Dahmer's murderous spree had come to an abrupt end.

Dahmer readily admitted to the murder of 15 young men in the state and to two further murders in Ohio. There still had to be a protracted trial, however, because he claimed he was insane. A jury had to decide whether he was a twisted madman or a calculating killing machine. The trial itself was the most gruesome America had ever witnessed, with a national audience of millions on TV lapping up stories of bizarre sex, sick killings, and grisly fantasies. As Dahmer's

Jeffrey Dahmer was escorted into a Milwaukee County Circuit Court in July 1991. He was given a life sentence, but declared that he would rather have had the death penalty.

- - - - - - - - - - - -

trial proceeded in the imposing Milwaukee courthouse, families turned out to curse the monster who had ruined their lives and killed their loved ones. One young woman, whose 19-year-old brother had been butchered in the Oxford apartments, had to be restrained by court officials as she made a dash for Dahmer, screaming, "I'll kill you." Others branded Dahmer "a devil" and asked the judge to ensure he never saw daylight again.

Toward the end of the trial, Dahmer stunned everyone by asking to make a statement, an articulate apology composed in his prison cell. Asking for "no consideration" and declaring he would rather have faced the death penalty, he said:

"It is over now. This has never been a case of trying to get free. I really wanted death. I hope God can forgive, I know society and the families

The door to Jeffrey Dahmer's apartment was sealed with evidence tape and locked after his arrest in 1991.

God. I should have stayed with God. I tried and failed and created a holocaust. Only the Lord Jesus Christ can save me from my sins."

The statement continued: "I pledge to help the doctors find some answers. I know my time in prison will be terrible but I deserve what I get because of what I did." Dahmer, who admitted to detectives that he had studied satanic scripts, read a passage from the Bible and declared: "Jesus Christ came in the world to save sinners, of whom I am the worst." He apologized to the victims' families, the probation officer he had hoodwinked, and even to the policemen who were fired because of him. He also apologized to his father and his stepmother Shari, who had sat through the trial, heads bowed in silence. He said:

"I regret that the policemen lost their jobs. I know they did their best. I have hurt my mother, father, stepmother, and family. I love them all so much. I take all the blame for what I did. I hurt many people. I decided to go through with this trial for number of reasons. I wanted to show they were not hate crimes. I wanted the world to know the truth. I didn't want any unanswered questions. I wanted to find out what it was that made me bad or evil. Perhaps if there are others out there, this might have helped them."

One man taking a particular interest in the court hearing was Dahmer's distraught father who had paid for an expensive criminal lawyer, Gerald Boyle, to act for his son. Lionel Dahmer could not conceal his feelings of remorse over the monster his boy had become. He said, "In retrospect I wish I had done more in terms of keeping in touch with what he was doing and visiting him more often. I don't know about feeling guilty for what he did but I feel guilty that I didn't do more. I feel a deep sense

never can. I promise to pray every day for their forgiveness. I have seen their tears. If I could give my life right now to bring their loved ones back I would. This was not about hate. I never hated anyone. I knew I was sick or evil, or both. Now I have some peace. I know the harm I have caused. I can't undo the terrible harm, but I have cooperated as best I could. I am very sorry. I know I will be in prison for the rest of my life. I will turn back to

of shame. I think any father who has some sense of responsibility feels the transfer of shame or the responsibility somehow for this. When I first heard about it, I could not associate him with what I was hearing was done. Absolutely not. I didn't think in my wildest dreams, he was capable of something like that. I didn't look at him and see a monster. He acts—under most conditions—polite, kind, and, courteous. I can only imagine in my mind those occasions when he attacked the victims, that was the monster who was out of control."

Jeffrey Dahmer was found guilty of all charges. He was only the fourteenth necrophiliac to be convicted in American legal history. The jury decided that he was not insane, disregarding testimony of psychiatric experts who said he was a psychotic who suffered from unstoppable urges brought about by the mental condition of necrophilia which made it impossible for him to obtain sexual gratification except from corpses. The judge sentenced him to consecutive prison sentences totaling 1,070 years. The state of Wisconsin has no death penalty.

Long after the Dahmer trial, Apartment 213, Dahmer's chamber of horrors, still lay vacant, as did the entire second floor. The management even took the name from the front of the building to discourage ghouls and sightseers. Jurors from the trial received counseling and victims' families pressed ahead with lawsuits against Dahmer and the city.

> **He was kept in isolation for his own protection but then managed to talk his way into a unit for prisoners with emotional problems**

Dahmer was taken to the maximum-security Columbia Correctional Institution, Wisconsin's toughest jail. At first, he was kept in isolation for his own protection but then managed to talk his way into a unit for prisoners with emotional problems. There, he was interviewed regularly by psychiatrists and became something of a "guinea-pig" in their exploration of what turns a mild-mannered man into a murdering monster.

Some experts claimed the emotional distance between Dahmer and his parents might have contributed to a feeling of abandonment. They said this was what sparked his killing spree. Dahmer actually told doctors that the reason he killed his victims was because he did not want them to leave him. One psychologist, Judith Becker, who testified for the defence at Dahmer's trial, said he had managed to fool everyone including his social worker and the three policemen who failed to pick up that there was anything amiss in his killing and torturing lair. Ms. Becker found it interesting that the pills Dahmer used to drug his victims were all prescribed by his own doctor. She said:

"We could learn a tremendous amount from studying Dahmer because necrophiliacs are extremely rare. I have not seen anywhere in the literature the successful treatment of this disorder. Dahmer indicated to me that he hated what he had been doing and talked about a nuclear explosion that had gone off inside him since he was caught.

Jeffrey Dahmer during his initial court appearance was said to be wearing the shirt of one of his victims.

He talked about killing himself. He said he was sorry for what he did and felt pain for the relatives. He said the fantasies had stopped—but there's no way of knowing if they will start up again."

In the end, Dahmer did not have to wrestle with this anxiety. He was beaten to death by fellow inmates on the open unit on November 28, 1993. Ten months later, in September 1995, his body was finally cremated—except for his brain. Dahmer's mother, Joyce Flint, agreed to the disposal of his body but asked that the brain be preserved for medical research, saying that "science can be aided" by studying the mind of her monstrous son.

ALBERT DE SALVO

In 1963 Boston was a city that experienced mass panic after realizing a violent sex maniac was in its midst.

Between 1962 and 1964 the man gained access to the apartments of 12 single women, raped and mutilated them, then strangled them with a ligature tied in a bow.

The murderer earned himself the historic nickname the "Boston Strangler." He became the first person to be given the media label "serial killer." Yet mystery still surrounds his identity. Although Albert De Salvo confessed to the murders, evidence since suggests he may not have committed them all.

De Salvo was born in Chelsea, Massachusetts, in 1931. As with many cold-blooded killers, his story starts with a childhood spent in violent circumstances. One of six children, he was regularly battered by his drunken father whose attacks on Albert's mother once included knocking her teeth out and breaking her fingers. Short of cash, De Salvo Sr. even sold Albert and two of his sisters to a local farmer for nine dollars. When they

eventually came home, the children were taught to steal and shoplift. Worse, their father would bring prostitutes home and make them watch as he had sex with them.

By the time he left home, the young De Salvo had developed a near obsession with sex; as well

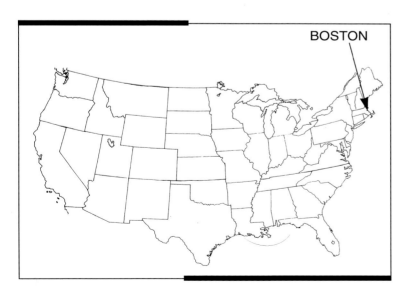

BOSTON

FACT FILE.

Name: Albert Henry De Salvo, aka the "Boston Strangler," the "Green Man," and the "Measuring Man"

Born: 1931

Location of killings: Boston, USA

Killed: 13 (disputed)

Modus operandi: strangulation followed by mutilation

Justice: De Salvo judged unfit to stand trial; received life sentenced in 1964 for lesser offenses; murdered in prison in 1973

as notching up many conquests among the neighborhood girls, he was happy to be the submissive partner in homosexual acts if the money was right. A regular offender in minor crimes, a brief spell in the army failed to change his ways and he had several brushes with authority because of his petty thefts. His sexual experimentation continued until he a met a girl, Irmgaard, while on a posting to Frankfurt, Germany. She was the daughter of a respectable Catholic family and, after their marriage, it seemed for a while as though the teenage De Salvo might build a normal life for himself.

However he was soon caught molesting a nine-year-old girl, although the crime was covered up; he was dishonourably discharged from the army but the case did not become public because the girl's mother feared it would bring shame on the family. After this disgrace, it seemed as if De Salvo had learned his lesson. Now settled in Boston with his wife and two children, and working as a house painter and handyman, he seemed to his neighbors to be a decent family man. Yet he was still secretly committing burglaries and seeking sexual satisfaction wherever he could get it.

It was when Irmgaard finally rejected his demands for sex five or six times a day that De Salvo took up a strange pastime. He hung around

> **❝❝It was when Irmgaard finally rejected his demands for sex five or six times a day that De Salvo took up a strange pastime❞❞**

De Salvo's identity as the "Boston Strangler" still causes controversy. He was convicted of sexual offenses and robbery and sent to prison for life.

student areas looking for apartments shared by several young girls. Then he would knock on the door and say he was from a modeling agency. Having impressed the gullible women, De Salvo would persuade them to have their vital statistics measured, naked as well as dressed. Sometimes De Salvo seduced the students or they him. None of the girls seemed to have complained about his visits, more about the fact that their modeling careers did not take off.

It was when De Salvo was arrested after one of his break-ins and police found not only house-breaking tools but a clipboard and tape measure on his person that he admitted he was the "Measuring Man" who had found notoriety in student quarters.

De Salvo was sentenced to two years for theft but served only ten months. What followed has given rise to the debate over whether De Salvo then became the Boston Strangler. If so, it was a very different man who was now on the streets. He broke into hundreds of homes throughout New England over the next couple of years, tying up and raping countless women. His attacks first earned him the name the "Green Man" because he always wore a green shirt and trousers.

The Green Man was soon to turn to murder. On June 14, 1962, he broke into the Boston home of 55-year-old Anna Slesers and strangled her with the belt of her dressing gown before arranging her body in an obscene pose. After he had finished, he tied the belt into a bow, a habit that was to become

Albert De Salvo arriving for his court appearance in 1967.

- - - - - - - - - - - -

his trademark. More elderly women became victims, including 65-year-old nurse Helen Blake, Mary Mullen, aged 85, Ida Irga, 75, and Jane Sullivan, 67.

Realizing they had a murdering sexual deviant on the loose—perhaps a man with a mother-hating complex—Boston police scoured their records and questioned every man they thought fitted the criminal profile. De Salvo was not one of them because, apart from the minor sexual assault when he was 17, his only recorded crimes were for theft. Those convinced that De Salvo was indeed the Boston Strangler say it was at this time he

decided to take a break from his killing spree, returning to it on his wedding anniversary on December 5, 1962.

Sexually fired up even more than usual, De Salvo needed a young woman to satisfy his fantasies. The victim was a tall and striking 20-year-old Sophie Clark, on whose door he knocked and then embarked upon his Measuring Man routine. When her back was turned, she was attacked by De Salvo who stripped, raped, and strangled her before posing her naked body complete with the bow under her chin. Three days later, police claimed, De Salvo paid another visit to one of the women who had fallen for his earlier Measuring Man tactics. Once inside the apartment of 25-year-old secretary Patricia Bissette, he strangled her with her own stockings.

After losing one of his prey—a young girl who fought back and escaped—the killer rapist became even more violent. One victim, 69-year-old Mary Brown was raped and killed by having her skull crushed before being left with a fork stabbed in her breast. Another, 23-year-old Beverly Samans, was tied to a bed, raped repeatedly, strangled, and stabbed 22 times.

By now, Boston was a city shrouded in fear. Women virtually barricaded themselves in their homes at night and few braved walking through the streets alone. Meanwhile, police took in numerous suspects for questioning but got nowhere. The way was open for the Boston Strangler to strike again. The victim was 58-year-old Evelyn Corbyn, followed by 23-year-old dress designer Joan Gaff, strangled with her black leotard. Among the statements De Salvo was later to make was the admission: "I don't know why I killed her. I wasn't even excited. And then I went home

Police worked out the possible escape routes that De Salvo
could have taken when he broke out of the state mental hospital where he was being held.

- - - - - - - - - - - -

and played with the kids and watched the report
of her murder on the TV."

The Boston Strangler struck again on January
4, 1964. It was to be the last time—and the most
evil. After gaining access to her flat, the killer tied
up 19-year-old Mary Sullivan and raped her. This
time, he used his bare hands to strangle before
propping the body up in a grotesque fashion on the
bed. Hardened police were never to forget the sight
when they discovered Mary's body. Her head rest-
ed on her right shoulder and her breasts and
sexual organs were exposed. She had been
assaulted with a broom. Semen was found on a
blanket. Between Mary's toes, the sick killer had
slid a card bearing the words "Happy New Year."

The killings ceased but the police investigation
went into top gear. Forensic psychiatrists were
asked to build a profile of the Strangler and more
than a few came to the conclusion that there were
two killers on the loose, one attacking young

Albert De Salvo broke out of the Bridgewater State Hospital in 1967 but was apprehended in Lynn, Massachusetts, the following day.

women and the other older women. Others suggested that the slayings were perpetrated by only one man, whose personality defect had altered over the time span of the murders, at first killing older women because of a mother-hatred fixation, then turning to younger victims once his need for revenge had been fulfilled. One of the psychiatrists, Dr. James Brussel, the "father" of American psychological profiling, suggested that the Boston Strangler was physically strong, a neat dresser, of Italian or Spanish descent, in his early 30s, clean shaven with a good head of hair—and a paranoid schizophrenic. He also forecast that he would be caught because his nature would make him boast about his crimes. His profile was a remarkably accurate picture of Albert Henry De Salvo.

De Salvo was eventually arrested in February 1965—but not for murder. Charged with house-breaking and sexual assault, his obviously disturbed state of mind resulted in him being committed to a hospital for the criminally insane "until further orders of the court."

Meanwhile, the police bid to uncover the Boston Strangler continued. Their big break came with a young woman's report of rape. For some reason, the Strangler had not killed her but had left after the attack, even apologizing for it. The woman's description alerted police to the man they were already holding. Their suspicions were confirmed when a fellow inmate of the mental hospital revealed conversations he had had with De Salvo. Convicted killer George Nassar, keen to claim a $100,000 reward for information leading to the Strangler, reported to his attorney, the renowned F. Lee Bailey, that De Salvo had confessed all. Extraordinarily, Bailey would soon be representing De Salvo in one of the America's most high profile court cases of all time.

Questioned by police again, 33-year-old De Salvo at first denied everything and demanded to speak to Irmgaard before answering further questions. She was brought to his cell and they whispered together before she told him loudly, "Al, tell them everything. Don't hold anything back." He heeded her advice, telling detectives, "I have committed more than 400 break-ins and there's a couple of rapes you don't know about." But at first he vehemently denied murdering anyone. Sobbing,

> **"No, no, no, I've done some terrible things with women but I have never killed anyone"**

he protested: "No, no, no, I've done some terrible things with women but I have never killed anyone."

During the ensuing seven months, De Salvo began to open up to his new lawyer. He told Bailey that he wanted "only to be found innocent by reason of insanity so I can go to a mental hospital." On Bailey's advice, he refused to give police a formal statement for the record but he nevertheless talked freely to them about the Strangler killings. He finally went on to admit murdering the 13 women that police had linked him with, and he added two more to the list and confessed to raping thousands more. He said he had felt remorse for his early killings. Before his first murder, of Anna Slesers, he had tried to rape and kill another woman but at the very last moment had fallen to his knees in front of her and tearfully begged her forgiveness. He had told her: "Oh God, what am I doing? I am a good Catholic man with a wife and children. I don't know what to do." Instead of calling the police, the intended victim had simply told him to go home. Similarly, De Salvo told police that he had almost spared his final murder victim, Mary Sullivan, as she begged him not to rape her. "She could have been my daughter," he mused.

De Salvo spoke about his crimes in 50 hours of tape recordings. The gruesome details he supplied, many never made public, convinced police that they had at last caught the Boston Strangler. The clincher was when a detective observed him tying his shoelaces with the exact loops that police had come to know as the "Strangler's Knot." Not everyone was convinced, however. One theory was that De Salvo had studied the murders out of a morbid fascination and had laid claim to them to bring attention to himself. Another theory reported by the Boston media was that the real Strangler was locked up with him in the mental institution and had passed on details of the crimes to the psychotic De Salvo. George Nassar, the fellow inmate who had befriended De Salvo and then reported his secret "confession," was a vicious and resourceful killer who was later convicted of a murder unrelated to the Strangler killings. The debate over whether De Salvo was the only maniacal killer prowling the streets of Boston still rages to this day.

In the event, Albert De Salvo was never charged with those crimes. His mental state allowed F. Lee Bailey to make a remarkable plea bargain, with De Salvo only admitting sexual assaults and robberies. He never stood trial for the crimes of the Boston Strangler, it being argued that the mental patient could not be prosecuted for murder or more serious rapes.

De Salvo served only a fragment of his life sentence at Walpole State Prison. On November 26, 1973, he was found dead in his cell, stabbed 16

"On November 26, 1973, he was found dead in his cell, stabbed 16 times, six knife thrusts piercing his heart"

times, six knife thrusts piercing his heart. The reason for his murder is unknown and a conspiracy of silence among his fellow prisoners ensured that the killer or killers were never identified.

Many feel the real secret of the Boston Strangler died with him. Albert De Salvo's family joined forces with a surprise ally, the family of victim Mary Sullivan, to cast doubt on whether De Salvo really was the Boston Strangler. They pointed to discrepancies between Mary's murder and the confession De Salvo withdrew later.

In December 2001, DNA obtained from De Salvo's exhumed body was compared to evidence found on Mary's body. The samples did not match. Lawyer Elaine Sawyer took up the case saying: "There is a culture in this country that likes to sweep things under the carpet and I believe this is what happened in the Strangler case. For nearly 40 years, Mary Sullivan's family could get no peace, believing her killer was still at large. But the police don't want to know." Now campaigners feel that if De Salvo was innocent of that murder, he could be innocent of other killings committed by the Boston Strangler. Adds Ms. Sawyer, "I think the whole theory that there ever was one Boston Strangler will be proved wrong."

NANNIE DOSS

Nowadays the signs would have been obvious but in the early days of the last century the deaths of so many in one family was put down to sheer bad luck.

It was not, of course, and the murderer was a wife and mother whose search for love became twisted and tortured. Nannie Doss was later to say: "I was searching for the perfect mate, the real romance of life." What she found instead was a childhood of sexual abuse and a string of husbands whom she found "dullards." So she killed them.

Nannie, a compulsive reader of romantic pulp fiction, married her first husband Charles Braggs (sometimes also referred to as George Frazer) in 1920 when she was just 15. Having fathered four children, he returned to their home in Tulsa, Oklahoma, one day to find two of them dying on the floor, allegedly poisoned. He walked out with one of the surviving pair, and made sure he never saw his wife again. The fourth child Florine was later reunited with her father after giving birth to a child which mysteriously died when in its grandmother's care. When her first husband walked out on her, Doss immediately took up with her second partner, Frank Harelson, who died of stomach trouble within a year. Husband number three, Arlie Lanning, survived until 1952 before succumbing to the same affliction. Number four, Richard Morton, died within a month of their 1953 marriage leaving a healthy insurance policy.

Her mother, her two sisters, and the nephew of one of her deceased husbands were added to the list of deceased. It transpired that she had disposed of her mother while nursing her through recuperation for a broken hip in 1953. The sisters each collapsed and died mysteriously while Nannie was paying them visits in the different towns where they lived.

It was only upon the death of Mrs. Doss's fifth husband, Samuel Doss, in Tulsa in July 1954 that an autopsy was ordered. It was discovered that there was enough arsenic in him to kill 20 men. At her trial, police estimated the total tally of her victims at 11. Nannie Doss explained that she had

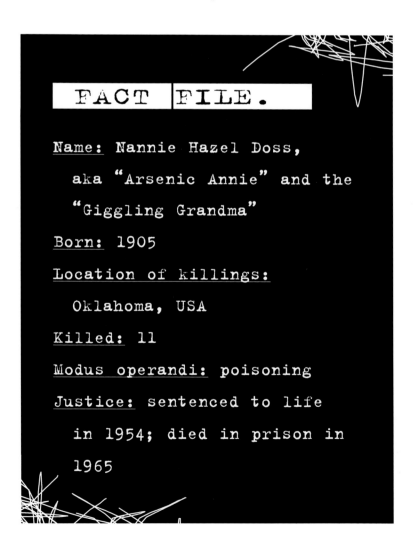

FACT FILE.

Name: Nannie Hazel Doss, aka "Arsenic Annie" and the "Giggling Grandma"

Born: 1905

Location of killings: Oklahoma, USA

Killed: 11

Modus operandi: poisoning

Justice: sentenced to life in 1954; died in prison in 1965

❝She had disposed of her mother while nursing her through recuperation for a broken hip❞

Nannie Doss, confessed killer of four of her husbands, seen leaving the County Attorney's office en route to jail.

poisoned the last four of her five husbands because they were "dullards." She said that although some of them had insurance policies, money was not her motive. She had simply found them boring and was seeking a soulmate who would live up to the standards of her fictional heroes. She was sentenced to life imprisonment and died of leukemia in 1965, leaving in her cell hundreds of well-thumbed true-romance magazines.

JOHN DUFFY

As many as 50 women in just four years were raped by John Duffy as he stalked lonely paths and isolated spots beside railway lines throughout the London area.

During that time he turned killer too, murdering three women. Duffy first raped in October 1982, repeating his violent attacks until his first murder on December 29, 1985, when he attacked 19-year-old secretary Alison Day as she got off a train in

> **❝Police found him loitering outside a station with a knife but let him go after he told them it was for a martial arts class❞**

Hackney, East London. Alison was garrotted with a piece of her own shirt and her body thrown into a river. It was later discovered that Duffy had an accomplice in this attack, as well as several others, but his identity was not revealed for another 14 years.

On April 17, 1986, four months after the murder of Alison Day, a Dutch schoolgirl, 15-year-old Maartje Tamboezer, was grabbed, raped, and strangled as she cycled through fields in East Horsley, Surrey. On May 18, 1986, Duffy killed his last victim, newlywed Anne Lock, a 29-year-old who worked for a London television company. She was snatched after getting off a train at Brookmans Park station.

During the hunt for the "Railway Rapist," police had Duffy at their mercy on two occasions. He was first questioned over the murder of Alison Day but was freed because he provided an alibi. On another occasion, police found him loitering outside a station with a knife but let him go after he told them it was for a martial arts class. Duffy panicked and, in a bid to cover his tracks,

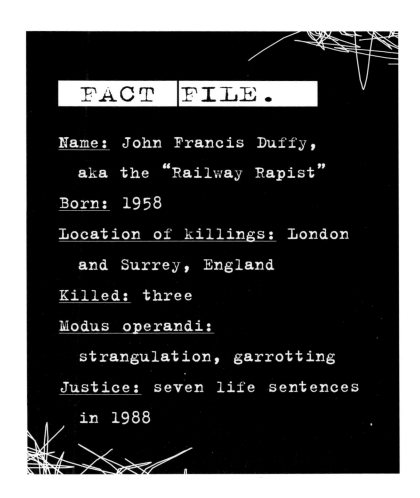

FACT FILE.

Name: John Francis Duffy, aka the "Railway Rapist"

Born: 1958

Location of killings: London and Surrey, England

Killed: three

Modus operandi: strangulation, garrotting

Justice: seven life sentences in 1988

"Duffy was a carpenter with a police record for raping his wife"

Duffy received seven life sentences in 1988.

admitted himself to London's Friern Barnet Mental Hospital claiming he had amnesia.

Police checked fingerprints on a million rail tickets in their hunt for the killer. They finally whittled possible suspects down to just 50 after analyzing semen traces at the murder scenes. Duffy had an unusually low sperm count which made him infertile—a factor police believe led to his resentment of women. A psychological profile of the killer, drawn up by behavioral scientist Professor David Canter, included the fact he was a martial arts fanatic, did semi-skilled work, and was likely to have a failed marriage behind him. Duffy was a carpenter with a police record for raping his wife. All this information supported police suspicions that Duffy was the killer and he became the first offender in English legal history to be

identified by Psychological Offender Profiling. Duffy was arrested on October 21, 1986, after raping a 14-year-old girl in Watford on the outskirts of London. Police found not only a selection of knives at his north London flat but fibers from Alison Day's coat, his victims' assorted house keys, and string identical to that used to bind the hands of Maartje Tamboezer. In 1988, Duffy was charged with seven rapes and the three murders, although it was later ruled there was insufficient evidence to convict him of Ann Lock's murder.

Duffy received seven life sentences. Eleven years later, police learned the identity of the man who had committed some of the attacks with Duffy. Decorator David Mulcahy was arrested on February 6, 1999, and sentenced to life imprisonment.

DONALD EVANS

What makes the case of Donald Evans unique is the disparity between the number of murders he claimed to have committed and the number with which he was charged—60 and two respectively.

Could anyone believe what the weird drifter said when he confessed to killing as many as 60? In the end, many considered his own violent death in jail was suitable justice.

Despite his confession, Evans was only ever convicted of two murders. The first was that of a homeless ten-year-old girl called Beatrice Routh whom he abducted from Gulfport, Mississippi, then raped and strangled her before dumping her body. Feeling some remorse for the killing, Evans confessed to police. He then embarked on a long tale of his other murders, started, he said, in 1977 when he was dismissed from the US Marine Corps.

Evans, originally from Galveston, Texas, certainly caught the attention of the Mississippi police who were holding him. For his confession to raping and killing six women in Florida, Illinois, and Texas as well as over 50 men and women in 22 states right across America, first led them to believe they had caught the notorious "Green River Killer." There had certainly been a spate of prostitute slayings in Washington State shortly after Evans' discharge from the Marines. Said Evans' legal adviser Fred Lusk, "There is a strong possibility that Evans is telling the truth. The count could go higher."

However, many felt that Evans was cashing in on the notoriety of cannibal killer Jeffrey Dahmer whose sick murders had shocked the world in August 1991, shortly before Evans decided to come clean about his own murder spree. Evans made a strange pact with police: he would try to locate the bodies of all his victims as long as was given the death sentence. According to Lusk, "He said he lived by the sword and wanted to die by the sword."

Evans was sentenced to death for the murder of Beatrice Routh, with an additional life sentence for kidnapping. In 1995, he was given a second life sentence after admitting to the killing of Ira Smith, a black woman, in Fort Lauderdale, Florida. The

FACT FILE.

Name: Donald Leroy Evans

Born: 1958

Location of killings:
  Mississippi and Florida,
  USA

Killed: convicted of two,
  confessed to as many as 60

Modus operandi: various,
  generally involving rape

Justice: stabbed to death
  while on death row in 1999

professed white supremacist caused outcry in the court by asking if he could wear a Ku Klux Klan robe.

In January 1999, while on death row at Parchman Prison, Mississippi, Evans, 41, was attacked by a fellow prison inmate and stabbed 17 times with a makeshift knife as he was being escorted to his cell. Corrections Department spokesman Ken Jones announced, "Evans was stabbed to death by Jimmie Mack, another death row inmate. Mack was being taken to the shower when the stabbing occurred." The prison authorities refuted that it was a racist killing, with white victim Evans being attacked by a black man.

Whatever the motive, there was little concern over the death of Evans, a self-proclaimed serial killer who kept changing his story and who had satisfied his murder and sex lust on a little girl.

Said District Attorney Cono Caranna who prosecuted Evans for the rape and strangling of Beatrice Routh, "We don't mourn him. We simply close his file. Everything I saw in his life was pure self-involvement and as close to evil as I've ever seen."

RAYMOND FERNANDEZ AND MARTHA BECK

Raymond Fernandez and his 200-pound lover Martha Beck were known as the "Lonely Hearts Killers" because they traveled the USA targeting vulnerable women, stealing from them and murdering more than a dozen in just two years.

FACT FILE.

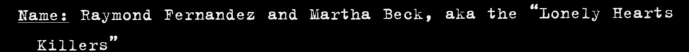

Name: Raymond Fernandez and Martha Beck, aka the "Lonely Hearts Killers"

Born: 1914 and 1920

Location of killings: Michigan, New York, and various states, USA

Killed: charged with three, suspected of 20

Modus operandi: various

Justice: both executed in the electric chair in 1951

Before meeting Beck, the Hawaiian-born Spanish-American had been a small-time conman. But after teaming up with his roly-poly paramour, the pair launched into a determined campaign to swindle the lovelorn—then kill them to get rid of the evidence.

Fernandez had already utilized his devious charm for the purpose of embezzlement several times before he met Beck in 1947. Wearing a cheap wig to cover his balding head, he would join a lonely hearts club and win over a fading female with his glib patter. He would suggest marriage and, if the victim had money, would deprive her of as much as possible before moving on. One woman who responded to Fernandez's flattering was Martha Beck, successful in her career as the head of a school for disabled children but entirely unsuccessful in love. When Fernandez discovered that the thrice-married divorcee had no hidden wealth, he tried to ditch her. But when she persisted, even threatening suicide, he accepted her as a very willing partner in crime.

Beck would at first stay in the background as Fernandez entrapped a gullible female. He would then introduce the starry-eyed lady to Beck, pretending that she was his sister. In many cases, Beck would move in to the woman's home along with Fernandez as marriage plans were made. This was the case with widow Delphine Dowling, 28, who in 1949 allowed Beck to stay with her and her two-year-old daughter at their house in Grand Rapids, Michigan. However, she delayed marrying Fernandez until she "was sure of Raymond's affections" and this did not suit the evil duo, who saw a swifter way of getting their hands on her money. Fernandez shot her in the head and Beck drowned her weeping daughter in a washtub.

Martha Beck being questioned by the prosecutor. She was the partner-in-crime to the "Lonely Hearts" killer Raymond Fernandez.

Police, tipped off by suspicious neighbors, found the bodies under a concrete slab in the cellar. They arrested the killers and linked them with the deaths of 18 other lonely hearts throughout the country, including 66-year-old Janet Fay, of Albany, New York, whose battered body was found cemented into a floor. With no death penalty in Michigan, the couple were extradited to New York to be tried for the Albany murder.

They were both electrocuted at Sing Sing prison on March 8, 1951, Martha Beck having difficulty squeezing into the electric chair. Although Fernandez had not felt up to enjoying his proffered last meal, Beck had just tucked into a double portion of fried chicken and potatoes.

ALBERT FISH

In his sickening, twisted mind, Albert Fish was simply doing God's work. To the good people of America who learned of his child murders, he was one of the most evil men who ever lived.

Incredibly, Fish, a painter and decorator, had six children of his own. But there was no paternal instincts shown when he preyed on other youngsters before kidnapping them and subjecting them to unspeakable cruelty.

Born in 1870, Fish was brought up in an

FACT FILE.

Name: Albert Howard Fish, aka Frank Howard and the "Moon Maniac"

Born: May 19, 1870

Location of killings: New York, USA

Killed: at least 15 children but tortured as many as 100

Modus operandi: used his kindly old man persona to ensnare children before killing them

Justice: died in the electric chair in 1936

orphanage in Washington D.C. He later claimed that abuse he suffered in childhood turned him into a sexual deviant and killer. "I saw so many boys whipped it took root in my head," he said. But Fish's perversions did not take hold of him until he was a married man aged 47 and his wife left him for a younger lover. Fish turned from devoted father and husband into a seeker of perverted sexual thrills and a child killer. He also started to indulge himself in a bizarre mixture of exhibitionism and masochism. He began to dance naked in the moonlight and harm himself with hot pokers, sharp needles, and nail-studded paddles. At some point, Fish's need to cause himself pain switched to a desire to inflict pain on children.

Changing his name to Frank Howard, Fish moved to New York. His first victim was ten-year-old Grace Budd who was killed on June 3, 1928. Grace was the daughter of a Manhattan family on whom Fish used his kind, fatherly act to win trust. He told her parents that he was taking her to a party but instead took the child to a derelict cottage. Armed with what he called his "instruments of hell," including a butcher's knife and cleaver, Fish strangled Grace and then dismembered her body. He carried parcels of her flesh home and cooked them in a stew. As he later told police, he ate the sickening dish over a period of nine days, during which he became constantly sexually aroused.

Grace was the first of Fish's many victims. It is thought he murdered at least 15 children, ate four and subjected yet another 100 or so to depraved acts without killing them. Mostly he

> **❝❝Armed with what he called his 'instruments of hell,' including a butcher's knife and cleaver, Fish strangled Grace and then dismembered her body❞❞**

stripped naked before pouncing on his victims. And although his painter's overalls were sometimes spattered with blood-red marks, no one asked any questions of the seemingly devout, though slightly eccentric, Christian.

All the while, Fish continued with his own violent self abuse. He drove as many as 29 needles into his genitals, set fire to cotton wool soaked in lighter fuel inserted in his rectum, ate excrement, and drank blood and urine. According to psychiatrist Dr. Frederic Wertham who examined Fish after his arrest: "There was no known perversion which he did not practice and practice frequently."

At the height of his killings, Fish became known as the "Moon Maniac" because of his habit of striking when there was a full moon. But at that time, no one could have possibly known the extent of his torturing and murdering ways, nor his activities as a cannibal and necrophile. Fish was always

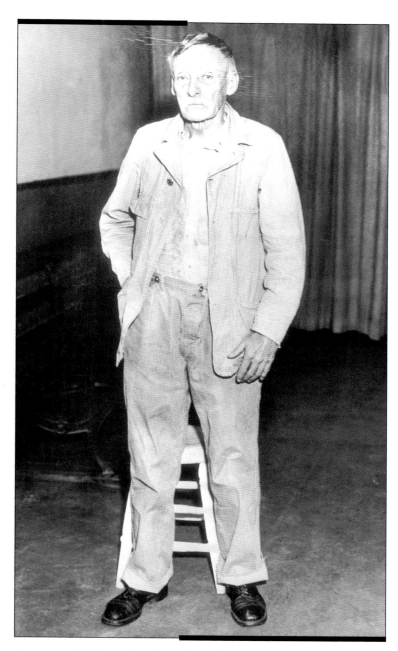

There was little indication that Albert Fish, thought of as a rather meek, retiring man, was to turn out to be a monster torturer, and murderer.

on the move, not only to look out for his next victim but for suitable places to take them. His work as a painter and decorator gave him access to many unused rooms such as basements and attics. It is thought that Fish abused children in several states, most of them from poor, black families. Fish said this was because parents didn't "make a fuss" if their children disappeared or arrived back home in a distressed state.

Fish was finally arrested after sending the parents of Grace Budd a letter in November 1934. It was a bold and arrogant gesture and proved to be his downfall. The letter said, "Some years ago, a friend of mine, Captain John Davis, shipped from California to Hong Kong, China, where at that time there was a great famine. It was dangerous for children under the age of twelve to be on the streets, as the custom was for them to be seized, cut up, and their meat sold for food. On his return to New York, my friend seized two boys, one six, the other eleven, killed and cooked and ate them. So it was that I came to your house on June, 3, 1928, and under the pretence of taking your daughter Grace to a party at my sister's, I took her up to Westchester County, Worthington, to an empty house up there and I choked her to death. I didn't fuck with her. She died a virgin."

To save money, Fish had reused an envelope sent to him and had tried, but failed, to completely erase an address on the back of the envelope. On December 13, police swooped on his room in a squalid New York boarding house. Now the 66-year-old serial killer was to gain notoriety not only for his heinous crimes but for being one of America's oldest perpetrators of them. The "Moon Maniac" was now also referred to in the press as "Thrill Vulture" and "Vampire Man."

Fish was brought to trial at White Plains, New York, on March 12, 1935, charged only with the

------- — — — — — — — —

Albert Fish's small cottage, where he confessed to murdering Grace Budd. Police dismantled the structure and dug the surrounding ground in search for bones of other possible victims.

An officer seeks a kitchen knife with an electromagnetic metal detector as evidence against Albert Fish.

- - - - - - - - - - - - - - -

murder of Grace Budd, as hers were the only remains he had led police to. His defence attorney pleaded that Fish was insane. Said one juror after the hearing: "I also thought Fish was insane but he deserved to be electrocuted anyway."

Despite numerous interviews with doctors, Fish could not give a reason for his horrific killings. He said he sometimes felt a need to "make a sacrifice" and told one doctor: "I killed Grace Budd to save her from some future outrage." He added: "I felt sure that an angel would have stopped me if I did the wrong thing."

After being found guilty of Grace Budd's murder, Fish confessed to several other crimes

The medical examiner directed police who were digging for bones at the spot in Westchester County where parts of Grace Budd were found.

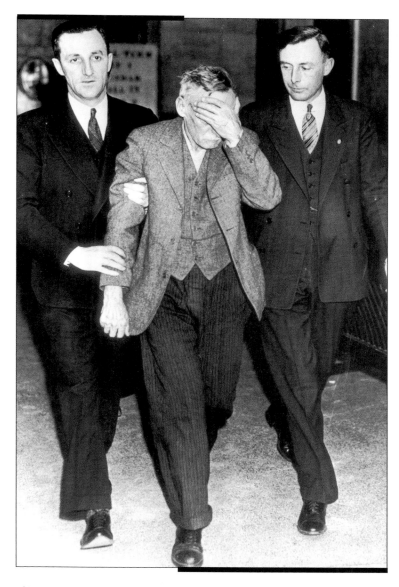

Albert Fish hid his face when entering the court faced with the charge of murdering 10-year-old Grace Budd.

including killing eight-year-old Francis McDonnell on Staten Island in 1924 and torturing, murdering, and cannibalizing four-year-old William Gaff in 1927. He reeled off dozens of other assaults and claimed to have violated as many as 30 children a year.

Fish went to the electric chair at Sing Sing prison on January 16, 1936. Eroding needles still embedded in his flesh first caused a short-circuit and a failed attempt to electrocute him. Wisps of blue smoke floated above his head before the second, fatal charge coursed through his body.

Said the sick old man before his death: "It will be the supreme thrill. The only one I haven't tried."

JOHN GACY

In March 1978, a 27-year-old Chicago man, Jeffrey Rignall, went to the police with a horrific story.

He told them that he had been approached by a fat man driving a flashy Oldsmobile car and had been invited to sit in the passenger seat for a smoke of cannabis. But as he held the joint, a handkerchief drenched in chloroform was stuffed into his face. He remembered regaining consciousness in the basement of his abductor's house where he was fastened to a homemade torture device which the fat man, who now stood before him naked, referred to as "the rack."

Over several hours, Rignall was beaten with whips and repeatedly raped. His attacker boasted that he was a policeman and would "just as soon shoot you as look at you." Weird sexual implements were used on the terrified hostage and the pain was so severe that he prayed that he would die quickly. But every time he blacked out, he would awake again to fresh tortures. He pleaded with the fat man to free him, promising to leave town and say nothing about his abduction. Chloroformed for the last time, Rignall awoke the following morning beneath a statue in Chicago's Lincoln Park. He was more dead than alive but was fully clothed, with his money and wallet still on him.

In hospital, Rignall was found to have suffered permanent liver damage as a result of the huge dose of chloroform he had inhaled. He was bruised

FACT FILE.

Name: John Wayne Gacy, aka the "Fat Man" and the "Killer Clown"

Born: March 17, 1942

Location of killings: Chicago, USA

Killed: 33

Modus operandi: strangulation

Justice: executed by lethal injection in 1994

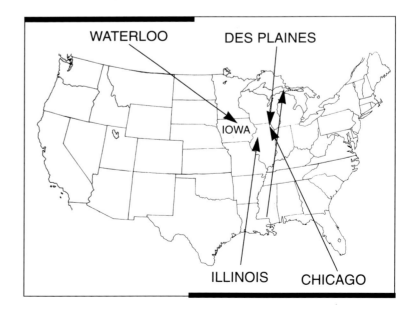

and bleeding internally and he was in severe mental trauma. Yet because he could give no accurate description of his assailant, the location of his house or the registration of his car, police held out little hope of making an arrest. Eventually Rignall decided to take matters into his own hands. In an astonishingly competent piece of detective work, he combed the city in search of the Oldsmobile car. His persistence paid off when the vehicle passed him as he staked out an expressway exit that was the only landmark he recalled from his journey in a chloroform-induced coma. He took down the license plate and followed the Oldsmobile until it turned into the driveway of 8213 West Summerdale Avenue, Des Plaines. Fearful to approach the occupant, he checked through real estate records until he established that the owner was named John Wayne Gacy Jr.

Rignall went back to the police with all this information, yet was told that it was not enough. The frustrated victim later claimed he almost had to beg detectives to question 36-year-old Gacy. In July, four months after the horrendous assault, they finally got round to interrogating him. It was to no avail. Gacy denied all knowledge of any homosexual rape and, as there were no witnesses to challenge his statements and alibi, senior officers felt that the case against him was wafer thin. A misdemeanor charge was brought but the case dragged on for a further five months. It was never concluded because, by then, Gacy had struck again—and been exposed as a mass murderer.

An initial check by Chicago police on Gacy's personal life had also drawn a blank. Detectives established that he had completed a good education at business school, going on to become a top shoe salesman with the Nunn-Bush Shoe

John Gacy, notorious killer of 32 people, was popular as a children's entertainer. He liked to dress as Pogo the Clown.

- - - - - - - - -

Company. He had become a leading light in the Junior Chamber of Commerce and was much in demand as a children's entertainer. His character was Pogo the Clown.

If police had dug further into Gacy's background, they would have uncovered sinister clues to his evil character. John Wayne Gacy Jr. was born in Chicago in 1942, the son of a Danish mother and Polish father. John Gacy Sr. was, by all accounts, an alcoholic monster who gave his son constant beatings, sometimes even hurling him

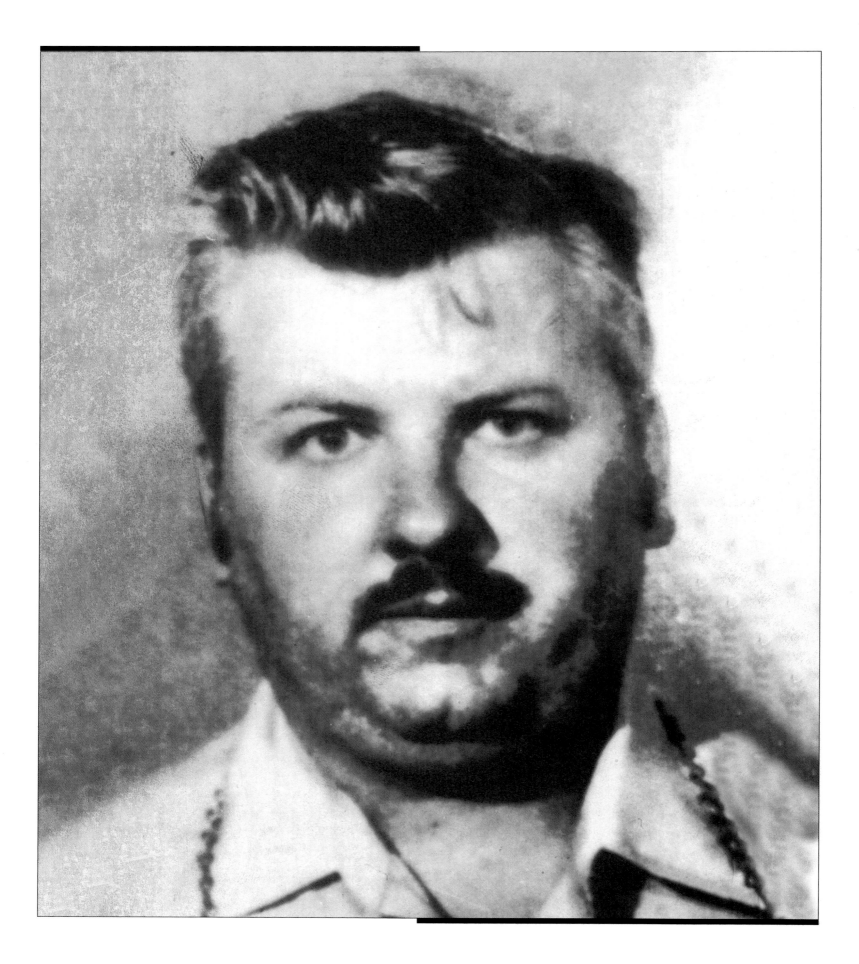

across the room in drunken rages. Labeled a "dumb sissy" by his father, young John was a sickly child. Hit on the head by a swing at the age of 11, he suffered blackouts throughout his teens until a blood clot on the brain was diagnosed and successfully treated. While suffering his father's wrath, John allowed himself meekly to be dominated by his mother and older sister and it has been speculated that this led to his resentment of women that influenced his behavior throughout his life.

While working as a shoe salesman, he met and married fellow employee Marlynn Myers in 1964 and she bore him two children. Her parents owned a fried chicken restaurant in Waterloo, Iowa, which Gacy successfully managed and he become a pillar of the local business community. Marlynn described him as "a likeable salesman who could charm anything right out of you."

The town was shocked when in 1968 he was charged with homosexual acts with one of his young workers. The terrified boy had been handcuffed while the 20-stone Gacy subjected him to a vicious attack. A further charge of hiring a thug to beat up the prosecution witness was dropped when Gacy plea-bargained himself a charge of sodomy and he was sentenced to ten years in prison.

Eighteen months later he was back on the

> **"The town was shocked when in 1968 he was charged with homosexual acts with one of his young workers"**

streets, his reputation as a model prisoner convincing his parole board that he was no longer a risk to the public. By then his marriage to Marlynn had ended. Upon his release, Gacy moved to the Chicago suburb of Des Plaines where he launched a successful building business. He was a worker for the Democratic Party and was once photographed with President Jimmy Carter's wife Rosalynn. In his spare time he performed as Pogo the Clown at charity events and children's parties.

In 1971, a year after his release from prison and while still on parole, Gacy was questioned by police for trying to force a teenaged boy into having sex. The case had to be dropped after the boy failed to turn up for the preliminary hearings. Gacy's parole officers in Iowa were not informed of the arrest, so the sexual deviant was formally discharged from parole later that year. In 1972, Gacy was married a second time to Carole Hoff, but this also ended in failure and she walked out on him in 1976. Police were later to learn how Hoff was puzzled by his lackluster sexual performance and terrified of his violent temper. Like his first wife, Carole said that Gacy had acted normally during the first few months of the marriage but had then begun to behave mysteriously, staying out all night in his car. Just before they separated, he had "started bringing home lots of pictures of naked men." Carole also said that she had complained constantly to her husband about the fetid smell that seemed to hang around the house.

- - - - - - - - - - - - -

Gacy always claimed that he was not a homosexual and that indeed he hated homosexuals. Despite the confessions that he made while in custody, he did not give evidence at trial.

The reason was not to become clear for a further two years—following the disappearance of a 15-year-old student named Robert Piest. On the evening of December 11, 1978, Robert set out for a job interview with a local building contractor who had suggested that there might be some vacation work for him. As he stepped out of the family home in Des Plaines, his mother urged him to return speedily. It was her birthday and a family party was getting into full swing. When there was still no sign of Robert by midnight, his worried mother phoned the police to report that he had not returned. He never did.

Unsurprisingly, the disappearance of Piest following his arrangement to meet John Gacy caused police to call at the builder's home. Asked about the missing youngster, his answers were unconvincing and, although there was no evidence to arrest him, police decided to put him under close surveillance. Nevertheless, the killer found the opportunity to remove Piest's body from West Summerdale Avenue and dump it in the Des Plaines River.

Gacy was well aware that he was being watched and on December 19 invited two officers who had been parked outside his house to join him inside for breakfast. As they did so, they noticed a foul smell that Gacy explained away as being a problem with his drains. At last, a warrant was speedily issued and a methodical search of the house undertaken. The smell that hung around had an awful familiarity. It was when police lifted the trapdoor that led to the crawl-space beneath the floorboards that they knew they had chanced upon one of America's worst serial killers. The stench of rotting flesh was unmistakable. Stored in the cramped void were seven corpses in different stages of decomposition. Later, eight more were dug out of crude lime pits in the garden. In total, the remains of 28 teenage boys were accounted for in the house and grounds. Gacy confessed that he had run out of space to store any more corpses. Another five victims, including Robert Piest, had been thrown into the Des Plaines River. Nine of the victims were never identified.

During questioning, it became clear that Gacy had used his building contracting business to attract young men seeking work. Yet although he bore all the signs of a closet homosexual, he always remained adamant that he was not gay. He justified his actions by telling police that he hated homosexuals and refused to accept the counter-argument that many of his victims were in fact heterosexual. Once he had raped them, it was enough. He could convince himself they deserved to die for their "homosexual activities."

Over the ensuing months, details of Gacy's modus operandi emerged. During his mysterious night-time sorties, he would frequent Chicago's

> **When police lifted the trapdoor that led to the crawl-space beneath the floorboards they knew they had chanced upon one of America's worst serial killers**

Greyhound Bus station looking for drifters to whom he would offer jobs with his construction company. "I wanted to give these people a chance," he said, "because young folk always get a raw deal. If you give them responsibility, they will rise to the occasion. They are hard workers and proud of their work." Fine and charitable words but what their boss was really looking for was teenage males to satisfy his perverted lust.

Gacy also frequented the city's notorious "Bughouse Square" where itinerants and rent boys tended to hang out. After making an assignation, he would invite his new friend back to his expensive ranch-style home where he kept a collection of police equipment, including badges and handcuffs. Gacy would offer to show his unsuspecting visitor the "handcuff trick" which, he said, would have him released within seconds. Once trapped, however, Gacy would tell them, "The way to get out of these handcuffs is to have the key; that's the only trick." He would then tie down the terrified captive and violently sodomize him. The handcuff trick was followed by the rope trick. Gacy would tie two knots in a length of cord and circle it round the victim's neck. A piece of wood was inserted through the loops and twisted slowly. The victim might take minutes to die.

John Gacy confessed his crimes to detectives on several occasions but he decided not to give evidence at his trial and sat stony-faced as the prosecution placed photographs of the 22 identified victims on a large board facing the jury. Chicago District Attorney William Kinkle described Gacy as a sick man who methodically planned and executed his many murders. The State of Illinois was at that time debating the reintroduction of the death penalty for various kinds of murder, and

John Gacy was connected with the murder of 22 identified young men. Police found the remains of several bodies under his home and garage.

- - - - - - - - - -

Kinkle asked that this be Gacy's fate. The defense lawyers entered a plea of insanity to the charges against him but it cut little ice with the jury. On March 12, 1980, they convicted him of murder.

Gacy survived for 14 years on death row through a long string of appeals. He was finally executed by lethal injection at a prison near Chicago on May 10, 1994.

GERALD GALLEGO

If family history can be said to have an affect on the mind of a killer, then the case of Gerald Gallego proves the argument.

Born in 1947, he never met his father because he was serving time in San Quentin. Gerald Gallego Sr was a three-times killer who, nine years later at the age of 28, became the first person to be executed in a Mississippi gas chamber after shooting two police officers. Gallego Jr. was first wed at 18, and by the age of 32 he was marrying for the seventh time—twice he had married the same woman.

Gallego first came to the attention of California police in 1978 when his daughter complained to them that he had been abusing her from the age of six. They tried to interview him but he went on the run with his latest fiancée, Charlene Williams.

> **❝The injuries had not killed her—but she had been buried alive❞**

Ten years Gallego's junior, she was bisexual, a polished violinist, had a genius-level IQ—and a drug habit. Charlene agreed to help fulfill Gallego's fantasy of finding the perfect sex slave. Driving a van, she would patrol the Sacramento area luring young girls into it with the promise of drugs. Once inside, Gallego would pounce on the girls, rape them, and murder them while Charlene sat coolly in the front seat.

One of their most horrific crimes was the murder of 21-year-old Linda Aguilar who was four months pregnant when Charlene pulled up in a van at Gold Beach, Oregon, and offered her a lift. Her body was found with her skull shattered and her legs and hands tied. A post-mortem revealed that the injuries had not killed her—but that she had been buried alive.

Gallego and Charlene, now bigamously mar-

FACT FILE.

Name: Gerald Armand Gallego

Born: July 17, 1946

Location of killings: California, Oregon, USA

Killed: 10

Modus operandi: with accomplice Charlene Williams, shooting and raping

Justice: sentenced to death in California in 1983 and in Nevada in 1984

ried, killed ten people before finally being identified. On November 2, 1980, Craig Miller and Beth Sowers were leaving a dance near Sacramento when a woman brandishing a gun forced them into the back of a van. A friend tried to follow them and took down the registration number of the killers' van.

Arrested, Charlene Gallego cracked when she realized that she faced a death sentence. She turned state's evidence for a maximum of 16 years in jail. She was freed in 1997. Gallego was tried in both California, where he was sentenced to death on June 22, 1983, and in Nevada, where on June 7, 1984, he was again condemned to death. Nevada's lethal injection sentence superseded that of California's gas chamber and Gallego was imprisoned at Carson City to await execution pending appeals.

Gerald Gallego was caught at the edge of a cornfield after bloodhounds sniffed him out from behind a tree and ended the manhunt for his arrest.

LUIS GARAVITO

The biggest manhunt in the history of Colombia began with the gruesome discovery of a grave containing the bodies of 25 boys, aged eight to 16 years, in a ravine beside an overgrown car park in the town of Pereira in 1997.

But police, initially believing they were seeking some kind of satanic cult, were to be even more sickened to discover the youngsters had been killed by one man. Luis Garavito was to go down in history as one of the world's worst serial killers.

Even today, no one is exactly sure just how

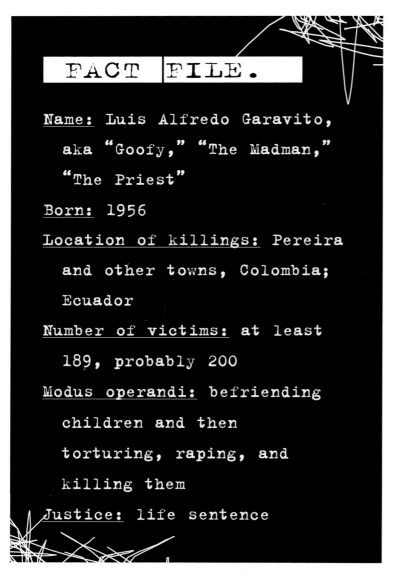

FACT FILE.

Name: Luis Alfredo Garavito,
aka "Goofy," "The Madman,"
"The Priest"

Born: 1956

Location of killings: Pereira
and other towns, Colombia;
Ecuador

Number of victims: at least
189, probably 200

Modus operandi: befriending
children and then
torturing, raping, and
killing them

Justice: life sentence

many children Garavito lured to their deaths. Police found 114 bodies. Garavito confessed to killing 140. But it is believed as many as 200 could have fallen into his evil hands.

Born in Colombia's western coffee-making region, Garavito was the oldest of seven children. As is the case with many who turn to murder in adulthood, the young Garavito was the victim of parental abuse. He was regularly beaten by his father and later claimed he was raped by two male neighbors. He left home when he was 16, having managed just five years of schooling, and worked first as a store clerk then as a street vendor selling religious icons and prayer cards. Other jobs included laboring and being a handyman. Considered something of a simpleton by those who knew him, Garavito's heavy reliance on drink was turning him into an alcoholic.

It is thought that he committed his first murder in 1992 but in Colombia, with one of the highest murder rates in the world, little was done about the discovery of a child's body. Neither did the authorities act when children first started to go missing. As Timothy Ross, a charity worker with juvenile prostitutes, said at the time: "Kids disappear all the time in Colombia, especially those from the poorer strata of society. And they tend to come from unstable homes anyway." Police later reported that it was because there was no one to notice that the children were missing or to inquire about their whereabouts that Garavito was able to go on killing for so long without being detected.

Garavito moved around the country once his killing spree had started in earnest in 1994. His prey were always poor or homeless children more than willing to wander off with him on the promise of money, food, drink, or drugs. Many of them were the children of street vendors who had been left unattended in parks and at city traffic lights to beg money from motorists. To win their confidence, Garavito would pretend to be a street vendor or beggar himself. He also posed as a cripple and even a monk.

Having gained a child's trust, he would then persuade them to go for a walk. This was often a long trek as he wanted to make his victim as tired as possible before pouncing. Then the child would be tied up, tortured, raped, and killed by having their throats cut. Sometimes Garavito would decapitate his young victims. What was consistent with each of the killings was Garavito's condition— highly intoxicated after a massive drinking binge. And he always knew the best overgrown areas where he could carry out his evil work.

Garavito's terrifying stalking and murdering of children carried on for five years. As his blood lust continued, he regularly changed his appearance, swapped jobs, adopted various false names, and even traveled to Ecuador and other neighboring countries to find more victims. But it was in Garavito's home country where most of the killings took place.

After the discovery of the remains of 25 boys in Pereira in November 1997, a nationwide task force was set up to uncover the supposed "satanic group" whom the police felt sure was responsible. Then another 16 bodies were found

Luis Alfredo Garavito confessed to killing over 100 children between the years 1994 and 1999.

- - - - - - - - - - - - -

just a few miles away. Yet another 27 were found in the bordering area of Valle de Cauca. The mutilated corpses, mostly male and aged between eight and 16, were found in the vicinity of more than 60 towns in 11 of Colombia's 32 provinces.

The concentrated effort of the task force finally linked Garavito with the serial killings. Police turned up a warrant that had been issued for his arrest following a child murder in the north central city of Tunja in 1996. After an 18-month hunt, Garavito was eventually tracked down in April 1999. He was living in the city of Villavicencio under an assumed name and was initially arrested on suspicion of the attempted rape of a

Thirty-six corpses of young people aged from eight to 16 were found in Pereira, Columbia.

- - - - - - - - - - - - - -

12-year-old boy that same month. But the 42-year-old monster, now dubbed "The Madman," "The Priest," and "Goofy" because of his prominent front teeth, confessed to killing 140 children. Police discovered that he kept a list of his victims.

Prosecutor Alfonso Gomez Mendez said evidence against Garavito was so strong that the murderer had no choice but to confess. Mendez said, "We know now that he passed himself off as a street vendor, monk, indigent, disabled person, or a representative of fictitious foundations for the elderly and children's education. In that way, he even gained entrance to schools as a speaker. This way of operating has no precedent in Colombia." One police officer described Garavito as "a cunning serial killer, a glib predator, and a solitary sadist." Chief government investigator Pablo Gonzalez said Garavito was "an assassin without brakes when it came to killing."

But the slowness with which police acted to catch one of the world's most notorious killers brought criticism from Colombia's poorer quarters. Many accused police officials of being indifferent, abusive, and corrupt. One victim's mother, Maria Consuelo Velez, said, "The police investigation came too late. When I needed them to help they did nothing. They should kill Garavito, not put him in prison where he'll get fat like a pig." In October 1998, Maria's 11-year-old son and eight-year-old nephew had gone out to sell newspapers but never returned. An aunt, Diana Velez, said that unlike many of Garavito's victims, the two boys had a loving home. She complained that for many months, authorities in Colombia's highly class-divided society had shown little interest in the child murders, adding, "If we were rich they would have looked high and low for the children."

There was further outcry when it was learned that a man had been arrested in connection with 29 child murders in December 1998. He was named as Pedro Pablo Ramirez but police refused to give details of the arrest—or to admit that the man calling himself Ramirez was more likely to have been Garavito.

Because the death penalty had been abolished in Colombia, Luis Alfredo Garavito, who eventually faced charges of killing 189 people, was sentenced to 835 years in prison.

The 12 palm trees planted as a memorial to the 25 children whose bodies were the first found are still growing strong at their site in Pereira. And brightly painted figures of children at play are carved into an overlooking hillside. Below them in the grass is a sign reading: "If we continue with the indifference and abandonment, we will never know what happened to the children of Pereira."

PEE WEE GASKINS

He earned his nickname of "Pee Wee" because he was a short man, only 5ft 3in tall, who tried to make up for his lack of height with fiery outbursts of temper.

But people in the tiny town of Prospect, South Carolina, stopped laughing at Pee Wee Gaskins when the body count in what was described as his own "personal graveyard" grew and grew. Born illegitimately on March 31, 1933, Gaskins soon entered a life of juvenile crime. His home environment became increasingly unhappy when his mother married one of her man friends who regularly beat the boy and his brothers and sisters. Gaskins was sentenced to reform school until his eighteenth birthday after a hatchet attack on a man who had caught him carrying out a burglary and, following his release in 1951, found work on a tobacco plantation before turning again to theft.

Just one year later, a series of arson attacks and an attempted murder put him back in jail, were he was sentenced to a further nine years for the manslaughter of a fellow prisoner he claimed had sexually attacked him. Paroled in 1962, Gaskins committed more offenses including the rape of a 12-year-old girl, served more prison sentences and was again out on parole in November 1968.

The full depths of Gaskins's evil emerged in 1975 when police investigating the disappearance of a 13-year-old girl encountered a wall of silence in his Florence County neighborhood. They couldn't believe that this man,

once treated as a joke, was now spreading fear and intimidation following strong rumors that a string of missing people were ending up in his very own "cemetery."

It was a tip-off from Walter Leroy Neeley, an old cell-mate and killer-accomplice of Gaskins, that led police to a remote wood east of Prospect. There they unearthed the bodies of three men and three women. Four had been

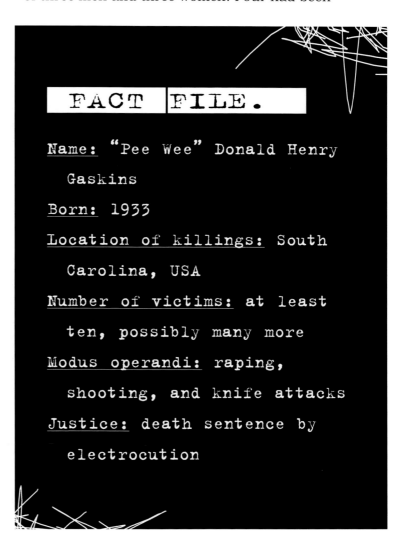

FACT FILE.

Name: "Pee Wee" Donald Henry Gaskins

Born: 1933

Location of killings: South Carolina, USA

Number of victims: at least ten, possibly many more

Modus operandi: raping, shooting, and knife attacks

Justice: death sentence by electrocution

Gaskins admitted to killing Peggy Cuttino, a girl from Sumter, but because of his lack of detail police were unable to confirm it.

- - - - - - - - - - - - -

shot and two had had their throats cut. A mile away, another grave yielded the heart-breaking discovery of the body of a woman and her baby.

Gaskins tried to escape across the state line but was arrested and eventually charged with the eight murders, plus that of another man, James Kony Judy.

Most of the victims were neighbors who, in Gaskins's mind, had offended him in some way. He actually confessed to at least 13 murders but bargained with police by offering his co-operation and avoided a death sentence, instead receiving nine terms of life imprisonment.

Police believe Gaskins committed his first murder in September 1969 when he tortured and disembowelled a girl hitchhiker he picked up along the Carolina coast. This was one of Gaskins's "coastal kills" in which he targeted strangers purely for sadistic pleasure. There were also what he called "serious murders" in which the victims were people he knew. These included his own 15-year-old niece, her 17-year-old friend and an eight-months pregnant woman aged 23.

Gaskins also raped and killed the woman's 20-month-old daughter, describing the abhorrent act as "the best sexual experience of my life." He later told police: "I am one of the few that truly understands what death and pain are all about. I have a special kind of mind that allows me to give myself permission to kill."

Gaskins was sentenced to nine life sentences but even in jail he carried on killing, accepting a contract to murder death-row inmate Randolph Tyner. He wired an explosive charge to Tyner's radio and detonated it. Gaskins now faced a certain death sentence. His own life was taken in the electric chair on September 6, 1982.

Before he died, Gaskins wrote his autobiography in which he bragged of committing 31 "serious murders" and "80 or 90 coastal kills"—the latter figures almost certainly exaggerated. Although his deliberate lack of detail about the murders meant police were unable to confirm the true number of victims, Pee Wee Gaskins still goes down in criminal history as one of America's most prolific serial killers.

EDWARD GEIN

Many serial killers have surpassed Edward Gein's body count but mercifully few have come close to equaling him in sheer, sickening, mental aberration.

Edward Gein in court. Remains of several bodies were found in his dilapidated Wisconsin home, where he lived alone for 12 years.

Half a century after his crimes, Gein's name has faded in American consciousness but his crimes never will. For few murderers can claim their evil deeds inspired blockbusting Hollywood movies. Gein is said to be the inspiration for the character of schizophrenic transvestite Norman Bates in Hitchcock's *Psycho* and, through his liking for wearing human skin, also resurfaced in *The Silence of the Lambs*. No film director, however, could ever hope to replicate the atrocities discovered at the remote, ramshackle house of horror that was Gein's family home.

Country boy Edward Gein's childhood

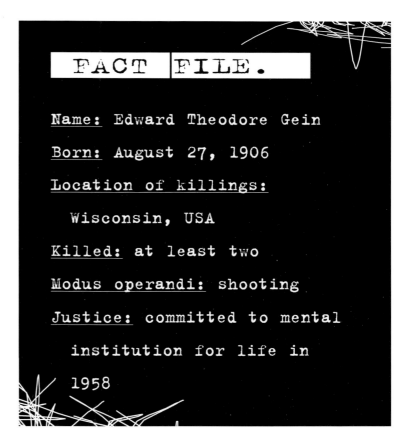

FACT FILE.

Name: Edward Theodore Gein

Born: August 27, 1906

Location of killings:
Wisconsin, USA

Killed: at least two

Modus operandi: shooting

Justice: committed to mental institution for life in 1958

undoubtedly shaped his weird future. Born in 1906, the son of a hard-drinking carpenter and a fiercely religious mother, he was raised on a lonely farmstead near Plainfield, Wisconsin. He grew up dominated by his possessive, woman-hating mother, so much so that neither he nor his elder brother Henry ever got close to a member of the opposite sex. There were precious few pleasures in his life; working the farm occupied him day and night for years and he gradually retreated further and further into a deviant fantasy world.

> **At first, he satisfied his curiosity by digging up female corpses from a local graveyard, aided by a simple-minded farmer**

Edward's father, George, died of alcoholism in 1940 and brother Henry died in a brush fire in 1944, leaving the youngest son with his devoutly Lutheran mother Augusta. Shortly after Henry's death, she suffered a stroke and Edward nursed her tenderly for 12 months until she finally died in December 1945. Edward was now left alone in the large, L-shaped house—and the lurking madman that lay within him took control. He kept his mother's corpse locked in her bedroom, the surroundings unchanged from the moment of her death.

Gein's interest in women's anatomy developed into an obsession, and soon he cast aside his medical text books to get a closer look at the real thing. At first, he satisfied his curiosity by digging up female corpses from a local graveyard, aided by a simple-minded farmer. Gein would touch the corpse's sexual organs and wear bits of their flesh. He preserved some parts of the bodies, skulls being mounted as ornaments and skullcaps used as bowls. Gradually his fetishism grew more extreme and he would arrange a dead woman's skin over a tailor's dummy as though he were somehow trying to resurrect his mother. He graduated to draping himself in the skin and would walk around the house wearing a woman's scalp on his head, a woman's chest over his own, and women's genitalia strapped to his groin.

Eventually the stench of rotting corpses became too much even for the sick grave robber and he sought fresher flesh. On December 8, 1954, Gein, then aged 48, committed his first murder. Mary Hogan, aged 51, disappeared from the saloon bar she owned in Pine Grove, Wisconsin, leaving only a pool of blood and a spent cartridge on the floor. Gein had waited until the bar was empty, shot her with a Mauser pistol, took her body outside to a sled which he dragged home through a snowstorm. There he dissected the corpse and skinned it.

Between then and his final killing three years later, Gein put paid to an unknown number of victims. It was not until November 16, 1957, that police caught up with the maniac in their midst. They were out looking for storekeeper Bernice Worden, and Gein's car had been seen parked near her Plainfield hardware shop. He was arrested after Mrs. Worden's son, the local sheriff's deputy, recalled that Gein had mentioned calling by her store to buy anti-freeze.

Gein was taken in for questioning and, while

A police officer examines the kitchen in the farm home of
Edward Gein. Police found skulls and other parts of human bodies in the house and the body of Mrs Bernice Worden in a shed.

safely in a cell, Wautoma County's recently
appointed sheriff, 32-year-old Art Schley, took the
opportunity of searching his house. They walked
around the back and pushed open the door of an
outbuilding where Gein seemed to spend most of
his time. As he entered the darkened room, Schley
felt something brush against his shoulder. He
spun round and pointed his torch at the bloody

stump of a headless corpse hanging upside down.
It was Bernice's headless body, hooked by the ten-
dons of her ankles onto the rafters. She had been
disembowelled and dressed like a deer hunted
from the surrounding woods.

Elsewhere around the Gein farm police found
a stomach-churning array of artifacts. There were
lampshades made of human skin; a hollowed-out
skull was used as a soup dish; skulls were stuck
on bedposts; a belt had been made of nipples; a
pair of slippers were of human skin; a blind-pull
was adorned with a pair of lips; nine vulvas, one

Edward Gein on his way to take a lie detector test at the Wisconsin State Crime Laboratory.

- - - - - - - - - - - - -

trimmed with red ribbon, were found in a shoe box; and the refrigerator was stocked with human organs. They found the remains of Mrs. Hogan—a death mask of skin and hair, alongside no fewer than nine others. Mrs. Worden's head was discovered ready to go into a cookpot along with her heart.

Edward Gein eventually explained to detectives what uses he made of these various human remains. He said he would dance by moonlight in his farmyard—with a woman's torso, tanned like leather, strapped around his body. He regularly oiled the skin to keep it supple. He admitted wearing skin from various dead women, eating their flesh, and playing with other parts of their bodies. He confessed to the Hogan and Worden murders but inexplicably was adamant in denying the relatively minor crime of stealing the cash register from Mrs. Worden's store.

The discoveries of the bodies of Mrs. Hogan and Mrs. Worden were grisly enough. But Gein also refused to explain how he came to possess the preserved private parts of two teenage girls, whose ages were put at approximately 12 and 18, which were found among his sickening collection. No girls of that age had been buried in the area during Gein's macabre activities. Detectives could only deduce that the remains were of live victims. Going back through their files, police turned up the suspicious disappearance of a schoolgirl in May 1947 and of another in November 1953. The latter, 15-year-old Evelyn Hartley, had been abducted while babysitting for a neighbor, the only evidence of her demise being a trail of bloodstains leading from the house.

There were also suspicions about the disappearance of two men who were known to have hired Gein as their hunting guide. Local farmer Victor Travis and his friend Ray Burgess set off on a deer hunt in the Wisconsin open season of November 1952 but only Gein returned. Police even speculated that Gein's brother Henry might have been one of his victims. Henry had died in a brush fire in 1944 but rescuers thought it strange that younger brother Edward had been able to lead them directly to where the body lay, with bruising to the forehead. However, an autopsy gave the cause of death as smoke inhalation.

As Gein was held awaiting trial, his farmhouse was first vandalized and then burned to the ground as villagers attempted to destroy the sickening memory of a cannibal in their midst. In January 1958, a judge found Gein "incompetent" for trial and he was kept in the Central State Hospital at Wapun, Wisconsin. A decade later, another attempt was made to have him answer to a court and in November 1968 he faced Judge Robert Golmar who sent him straight back to hospital, declaring him insane. He passed away peacefully

Edward Gein, surrounded by journalists and police officers on his farm after the discovery of human skulls and parts of female bodies.

at the age of 78 in the Mendota Mental Health Institute on July 28, 1984. He was buried in an unmarked grave alongside his mother.

HARVEY GLATMAN

California Highway Patrol officer Thomas F. Mulligan was riding his motorcycle through the darkened streets of Tustin, south of Los Angeles, when his head-lamp illuminated a couple struggling beside a parked car.

By the time he had drawn to a halt, the woman, who was disheveled and in a state of obvious terror, was holding a pistol aimed at the man who was squirming in pain. In fact, she was about to shoot him dead.

Mulligan barked a warning to the couple as he drew his own gun and cautiously approached. The pair put their hands up. The woman then blurted out the story of her terrifying ride through the night with a man intent on raping and murdering her. Her name was Lorraine Vigil and the spirited fight she had put up had almost certainly saved her and others from death at the hands of serial killer Harvey Glatman.

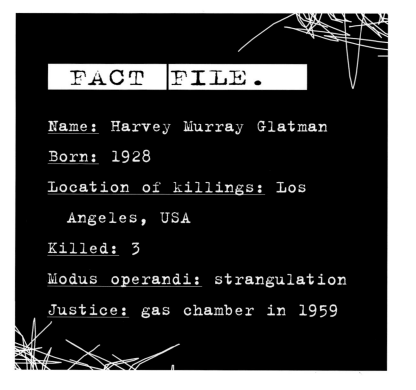

FACT FILE.

Name: Harvey Murray Glatman

Born: 1928

Location of killings: Los
   Angeles, USA

Killed: 3

Modus operandi: strangulation

Justice: gas chamber in 1959

Harvey Murray Glatman was born in Denver, Colorado, in 1928 and grew up a mommy's boy who did not mix easily with other children. His appearance was not prepossessing, mainly because of his jug-handle ears, and as a teenager he found himself being shunned by girls. At 17, he ordered a fellow student to undress at gunpoint and was arrested but fled the state when granted bail.

He ended up in New York where he became a street mugger and burglar before his further arrest. He spent five years in Sing Sing where he received psychiatric treatment before returning to his doting mother in Denver. She paid for further treatment and funded a course as a TV repair man, finally setting him up with a business in Los Angeles. But Glatman yearned for a more glamorous life and, using false names and credentials, posed as a professional photographer to get close to beautiful women. Three of them were to die at his hands.

His first victim was blonde model Judy Ann Van Horn Dull whom he arranged to meet for a picture shoot on August 1, 1957. Calling himself Johnny Glynn, he picked her up at her flat and drove her to his makeshift Hollywood studio where he took some bondage shots, supposedly for the cover of a crime magazine. Having tied her up, he raped her before driving her into the desert. There he took further erotic photographs while holding her at gunpoint. Finally he tied a noose around her

Harvey Glatman confessed to raping and strangling three women and burying their bodies in the desert.

- - - - - - - - - - - - -

neck, attached the other end to her feet and slowly throttled her. Her body was found in a shallow grave five months later by a rancher and his dog.

Now calling himself George Williams, Glatman targeted his next victim: Shirley Bridgeford, 24, a divorcee and mother of two, whom he met through a dating agency. On March 9, 1958, he drove her into the desert, tied her up, raped her, and took photographs of her lain across the same blanket on which he had killed Judy Dull. Ordering her to lie face down, he tied a rope around her neck and garrotted her.

Glatman waited only four months before seeking out his third victim: stripper and model Ruth Mercado who offered her services through newspaper advertisements. On July 23, the killer arrived at her apartment for a photo session but instead tied her up and bundled her into his car. He again drove into the desert, where he held her overnight and the following day, raping her repeatedly before strangling her. As with his earlier victims, he photographed his sordid attacks right to the moment of death.

The killing spree would almost certainly have continued if it had not been for the fact that Glatman's next victim, 27-year-old model Lorraine Vigil, was as tough as he was. Phoning her model agency and using the name Frank Johnson, he picked her up from her apartment and told her he was taking her to his studio. Instead, to the girl's growing alarm, they drove south out of Los Angeles. On a dark sidestreet in Tustin, he pulled a gun and tried to tie her up.

But Lorraine made a lunge for the door. As the pair tumbled onto the roadway, the gun went off, grazing Lorraine's thigh, yet the brave girl continued to fight back, sinking her teeth into her assailant. Glatman dropped his pistol and quick-thinking Lorraine turned the tables on him by seizing it and aiming it at his head. Just as she was about to pull the trigger, highway patrolman Mulligan arrived on the scene.

When photographs of the dead girls were found at his home, Glatman confessed. His lawyers suggested he plead insanity but he declined and was sentenced to death. The ugly, jug-eared killer was led into the San Quentin gas chamber on September 18, 1959.

BELLE GUNNESS

Brynhilde Paulsdatter, a stonemason's daughter from Trondheim, Norway, migrated to the United States in 1883, joining her sister and brother-in-law in Chicago and Americanizing her name to Belle and sometimes Bella.

A year later, at the age of 25, she married another Norwegian immigrant, Mads Sorenson, and the couple began to experience an amazing decade of bad "luck." First they opened a baker's shop, which burned down within a year. Fortunately for them, it was heavily insured. So was their home, which burned down shortly afterward. In fact, everything Belle touched seemed to turn to ashes. Another

home burned down before the couple moved in to a fine house in Chicago's Alma Street. During this period of domestic disasters, Belle lost not only property but also members of her family. Daughter Caroline passed away in 1896 and son Axel in 1898, both from "acute colitis." Finally, in 1900, husband Mads died in a manner suspiciously like poisoning after suffering a period of horrific convulsions. Although his body was later exhumed, no evidence of foul play was detected. Sorenson was, of course, insured.

With her two remaining daughters and a foster daughter, Belle moved to Indiana, where she married widower Peter Gunness, and they settled on a lonely farm near the town of La Porte. He was persuaded to take out heavy life insurance and was dead within eight months of the nuptials.

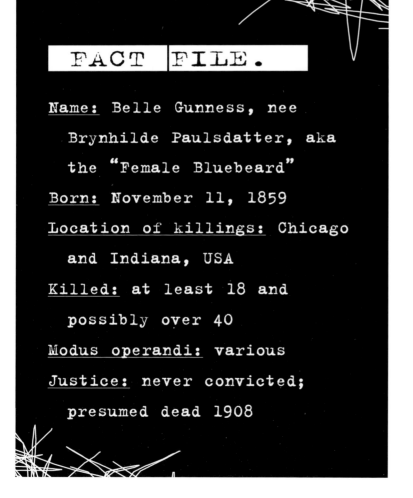

FACT FILE.

Name: Belle Gunness, nee
  Brynhilde Paulsdatter, aka
  the "Female Bluebeard"

Born: November 11, 1859

Location of killings: Chicago
  and Indiana, USA

Killed: at least 18 and
  possibly over 40

Modus operandi: various

Justice: never convicted;
  presumed dead 1908

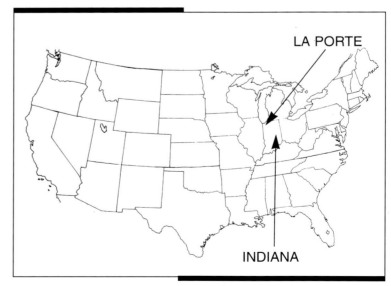

LA PORTE

INDIANA

According to his widow, a sausage grinder fell from a shelf that he was sitting under and split his skull. It is far more likely that his fat, ferocious wife hit him over the head. For that was also the fate of the 14-year-old foster daughter, Jennie, murdered after she had gone to the police to report her suspicions about Mr. Gunness's death. Luckily for the bereaved widow, they had not believed her. Belle's cover story was that the girl had been "sent away to finishing school."

As a widow in her fifties, Gunness tried to run the farm with a string of hired helpers. One of them was handyman Ray Lamphere who soon became her lover. But she needed more than muscle power; she needed money. Her method of attracting fresh finance was quite simple: she placed advertisements for suitors in the matrimonial columns of newspapers, particularly those printed in Norwegian for an immigrant readership. The following are samples of the temptress's lure:

"RICH, good-looking woman, owner of a big farm, desires to correspond with a gentleman of wealth and refinement, object matrimony. No replies by letter will be considered unless the sender is willing to follow an answer with a personal visit. Triflers need not apply."

"WANTED: A woman who owns a beautifully located and valuable farm in first-class condition wants a good and reliable man as partner in the same. Some little cash is required, for which will be furnished first-class security."

Prospective suitors who answered the advertisements would be invited to stay at the farm to experience her country hospitality first-hand. They were always asked to bring along a sum of money to prove their willingness to invest in the property. Belle would feed them, sleep with them, drug

Belle Gunness was accused of killing the men who visited her farm after answering her advertisement for a husband. She managed to take their money before they died.

- - - - - - - - - - - - -

them, steal their savings, and then hack them to death with a meat cleaver.

There is some evidence about the fate of a few of them. There was fellow Norwegian immigrant John Moo, from Wisconsin, who brought along $1,000 in cash to pay off Belle's mortgage. He vanished from the scene after just a week. Then there was George Andersen, another Norwegian, who traveled from Missouri with a hefty wad of cash. All notions of romance evaporated, however, when the hopeful middle-aged farmer met the portly, harsh-featured, middle-aged widow, who was anything but the gentle beauty he had imagined. He awoke in his guest quarters in the middle of the night to find Belle standing over his bed—and fled into the night, taking the first train out of La Porte in the morning. Ole Budsberg was another suitor, who stayed longer than Andersen—in fact, he stayed forever. Budsberg, an elderly widower, was last seen withdrawing his life's savings from a bank in La Porte on April 6, 1907. After his disappearance, his sons contacted Mrs. Gunness asking when she had last seen him; she replied that she never had.

Fascinating evidence survives about the fate of the last in the long line of Belle's hapless suitors. Andrew Helgelein carried out a lengthy correspondence with Gunness from his home in South Dakota, receiving some highly romantic letters in return. It is easy to imagine the vision of loveliness that poor old Helgelein must have dreamed up of the temptress Gunness:

"To the Dearest Friend in the World, No woman in the world is happier than I am. I know that you are now to come to me and be my own. I can tell from your letters that you are the man I want. It does not take long to tell when to like a person, and you I like better than anyone in the world I know. Think how we will enjoy each other's company, you, the sweetest man in the whole world. We will be all alone with each other. Can you conceive of anything nicer? I think of you constantly.

"Belle would feed them, sleep with them, drug them, steal their savings, and then hack them to death with a meat cleaver"

When I hear your name mentioned, and this is when one of the dear children speaks of you, or I hear myself humming it with the words of an old love song, it is beautiful music to my ears. My heart beats in wild rapture for you. My Andrew, I love you. Come prepared to stay forever."

A final tempting letter from the widowed seductress was sent to Helgelein in December 1907. Filled with florid comparisons with Scandinavian royalty, it read:

"To the Dearest Friend in all the world, I know you have now only to come to me and be my own. The King will be no happier than you when you get here. As for the Queen, her joy will be small when compared with mine. You will love my farm, sweetheart. In all La Porte County, there is none that will compare with it. It is on a nice green slope near two lakes. When I hear your name mentioned, my heart beats in wild rapture for you. My Andrew, I love you." Then, as an afterthought, she thoughtfully added: "Be sure and bring the three thousand dollars you are going to invest in the farm with you and, for safety's sake, sew them up in your clothes, dearest."

Poor gullible Andrew Helgelein made the journey to Indiana and, like so many others before him, was never seen again. He was, however, probably the last suitor to vanish within the grounds of the La Porte farm. Belle's one-woman crime wave ended the following year, 1908, although the circumstances surrounding her demise are still shrouded in mystery.

On the night of April 28, the farmhouse was burned to the ground. Belle's former handyman and lover, Ray Lamphere, was seen running from the scene. This clearly pointed the finger of suspicion at him, for he had recently fallen out with his employer and had complained to locals that she had unjustly fired him. Belle, for her part, had gone to her lawyer and complained that Lamphere had threatened to kill her and burn her house down and that she and her family were in fear for their lives.

After the threatened blaze came to pass, police arrested Lamphere on the assumption that he had burned the farm in revenge. He was later jailed for arson but murder charges against him had to be dropped—for the very good reason that the real culprit was almost certainly Belle Gunness herself.

It is likely that Lamphere had been not only the widow's lover but an accomplice in some of the earlier murders of her suitors. If they had fallen out in recent months, it is strange that their quarrel was played out in such a public fashion. And although Lamphere might have lit the match that destroyed much of the evidence, the burning of the farmhouse was far more in Belle's interests than her handyman's.

The scenario that emerged following the blaze was that Gunness had at last realized she had overplayed her hand. Andrew Helgelein's brother, Asle, had started making inquiries about his missing sibling. Belle wrote back telling him that Andrew had left her after his visit to the farm and that she was distraught not to have heard from him again. In a foolhardy moment, she then wrote again to Asle suggesting that he too visit her and that, if he supplied some funds toward the cost, she would launch a state-wide search for her miss-

The murderous career of Belle Gunness was not only notorious but ended mysteriously. Police closed their files after finding her corpse but it is doubtful whether it was actually her.

ing lover. When that greedy ploy failed to convince him, Belle panicked and left Lamphere to burn the evidence.

Forty bodies were discovered in and around the burned-out farmhouse, including that of Andrew Helgelein. Fourteen male corpses were found in a hog pen. And, most tragically, among the ashes in the basement of the house were the charred bodies of Gunness's three children: Myrtle, aged 11, Lucy, nine, and Philip, five. Alongside them lay the headless body of a woman—at first presumed to be that of Belle because her false teeth were recovered nearby. Forensic experts, however, pointed out that the corpse was considerably shorter and lighter than the strapping widow. There were also traces of poison in it. It seems that Belle Gunness had lured yet another victim to the farm, this time a woman, and had callously murdered her alongside her own children in order to conceal her escape.

Ray Lamphere was tried for murder and arson on May 22, 1908. He admitted torching the farm but vehemently denied killing Belle and her three children. The murder charges had to be dropped but he was jailed for 20 years for arson. He died in prison from consumption on December 30, 1909. He left behind him a deathbed confession. He told a fellow prisoner and a prison chaplain that, although he had not killed anyone, he had helped Belle Gunness bury many of the bodies.

By his count, she had murdered 42 people at the farm in four years and acquired more than

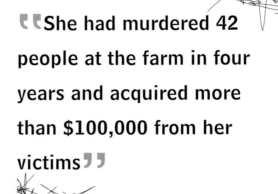

❝She had murdered 42 people at the farm in four years and acquired more than $100,000 from her victims❞

$100,000 from her victims. Her modus operandi was to feed the visiting suitor a hefty meal then creep up to their bedroom in the middle of the night and chloroform them in their sleep. So strong was she that she would carry the body down to the cellar, place it on a table and dissect it. The body parts would be distributed around the farm. If she tired of this task, she would sometimes simply hack at the corpse with a meat cleaver and dump it straight into the hog pen.

Belle Gunness had discussed with Lamphere the notion of faking her own death. He had gone along with the plan, agreeing to burn down the farm before meeting up with Belle and her children on the road out of town. But in a final act of betrayal, the widow had fled without him—after first murdering her own children. The last that Lamphere saw of her was her cart disappearing down a woodland track.

Given the certainty that Belle Gunness faked her own "death" and that she had grown accustomed to killing for profit, it is quite possible that she might have continued quietly adding to her murderous tally elsewhere in America for many years afterward.

FRITZ HAARMANN

Fritz Haarmann adored his mother, who became an invalid soon after he was born. He played with dolls and dressed in his sister's clothing.

This did not endear him to his father, a mean and moody locomotive stoker nicknamed Sulky Olle, who tried to get his boy committed to an asylum on the grounds that he had a feeble mind. The doctors refused, insisting that the chubby child was not mentally ill. Rejected by his father, young Fritz soon found himself wandering around Germany getting involved in petty crime. He was viewed by other crooks as a simpleton who tried hard to please and he got a reputation among police for coming quietly when arrested, often with a laugh on his lips.

But Haarmann's seeming good humor hid a depravity almost beyond imagination. For Fritz Haarmann preyed on young boys, especially those who were homeless with no family to report them missing. He would seduce or rape them—before dispatching them, vampire style, with a savage bite to their throats.

His killing ground was Hanover, where

Haarmann settled in 1918 when he left jail after serving a five-year jail sentence to find himself thrown into the chaos of post-war Germany. Haarmann quickly realized that he had his own niche in this sinister, twilight world of villains and conmen, black marketeers and swindlers. He found himself drawn more and more to Hanover's

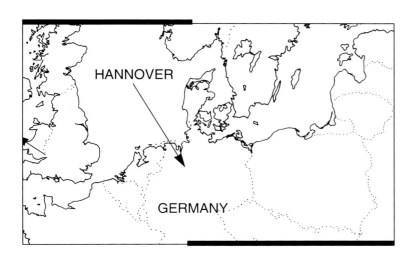

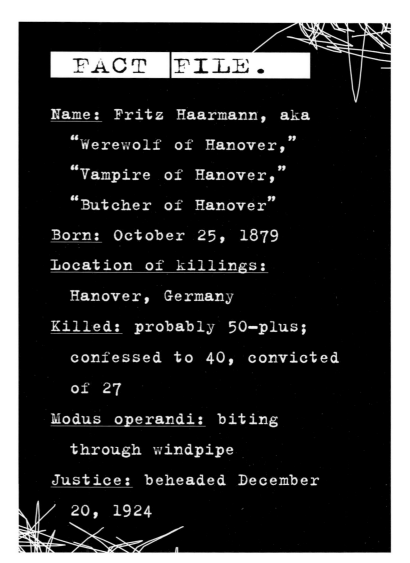

FACT FILE.

<u>Name:</u> Fritz Haarmann, aka "Werewolf of Hanover," "Vampire of Hanover," "Butcher of Hanover"
<u>Born:</u> October 25, 1879
<u>Location of killings:</u> Hanover, Germany
<u>Killed:</u> probably 50-plus; confessed to 40, convicted of 27
<u>Modus operandi:</u> biting through windpipe
<u>Justice:</u> beheaded December 20, 1924

Fritz Haarmann picked up young men arriving at the station in
Hanover before luring them to their death.

central station to watch the drifters arrive, many
of them young and vulnerable and desperate to see
a friendly face. Haarmann was that face. He would
be there every night, offering sweets, cigarettes,
and chocolate to the new arrivals. The relief and
gratitude would shine out from their eyes as he
offered them shelter and a mattress for the night.

Haarmann was good at lending an ear to these
boys, some only 12 years old. By listening to their
stories he would win their confidence and soon
even the welfare workers at the station began to
see him as one of their team. Police knew about his
underworld and black market connections but

Haarmann convinced detectives he could be a useful informer. Consequently his activities as fence
and petty thief were left undisturbed while he provided his friends in the police with intelligence on
planned robberies and hideouts. As his personal
wealth increased, he set himself up as a second-
hand clothes dealer and meat hawker. Housewives
would come running to buy his keenly priced joints
and he got a reputation for always having plenty
of stock in an economy still reeling from the war.

When, in September 1918, the parents of 17-
year-old Friedel Rothe reported that he had gone
missing, detectives did not overly exert themselves.
This sort of thing happened all the time. Even
when an informer mentioned he had seen someone answering Rothe's description in a billiards
room with Haarmann, the officers didn't get excited. They did not even want to question their friend
Fritz, though finally they agreed to do so. Years
later, during his trial, Haarmann was to boast:
"When the police examined my room the head of
the boy Friedel was lying wrapped in newspaper
behind the oven."

That close shave served only to convince
Haarmann that he was unstoppable. The following
year he teamed up with an accomplice, Hans
Grans, 20, son of a librarian. Grans regarded himself as Haarmann's social superior and was happy
to let everybody know it. Slowly he began to wield
a terrible influence on the older man, once even
instructing him to murder a boy "because I like the
clothes he's wearing." The two men lived in a sidestreet called Rothe Reihe (Red Row) close to the
River Leine. They became callously casual about
their grisly deeds, often carting around buckets of
blood in front of neighbors and chopping up bodies so that everyone could hear. But still

Haarmann's cover remained intact. He was a butcher. His behavior, thought the locals, was entirely normal.

But the crimes were now becoming so outrageously blatant that time was running out for the murderous duo—as panic began to sweep the streets of Hanover. In the spring of 1924, the city found itself sucked into the kind of werewolf scare that should have died out in the Middle Ages. It started with housewives complaining about cuts of meat they had bought. The joints looked, smelled, and tasted odd, the women said. There were rumors that a vampire or werewolf was on the loose. Could the meat possibly be human flesh? The police were quick to crush such rumors. Offending joints were pronounced to be pork and senior officers blamed the scare on "mass public hysteria."

Then, on May 17, children found a human skull on the banks of the River Leine. It was to be the first of many; one pathologist later claimed the river had washed up the remains of at least 27 dismembered murder victims. Yet at this stage police still did not want to accept publicly that a serial murderer was on the loose. Incredibly, detectives put out a statement to the press claiming the bones found had been placed near the river by medical students as a sick prank. In their desire to quell public anxiety, they were guilty of a huge misjudgment. For they were dealing with a ruthless sex slayer whose appalling depravity meant that he would kill again and again until caught.

" When the police examined my room, the head of the boy Friedel was lying wrapped in newspaper behind the oven "

Newspapers, critical of police efforts, now described Hanover as a town to which hundreds of youngsters would gravitate—and vanish. One writer even suggested 600 people had disappeared in the city inside a year. The furor over the finding of the skull and bones by the river at last spurred the police into action. Underworld sources were questioned at length. Runaways were asked to identify anyone who had tried to befriend them. More and more, the finger of suspicion began to point at Haarmann.

At last detectives put him under observation. On the night of June 22, 1924, he was on his usual beat in the station when he accosted a teenager called From. They quarreled, began to fight, and the police moved in to arrest the man they knew as one of their best "grasses." A search of his flat revealed blood-splattered walls and heaps of clothes of varying sizes. Haarmann tried to stay calm. "What do you expect?" he asked his interrogators. "I am a butcher and I also trade in second-hand clothes."

Parents of the missing children were invited to the flat to look at the clothes. One mother couldn't see anything she recognized—until she spotted the son of Haarmann's landlady. He was wearing the coat that had belonged to her boy. The evidence was now overwhelming and Haarmann knew it. He broke down and confessed everything.

The trial of Haarmann and Grans began on December 4, 1924. They were jointly charged with the murders of 27 boys aged between 12 and 18 and the case became the biggest news story in Europe. Haarmann showed glimpses of his callous ways right from the start. He was shown pictures of his victims and asked if he had been responsible for their deaths. "Yes, that might well be," he would say of one photo. "I'm not sure about that one," he would claim occasionally. But when a court official held up a picture of young Hermann Wolf, Haarmann turned scathingly on the boy's distraught father, who was sitting in court:

"I should never have looked twice at such an ugly youngster as, according to his photograph, your son must have been. You say your boy had not even a shirt to his name and that his socks were tied on to his feet with string! Deuce take it, you should have been ashamed to let him go about like that. There's plenty of rubbish like him around. Think what you're saying man. Such a fellow would have been far beneath my notice."

One court reporter filed this moving account of the scenes as Haarmann stood in the dock: "Nearly 200 witnesses had to appear in the box, mostly parents of the unfortunate youths. There were scenes of painful intensity as a poor father or mother would recognize some fragment or other of the clothing or belongings of their murdered son. Here it was a handkerchief, there a pair of braces, and again a greasy coat, soiled almost beyond recognition, that was shown to the relatives and to Haarmann. And with the quivering nostrils of a hound snuffling his prey, as if he were scenting rather than seeing the things displayed, did he admit at once that he knew them."

- - - - - - - - - - - - - - - - - -

Fritz Haarmann's seedy bedroom where the victims' parents were later to identify fragments of clothing belonging to their sons, all missing presumed dead.

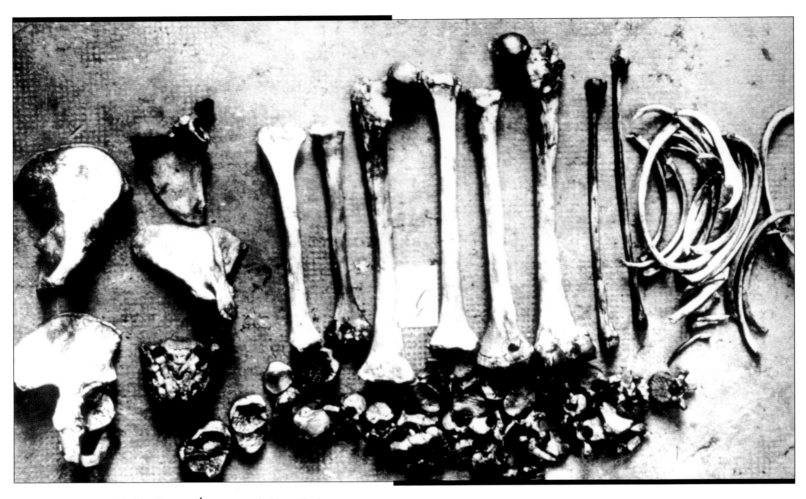

Bone fragments of Fritz Harmann's young victims that were found on the banks of the River Leine.

- - - - - - - - - - - -

At one point an exchange between the prosecution counsel and Haarmann filled the courtroom with an electric tension. When counsel asked, "How many victims did you kill altogether?" Haarmann said casually: "It might be 30, it might be 40. I really can't remember the exact number." When the lawyer asked, "How did you kill your victims?" Haarmann replied without emotion: "I bit them through their throats."

Damned out of his own mouth, Haarmann was found guilty on December 19, 1924. His last words to the court were screamed with a ferocity that belied the psychiatrists' insistence that he was sane: "Do you think I enjoy killing people? I was ill for eight days after the first time. Condemn me to death. I ask only for justice. I am not mad. It is true I often get into a state when I do not know what I am doing, but that is not madness. Make it short, make it soon. Deliver me from this life, which is a torment. I will not petition for mercy, nor will I appeal. I want to pass just one more merry evening in my cell, with coffee, cheese, and cigars, after which I will curse my father and go to my execution as if it were a wedding."

The monster, variously nicknamed the "Vampire of Hanover," "Werewolf of Hanover," and "Butcher of Hanover," had his last wish speedily granted. He was beheaded the next day—and Hanover rejoiced.

JOHN HAIGH

When John George Haigh went to the gallows at Wandsworth Prison, the riddle of the Acid Bath Murders died with him.

Convicted of six killings, he voluntarily added another three to the tally. His aim, it was assumed, was to make his crimes sound like the actions of a madman, committed to fuel his supposed lust for cannibalistic practices. Had he been found guilty but insane, he would not have faced execution at the hands of hangman Albert Pierrepoint that Wednesday morning on August 10, 1949.

But however many victims Haigh claimed, the total would have been more but for one fatal error on his part. The careless oversight was, in fact, totally out of character for the meticulous, calculating serial killer brought up in a strict, religious household.

Young George's parents were both followers of the Plymouth Brethren sect but they failed to inculcate him with their religious beliefs. He later said that he had developed a taste for blood when, beaten savagely by his parents, he enjoyed licking his wounds. "Once acquired, the taste obsessed me. An appetite was unleashed."

The boy grew up to be an intelligent, if socially backward, young man with a skill in forgery. A confidence trickster specializing in fraudulent hire purchase deals and selling cars he didn't own, he acquired a healthy bank balance, a gleaming sports car, and a pretty wife. He lost all this when he was jailed for fraud in 1934 and again in 1938. He never saw his wife again after separating from her just eight months into their marriage. "Ninety per cent of women are definitely repellent at close

quarters," he later said, though denied being homosexual.

Within the bleak fortress of Dartmoor prison, Haigh learned new skills. He studied chemistry and so worked in the tinsmith's shop where he had access to sulphuric acid. The idea of dissolving bodies in acid began to take shape. He would experiment on small animals brought in as pets by prisoners on outside work parties. He made careful notes about the time taken for acid to dissolve flesh and bone.

FACT FILE.

Name: John George Haigh
Born: July 24, 1909
Location of killings: London
  and Sussex, England
Killed: six, possibly nine
Modus operandi: coshing or
  shooting, then immersion in
  acid
Justice: hanged August 10,
  1949

Haigh claimed to be a vampire who drank the blood of his victims, but his plea of insanity was dismissed by the court. He was sentenced to death.

- - - - - - - - - - - -

Haigh avoided military call-up during World War II by volunteering for fire-watching duties, while working for a Mr. McSwann who ran a pin-table saloon empire from his home in south-west London. By 1944 Haigh had set up his own business repairing pin-tables. One of the regular callers at his basement in London's Gloucester Road was his former employer's son, Donald McSwann, who was seeking help in dodging the draft.

One night Donald failed to return from a visit to the flat. Haigh had staved his skull in with a pin-table leg and dissolved the body in a 40-gallon

water butt filled with acid. The little that was left of Donald McSwann had been poured down a drain in Gloucester Road. Haigh told the boy's parents that he had gone into hiding to avoid his call-up papers. He could explain the situation better, he assured them, if they would call and see him. They did—and never returned home. Their remains also went down the drain.

Using forged papers, Haigh managed to seize

> ❝Haigh had staved his skull in with a pin-table leg and dissolved the body in a 40-gallon water butt filled with acid❞

control of the couple's assets to the tune of £4,000, then a small fortune. He lived in comfort at the respectable Onslow Court Hotel nearby. With money came a passion for gambling, however, and Haigh's debts mounted. He decided that new victims were needed for his bubbling baths.

Haigh had got to know a Dr. and Mrs. Henderson after putting in a spurious offer to buy their house in London's Ladbroke Square. Although they eventually sold to another buyer, some of his infectious charm rubbed off and the Hendersons later invited him to join them for a short break in Brighton. One afternoon the doctor decided to accompany Haigh on the short drive to Crawley, where the killer's repair workshop was now based. The doctor was murdered at the first

Detectives looked for remains at the grounds of the factory in Crawley used by murderer John Haigh.

- - - - - - - - - - - - -

convenient moment and his body consigned to the acid vat.

Mrs. Henderson was fetched on the pretext that her husband had fallen seriously ill. Haigh smashed her over the head and heaved her body into the bath. It was then absurdly straightforward for the couple's murderer to forge a letter giving authority over their assets. Later that year, 1948, he banked around £7,000.

Haigh's final victim was a fellow resident of the Onslow Court Hotel, 69-year-old colonel's widow Olive Durand-Deacon. Haigh had already had the audacity to sell her Mrs. Henderson's crocodile-skin handbag for £10. Now he was hatching a plan

to get his hands on her assets and £1,000-a-year income.

The charmer—whose appearance resembled that of the heartthrob of the day, Errol Flynn—began ingratiating himself to Mrs. Durand-Deacon, escorting her to literary lunches and presenting himself as the perfect dinner table companion. When invited to visit his business in Crawley, she agreed but got only the briefest of inspections before Haigh shot her in the back. He then removed her jewels and Persian lambskin coat, trussed her up and heaved her 14-stone bulk into one of his water butts before squirting the acid in with a stirrup pump.

In a letter written later from his prison cell, Haigh claimed he had stamped the widow's crucifix into the earth before slitting her throat with a

Haigh murdered his victims and then disolved their bodies in sulphuric acid.

- - - - - - - - - - - - - - - -

penknife and gorging himself on her blood. It had then taken him two hours to dispose of the body in the vat of acid. He wrote: "It is a fatiguing business getting a 14-stone carcass into an oil drum. I'm not a very strong man." Yet, despite these problems, his crime seemed to have gone according to plan.

Haigh appeared as concerned as the other hotel residents when the widow disappeared. When one of her friends suggested going to the police station, he went too. The woman desk sergeant, instantly suspicious of the dapper conman, ran a check on him and discovered that he had several previous convictions. Suddenly the helpful neighbor was in the frame for murder.

Haigh had become over-confident. He had forgotten to allow for the long time that body fat can take to dissolve completely in sulphuric acid. False teeth are equally resistant. Police found the remains of both in soil at the back of the Crawley yard when they were called in by a friend of Mrs. Durand-Deacon who knew of her appointment with Haigh.

The killer had also been careless. He had taken his victim's lambskin coat to the cleaners and left the ticket lying around in his workshop. Police knew Mrs. Durand-Deacon had been seen in a lambskin coat shortly before she went missing. They were also interested in the revolver, vats of acid, rubber gloves, and other protective clothing they found lying around in Haigh's lair.

If the body of Mrs. Durand-Deacon had been allowed to remain in her acid bath for a further couple of weeks, all remnants of the widow would have disappeared. But in the vile slime through which police scientists sifted there were still the identifiable bones of a left foot the same shoe size as the old lady's, fragments of arthritic bone joints, three gallstones and the plastic handle of a handbag.

On March 2, 1949, John Haigh was charged with murder after police presented him with damning evidence that he had sold some of Mrs. Durand-Deacon's jewelry. For a while, Haigh remained tight-lipped. Then he suddenly asked his police interrogators: "Tell me frankly, what are the chances of anyone being released from Broadmoor?" He was referring to the top-security hospital for the criminally insane and was apparently considering his chances of being sent there rather than to the gallows. After a further silence, he continued: "Mrs. Durand-Deacon doesn't exist. I have destroyed her with acid. How can you prove murder if there is no body?"

Haigh then made a full confession to the murders police were investigating. But he went on to add a further three victims to the murder toll: a man and a woman in the Gloucester Road area and another woman at Crawley. Police did not believe him, especially after he went on to talk about recurring nightmares he had had since childhood, involving forests of crucifixes and chalices of blood. Haigh went on to spice up his accounts of his murders with stories about how he drank the blood of

Haigh made a full confession to the murders on his arrest, but his attempt at convincing the authorities that he was insane, in order to avoid a death sentence, failed.

– – – – – – – – – – –

his victims before dissolving them. He believed it would help him escape the gallows on the grounds that he was insane. He was wrong.

John George Haigh was not the first killer to realize the useful properties of acid in disposing of a body. He was, however, one of the most prolific dissolvers and, but for one careless oversight, would almost certainly have gone on to claim the lives of many more unfortunates charmed by his plausibility. Right to the moment of his death on the gallows on August 10, 1949, he relished the title bestowed on him by the press: "The Acid Bath Murderer."

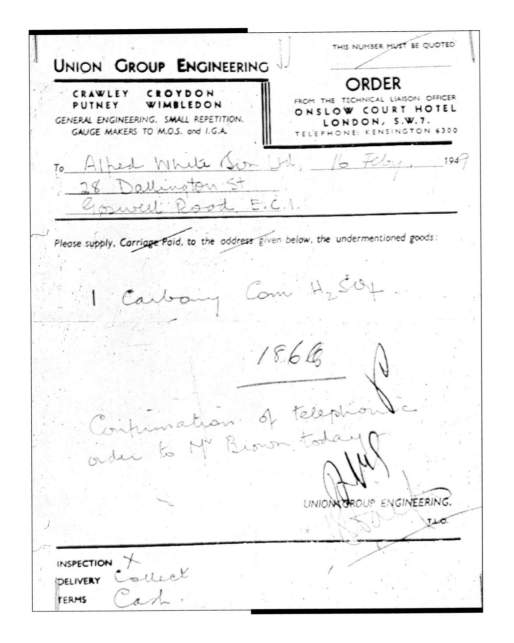

Haigh's order for sulphuric acid was used as an exhibit at his trial.

> **He would soon be immortalized as a waxwork in Madame Tussaud's Chamber of Horrors—a venue close to his heart as it was a place he had regularly visited with girlfriends**

Hours before he was due to hang, Haigh made the most bizarre of several last requests. He told his jailers that he would soon be immortalized as a waxwork in Madame Tussaud's Chamber of Horrors—a venue close to his heart as it was a place he had regularly visited with girlfriends.

Could the owners of Tussaud's be presented with the clothes he wore throughout his trial: his green hopsack suit, green socks, and red tie with green squares? He was also very keen that his suit trousers should be properly pressed. His wishes were granted a few days after his execution.

ARCHIBALD HALL

Archibald Hall thought of himself as the "Perfect Gentleman." Indeed he wrote a book entitled exactly that and on passing acquaintance, his boast was quite believable.

Working as a butler and using the name Roy Fontaine, Hall was charming, attentive, witty, immaculately dressed, and impeccably mannered—he was the epitome of the gentleman's personal assistant. He might almost have modeled himself on P. G. Wodehouse's immortal manservant Jeeves. But in reality, Hall was a bisexual seducer, burglar, forger, conman, jewel thief, jailbird, and murderer.

Born in a Glasgow tenement in 1924, Hall, the son of a post office sorting clerk, lacked for little but was never well off. He did, however, get a taste of the good life at the age of 16 when he was seduced by an older woman who took him to the best hotels and bought him fine food and wine. He determined that this elegant lifestyle would be his from then on, whatever he had to do to get it.

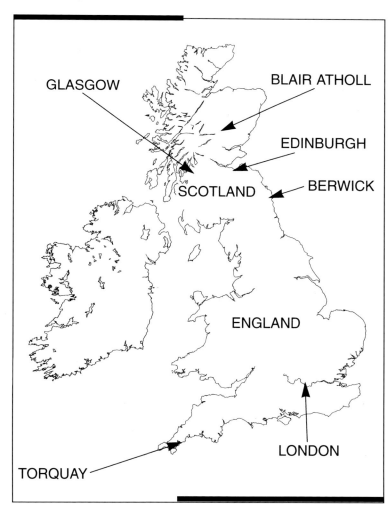

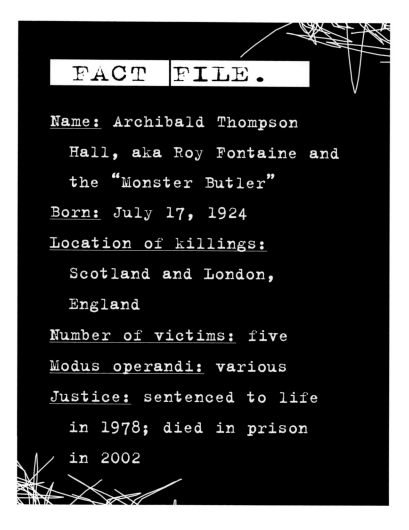

FACT FILE.

<u>Name:</u> Archibald Thompson Hall, aka Roy Fontaine and the "Monster Butler"

<u>Born:</u> July 17, 1924

<u>Location of killings:</u> Scotland and London, England

<u>Number of victims:</u> five

<u>Modus operandi:</u> various

<u>Justice:</u> sentenced to life in 1978; died in prison in 2002

Archibald Hall had many previous criminal convictions but still managed to secure a job as a butler before going on to become a serial killer.

His criminal career started in a small way, by cheating the Red Cross. He became a regular and successful collector for them, but when he went out on the streets, he always took two tins. Into one went the notes and the higher denomination coins, while he made sure that the tin he handed in was always full—albeit only with pennies. From this, it was a small step to outright theft, and in 1943 he embarked on a crime spree in Scotland and England.

Jailed for 60 days in Glasgow in 1943, he was again in trouble with the law a year later when he was arrested for housebreaking. This time he was adjudged to be mentally unstable. Twice he was sent to mental hospitals following petty crime sprees, twice he escaped and remained at liberty for 28 days, which in Scottish law established his ability to look after himself, so he could not be classed as unstable. His freedom did not last long.

Following further burglaries, he was certified insane in 1944 and sentenced to be detained indefinitely. Released in 1946, he drifted to London, where he soon found himself in court again when he was jailed for two years for forgery and housebreaking. He asked for another 51 offenses to be taken into consideration. In 1949 and again in 1951, Hall was sent to jail for shop breaking and forgery.

Upon his release, Hall reinvented himself and embarked on a new career as a "gentleman's gentleman." With forged references, he answered an advertisement placed by a shipping executive in Stirlingshire. He was turned down because the executive recognized one of the names among the referees—that of a blind man who could neither read nor write.

Undaunted, Hall, now calling himself Roy Fontaine, took his phoney references to a neighboring country home and got a job as a butler. It was a career that would give him many opportunities to exercise his true calling, thieving, which he now combined with confidence trickery. Eventually, it would lead to gruesome murder.

Among the conman's stunts over the following five years were standing in for his unwitting employer at a royal garden party, posing as a rich Arab in order to fool jewelers into parting with gems, and playing the part of a wealthy American to gain access to top-notch functions.

Justice caught up with the agile swindler in 1956 when he was sentenced to 30 years for a string of theft-related offenses. Released on parole in 1963, he was back inside again the following year. He escaped and was on the run for two years before his recapture, when a further five years were added to the original ten of his sentence. Nevertheless, he won parole in 1973, only to be jailed again in 1974. In 1977, again with forged references, Hall obtained a post as butler to Lady Peggy Hudson in Scotland's border country. On his recommendation, David Wright, a homosexual lover from prison, was taken on as gardener. Wright and Hall soon quarreled, however, as Wright wanted to rob the property immediately, while Hall had far bigger plans. The disagreement was to lead to murder.

While Lady Peggy was absent, Wright stole an expensive ring. Hall immediately tracked it down to a girlfriend of Wright's and took it back. The following night he was awoken dramatically by a gunshot as a drunken Wright tried to kill the sleeping Hall, missing him by a fraction of an inch. Hall calmed the man down and disarmed him, but he realized that he would always be in danger of blackmail, exposure, or worse as long as Wright lived. The following day the two men went out shooting rabbits. Hall waited until his companion's gun was empty then cold-bloodedly shot him, burying his body under a pile of stones in a stream. A week later, by great good fortune, his employer

> **"Hall waited until his companion's gun was empty then cold-bloodedly shot him, burying his body under a pile of stones in a stream"**

received an anonymous letter exposing Hall's criminal past and he was dismissed.

Hall's next post was with the wealthy Walter Scott-Elliott and his wife Dorothy at their home in London's Chelsea. At 82, the former Member of Parliament for Accrington had to take a number of drugs, which left him vague and almost helpless. He was an easy mark for Hall, who persuaded the old man to sign blank cheques with which to pay the household bills. Hall now called in two accomplices: Mary Coggle, who forged credit cards, and petty thief Michael Kitto. The three planned to rob and defraud the Scott-Elliotts, though at this stage it is unlikely that any of them had murder in mind.

Hall took Kitto to look round the house on December 8, 1977, while Mrs. Scott-Elliott was in a nursing home. However, she returned a day early and surprised the pair in her bedroom. In a panic, Hall knocked her down and suffocated her to stop her screams. Her husband, who had been awoken, was told she had had a nightmare and returned to bed. The next day Hall and Kitto filled the boot of a hired car with Mrs. Scott-Elliott's body, along with a haul of valuable antiques and jewelry. Mary Coggle put on the dead woman's furs and impersonated her well enough to fool the well-drugged Scott-Elliott. They drove to a cottage near Carlisle, which Hall had rented the month previously. The strangely assorted party then drove another 200 miles into Scotland, and at Glen Afric, near Blair

A victim's body murdered by Hall and his accomplices was found
behind a farmhouse.

- - - - - - - - - - - - -

Athol, they murdered the old man and buried him
in bushes.

Hall later wrote in his autobiography: "I
wrapped a scarf round his neck but he struggled
and fell to the ground. I put my foot across his
throat and barked at Kitto, 'Get the spade!' He
crashed it down on the old man's skull, killing him.
We then dug a shallow grave and buried him. Kitto
and Mary were now my accomplices. We had all
dipped our hands in blood."

Back at the cottage, the accomplices began to

fall out. Hall and Coggle disagreed over the mink
coat, she wanting to keep it but Hall considering it
too easily identified. In the course of the row, Hall
attacked her with a poker, striking her several
times across the head. The two men finished her
off by suffocating her and dumping the body in a
stream. They then returned to London to ransack
the Chelsea house.

The following month, Hall's brother Donald, 17
years his junior, appeared on the scene. Recently
freed from jail, Donald became curious about his
brother's new affluence and, after an argument,
Hall and Kitto killed him with chloroform. Again,
the two hired a car, put the body in the boot and,
with false plates, drove into Scotland. Unbeknown

to them, however, the body of Mary Coggle had been found on Christmas Day and when the two killers checked into a hotel at North Berwick, the manager became suspicious of them. While they

> **"He asked for a glass of water and tried to commit suicide with a pill secreted in his rectum"**

ate, he telephoned the police, who ran a check on the car, discovered that it had false number plates and arrested them.

Hall escaped, hailed a taxi but was apprehended at a road-block. Back at the police station, he was told that a body had been found in the boot of the car. He asked for a glass of water and tried to commit suicide with a pill secreted in his rectum. The bid was foiled after a dash to the Edinburgh Royal Infirmary. Two days later Hall again tried to kill himself.

Hall and Kitto both cracked under interrogation. They were tried twice, in England and Scotland, and both received life sentences. Kitto was to serve a minimum of 15 years, but in Hall's case, there was to be no chance of parole. His life of crime over, Hall languished in high-security prison wings, from where he hinted at further crimes for which he had not been charged. He claimed that he had been involved in two further killings—of an American helicopter pilot and a

On his arrest Archibald Hall tried to kill himself unsuccessfully. He was imprisoned with no chance of parole.

Preston garage worker—though he steadfastly refused to give further details of the deaths.

From his cell at Full Sutton Prison, Humberside, he wrote an autobiography which was successfully published in 1999 with the title *A Perfect Gentleman*. In it, he said: "Death will be my release. Not until I am dead can I escape these walls. To anyone who thinks they have the capacity for murder, I urge you to think again. My life is an impoverished nightmare. Let it be a lesson to you." He was right, for he died in jail in October 2002.

MYRA HINDLEY AND IAN BRADY

Even today, in a world hardened by violent crime, the vile deeds of Myra Hindley and Ian Brady set them apart as monsters of a very special breed.

With her lover, Ian Brady, they were objects of hatred like no other murderers in British history. But it was Hindley, because she was a woman and because her crimes were against children, who aroused the greatest revulsion. Almost four decades after her crimes, Hindley's death in prison in November 2002 was still front-page news. "The Devil," was one headline. "At last Myra is where she belongs: HELL."

Myra Hindley and Ian Brady, destined to be forever known as the "Moors Murderers," lived out their obscene fantasies in the Manchester area between 1962 and 1965. During that time, they abducted, tortured, and murdered at least five, possibly eight, children or teenagers. Most of the

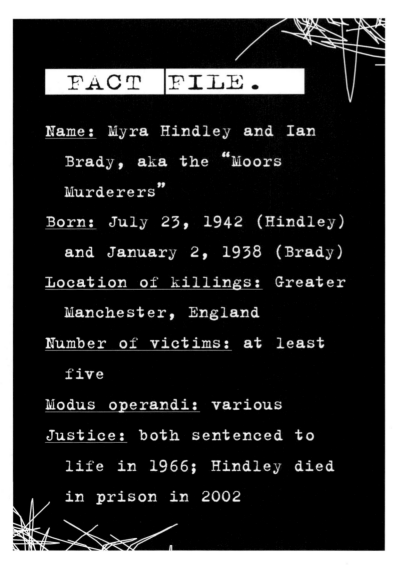

FACT FILE.

Name: Myra Hindley and Ian Brady, aka the "Moors Murderers"

Born: July 23, 1942 (Hindley) and January 2, 1938 (Brady)

Location of killings: Greater Manchester, England

Number of victims: at least five

Modus operandi: various

Justice: both sentenced to life in 1966; Hindley died in prison in 2002

Myra Hindley (top left) and Ian Brady (top right) have become synonymous with the concept of "evil." The body of Keith Bennett (below left) was never found, but Pauline Reade (below right) was found buried on the Saddleworth Moor in July 1987.

- - - - - - - - - - - - - - - - - -

bodies were buried on the bleak Saddleworth Moor on the outskirts of the city.

It was as if Brady and Hindley had met through some dark destiny. Brady, born in 1938, was the illegitimate son of a Glasgow waitress. A sullen, moody boy, his first court appearance was for burglary in 1951 when he was 13. He was put on probation twice. In 1954 he moved to Manchester to live with his mother and her new husband. He took a job in a brewery but was caught stealing lead and served a year in an institute for young offenders. After his release, it seemed Brady had finished with his criminal ways and he settled into a job as a clerk. But his mind was becoming more and more twisted. And as his obsession with sadism grew, typist Myra Hindley walked into his life.

Hindley and Brady worked for the same company, a chemical supply firm. Their paths first crossed in 1961 when she was 19. Hindley meticulously kept a diary after making Brady's acquaintance. One entry read: "Ian wore a black shirt and looked smashing. I love him." Their affair began a year later. The satanic hold Brady had over Hindley has never been understood. But right from the start, she eagerly participated in his fetishes. They both wore leather and acted out Nazi crimes together. They took pictures of themselves having sex and with whips.

But this was not enough for the evil couple. Brady wanted to inflict his perversions on the innocent and Hindley was a more than willing partner.

> **❝He was held down and molested by Brady before being strangled and buried in the boggy soil❞**

She was a woman without mercy, a woman who could stand by and do nothing as her sadistic lover toyed with his victims—then took part in their torture and death.

In July 1963, 16-year-old Pauline Reade, from the Gorton area of Manchester, disappeared. As with all their victims, Hindley was the one who lured her into Brady's clutches. Pauline was told by her neighbor Hindley that she had lost a glove on Saddleworth Moor and wanted the girl to help her search for it. Brady, who was following them, raped Pauline then hit her over the head with a shovel before cutting her throat. Four months later, Brady told Hindley "It is time to do another one" and 12-year-old John Kilbride went missing. The boy was said to have gone with the couple "like a lamb to the slaughter." Once on the moor, he was held down and molested by Brady before being strangled and buried in the boggy soil.

Another 12-year-old, Keith Bennett, vanished in June 1964. It later emerged that Hindley had asked him to carry some boxes of shopping for her before Brady used the lost glove story to lure him onto the moor. There the boy was abused and strangled, Brady taking photographs of the body before burying it. Ten-year-old Lesley Ann Downey disappeared while attending a Christmas fair on

Mrs. Downey watched the searchers as they looked for her daughter after Brady and Hindley were accused of her murder.

Detectives examine articles found during a search for clues in the Moors Murder case.

- - - - - - - - - - - - - -

December 26. She was taken to Brady's home and forced to pose nude for pornographic photographs before being sexually tortured and strangled.

It was ten months before Brady and Hindley struck again. In October 1965, Brady met 17-year-old Edward Evans. There was a special reason why Brady wanted to entice this victim to his home, where he had also invited Hindley's brother-in-law David Smith. Brady had talked to Smith about previous murders but then became fearful that he would go to the police. It was vital that Smith was present at the murder of Evans, so that he too would be implicated. In front of the horrified Smith, Brady then launched his fatal, bloody attack on Evans with a hatchet. Brady also ensured that Smith's fingerprints were on the hatchet. After the murder, Brady boasted to Smith: "It's the messiest yet. It normally only takes one

blow." Edward's body was wrapped in plastic and taken upstairs. Smith later recalled that the couple then sat around laughing and drinking wine, Hindley still wearing her blood-soaked shoes.

Brady's attempt to involve Smith was a fatal mistake. What he had witnessed so disturbed him that he went to the police. Arrested, Brady tried to put the blame onto Smith and to keep Hindley in the clear. Under questioning, Brady made mistakes and the police were able to trip him up on several of his denials. Hindley, however, was a tougher nut to crack and never wavered under interrogation. She simply stated: "I didn't do it. Ian didn't do it. I am saying nothing." Hindley was not arrested for four days following the murder of Evans and in that time she managed to destroy some of the evidence. But the case against them was already solid by then.

When Brady's house was searched, a book with John Kilbride's name in it was found, together with nine pornographic pictures of Lesley Ann Downey. A ticket led police to a luggage locker at Manchester Central railway station. The two suitcases that were found contained sex and torture books, whips, coshes, and other items used for perverted activities. Yet another photograph, of Hindley posing next to John Kilbride's shallow grave on Saddleworth Moor, enabled police to locate the grave not only of the boy but of Lesley Ann Downey.

The trial of Hindley and Brady began on April 19, 1966, at Chester Assizes. According to Hindley's confession, Brady told her that he had strangled John Kilbride with a thin piece of string and had cut Pauline Reade's throat. But it was the production of a cassette tape that was the most damning evidence. No one who sat in court that day would ever forget the harrowing recording played to them. It was of a little girl's voice, begging for her mother and pleading for mercy. The child's plaintive cries were accompanied by the obvious sounds of torture and sexual assault. The recording was of Lesley Ann Downey, at ten the youngest victim, and was made by the evil couple themselves as the little girl was put to death.

Hardened cops had wept when they had first listened to the tape. A senior detective screamed "Turn it off, turn it off" as he covered his ears from the sound of the child's pleading and sobbing. When played in court, hardened reporters were reduced to tears. The courtroom heard Lesley saying: "Please take your hands off me a minute, please. Please, Mum, please. I can't tell you. I cannot breathe. Please God. Why? What are you doing with me?" Throughout the horrific sixteen-minute tape, there was Hindley's voice, coldly ordering the child to "shut up," "come on," and "sit down and be quiet." The tape ended with a scream and a loud

> " Two suitcases that were found contained sex and torture books, whips, coshes, and other items used for perverted activities "

cry and then the sound of a favorite song of the time, *The Little Drummer Boy*.

The case against Brady and Hindley was the most horrific to have ever come before a British court. The judge said of the killers: "They are evil beyond belief." On May 6, the couple were found guilty of killing Edward Evans and Lesley Ann Downey. In the cases of Pauline Reade and Keith Bennett, the Department of Public Prosecutions decided against a new trial, although both Brady and Hindley had implicated themselves by their statements. Both were given life sentences.

Little Pauline Reade's body was found on the moors in July 1987. Keith Bennett's body still lies there. During his time in prison, Brady "confessed" to five other murders, including "bricking" a man on wasteland behind Manchester's Piccadilly railway station, stabbing a man under railway arches in Glasgow, throwing a woman into a canal in Manchester, shooting and burying an 18-year-old youth on Saddleworth Moor, and shooting a hiker at Loch Long, Scotland. But it was difficult to give too much credence to this information from Brady, who was diagnosed as suffering from a paranoid psychosis.

Brady stated that he never wanted to be released and even went on hunger strike in an attempt to end his life. Myra Hindley, by contrast, campaigned for her release as a totally reformed character and managed to entice a small band of

The searches on Saddleworth Moor spanned the decades. Here
police discover the remains of one of the victims in 1968.

sympathizers to her cause. However, the killer was seen by others as a cold, calculating, and manipulative woman. She became Britain's longest-serving female prisoner because of her "whole life" sentence and, after 36 years in jail, she died on November 15, 2002, from a chest infection made worse by previous bouts of angina and a stroke. At 60, she was still the most reviled woman in Britain.

JAVED MUGHAL IQBAL

Attempting to ensure that the punishment fitted the crime was at the forefront of a judge's mind when he passed sentence on a maniac who murdered at least 100 children.

Mirroring the fate of his innocent victims, Javed Iqbal Mughal was sentenced to be strangled 100 times in a public park, cut into 100 pieces, and thrown into an acid bath. A teenage accomplice was also handed the same retribution of death and mutilation. Two younger boys involved in the slaughter were jailed. Bizarrely, as well as his multiple-death sentence, ringleader Iqbal was also sentenced to prison for 700 years, being seven years for each of the bodies he had been proved to have dissolved in acid.

Iqbal, 42, had been the target of Pakistan's biggest ever manhunt. In a sickening rampage, he plucked children from the streets of Lahore, sexually abused them, throttled them, and then hacked their bodies to bits. He confessed to the killings in a letter to a newspaper which mocked police for failing to catch him, then went on the run. Police swooped on his home in the city and found a huge vat of acid but the remains of only two children. But they found photographs of 100 missing youngsters and tearful parents identified many of them from clothes found in the house.

After a month on the run, Iqbal gave himself up. He told his captors: "I have no regrets. I killed 100 children. I could have killed 500. This was not a problem, nor was the money. But I pledged to kill 100 and I never wanted to violate this."

In court, Iqbal denied his confession and pleaded not guilty to murder as relatives of the dead held a vigil outside. He was also charged with abduction and sodomy, in connection with a separate case involving two brothers who were still alive. Iqbal's three accomplices, all in their teens, also denied charges of murder, abduction, and sodomy.

FACT FILE.

Name: Javed Mughal Iqbal

Born: 1958

Location of killings: Pakistan

Killed: at least 100 children

Modus operandi: (with young accomplices) strangulation; bodies dissolved in acid

Justice: sentenced to "be strangled 100 times, cut into 100 pieces, and thrown into a bath of acid" although this was not carried out

Javed Iqbal was led to court in chains. He was sentenced to be strangled, cut into pieces, and thrown into acid for murdering and mutilating children.

However, the court heard evidence from a shopworker who had sold one of them, 18-year-old Shahzad Sajid, sulphuric and hydrochloric acid. It was used to fill vats into which Javed tipped the remains of the 100 teenagers he had murdered. Only 25 ill-fated children out of the 100 were identified by their parents, mainly by their belongings which the murderer had kept in five sacks.

The parents' fury at the lack of police efforts to catch the killer earlier were given voice by the judge in the case, Allah Buksh Ranjha. He told the court: "I want to express my opinion regarding the irresponsible and indifferent attitude of police who miserably failed to search for even a single boy who left his house on some pretext and rather they avoided their liabilities in such a manner that every legal heir appearing before the court complained that they approached the police for registration of their missing child but the police refused to do so. This is an alarming situation and

I will write separately to the authorities concerned."

On March 16, 2000, Iqbal was found guilty of 100 murders and Sajid of 98. The third accused, named as Nadeem, aged about 15, was found guilty of complicity in 13 killings and the youngest boy, 13-year-old Sabir, of complicity in three killings. Being minors, Nadeem and Sabir, the latter wearing a prayer cap, were spared the death sentence and instead given extended jail sentences of 162 and 42 years respectively.

The judge then handed down his astonishing sentence on the two prime movers. He directed that for killing 100 children, Javed Iqbal Mughal and Shahzad Sajid should, in the presence of the relatives of the boys, be strangulated with the same iron chain which they used as weapon of offense, their bodies to be cut up—into 100 and 98 pieces respectively—and put into a drum containing acid as they did with those of the dead children. The court recommended that "to set a horrific example," the sentence should be executed at an open place, preferably a public park.

The punishment, meted out under Section 302-A of the Pakistan Penal Code, was described as the first sentence under Islamic "Qisas" law. All four accused heard the verdicts calmly—although Iqbal seemed to protest at one point that some others who had been questioned by police should have been with them in the dock. The two minors were seen smiling as they left the courtroom.

Casting doubt on whether the full horrific death sentence on Iqbal and his co-conspirator would ever be carried out, Pakistan's Interior Minister, Moinuddin Haider, said later: "Pakistan is a signatory to international conventions which do not allow these things."

COLIN IRELAND

In London, during the spring of 1993, a serial killer was very publicly on the rampage.

As Colin Ireland's hideous acts were reported week by week in the newspapers, he would telephone detectives to taunt them. "I've got the book," he would say. "I know how many you have to do." After the fifth victim was found, he boasted: "I've done another one." The book was the FBI handbook by Robert Ressler, which stated that only someone who had murdered "one over four" could count as a serial killer. Colin Ireland wanted nothing more than that notoriety. Later, after he confessed to his five murders, he told police he had just wanted the thrill of fame.

❛❛I've done another one❜❜

Ireland, a six foot, 210-pound survival enthusiast with two failed marriages behind him, was obsessed with the crimes of the Yorkshire Ripper, Peter Sutcliffe, and sex killer Donald Neilson. He also loved watching the film *Silence of the Lambs*, relishing the malevolent evil conjured up by Sir Anthony Hopkins. He told police that homosexuals were a good target for him because they attracted little public sympathy. But the idea that he killed purely for fame is only part of the truth. He nurtured a lingering hatred toward homosexuals after being sacked at Christmas

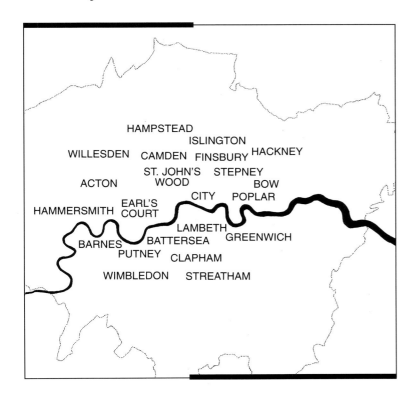

FACT FILE.

Name: Colin Ireland
Born: 1954
Location of killings: London, England
Killed: five
Modus operandi: strangulation
Justice: given five life sentences in 1993

1992 from the night hostel for the homeless where he worked in Southend, Essex, after a row with a gay man. He moved to London intent on revenge against all homosexuals—and he knew only one way to work it out.

Ireland launched his reign of terror in the spring of 1993. His stalking ground was the Coleherne pub in West London's Earl's Court district. There, on March 9, he met 45-year-old theater director Peter Walker and was invited back to his apartment for a sadomasochistic sex session. Ireland, aged 39, had come equipped with his own cord, knife, and a pair of gloves. At Walker's apartment, he told his victim to lie naked on his bed and then tied him firmly down before whipping him, placing a plastic bag over the man's head, and suffocating him. Two days later he rang the Samaritans and a newspaper asking if someone could go round to the address to free Walker's two pet dogs trapped inside.

In a later confession to detectives, Ireland said, "I had gone there (the Coleherne pub) with the idea that if someone approached me something would happen. It would be some sort of trigger—a stepping over the line in a way." Now that line was crossed and Ireland soon struck again. On May 29, he picked up a 37-year-old librarian, Chris Dunn. At Dunn's apartment, Ireland handcuffed him to the bed, beat him with a belt, and held a cigarette lighter to his testicles before strangling him. When found the following morning, Dunn was naked apart from a black harness. Arrayed around him were the implements he used for a night of "pleasure:" belts, a cane, a truncheon, and other kinky equipment used for sadomasochistic sex.

Third to die was Perry Bradley III, a 35-year-old businessman whose father was a US

Colin Ireland picked up his first victim at the Coleherne Pub in West London's Earl's Court area.
– – – – – – – – – – – –

Congressman. Friends later insisted he was not gay, though the facts suggest he was certainly bisexual in his tastes. Bradley was also picked up at the Coleherne, on June 4, and again Ireland was invited home, this time to a smart apartment in Kensington. Once tied and handcuffed to the bed, Bradley was informed that he was going to be robbed but that if he cooperated he would be all right. That night, Bradley eventually fell asleep. Ireland admitted in his statement: "I sat there in the room and thought about it and at one point I was thinking of letting him go. Then I thought, 'It's easier to kill him.' I walked round and pulled the noose."

Ireland's next pick-up four days later followed a similar pattern. Andrew Collier, a 33-year-old warden at an old people's home, ended up being spread-eagled on his own bed, beaten black and blue, and strangled. In an additional, sickening twist, Ireland broke the neck of his victim's cat Millie. The killer said later that he had been outraged to discover from papers he was rifling through at the flat that Collier was HIV positive. He had not, he said righteously, even been offered a condom by the man. He told police: "I went fucking crazy. I burned certain areas of his body. He loved that cat, it was his life, so I did the cat with a noose and draped it over the body." In fact, the cat's tail was stuffed into Collier's mouth and the cat's mouth was around the dead man's penis. As he later explained: "I wanted him to have no dignity in death. It was a way of saying to the police, 'What do you think of that?' It was like a signature to let them know I'd been there. I was reaching a point where I was just accelerating. It was just speeding up, getting far worse."

After the Collier killing, Ireland phoned police and asked them: "Are you still interested in the death of Peter Walker? Why have you stopped the investigation? Doesn't the death of a homosexual man mean anything? I will do another. I have always dreamed of doing the perfect murder."

> **"I went crazy. I burned certain areas of his body. He loved that cat, it was his life, so I did the cat with a noose and draped it over the body"**

Ireland then referred to the call he had made about Walker's dogs. "I pissed myself when I read I was an animal lover. I thought I would give you lot something to think about, so I killed the cat."

Ireland, now clearly oozing confidence in his ability to kill at will, could not have known that he had already made his first mistake. Normally so punctilious about wiping his victims' homes clean of clues, he had missed a single fingerprint on Collier's window security grille. The reign of terror which had gripped London's gay community was almost over.

On June 13, Ireland killed for the last time. Emmanuel Spiteri, a 42-year-old chef, was tied up and tortured in an attempt to make him disclose his cash card number. Spiteri screamed back: "You will just have to kill me." Ireland said later: "He was a very brave man but I couldn't allow him to stick around."

Within days, police knew the face of the killer. Checks on Spiteri's usual haunts took them to Charing Cross station where a security video had caught him and Ireland walking together. Ireland later went to police admitting he had been with Spiteri that night but claiming that a third man had been at the chef's apartment. The story was quickly demolished. Police recognized Ireland's voice from the anonymous phone calls and, more damning, his fingerprints matched ones left on the grille on Collier's window.

The game was up. On his way to a magistrates

court for a routine remand hearing, Ireland confessed to all five murders. At the Old Bailey in December 1993, Lord Justice Sachs told him: "You are an exceptionally frightening and dangerous man. In cold blood and with great deliberation, you killed five of your fellow human beings in grotesque and cruel circumstances. The fear, brutality, and indignity to which you subjected your victims are almost unspeakable. To take one human life is outrageous. To take five is carnage. You expressed a desire to be regarded as a serial killer. That must be matched by your detention for life." Colin Ireland was given five life sentences and told he would never be released from prison. He had found his place in British criminal history.

After the trial, the two women who knew him best attempted to explain what was in the mind of Ireland the monster. His former wife Virginia Zammit, a disabled sportswoman who held British records for wheelchair athletics, said Ireland was a Jekyll and Hyde character, torn between good and evil. "He told me it was a battle between two forces. He just felt the evil force was so powerful. He always hated gays; I don't know why, I just assumed something might have happened to him when he was younger."

His second wife, former pub landlady Jan Young, agonized: "I was hooked from the second I set eyes on him. He was like a mercenary in a war movie. I thought of him as an exciting stranger with an edge of danger to him. He had a lovely voice, soft and well-spoken, but his eyes were intense. They were so dark they were almost black. And they gave away nothing—they seemed to burn

Six-foot tall Colin Ireland was a survival enthusiast.
— — — — — — — — — — — —

through you. If he lost his temper, he would pin me against the wall and shout and spit. Women regulars found him sinister and creepy and threatened to stop coming to the pub. But I was besotted with him. Why was I so blind? Why did I not see evil in him?"

Colin Ireland launched his reign of terror in the spring of 1993 in the Earl's Court district of London.
— — — — — — — — — — — —

JACK THE RIPPER

Never has there been such a tantalizing murder mystery as that of Jack the Ripper. Over a century later, speculation is still rife over the true identity of the night-time prowler who stalked and murdered on the streets of London.

Since his skilled slayings shocked England in 1888, provoking outrage from Queen Victoria, researchers have endlessly poured over the few, juicy clues that he left behind. And rather than interest in him waning, investigation has, if anything, intensified over the years, guaranteeing the killer an indelible place in history.

The shadowy fiend who became known as Jack the Ripper was very far from being the most prolific murderer in the annals of crime. Although particularly gory—each slaying was followed by mutilation with surgical precision—this "minor" serial killer put paid to no more than five humble prostitutes. Yet his brief reign of terror has become perhaps the most enduring murder mystery for forensic experts, police, historians, and amateur sleuths. In fact, the story of Jack the Ripper raises two mysteries: the first being his identity, the second being why his notoriety has continued to fascinate us for more than a century. The Ripper's brief crime wave was quickly forgotten after the turn of the century, yet in recent years many books have been written about him.

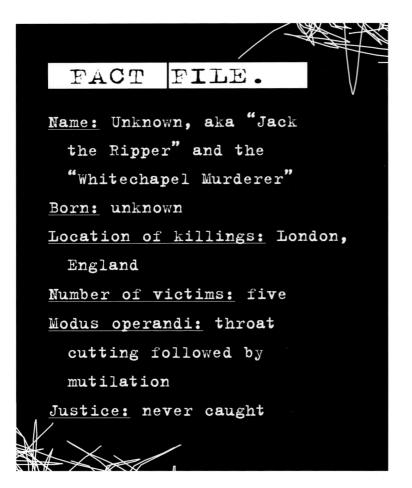

FACT FILE.

Name: Unknown, aka "Jack the Ripper" and the "Whitechapel Murderer"

Born: unknown

Location of killings: London, England

Number of victims: five

Modus operandi: throat cutting followed by mutilation

Justice: never caught

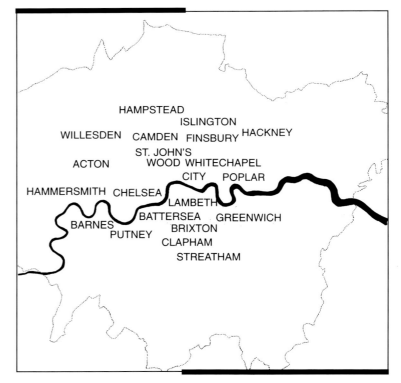

Speculation as to his identity is rife and often wildly wide of the mark, which has resulted in Jack being credited with many more names than the number of his victims. Was the murderer a self-styled purger of prostitutes who plied their sad

> **Most were subjected to appalling savagery, being mutilated and dissected in a manner that suggested a perverted sexual motive**

trade under the gas lights of London's East End? Was he a Jewish ritual slaughterman, as some clues suggested? Was he a surgeon who had turned his talents to butchery? Was he a mortician, skilled in the art of disembowelling? Was he a policeman, his nightly beat giving him the perfect alibi to be out on those dank, dark streets? Was "he" in fact a "she"—a midwife with a grudge? Or, most extraordinarily of all, was the killer a deranged member of the British Royal Family?

Amid this endless debate, it is easy to forget that Jack the Ripper's reign of terror was short and swift. It lasted less than three months. Between August 31, 1988, and November 9, 1988, five prostitutes were murdered. Each was attacked from behind. Each had their throats cut. Most were then subjected to the most appalling savagery, being mutilated and dissected in a manner that suggested a perverted sexual motive. Then just as suddenly as the slayings started, they stopped.

Contemporary illustrations of the police investigation into the Jack the Ripper murders highlight the lack of insight and bumbling detective work.

Jack's first victim was Mary Ann Nichols, a 42-year-old prostitute who plied her trade in the Whitechapel area of the East End. "Pretty Polly," as she was known, approached a tall stranger with the invitation: "Looking for a good time, mister?" If the stranger had accepted, a sum of four pence would have exchanged hands. Mary would have spent it in one of the gin shops of the area. Instead, the man put his hands around her throat to stop her crying out, then dragged her into the darkness of an alleyway. Within seconds he had cut her from ear to ear.

A police surgeon who examined the body said:

A contemporary illustration of the discovery of one of Jack the Rippers victims by police.

- - - - - - - - - - - -

"Only a madman could have done this. I have never seen so horrible a case. She was ripped about in the manner only a person skilled in the use of a knife could have achieved." The residents of Bucks Row, where Mary Ann Nichols' body was found, were so ashamed of their sudden notoriety and so outraged by officials who dubbed the street "Killer Row," that they petitioned to have it renamed. It was duly renamed Durward Street and remained so until it was demolished many years later.

Police put Mary's murder down to one single, frenzied attack. Then a week a later, on September 8, another prostitute, 47-year-old "Dark Annie" Chapman, was butchered in Hanbury Street, near Spitalfields Market. Her few pitiful possessions had been laid out neatly alongside her disemboweled corpse. Also alongside her were her entrails, slashed out of her in a sexual frenzy. A witness who dashed to scene after hearing the cry "Murder" said: "I jumped off my cart, being a lad, and joined the crowd—and there she was, all her entrails steaming hot."

Shortly afterward a Fleet Street news agency

" Her face had been hacked off and her ears were missing "

received the following letter: "Dear Boss, I keep on hearing that the police have caught me. But they won't fix me yet. I am down on certain types of women and I won't stop ripping them until I do get buckled. Grand job that last job was. I gave the lady no time to squeal. I love my work and I want to start again. You will soon hear from me with my funny little game. I saved some of the proper stuff in a little ginger beer bottle after my last job to write with but it went thick like glue and I can't use it. Red ink is fit enough, I hope. Ha, ha. Next time I shall clip the ears off and send them to the police, just for jolly."

Victim number three was 44-year-old Elizabeth "Long Liz" Stride. Her body was found in Berner Street, Whitechapel, on September 30. Police believe the killer had been disturbed in his grisly work because, although the victim's throat had been cut, her body was otherwise untouched.

The Ripper's fourth victim was discovered on the same day, not far away in Mitre Square. This time the Ripper achieved the bestial satisfaction he seemed to crave. Catherine Eddowes, a drunkard

in her forties who had just been released from police cells after causing an affray, was disemboweled and her intestines draped across her right shoulder. Her face had been hacked off and her ears were missing. A trail of blood led from Catherine's corpse to a torn part of her apron. On a nearby wall was scrawled in chalk: "The Jewes

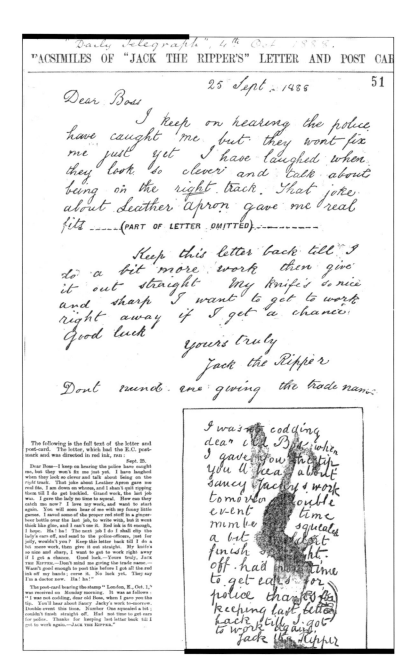

A series of letters starting "Dear Boss" were sent to a Fleet Street news agency claiming to be from "Jack the Ripper."

(sic) are not men to be blamed for nothing." The Ripper's final victim was Mary Kelly, younger than her predecessors at just 25 years of age. Mary, also a prostitute, had accosted a man on the night of November 9. He was described as being tall, dark, with a moustache and a deerstalker hat. Poor Mary was butchered not in the street but in her own tiny apartment, where the Ripper spent hours grotesquely mutilating her. The following morning her landlord knocked on her door to demand his rent. After discovering her remains, he told police: "I shall be haunted by this sight for the rest of my life."

Terror had by now gripped the East End. Vigilante groups were formed and a host of accusations were bandied about. Was the Ripper a mad surgeon? Was he a Jewish ritual slaughter-man, as the writing on the wall seemed to suggest? Was he a policeman on his nightly rounds?

One suspect was revealed by Inspector Robert Sagar, who played a leading part in the Ripper investigation. Shortly before his death in 1924, Sagar said, "We had good reason to suspect a man who lived in Butcher's Row, Aldgate. We watched him carefully. There was no doubt this man was insane. After a time his friends thought it was advisable to have him removed to a private asylum. Once he was removed, there were no more Ripper atrocities."

After the slaying of poor Mary, London held its

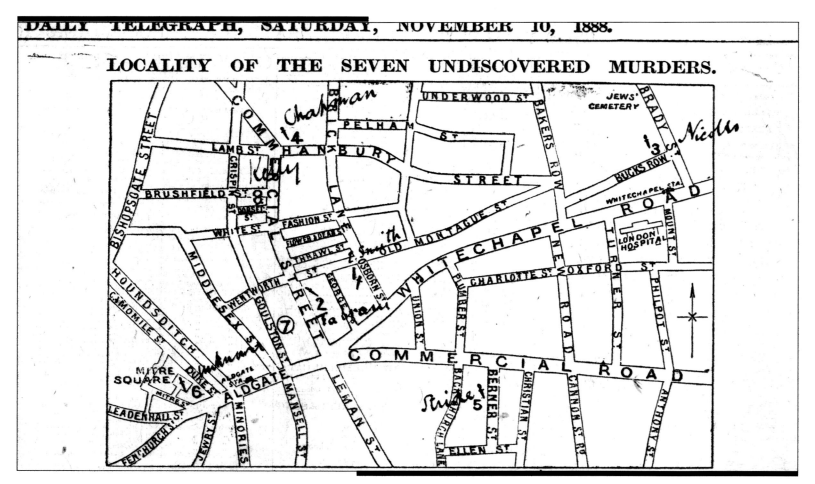

DAILY TELEGRAPH, SATURDAY, NOVEMBER 10, 1888.

LOCALITY OF THE SEVEN UNDISCOVERED MURDERS.

The Jack the Ripper murders were reported in detail in the newspapers at the time. This map pinpoints the location of victims.

POLICE NOTICE.

TO THE OCCUPIER.

On the mornings of Friday, 31st August, Saturday 8th, and Sunday, 30th September, 1888, Women were murdered in or near Whitechapel, supposed by some one residing in the immediate neighbourhood. Should you know of any person to whom suspicion is attached, you are earnestly requested to communicate at once with the nearest Police Station.

Metropolitan Police Office.
30th September, 1888.

Printed by M. Corpodale & Co. Limited, "The Armoury," Southwark.

As part of the police inquiries, this notice was published and distributed on September 30, 1888.

- - - - - - - - - - - - - - -

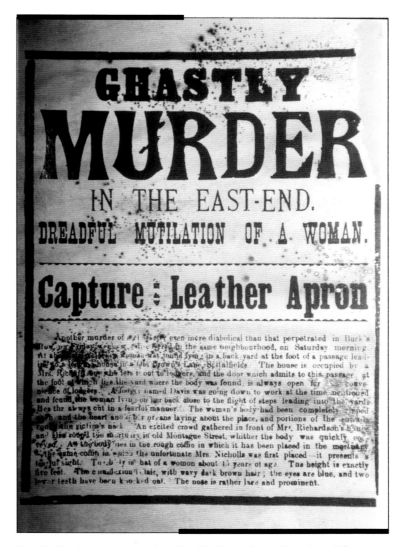

The *Daily Express* reports the finding of another horribly mutilated body in the East End.

- - - - - - - - - - - - - - -

breath. The populace awaited news of another horrible murder. But it never came. The killings had ended as suddenly as they had begun. The Ripper fever died down—for half a century. Then, for some reason, fascination with the case slowly began to grow again. The pursuit of the Ripper's identity became a fresh fascination for modern-day criminologists. Books, articles, and television programs continue to speculate about the true identity of Jack the Ripper—and come up with a bewildering array of solutions. The suspect favored by several authors of Ripper investigations is Montagu (sometimes also spelled Montague) John Druitt. In their book *The Ripper Legacy*, authors Martin Howells and Keith Skinner say that Druitt, an impoverished barrister, had been trained in medical skills as a young man. He was unstable and his family had a history of mental illness. His body was found floating in the Thames a few weeks after the murder of Mary Kelly.

Richard Gordon, famous for his *Doctor In The House* series of comic novels, was an anaesthetist before turning to writing. In 1980 he retraced Jack's steps through the East End and observed: "The victims died by having their throats cut. The vein in the neck is only three or four inches from the heart and, given that the victim is apprehensive, the heart would be pumping at enormous pressure. It always does when you're frightened. That meant the villain chloroformed his victims first, because that slows down the heartbeat." For this reason, said Richard Gordon, the Ripper was not only a doctor but an anaesthetist like himself.

The most original theory, however, came from author William Stewart who suggested that Jack was really Jill the Ripper, a midwife and abortionist who went mad after serving a jail sentence for prostitution. Other names put forward include William Bury, hanged for murdering his prostitute wife five months after the last Ripper attack, and Aaron Kosminski, a Polish Jewish hairdresser from Whitechapel who hated prostitutes and was committed to an asylum in 1890.

❛❛The vein in the neck is only three or four inches from the heart and, given that the victim is apprehensive, the heart would be pumping at enormous pressure. It always does when you're frightened❜❜

Almost unbelievably, another suspect was a member of the British Royal Family. The finger of suspicion fell on Queen Victoria's grandson, Prince Eddy—or, to give him his full title, Albert Victor Christian Edward, Duke of Clarence and Avondale, heir to the throne and great-uncle of the present Queen. Certainly, the talk at the time was that the prince was a bisexual who had turned criminally insane after contracting venereal diseases. According to renowned forensic psychiatrist Dr. Harold Abrahamsen in his book *Murder And Madness: The Secret Life Of Jack The Ripper*, the prince was supposedly aided and abetted in his dark deeds by his mentor, tutor, and woman-

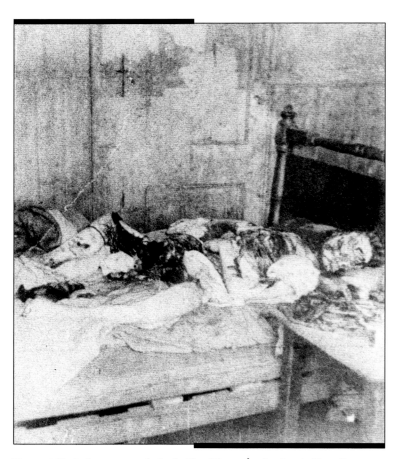

The mutilated corpse of Jack the Ripper's last victim, Mary Kelly, as police found her in Miller's Court.

hating homosexual lover James Stephen. Prince Edward died in 1892 of brain damage brought on by syphilis, although the official announcement described his fatal ailment as pneumonia.

Excitement among Ripper hunters was rekindled in 1993 when a diary was said to have been discovered under floorboards of a house in Liverpool, proving that wealthy cotton broker James Maybrick was the killer. The discovery was enough to fire up one publishing house but the claims and the "Ripper Diary" itself were derided by experts.

The principal expert contracted by one newspaper to disprove the diary's authenticity was author Melvin Harris, who himself wrote one of the best-researched books on the subject. In *The True Face Of Jack The Ripper*, Harris named as his prime suspect Robert D'Onston Stephenson, born April 20, 1841, the son of a wealthy Hull mill owner. As a youth, Stephenson became obsessed with witchcraft and, in his own words, the "black arts." He embarked on a tour of Europe, ending up in southern Italy, where in 1860 he joined Garibaldi's uprising as a medical officer. There he learned a further art: crude field surgery. He reveled in the adventure and particularly the butchery.

Once the war was over, Stephenson sailed to West Africa where, he boasted later, he killed a black woman in cold blood because he believed she was a witch doctor. Returning to Hull in 1863, he took a post as a customs officer but began consorting with prostitutes. He contracted venereal disease and was banished from home. He left in disgrace for London where, to spite his parents, he married their illiterate serving girl and changed his first name to Roslyn.

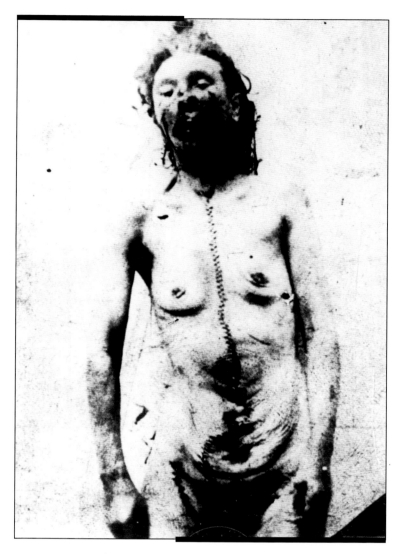

Jack the Ripper's victims were horrifically mutilated and their internal organs removed.

Author Melvin Harris believes that Mrs. D'Onston Stephenson, who disappeared in 1887, was butchered by her husband. From wife murder, it was but a short step to the killing of the five Whitechapel prostitutes the following year. The devious Stephenson then became a self-professed expert on the crimes and persuaded the Pall Mall magazine to publish his articles, which examined the slayings with a strange authority and detail. In his later years, Stephenson experienced a religious conversion and, seemingly by way of atonement,

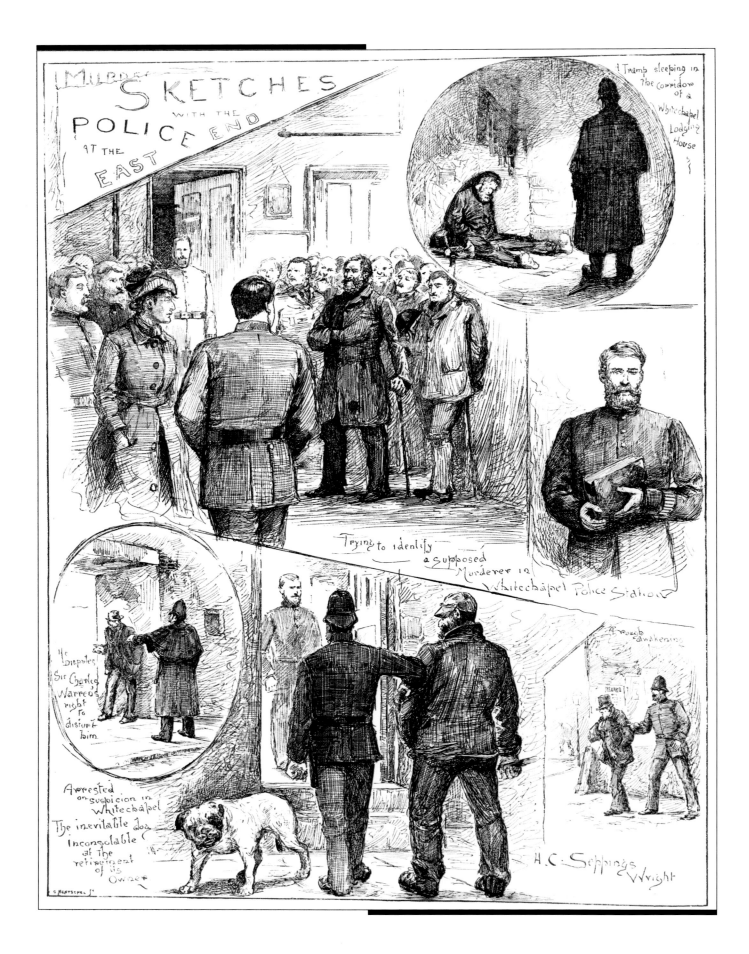

wrote a tortuous study of the earliest translations of the Gospels. He completed his book in 1904 and thereafter vanished without trace. No death certificate for him has ever been found—leaving yet another mystery for the modern-day "detectives" seeking the true identity of Jack the Ripper.

In 1996, a television documentary put forward the theory that the Ripper was an American, a New York doctor named Tumblety, who was so incensed when he discovered that his wife was a prostitute that he embarked on a deranged vendetta against "fallen" women. Tumblety visited London several times to raise funds for the Irish republican cause, one such visit coinciding with the Ripper attacks. He fled the city soon after the last killing, while awaiting trial for indecently assaulting four men. On his death in 1903, a collection of preserved female reproductive organs were found among his possessions.

In December 2002, another, surprising name was put forward. Crime writer Patricia Cornwell declared that the culprit was Walter Sickert, the Impressionist artist whose works are displayed in museums and galleries around the world. The author, who has made millions from her fictional crime stories, investigated Sickert because he had been previously put forward as a suspect. She studied his paintings which she said reflected the murder scenes, and his letters which she says were written on the same stationery as the Ripper's. She also claimed there was a DNA link between the two. Interviewed about her book *Portrait of a Killer: Jack the Ripper*, Miss Cornwell said: "Sickert led a horrifying double life, painting by day and killing by night. I am 100 per cent certain that this case is now closed." In that belief, Miss Cornwell was mistaken, for the case still remains very much open.

Even today, with most of the crumbling old workers' homes gone, the taverns replaced with office blocks, and the gas lamps ripped out in favor of electric ones, the East End has become a lurid shrine for Ripper enthusiasts. Tourists are escorted on guided tours of the streets where the maniacal Jack dispensed with his victims, and sip beer afterward in a pub named after him. Books are still being churned out and TV documentaries posing the same questions about just who was Jack the Ripper are still being made. More than a century later no one has come up with the definitive answer.

> **" "Tourists are escorted on guided tours of the streets where the maniacal Jack dispensed with his victims, and sip beer afterward in a pub named after him " "**

Circulations of lurid London news-sheets soared as the capital walked in fear of Jack the Ripper.

JACK THE STRIPPER

There are close parallels between the slayings of Jack the Ripper and of another killer whose exploits three quarters of a century later gave rise to a similar nickname.

The scalpel-wielding Ripper may well have been the first notorious murderer whom we would now brand as a serial killer but his near-namesake Jack the Stripper, although less well known, was equally adept at bringing terror to the streets of London. They both targeted prostitutes. They got their sexual kicks out of the act of killing, which in both cases was peculiarly horrific. Thirdly, neither was ever caught. Indeed, the Scotland Yard files remain open on both murderers to this day.

The Stripper killings began in 1964, 76 years after the horrors unleashed by the Ripper in the East End. All were concentrated within a few miles of each other in the West London suburbs and, though it remains unclear exactly how many were the work of the same man, police suspect the tally was six or more. There is doubt over the numbers because the first possible victims did not entirely fit the killer's modus operandi.

On June 17, 1959, the body of prostitute Elizabeth Figg was dragged out of the Thames. Many police believe she was the Stripper's first victim, although she had been manually strangled, a mode of death which does not precisely conform to the Stripper's usual method of dispatch. On November 8, 1963, the body of 22-year-old Gwyneth Rees was found in a shallow grave on the banks of the Thames. She had been sexually assaulted and was naked apart from one stocking. Again, there is suspicion but no proof that she was a victim of the Stripper.

A more certain victim of the mysterious killer was Hannah Tailford, who also appeared to have died from drowning after her body was recovered from the River Thames at Hammersmith, West London, on February 2, 1964. Hannah, aged 30,

FACT FILE.

Name: never identified, aka "Jack the Stripper" and the "Hammersmith Nudes Murderer"

Born: unknown but probably around 1920

Location of killings: London, England

Killed: at least five, possibly seven

Modus operandi: asphyxiation during sex

Justice: never caught; prime suspect committed suicide

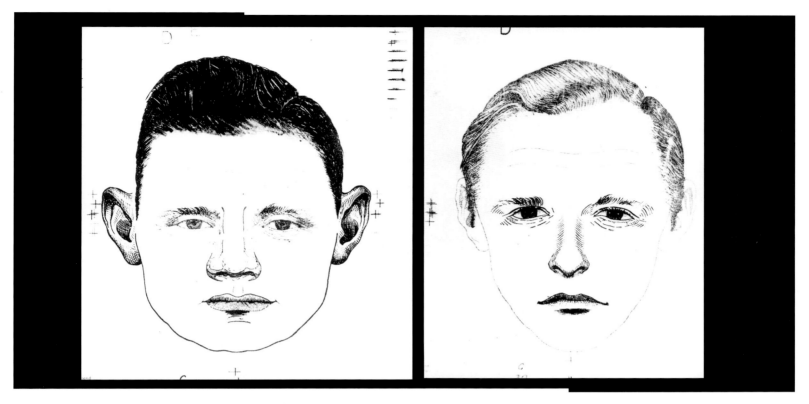

Police identikit of the two men who were the last to be seen
with Margaret McGowan at a Kensington car park.

who sometimes used the pseudonyms Ann Tailor,
Theresa Bell, or Hannah Lynch, had been clinical-
ly depressed, which initially led police to assumed
she had committed suicide. An inspection by a
pathologist soon put them right. She was naked
apart from her stockings, her panties had been
stuffed down her throat and her stomach contained remnants of a large undigested meal. In the
pathologist's experience, suicides did not first
indulge in feasts.

The recovery of another nude prostitute's body
from the Thames on April 8 began to sound alarm
bells at Scotland Yard. But there was no obvious
link between the girl, 26-year-old Irene Lockwood,
and the other possible victims. When a 24-year-
old man walked into a police station and admitted
killing Irene Lockwood, the case was also put down

as an isolated incident. A question mark still hangs
over it, however, for when the self-accuser was
brought to trial, he retracted his confession and
was acquitted for lack of evidence.

Since the oldest profession is also a dangerous
one, there seemed nothing particularly unusual
about a number of prostitutes being found dead in
London over a period of months. But police atti-
tudes hardened on the morning of April 24, 1964
when the naked body of 22-year-old Helene
Barthelemy was found lying amid rubbish at a
sports ground in Acton, West London. She too
was a prostitute but, unlike the other unfortunate
girls, her body did yield some forensic clues.
Helene had clearly been choked to death. Her skin
showed up microscopic traces of industrial paint
and there were heat marks on one side of the body
suggesting it had been stored close to machinery.
Perhaps the killer had kept the corpse in a garage
or warehouse to await disposal. There were

Detectives inspect a house at Hammersmith Grove during the investigations in 1964.

- - - - - - - - - - - - - -

other, sinister forensic discoveries. Four teeth had been knocked out of Barthelemy's mouth with considerable force, one of which had remained lodged in her throat. And one of her last acts on earth had been to perform fellatio on a man; traces of sperm were recovered from the back of her mouth.

Over the following months, the clues from this woman's death surfaced again in the murders of three more prostitutes. The next victim was found early on the morning of July 14, her nude body bizarrely arranged on a garage forecourt with legs crossed and chest slumped forward. Mary Fleming, from Notting Hill, had been asphyxiated; in other words, her killer had not put his hands around her neck to choke her but had stopped her air supply by other means. At a press conference, a Scotland Yard spokesman likened it to the effect of pushing a small apple into the back of the throat. The policeman was being coy—the Stripper actually murdered his victims during fellatio by thrusting his penis into their mouths while gripping their hair to prevent escape.

On November 25, the body of prostitute Margaret McGowan, missing for almost a month, turned up on a rubbish dump in fashionable Kensington. Her death attracted exceptional media interest because of her links with high-class procurers in the London sex market. Through them, the press uncovered a connection with characters on the edge of the John Profumo–Christine Keeler sex scandal that had almost brought down the British government. Margaret had also been a friend of both Helene Barthelemy and Mary Fleming. Again there were the tell-tale clues: asphyxia, a dislodged tooth, sperm in the throat, and flecks of paint on the skin.

The Stripper's last victim was discovered on February 16, 1965, in bushes alongside an industrial estate in Acton. This time the body had been kept so close to heat that it was almost mummified. Forensic examination confirmed that Bridget "Bridie" O'Hara had lost several teeth, had sperm in her throat, and metallic paint on her skin. She bore all the terrible trademarks of the murderer.

As public hysteria mounted, the hunt for the killer now known as "Jack the Stripper" went into overdrive. The man in charge, Chief Superintendent John Du Rose, a policeman with an enviable reputation for cracking major murder mysteries, soon got his first big break. Scientific tests showed that the body of Bridget O'Hara had been dumped almost on the killer's doorstep. The Heron Trading Estate where it was found contained a spray-paint shop from which airborne flecks of paint were carried onto a transformer. This, the police believed, could well have been the source of heat that had dried her body. Du Rose was certain the killer was based on the estate and

"The body had been kept so close to heat that it was almost mummified"

his detectives questioned all 7,000 workers, paying particular attention to night staff because the Stripper needed the cover of darkness to dump the bodies.

Yet still there was no breakthrough. Du Rose then decided on a clever but somewhat devious ploy to try to flush out the killer. He called a press conference at which he announced that the hunt had been narrowed to 20 suspects. Later he said the number had been halved. Finally he bluffed his way through a statement that only three names were left in the frame. The psychological pressure on the murderer worked—O'Hara's was the last killing in the series.

In March 1965, a month after the O'Hara murder, a West London man gassed himself with the exhaust from his own van, leaving a note saying: "I cannot stand the strain any longer." There was nothing to connect the suicide of this quiet family man in his mid-forties to any of the murders and it went unnoticed by the Stripper squad. But as time passed and they realized that the killer had not struck again, they checked on all the suicides of men in the area since the last murder. To their shock, they discovered that this particular suicide victim had been a night security guard whose patrol had regularly taken him onto the Heron Trading Estate at Acton. His family were interviewed and an intensive search made of his home. No evidence was ever discovered that he was the notorious Jack the Stripper but, since the peculiar fashion of his killings was not repeated, police

Police discovered a woman's body in the Thames at
Chiswick, London, in 1964, who was suspected to be one
of Jack the Stripper's victims.

- - - - - - - - - - -

drew their own conclusions. Two months after the
suicide, John Du Rose began scaling down the
Stripper murder investigation. The following year,
his squad was disbanded altogether. Scotland Yard
never publicly named the man who had committed
suicide but detectives privately confirmed their
certainty that he had been the killer.

In his memoirs, *Murder Was My Business*, Du
Rose clearly affirmed that the suicide victim had
been his prime suspect, saying that "the man I

wanted to arrest took his own life." But he added:
"Because he was never arrested or stood trial, he
must be considered innocent— and will therefore
never be named." Du Rose also gave a fascinating
insight into the mind of a serial killer. He said that
the first of the Stripper's killings may have been an
accident. By choking the prostitute with his penis
during a frenzied orgasm, it could have been
argued that he was guilty only of manslaughter.
But Du Rose added: "When he continued to
indulge in his particular perversion, well knowing
that the girls concerned would die, he must have
recognized that he was fulfilling himself as a
murderer."

HELENE JEGADO

The true nature of serial killer Helene Jegado was not suspected until the French peasant girl entered a convent.

Previously employed as a domestic servant, she took holy orders when she was in her early twenties. She was expelled from her first convent for stealing and from her second when fellow nuns mysteriously fell sick from her ministrations. Unfortunately, no official report was made of these incidents.

Helene Jegado was born to illiterate peasants and orphaned in childhood. Taken into domestic service, she worked all over northern France, principally for members of the clergy. But every job she took provided new temptations. She was a kleptomaniac who covered up her petty thieving by the simple expedient of poisoning potential witnesses against her. That is what happened when she became a nun but it is very likely that she had already practiced her black arts on her former employers.

When she was cast out of her second convent in 1833, Helene Jegado offered herself for employment as a cook and in the next decade murdered at least 23 people. Her victims included her masters, mistresses, their relatives, her fellow servants, as well as her own sister. She would mix arsenic with their food then, upon their agonizing deaths, would go into convincing mourning. "Wherever I go, people die," was her constant lament as she moved from job to job.

In 1849, while working as cook for a family in Rennes, Jegado was caught stealing and was asked to find another position. Before packing her bags and leaving, she poisoned the entire household, although on this occasion no one died. She got a job elsewhere in the city working for a university professor but before long one of his servants had died mysteriously. When in July 1851 another young servant girl expired, Professor Theodore Biddard's medical knowledge raised his suspicions and caused an autopsy to be ordered. Arsenic was found in the victim's body and Jegado was arrested.

Hauled before a magistrate, Jegado gave the game away by protesting her innocence before details of the murder had even been put to her. Initially accused of 17 killings, including her sister's, the poisoner was eventually brought to court on only three charges of murder and three of attempted murder. However, the true total of her victims was believed to have been nearer 60. Found guilty in December 1851, she was led to the guillotine one wintry morning.

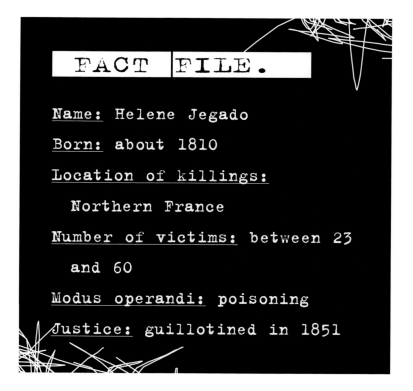

FACT FILE.

Name: Helene Jegado

Born: about 1810

Location of killings: Northern France

Number of victims: between 23 and 60

Modus operandi: poisoning

Justice: guillotined in 1851

PATRICK KEARNEY

On July 13, 1977, two men walked into a Californian police station, pointed to a wanted poster showing a pair of murderers and announced: "We're them!"

The couple were Wayne Kearney, aged 37, and his best friend David Hill, 34, and the confession they made that day ended the hunt for California's "Trash Bag Killer." The case against Hill was eventually dropped for lack of evidence but Kearney was firmly identified as the murderer who had left bodies galore in plastic garbage bags on roadsides between Los Angeles and San Diego.

Kearney did not look like the stereotypical serial killer—if there is such a thing. In his ordinary life, he was an electronics engineer for Los Angeles

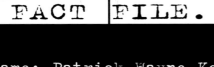

FACT FILE.

Name: Patrick Wayne Kearney,
aka the "Trash Bag Killer"

Born: 1940

Location of killings: Los
Angeles; California, USA

Killed: 32 plus

Modus operandi: shooting

Justice: sentenced to life
sentences in 1977

Hughes Aircraft Co., a man who shyly hid behind thin-rimmed spectacles and who liked to carry out his work projects without any small talk with colleagues. But by the time he and Hill had handed themselves in to police that day at Redondo Beach, Kearney was already linked with the murders of at least 32 men.

Kearney and Hill had been roommates for 15 years, forging a gay friendship that festered with a fascination for violence. Their first victim, as far as police were aware, was 21-year-old Albert Rivera whose body was found in April 1975. Next was 24-year-old Arturo Marquez, followed by many more. All the victims were drifters, young men who frequented the homosexual cruising areas and seedy bars of Los Angeles. No one would report them missing. All came to a similar end, stripped naked, shot in the head with a small-caliber gun, dismembered, and their body parts packaged in plastic garbage bags and left by the roadside.

Police realized that the killings, from 1975 to 1977, seemed to happen in batches, with several gay men being murdered within a few days, followed by a short break. But despite trawling homosexual haunts, they gleaned little from a twilight society with a deep-rooted distrust of police. There was the odd witness willing to talk, however, and the disappearance of the men seemed inextricably linked to the company of two particular, mysterious prowlers. They were, of course, Kearney and Hill.

The duo's last known victim was 17-year-old John Le May who had waved cheerily to his parents as he left his home to meet an acquaintance he named only as Dave. Five days later, on March 18, 1977, Le May's body, hacked to pieces, was found beside a highway south of Corona. Police questioned Le May's gay friends, one of whom was able to identify "Dave" as David Hill and supply an address for him and his roommate, Kearney.

When police raided their shabby home close to Redondo Beach, they found a hacksaw smeared with blood. Close examination throughout the house revealed hair and carpet samples matching those found on tape used to bind their victims. By this time, however, Kearney and Hill had realized that police were closing in on them and had fled to Mexico. It was only the persuasion of family members that made them return to California and turn themselves in.

To the great disappointment of investigating officers, the charges against David Hill were dropped through lack of evidence. Kearney assumed full responsibility for the murders, saying that killing "excited me and gave me a feeling of dominance." Kearney was charged with the murder of three men: Albert Rivera, Arturo Marquez, and John Le May whose blood was on the hack-

Patrick Kearney arriving at the Criminal Courts building in Los Angeles. He pleaded guilty to 18 murders of young boys and men to avoid the death penalty.

saw blade. At his trial on December 21, 1977, he pleaded guilty and was sentenced to life by Superior Court Judge John Hews.

That was not the end of the case, however. Police wanted more confessions from Kearney and, in return for full details of his other killings, he was spared the death penalty. He signed confessions to 28 murders in total. He was brought back into court on February 21, 1978, to plead guilty before Judge Dickran Tevrizzian Jr. to the murders of 18 boys and young men and to provide information relating to a further 11 gay victims, bringing the probable total of his victims to 32. They included two children, aged five and eight. Kearney was incarcerated in California's Calipatria State Prison where he became an enthusiastic writer of letters to his many pen pals.

EDMUND KEMPER

Edmund Kemper was born on December 18, 1949, and like many criminals was the product of a stormy marriage.

But though his mother and father did lavish some attention on him, the friendless Kemper was far from a normal child. It was after his parents finally separated when he was nine that Kemper practiced the savage killings he would carry out in later life. He tortured and killed animals and lost himself in fantasies that combined sex and violence. On one occasion, Edmund buried his family's pet cat alive in the garden of his home in North Fork, California, then dug up the body, cut off the head and took it to his bedroom. Decapitation was to become the adult Kemper's trademark.

Kemper committed his first murder when he was just 15 years of age. It was August 27, 1964, and he had just returned from a visit to his mother, arriving back at the home of his grandmother, Maude Kemper, with whom he lived most of the time. Finally getting his hands on the gun Maude had always managed to keep away from him, Kemper shot her three times. When his grandfather returned home, he too was shot in the back of the head.

A confused Kemper then called his mother, saying: "There has been an accident. Grandma's dead. So is Grandpa." Kemper's mother told him to give himself up. After telling police he had often thought about killing his grandmother and only shot his grandfather as an act of mercy, Kemper was diagnosed as paranoid and psychotic and was committed to Atascadero State Hospital. He had not even reached his sixteenth birthday.

Sending Kemper to such a place might have been the worst thing the doctors could have done. There he listened as inmates, mostly rapists, talked about their crimes and fantasies. Kemper filed away useful information—mainly about how not to get caught. While putting on a good act at having "found God," he was really preparing himself for a future filled with bloodlust and unnatural sexual acts.

FACT FILE.

Name: Edmund Emil Kemper, aka "Co-Ed Killer," "Genius Giant," and "Headhunter"

Born: December 18, 1949

Location of killings: Los Angeles and central California, USA

Number of victims: ten

Modus operandi: strangulation, stabbing, decapitation

Justice: life imprisonment

Kemper was released in 1969 and went back to school at a community college near Atascadero. It was here that he decided he wanted to become a policeman. It was also the time that Kemper was to harbor yet another grudge against society when his height, 6ft 8in, went against him and he was told he was too tall to join the police force. So when he was returned to his mother against the recommendation of doctors at his former prison, the seeds were already sown for further murders.

Kemper's mother had already married again and then divorced and was working as an administrative assistant at the University of California. To her colleagues she was competent and pleasant. To her son, she was a relentless nag who accused him of going soft after the father he adored had left them.

Kemper still held a fascination with police work and often escaped his mother by going to the Jury Room, a local bar frequented by off-duty police officers. He enjoyed discussions about guns that the officers were happy to involve him in. Treating them with great respect, Kemper became a regular member of the group and earned himself the nickname "Big Ed."

Kemper finally found work as a laborer with the Highways Division. This enabled him to escape his mother's sharp tongue and move into an apartment with a friend. He bought a car which, with its radio transmitter and large whip aerial, looked like an unmarked police vehicle. It was in this that Kemper gave lifts to girl hitchhikers. Unknown to the girls, this was all a rehearsal for Kemper. He was learning how to win people's trust and already he was fantasizing about what it would be like to kill a young woman.

To move closer to his goal, Kemper customized

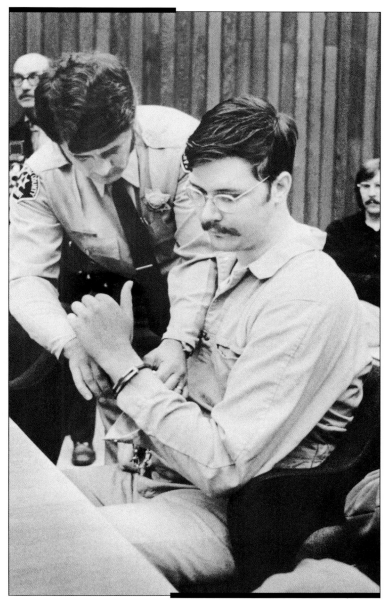

An officer removes manacles from Edmund Kemper in court. The jury took five-and-a-half hours to reach a verdict of guilty for eight counts of murder.

his car. He fixed the passenger door so it could not be opened from the inside and stored plastic bags, knives, and guns in the boot. But still he bided his time, regularly giving girls lifts but letting them leave his car unharmed. It is believed Kemper carried as many as 150 girls in his car until May 7, 1972, when he decided he was ready to kill.

Mary Ann Pesce and Anita Luchese were students at Fresno State College and were hitchhiking to Stanford University after a couple of days in Berkeley. They never reached their destination and although their families filed missing persons' reports, police assumed the girls had joined the hundreds of runaways in the area whom they dealt with every year. In fact, Mary Ann and Anita were the first victims of Kemper's killing spree. First he forced Anita into the boot of his car while he put a plastic bag over Mary Ann's head before strangling and stabbing her and then slashing her throat. Anita was then stabbed to death. Unsure what to do with the bodies, Kemper drove around for several hours before taking them to his home. There he undressed Mary Ann and cut her into pieces. He cut the heads off both girls.

Kemper's next victim was Aiko Koo, a 15-year-old dancer of Korean descent, who made the mistake of thumbing a lift to her dance class on September 14, 1972. Although quickly realizing Kemper intended to harm her, the dance student could not save herself. Kemper taped her mouth and suffocated her before raping her. He then drove to a local bar for a few beers with Aiko's body still in the boot of his car. Later that night, Kemper

> **He forced Anita into the boot of his car while he put a plastic bag over Mary Ann's head before strangling and stabbing her and then slashing her throat**

took the body back to his apartment and decapitated it. The hands were also cut off.

Even when he moved back home with his mother, Kemper could not give up his killing habits. He picked up Cindy Schall on January 8, 1973. After driving her into the hills near Watsonville, he forced her into the car boot and shot her with a gun he had purchased that day. Then he drove the body back to his mother's home, had sex with it and again cut off the head which he buried in the backyard. He later threw various body parts off a cliff.

After a furious row with his mother on February 5 that same year, Kemper stormed out of the apartment and picked up Rosalind Thorpe and then Alice Lui. This time Kemper did not even drive to a secluded spot to carry out the murders. Instead, he calmly shot Rosalind as they drove along and then turned the gun on Alice who was sitting in the back seat. Both bodies were bundled into the boot and decapitated—but only after Kemper had stopped to buy petrol. Alice's headless body was dragged inside his mother's apartment where he abused it. Knowing it would help him avoid capture, Kemper removed the bullets from both heads, just as he had done with his previous victims. He then drove around the area disposing of various body parts.

Incredibly, throughout his depraved killing spree, Kemper was seen regularly by psychiatrists who felt he was adapting well to the outside world.

- – – – – – – – – – – – – –

Edmund Kemper towered above police officers as he was escorted into court. At one time he wanted to join the police, but he was rejected, being told he was too tall.

His mother was unaware of his depraved activities. Neither could she have guessed she would be the next victim of the man now dubbed the "Co-Ed Killer." That Easter Sunday, about a month after his last killings, Kemper struck his mother on the head with a hammer as she lay asleep in bed. Then he slashed her throat and, as a final gesture to acknowledge her constant nagging, he removed her larynx and threw it into the waste disposal unit. He later told police a bit of the larynx flew out, adding: "Even when she was dead, she was still bitching at me. I couldn't get her to shut up."

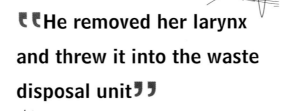

"He removed her larynx and threw it into the waste disposal unit"

Kemper hid his mother's body in a cupboard and cleaned the house. He then came to a strange decision. He decided that if another body was found in the house, he would not automatically be the prime suspect. So he called Sally Hallet, a friend of his mother's and invited her for dinner. When Sally arrived, Kemper strangled her with the scarf he had taken from Aiko Koo and stripped her naked. Some time later, Kemper sexually assaulted the body.

The next morning, Kemper left the apartment in Sally's car that he dropped off at a garage before renting another vehicle. He drove for 18 hours and, even though he was stopped by police for speeding, he remained so calm no one could have guessed what heinous crimes he was guilty of. In Pueblo, Colorado, Kemper rang his friends at Santa Cruz Police Department and started to make his shocking confession. It took several phone calls before anyone believed he was not a crank confessing to crimes he did not commit.

Brought back to his hometown, Kemper led police to the various places he had deposited his victims' body parts. These included the spot where he had buried Mary Anne Pesce's head. Neither Anita Luchesa's head nor body were ever found. Hardened police officers were sickened when they saw the evidence of Kemper's murders and they recoiled in horror when Kemper said he killed his victims simply so he could have them all to himself.

When his case came to court on October 25, 1973, Kemper pleaded insanity but prosecution witness Dr. Joel Fort, who had monitored him since the slaughter of his grandparents, said the killer was not a paranoid schizophrenic but an attention seeker obsessed with sex and violence. Dr. Fort said there was no question that Kemper—now dubbed "Genius Giant" in the press because of his clever cover-ups of the killings and exceptional IQ—would kill again if allowed to go free.

During the three-week trial, no one, including Kemper's family and friends, could convince the jury that he was insane. After being out for five hours, the jury found Kemper guilty of first-degree murder on all eight counts and he was sentenced to life imprisonment at Folsom maximum-security jail. This was despite his pleas to be tortured to death.

RANDY KRAFT

The murderous rampage of Randy Kraft occurred in California during the 1970s and 1980s, and although it coincided with an epidemic of slayings in that state, Kraft's case stands out.

His contemporaries included Patrick Kearney, the "Trash Bag Killer," Lawrence "Pliers" Bittaker, Douglas "Sunset Strip Slayer" Clark, and William Bonin, also nicknamed the "Freeway Killer." Indeed, Kraft ended up on San Quentin's death row with the last three. Together they were responsible for about 100 murders—with Kraft accounting for no fewer than 67 of them. What is also extraordinary about Kraft is the lengths to which he went to avoid justice: delaying his trial for five years, having it drag on for a record 13 months, and further prolonging his stay on death row by legal maneuvers.

Another reason why Kraft stands out from other serial killers is that he enjoyed a highly successful business career. A computer expert, he traveled the West Coast and elsewhere, sorting out companies' technology problems and earning himself a large salary which in 1980 amounted to over $50,000 a year. It was on these business journeys that Kraft, a homosexual, picked up partners and murdered them.

His first confirmed victim was Edward Moore, a 20-year-old Marine whose body was found near Seal Beach, California, in December 1972. He had been strangled and sexually assaulted. He had been spared sexual mutilation—a perversion that was increasingly to become Kraft's sickening trademark. Further murders attributed to Kraft included three in 1975, another in 1976, the

victim on this occasion being castrated, four in 1978, and two in 1980. In 1983, no fewer than three Marines were found strangled and mutilated. It was later established that some of his victims had been alive and conscious while Kraft hacked at their genitals.

In the early hours of May 14, 1983, two Orange

FACT FILE.

Name: Randy Steven Kraft, aka the "Scorecard Killer" and the "Freeway Killer"

Born: March 19, 1945

Location of killings: California, Oregon, Michigan, Ohio, New York, and Washington D.C., USA

Killed: convicted of 16, believed to have killed 67

Modus operandi: various, with mutilation

Justice: sentenced to death in 1989; delayed by appeals

Randy Kraft listening to testimony in a prelimary hearing at a court in California. It is believed he killed over 60 people.

County Highway Patrol officers stopped a car that was being driven erratically, suspecting the driver to be drunk. Rather than stay in the vehicle, as is normally the case, the driver got out of the car and walked toward the officers with a smile on his face. He gave his name as Randy Kraft and said he was a computer engineer on a business trip. Still suspicious, the officers walked him back to his vehicle, where they found a body in the passenger seat. Terry Gambrel, a 25-year-old Marine, had died either of strangulation or an overdose of drugs.

Also in the car was a briefcase containing a notebook cataloguing Kraft's sexual encounters and 47 photographs of young men, some naked, some dead. Among those pictured were victims whose deaths were on the police "unsolved" list. Hitchhikers Roger de Vaul and Geoffrey Nelson had

been found dead in February 1983, another hitchhiker Eric Church had been found dead in March 1983, and Marine Robert Loggins had been found in September 1980.

Shortly before his death, 19-year-old Loggins had been confined to barracks for drunkenness and his body, discovered near the El Torro military base, had a deadly level of alcohol and prescription drugs in the bloodstream. Consequently, the Marine's death had been logged at the time as accidental. Now police had in their possession a photograph of Loggins lying naked and apparently dead on a couch in Kraft's home. In a search of the house, in Huntington Beach, police found property and fibers that helped identify further victims: three from Oregon and one from Michigan, both in locations where Kraft visited in his work. It was suspected that he had also killed on business trips to New York, Washington, and Ohio.

Police now set about deciphering the entries in the notebook found in Kraft's car. It was apparently a "scorecard" showing that Kraft had killed both singly and sometimes with an unnamed partner. More than 20 on the death list remain a mystery to this day but others led to detectives to piece together the last hours of a number of confirmed victims.

Hitchhiker Michael O'Fallon, 17, was dumped near Interstate 5 near Salem, Oregon, in July 1980. Although he had overdosed on drugs and alcohol, his death had been caused by strangulation. Bound with his own shoelaces, he had also been tortured with a cord knotted round his scrotum. Another 17-year-old hitchhiker, Michael Cluck, 17, was dumped along the same highway near Goshen, Oregon, in April 1981. He had been beaten to death after being sodomized. Two victims retrieved from a ditch beside the Hollywood Freeway, Los Angeles, in July 1981 were identified as 13-year-old Raymond Davis and 16-year-old Robert Avila. The following month, 17-year-old Christopher Williams was found dead in the San Bernardino Mountains; he had been drugged and had then had paper stuffed up his nostrils to suffocate him.

In November 1982 the killer was back in Oregon, where the strangled body of Brian Whitcher, 26, was found near the I-5 outside Portland. The following month, Kraft was in Grand Rapids, Michigan, for a computer conference when he stopped at his hotel bar and struck up a conversation with cousins Dennis Alt and Chris Schoenborn. Their bodies were found together in Plainfield Township two days later, both drugged and strangled. Alt's trousers had been pulled down to expose his genitals. Schoenborn was completely nude, a ballpoint pen with the hotel logo on it stuck through his penis and into his bladder.

By the time the cousins' bodies were discovered, Kraft had returned to Oregon and had murdered again. The body of 19-year-old Lance Taggs was dumped close to the spot where Brian Whitcher had been found. He had been doped with Valium and had a sock forced down his throat until he choked to death. That same month another victim was discovered at the roadside near Hubbard, Oregon. Hitchhiker Anthony Silveira, 29, had been strangled, brutally sodomized, and left with a plastic toothbrush in his anus.

In January 1983, Kraft was in California, where one of the men later identified from his

> ❝ **Kraft didn't confess to any of the murders.** ❞

photographs, 21-year-old Eric Church, was found bludgeoned to death beside the 605 Freeway. Hitchhiker Mikael Laine, 24, was abducted near Ramona, Orange County, shortly afterward. And in February, two other victims, 18-year-old Geoffrey Nelson and 20-year-old Roger de Vaul, were found.

Kraft didn't confess to any of the murders. By playing a clever legal game, he managed to delay his trial for five years. When it eventually began in Orange County, it set further records for length (13 months) and cost ($10 million). Kraft was finally convicted of all 16 counts of murder in May 1989. It took a further four months of legal maneuvering before sentencing could be ordered and another three months before the jury formally recommended the death penalty on November 29.

He remained on death row raising a string of appeals and other litigations, all of which failed but all of which delayed his execution. One of his legal actions was to claim that the gas chamber violated the US Constitution's religious principles by forcing someone to "actively participate in his own killing." Another failed lawsuit was a $60 million libel action against author Dennis McDougal, claiming that a book he had written about Kraft besmirched his "good name" by unfairly portraying him as a "sick, twisted man" and thereby harmed his prospects for future employment! He took his libel action as far as California's Supreme Court before it was dismissed in June 1994. On August 11, 2000, that same court heard another in the long-running legal saga of Randy Kraft— upholding his original trial's sentence of death.

JOACHIM KROLL

Joachim Kroll's reign of terror as "the Ruhr Hunter" was brought to an end not by any great feat of German detective work but because (like the more notorious Dennis Nilsen a few years later) he blocked the drains with the body parts of his victims.

Police arrived at his apartment during routine inquiries into the disappearance of a small child. They had been told that a lavatory attendant had warned a neighbor not to use a particular toilet because it was "stuffed up with guts." It was in fact blocked with the remains of a four-year-old child.

When police searched Kroll's rooms in the

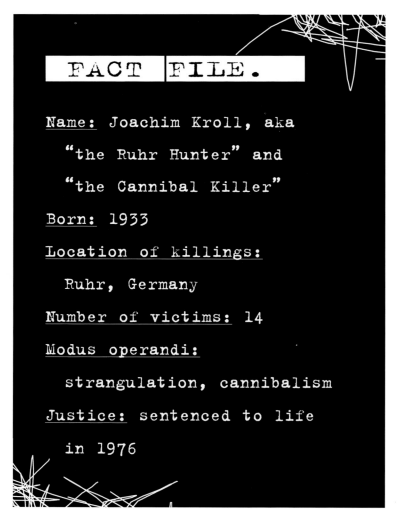

```
FACT FILE.

Name: Joachim Kroll, aka
  "the Ruhr Hunter" and
  "the Cannibal Killer"
Born: 1933
Location of killings:
  Ruhr, Germany
Number of victims: 14
Modus operandi:
  strangulation, cannibalism
Justice: sentenced to life
  in 1976
```

Duisberg suburb of Laar, they found pieces of flesh on plates in the refrigerator. On the stove was a stew of carrots, potatoes, and a tiny human hand. Plastic bags were also filled with the flesh of his victims. Knoll, aged 43, small and balding with tinted glasses, admitted killing at least 14 young women between 1955 and 1976. A simple-minded man, however, he told detectives that he had killed so many people that he could not remember all the details.

All Kroll's murders took place in the Ruhr area and the ages of his victims ranged from four to 19. Most had been raped and slices of flesh taken from their bodies. A clue to the cause of his sickening crimes was an interview in which he told police that as a young man he had been unable to have sex with a conscious woman. He said he had begun raping women at the age of 22. Having identified a victim, he would stalk her for days waiting for the right opportunity to pounce. He said the first girl he had killed had been a 19-year-old whom he had lured into a barn near the village of Walstedde and strangled in 1955. It was only four years and four victims later that he began cannibalizing the bodies. After raping and strangling a 16-year-old girl on the outskirts of Essen, he carved some slices from her buttocks with the aim of saving money on his weekly food bill.

Newspapers now labeled the Ruhr monster

"the Cannibal Killer" and Kroll began to live up to this notoriety. His next two victims were both 13-year-old girls from whose buttocks, thighs, and forearms he carved steaks for his dinner table.

Kroll's most pathetic young victims were little more than babes whose murders, ten years apart, indicate the long duration of the reign of terror that gripped the Ruhr. In December 1966, Kroll strangled five-year-old Ilona Harke in a park at Wuppertal, raping her and carving chunks of flesh from her buttocks and shoulders. In 1976, he abducted four-year-old Marion Ketter from a Duisberg street, took her to his apartment and cut up her body.

At this time, Kroll was working as a lavatory attendant in the block of apartments where he lived. When he told a neighbor not to use a top-floor toilet, the man asked why. The chilling response was: "Because it is blocked up with guts." A plumber was called and, to his horror, removed from the drains the internal organs of a child. They were the remains of Marion Ketter.

At first, police could not connect Kroll with any killings during the ten-year gap between the deaths of Ilona Harke and Marion Ketter. But Kroll himself helpfully filled them in with details of several slayings across the country. He had remained free because, although mentally retarded, he had developed an animal cunning that made him spread his crimes and cover his tracks. And he did not always cannibalize his victims.

In two cases, bungling cops had attributed the murders to completely innocent men. When a woman's naked body was found in a park in Marl, her boyfriend was thrown into the cells accused of strangling her after a lover's tiff. When a 13-year-

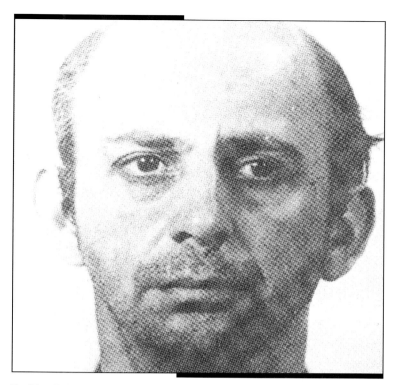

Kroll admitted killing at least 14 young women between 1955 and 1976. He told police he only ate victims who were young and tender.

old was found raped and strangled in Breitscheid, a villager was arrested because his blood type matched that of the unknown killer. The stigma of suspicion was only lifted from the young man's shoulders after Kroll was arrested and confessed six years later.

In his interrogation, Kroll tried to explain his sick habits by complaining to police about the price of meat in West German shops. He told them he only ate victims he considered to be young and tender—and when detectives checked through the files they found that the skinnier of the killer's victims had been left with their bodies intact. Kroll was officially declared a mental defective and was incarcerated for life in a secure hospital for the criminally insane.

PETER KÜRTEN

The blood lust and urge to kill could have been born within Peter Kürten.
Or they could have been planted by his childhood experiences.

One thing is certain, he deserved the chilling nick-name of the "Vampire of Düsseldorf." Born in 1883 into a family of 13 children, there was little chance of finding much moral guidance at home. His father was a bullying alcoholic who relished any opportunity to beat his 13 children. On occasions he would rape his wife in front of them and commit acts of incest with his daughters. It was one

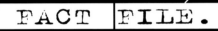

FACT FILE.

Name: Peter Kürten, aka
"Vampire of Düsseldorf"
Born: May 26, 1883
Location of killings:
Düsseldorf, Germany
Number of victims: confessed
to nine murders, seven
attempted murders, and 53
other attacks
Modus operandi: various but
preferred stabbing
Justice: guillotined July 2,
1932

such explosion of brutality that finally put the evil parent behind bars, albeit only for three years.

Peter Kürten was just nine years old when he was initiated into perversion and pain after a dog catcher showed him the "pleasures" of bestiality and of torturing animals. Kürten realized his great-est sexual kick was derived from spurting blood. The Vampire of Düsseldorf's reign of sadistic mur-der and sexual depravity had begun.

Kürten was ten years old when he committed his first murder. Playing with two other boys on a raft on the Rhine, he decided to drown one of them. He pushed the helpless youngster into the water, laughing at his cries for mercy. When the other boy dived in to save him, Kürten pushed him under the raft and held him below the surface. The true facts of this double murder were only to emerge many years and many killings later.

The teenage Peter Kürten obtained his sexual thrills from animals, stabbing them at the moment of orgasm. He then began an affair with a prosti-tute almost twice his age. A masochist, she took pleasure in the sexual abuse her new-found lover inflicted upon her. Kürten saw that the brutality with which he treated animals could be refocused on people. His apprenticeship as sadist and tor-turer was complete.

A few months after this relationship began, Kürten received a two-year prison sentence for stealing. He retreated further into his depraved fantasy world and even made sure he disobeyed prison regulations to get himself sentenced to solitary confinement, which he regarded as the perfect environment to conjure up his sick daydreams. Years later, these would be regaled to a hushed

> **When my desire for injuring people awoke, the love of setting fire to things awoke as well**

court: "I thought of myself causing accidents affecting thousands of people and invented a number of crazy fantasies such as smashing bridges and boring through bridge piers. Then I spun a number of fantasies with regard to bacilli which I might be able to introduce into the drinking water and so cause a great calamity. I imagined myself using schools or orphanages for the purpose, where I could carry out murders by giving away chocolate samples containing arsenic which I could have obtained through housebreaking. I derived the sort of pleasure from these visions that other people would get from thinking about a naked woman."

Out of jail, Kürten decided to wage a personal vendetta against what he saw as the "sick" society around him. He embarked on a series of arson attacks which, he later explained, coincided with his first urges to attack and kill. "When my desire for injuring people awoke, the love of setting fire to things awoke as well. The sight of the flames delighted me, but above all it was the excitement

A map of the vicinity where Peter Kürten disposed of 17 of his victims.

- - - - - - - - - - - -

of the attempts to extinguish the fire and the agitation of those who saw their property being destroyed."

His first attempted sex murder occurred in the woods at Grafenburg, Düsseldorf. Kürten beat a girl severely before and during intercourse, leaving her half dead. No body was ever found and the poor victim probably dragged herself home too terrified to report the attack.

On May 25, 1913, Düsseldorf was shaken by the foulest murder in living memory. Eight-year-old Christine Klein was found dead in bed with her throat cut. She had been raped. The truth behind

Peter Kürten was labeled the "Vampire of Düsseldorf," an apt title for one who relished the taste of blood since childhood.

Christine's death would remain hidden for 17 years. In the end, it was Kürten himself who recalled: "I had been stealing, specializing in public bars or inns where the owners lived on the floor above. In a room above an inn at Cologne-Mulheim, I discovered a child asleep. Her head was facing the window. I seized it with my left hand and strangled her for about a minute and a half. The child woke up and struggled but lost consciousness. I had a small but sharp pocket knife with me and I held the child's head and cut her throat. I heard the blood spurt and drip on the mat beside the bed."

Despite his love of killing, Kürten did not want to go to war to spill the blood of the Kaiser's enemies. His army career lasted barely a day before he deserted and he spent the entire conflict in jail for that and other petty criminal offences. On his release in 1921, he masqueraded as a good, hard-working German. He married a prostitute — threatening to kill her if she did not become his wife — and worked as a molder in a factory.

In 1925 the couple moved into the center of Düsseldorf and once more the lust for blood took hold. Kürten enjoyed regular flings with a string of mistresses. The women discovered they had met a man who loved sex and sadism in a way none had ever experienced before. They all kept his secret, perhaps too afraid to speak out.

They were right to be worried. Kürten's idea of a sexual kick was to stab his mistresses with a knife or scissors and achieve orgasm as he watched their blood pouring out. He switched his target to strangers, often drinking their blood. Once he sated himself by pressing his lips to the throat arteries of a victim; in another he drank from a wound on the side of a girl's head. He would even lick blood off their hands and claimed that during one frenzied attack he drank so much that he was sick.

By mid-summer of 1929, Düsseldorf police realized they were dealing with a major serial killer and sexual deviant. The man clearly acted like a mad vampire, but he was also clever. He made sure he didn't stick to the same districts and was careful to vary the style of his attacks to ensure he kept one step ahead of the detectives hunting him. The tactic worked well. Police files linked 46 crimes of deviancy, including four murders, but could not identify the culprit.

Düsseldorf was gripped by fear. Was there really a vampire in their midst? People had seen the evidence with their own eyes and were taking no chances. Children did not go off alone, women were escorted everywhere by their menfolk, and by nightfall most families preferred to stay indoors.

> **❝Kürten's idea of a sexual kick was to stab his mistresses with a knife or scissors and achieve orgasm as he watched their blood pouring out❞**

However, on August 23, 1929, hundreds of people did brave the night to attend one of the highlights of the city's year: the annual fair in the Flehe suburb. The bright lights, military music, wurst stalls, and beer kellers were hard to resist. Peter Kürten embarked upon a 12-hour orgy of sadism and killing.

Just before 10.30pm two foster sisters, Gertrude Hamacher, aged five, and Louise Lenzen, aged 14, took a last look at the fair and headed home through some nearby allotments. They did not see the shadowy figure who followed them. Then Louise heard a gentle voice behind her. "Oh dear," said the man, "I've forgotten to buy some cigarettes. Look, would you be very kind and go to one of the booths and get some for me? I'll look after the little girl." Louise took some money and ran back to the fairground. The stranger picked Gertrude up, bundled her behind the beanpoles and strangled her. He then slashed her throat with

A street in Düsseldorf during the 1930s when Peter Kürten was at large. During the evening the locals became a lot more vigilant, choosing to stay indoors and going nowhere alone.

a Bavarian knife. When Louise returned, she too was attacked. Her screams were lost in the music from the fairground. After strangling her, Kürten cut her throat.

The following morning, servant girl Gertrude Schulte, 26, met a man who offered to take her to the nearby Neuss fair. Foolishly she agreed. The man, who called himself Fritz Baumgart, suggested they take a stroll through the woods. A few minutes later he roughly pulled her toward him and tried to have sex. She screamed: "I'd rather die"— only to hear her gleeful attacker snap back: "Well, die then." With that, he began stabbing her in the neck and shoulders with a knife and gave

Kürten was ten when he committed his first double murder. He was playing on a raft on the Rhine, shown here in 1924, when he decided to drown and kill the two boys he was with.

- - - - - - - - - - -

one final thrust that snapped off the blade, leaving it embedded in her back. Despite her agony and appalling injuries, Gertrude was saved. A rambler heard her cries and called for the police and an ambulance. But Peter Kürten had vanished.

On another day, within the space of 30 minutes, Kürten attacked and wounded an 18-year-old girl, a 37-year-old woman, and a 30-year-old man. He exchanged his Bavarian dagger for a slimmer, sharper blade, then moved on to a cudgel that he employed to hammer two more servant girls to their deaths. The only thing that

linked the attacks was their unspeakable brutality. One five-year-old victim, Gertrude Albermann, was found to have 36 separate wounds on her little body.

Gertrude was the last of the Düsseldorf Vampire's murder victims, though the frenzied assaults continued in the city throughout the winter. Some wealthier people even left for country retreats until the monster was caught. Most had no such option. Girls like Maria Budlick, a 21-year-old maid, needed work. Maria knew there was a sex fiend at large. She never dreamed she would meet him so quickly.

On May 14, 1930, she stepped off a train at Düsseldorf central station, where a kindly-looking man offered to guide her to the nearest women's hostel. But as they entered the Volksgarten Park, Maria became anxious. She told the man she would not walk through the trees with him. During

> **Peter Kürten smiled back and invited her home for a glass of milk and a ham sandwich**

the ensuing argument another voice came out of the shadows: "Hello, is everything all right." Maria almost wept with relief. As her disgruntled escort left, she turned to the gentleman who had come to her aid. Peter Kürten smiled back and invited her home for a glass of milk and a ham sandwich.

Afterward, Kürten walked Maria to the hostel. In the Grafenburg Woods he grabbed her by the throat, forced her up against a tree, and tried to rape her. Slipping into unconsciousness, Maria felt Kürten release his grip. He hissed: "Do you remember where I live, in case you ever need my help again?" Maria managed to sob out a single word: "No." It probably saved her life. Kürten left and Maria managed to stagger back into the city.

Incredibly, she did not contact the police; instead she wrote a letter to a friend in her hometown of Cologne recounting her dreadful experience. For some reason it was undelivered and within a few days it found its way back to Cologne Post Office where it was opened so that it could be returned to its sender. An official read the

contents and realized the importance of Maria's ordeal. He contacted police and the following day a frightened Maria was gently questioned by a detective.

She had lied to Kürten about remembering his address and knew it was somewhere in Mettmannerstrasse. Under police escort, she returned there and correctly identified the house as number 71. While detectives waited outside, Maria asked the landlady if a "fair-haired, rather sedate man" lived there. The woman showed her to the fourth floor, unlocked a door, and Maria Budlick recognized the room instantly. Then, walking back downstairs, she met the man who haunted her every waking moment. Kürten looked

Frau Meiner was one of the victims of Peter Kürten. She is shown here in November 1929.

stunned but calmly continued to his room before leaving again unseen. Maria ran outside, calling to the police: "That's the man who assaulted me in the woods. His name is Peter Kürten."

Far from panicking, Kürten strolled to the restaurant where his wife worked and invited her to join him for a meal. As they ate, he calmly informed her: "I am the man sought by the police. I am the monster of Düsseldorf." Frau Kürten stopped eating but the killer continued—even finishing his wife's food.

On the morning of May 24, 1930, Frau Kürten told her dark secret to the local police, adding that she had arranged to meet Kürten at 3pm outside St. Rochus Church. Plain-clothes officers were waiting and on his arrival Kürten was surrounded by four of them pointing pistols. With a broad smile he assured the men: "There is no need to be afraid."

When Kürten's trial opened on April 13, 1931, thousands pushed and shoved around the converted drill hall of the Düsseldorf police headquarters to catch a glimpse of the fiend who had terrorized their streets. What they saw amazed them. This was no half-man half-beast. He looked a normal—a doctor perhaps, or civil servant. But Kürten had admitted 68 horrible crimes, including

> **❝I am the man sought by the police. I am the monster of Düsseldorf❞**

nine murders and seven attempted murders, and the court was taking no chances. Throughout his trial, he was kept under armed guard, surrounded by a shoulder-high wooden cage.

Kürten's account of his atrocities damned him more effectively than could any barrister. It was left to his counsel, Dr. Wehner, to persuade the jury his client was mad and so save him from the guillotine. It was a hopeless task, given that the nation's most distinguished psychiatrists had already pronounced him fully sane. Even Dr. Wehner appeared to give up the ghost when he addressed the court in these words: "Kürten is the king of sexual delinquents because he unites nearly all perversions in one person. He is a riddle to me. I cannot solve it. He killed men, women, children and animals, killed anything he found."

On July 1, 1932, Kürten walked to the guillotine in the yard of Klingelputz Prison. After his last meal, of veal, fried potatoes, and white wine, he spent a few final moments with the prison psychiatrist. "Tell me," Kürten asked the doctor casually, "after my head has been chopped off, will I still be able to hear, at least for a moment, the sound of my own blood gushing from the stump of my neck? That would be the pleasure to end all pleasures."

ILSHAT KUZIKOV

He was a vile monster who never really faced justice. But then Ilshat Kuzikov was mad.

He had to be, because he was one of the most sickening and notorious serial killers whose bloodlust was only truly satisfied with the taste of his victims' flesh. Kuzikov was a street sweeper in St. Petersburg, Russia, where he carried out the slaughter and eating of fellow humans for five years, between 1992 and 1997. Yet like most of his kind, he appeared perfectly normal. Although on the register at his local psychiatric hospital, neighbors in Ordzhonikidze Street recalled him as a cheery, likeable man who was always ready to help elderly locals with jobs around the house. Despite this, Kuzikov did not have many friends, preferring the company of his cat Dasha, to which he was totally devoted.

In November 1992 a piece of human torso turned up in the basement of a house close to Kuzikov's home. Police failed to link him to the crime, just as they failed to make the connection two years later when the severed head of a vagrant was found in a communal rubbish dump on Ordzhonikidze Street. But in August 1995, another severed head was found, this time belonging to one of Kuzikov's fellow psychiatric patients, Edik Vassilevski. Police realized the two men were friends and made 35-year-old Kuzikov their main suspect.

When they broke into his house, they found a fizzy-drink bottle full of blood, an old gherkin jar used to store dried skin and ears, and an aluminum cooking-pot containing Edik's last remains. He had been cut up for Russian-style kebabs. Kuzikov told police, "You know, I always wanted to be a surgeon, but it's better to be a cannibal. If you're a surgeon you have to put the body back together and you stop having any control over it. But a cannibal kills and then he can do what he wants with the body. After he kills, he owns it forever."

Psychologists said Kuzikov was a sexual sadist for whom cannibalism was the ultimate way of controlling his victims. His targets always seemed to be male acquaintances. Medical experts and police alike feared there were many more victims than the three they could positively link to Kuzikov. He was declared insane and incarcerated in an institution in 1997.

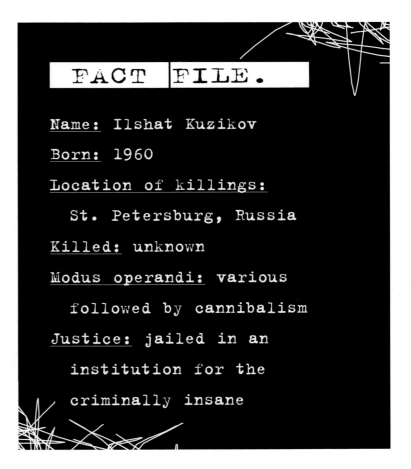

FACT FILE.

Name: Ilshat Kuzikov

Born: 1960

Location of killings:
St. Petersburg, Russia

Killed: unknown

Modus operandi: various
followed by cannibalism

Justice: jailed in an
institution for the
criminally insane

LEONARD LAKE AND CHARLES CHITAT NG

It was no decent hobby for a mother to encourage her young son to take up the photographing of naked young girls.

Even the sisters and cousins of Leonard Lake were filmed, his mother explaining that it would teach him to take pride in the human body. But if there had been any such pride, it was soon to evaporate, replaced instead by an obsession with pornography. He initiated his sisters into sex games, as his

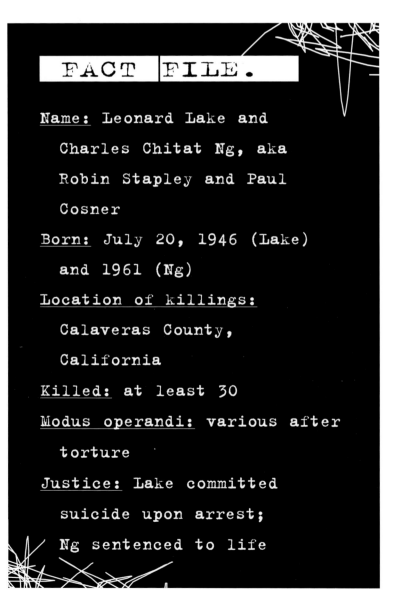

FACT FILE.

Name: Leonard Lake and Charles Chitat Ng, aka Robin Stapley and Paul Cosner

Born: July 20, 1946 (Lake) and 1961 (Ng)

Location of killings: Calaveras County, California

Killed: at least 30

Modus operandi: various after torture

Justice: Lake committed suicide upon arrest; Ng sentenced to life

"reward" for protecting them from the violence of another brother. Much later, worse perversions that had lain dormant within Lake were to come out in an explosion of terrifying serial slavery, savagery, and slaughter. Leonard Lake kidnapped people at random and then filmed their terror, culminating in their death as he directed his own chilling "snuff" videos.

Leonard Lake was born in San Francisco on July 20, 1946, into a family that had a history of mental disorders and alcoholism. At the age of six, poverty forced his parents to send him temporarily to live with his grandparents, where he received a tough, militaristic upbringing. Meanwhile his younger brother Donald, an epileptic, remained at home, becoming something of a mother's boy. But despite the attention he received from her, Donald developed a cruel streak that he exercised on animals and on his sisters. He started setting fires and, had he not himself been murdered, as we shall see, he might also have become a serial killer.

As a youngster, Leonard Lake was obsessive. He studied and experimented with pet mice, tracing genetic features through numerous generations. Through such single-mindedness, he became a self-taught geneticist. He showed no such dedication in adulthood, however, for in the 38 years and 11 months of his perverted life, his various jobs included being a trader, teacher, fireman, and circus showman. He joined the Marine Corps in 1966 and served a noncombatant tour in

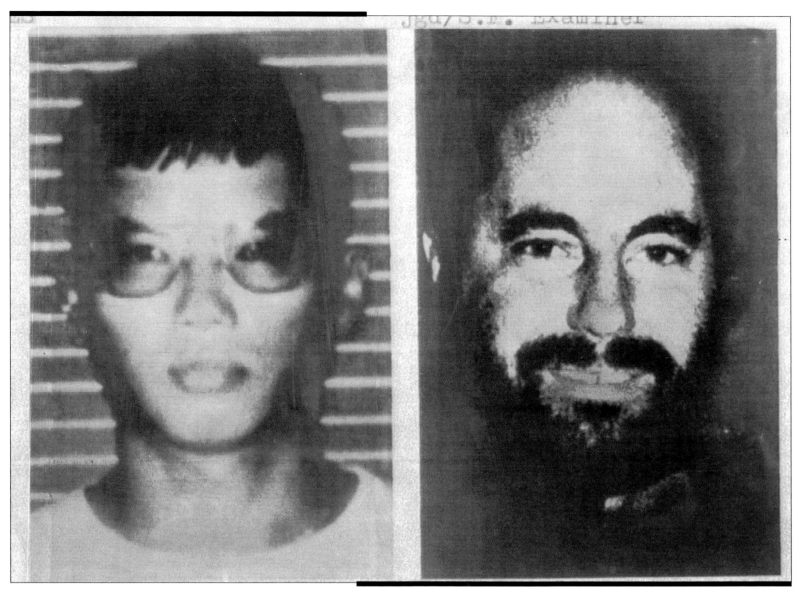

Lake first met Ng in California. Ng was to become an enthusiastic partner during the sickening series of killings that followed.

- - - - - - - -

Vietnam as a radio operator. During his service he underwent two years of psychiatric therapy at Camp Pendleton for unspecified mental problems before his discharge in 1971.

Lake moved to San Jose and got married, but this semblance of normality did not prevent him getting a reputation as a sexual pervert with an obsession with guns. Lake was known to enjoy

making his own bondage films featuring several woman partners including his wife. It was no surprise to anyone who knew the couple that the marriage ended. In 1980, Lake received a year's probation after being found guilty of stealing from a building site. By August 1981, he was married again and moved to a commune in Ukiah, California, where residents wore Renaissance-type costumes and led an archaic and bizarre lifestyle. He was one of a team there that created a "unicorn," grafting a single horn on the head of a goat.

It was soon after arriving at the commune that

Leonard Lake and his former wife, Cricket. She appeared in some of his earliest videos.

- - - - - - - - - - - -

Lake met Charles Chitat Ng, the son of wealthy Chinese parents and the man who would be an enthusiastic partner in the sickening serial killings. It was Ng, however, who unwittingly led police to discover the evil duo's house of horrors. The sequence of events that led up to the exposure of Lake and Ng as among the globe's most perverted and brutal killers were largely accidental.

They began in June 1985 when police officer David Wright got a radio call to go to a San Francisco hardware store where a young Chinese man was refusing to pay for a $75 vice. When the policeman arrived, he found that the Chinese man had run away but that his friend, a burly, bearded caucasian, was desperately offering to settle the bill. The store manager was ready to accept the cash but the policeman became suspicious when the man refused to reveal his identity.

His driving licence gave his name as Robin Scott Stapley. When a call was made to the station, the computer revealed that Stapley was a 26-year-old who had disappeared without trace some months previously. A check on the mystery man's car license plate revealed that it belonged to a local businessman, Paul Cosner, another missing person who had last been seen by his girlfriend some weeks previously when he went out to sell the car to a "weird-looking" man prepared to pay cash. Wright arrested the stranger and searched the car. He found a small handgun and a quantity of pornographic pictures.

Back at the police station, the man was calm. He asked for a glass of water and a pencil and paper to write out a statement. But when he was alone, he calmly took the cyanide pill that he always carried with him, washed it down with a gulp of the water, and scribbled a note to his ex-wife, a dubious character called Cricket Balazs. It read: "260. Tell Mama, Fern, and Patty I'm sorry." Then he called the detectives back, revealed that his real name was Leonard Lake—and fell forward unconscious. He had swallowed a cyanide capsule he always kept with him. He never came round and died four days later.

Meanwhile, mystified police followed up the only clue they had: an electricity bill found in Lake's pocket, made out to Charles Gunnar with an address in Wisleyville, Calaveras County, 150 miles east of San Francisco. The local sheriff, Claude Ballard, confirmed that Gunnar owned a small ranch in the area that he shared with a young Chinese man. He now realized that the man he knew as Gunnar must, in fact, be Lake. Sheriff Ballard had been taking an interest in the ranch because Lake advertised furniture and TV sets for sale on a regular basis. He had thought some of the articles might be stolen property.

Ballard recalled that what had first drawn his

❝I love you. Please forgive me. I forgive you❞

attention to the ranch was the sale of furniture belonging to a couple called Lonny Bond and Brenda O'Connor. Lonny and Brenda had been neighbors of Lake, but they had suddenly disappeared without trace, as had their six-month-old baby, Lonny Junior. Lake had claimed they had left him their furniture to settle a debt. In the light of the new information Ballard received from San Francisco, he recalled another mystery disappearance from a local camp site, when a couple vanished leaving their tent, equipment, and even a pot of coffee boiling on the stove.

Hackles rising, officers prepared to raid Lake's home in Blue Mountain Road in rural, wooded Wisleyville. The two-bedroom cabin was set in three acres. From outside it seemed idyllic. But what they were to find inside would turn the stomachs of the toughest of cops who, until then, had thought they had seen it all. They had stumbled upon a chamber of horrors: a den of lust, torture, and agonizing death. Leonard Lake, who had died a few hours before his 39th birthday, had kidnapped, raped, tortured, killed, and mutilated at least 30 people. And he had faithfully recorded the gruesome details of most of them in diaries, photographs, and on film.

Inside the house, the police soon found grim pointers to further horrors. Military camouflage suits hung beside women's clothes in the closets; chains and manacles were attached to brackets on the walls; a blood-stained chainsaw was found in an outhouse. In the master bedroom they saw hooks in the ceiling and walls and in a box they found shackles. Inside one closet they found women's underwear and flimsy nightgowns.

Outside, a searcher discovered bones. They had been burned but were still recognizable as human. As the hunt continued, shallow graves were unearthed and more charred bones and decomposing human remains were carted away in bin liners. As the men toiled in the summer heat, they became covered in a film of dust that stuck to their sweating faces. They were sickened to realize it was human ashes. Officer Wright's shoplifter had turned into the most prolific serial killer of recent history.

> **"They were sickened to realize it was human ashes"**

It was a day or so before police pushed aside a stack of barrels and found the dungeon. A trapdoor lead into an underground bunker, dug securely into the hillside—in it was found all the paraphernalia of a modern torture chamber. Lake, it turned out, was a "survivalist;" he believed the holocaust was coming and had stocked a bunker with guns and food with which he would survive a nuclear war. In the meantime, it served to fulfil his other fantasy: that of domination over women. In his twisted mind, he saw himself as a future savior of a world peopled by his sex-slaves.

To this end, his bunker doubled as a prison. As well as sleeping, living, and toilet facilities, there were rooms that looked for all the world like jail cells, complete with shackles and leg-irons. There were also pictures adorning the walls of naked and semi-clad women. Some of the pictures appeared to be of newly-dead corpses, their faces twisted in pain.

Even worse was to come. With the principal character dead and his accomplice on the run, the police took the bunker apart in an effort to uncover the grim truth. They had long since realized they were dealing with a monster but still they were unprepared for what they found next. Lake's dungeon was also a movie studio. Lake had been the director and co-star in his own "snuff" videos, pornographic home movies in which the victim, almost invariably a woman or a child, is subjected to sadistic sexual practices or ritual torture and, as a climax, is killed while the camera lingers over the gruesome, graphic details. Lake had not just satisfied his blood lust, he had made a lucrative income from it. For, as it transpired, this was also the center of a perverted mail-order business based on his cruel, warped fantasies.

The worst was revealed in Lake's own video library. Shocked police who viewed the films took it in turns to leave the room as one after the other became sickened by what he saw. One film, labeled only "M Ladies Kathy/Brenda" opened with a young woman, hands cuffed behind her back, sitting on a chair in the cabin. A menacing, disembodied voice off-camera tells her: "Mike owes us and he can't pay. We're going to give you a choice, Kathy. You can cooperate and in approximately 30 days we'll either drug you or blindfold you and let you go somewhere in the city. If you don't co-operate, we'll put a bullet in your head and bury you some place. No witnesses. While you're here, you'll wash for us, you'll clean for us,

The painstaking search in Wisleyville took over a week and police uncovered many human remains in Lake's death ranch.

- - - - - - - - - -

you'll fuck for us. That's your choice. It's not much of a choice unless you have a death wish."

Lake, heavy-set, bearded, and balding, then comes into view to put leg irons on Kathy. "My name you don't know," he tells her, then adds, "It is Charlie." As he speaks these words, another person enters the frame. It is Ng, the man who inadvertently set the investigation in motion with his bungled attempt to steal a $75 vice. Lake removes the handcuffs and orders Kathy to strip. The woman, later identified as missing person Kathy Allen, removes her outer clothes and her

bra, but is reluctant to take off her panties until Ng points to the gun on the table. Finally, shaking and crying, she strips naked and is sent to take a shower with Ng.

A later scene in the video has Kathy strapped, still naked, to a bed. It is four days later and Lake is threatening her as he takes pornographic photographs. He tells her that Mike (her boyfriend) is now dead, and soon it will be her turn. The scene shifts back to the cabin, where a young woman called Brenda sits shackled in a chair as Kathy did before her. Beside Brenda, holding a vicious-looking knife, stands Ng. As Lake gives Brenda the same instructions he gave Kathy, Ng uses the knife to cut away Brenda's blouse. This time though, the

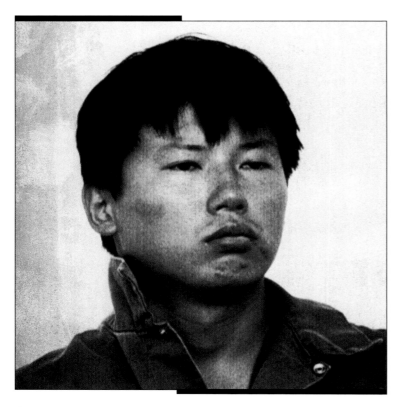

Ng was the son of wealthy Hong Kong parents but was a kleptomaniac and was sentenced to 27 months in a military jail. He
escaped and returned to San Francisco where he met Lake.

threats carry more menace. Lake tells Brenda that her baby has been given to a family in Fresno. She becomes hysterical and begs for the return of the child. Lake and Ng laugh.

"Why do you guys do this?" she asks plaintively.

"We don't like you," says Lake.

As Ng removes the shreds of her blouse she pleads: "Don't cut my bra off."

"Nothing is yours now," says Lake.

"Give me back my baby. I'll do anything you want."

"You'll do anything we want anyway."

Ng slowly cuts away the woman's bra. At last the sickening tape comes to an end.

It was the last that was ever seen of Kathy Allen

and Brenda O'Connor. Their remains were subsequently found with those of 19 others in shallow trenches near the cabin. Also found were the teeth of Lonny Junior, the child Brenda had pleaded so desperately for.

It was not the only film police had to sweat through as their rage and frustration mounted. There was a collection of films depicting all manner of ritual tortures, rapes, and degrading sex acts. Many of them culminated in the horror of real on-screen murder. These, along with a lucrative drug trafficking sideline, were the basis of Lake's income. There were also pictures of naked women in chains, pictures of bodies, their faces frozen in their death agonies. And there were bags of human bones that had been boiled down to a soup. Not all the victims had died in the torture chamber. Some had been set free in the grounds, only to be tracked down and murdered with hunting rifles. Others were doused with petrol and burned alive.

In a cabinet, police found full records of Lake's twisted trade, on film, in pictures, and in two 500-page journals in his own hand. A passage in one journal read: "The perfect woman is totally controlled, a woman who does exactly what she is told and nothing else. There is no sexual problem with a submissive woman. There are no frustrations, only pleasure and contentment."

What could explain Leonard Lake's macabre fixation with wanton murder and the subjugation and degradation of women? His strange home life as a youngster obviously played a part. His "survivalist" obsessions provided a further clue. Another of his compulsions was for cleanliness, washing and showering many times a day. In his torture videos, the victim was always made to shower before the degrading and bloody action began in earnest. And all the while, Leonard Lake lived in a world of fantasy, dreaming of Vikings, Valhalla, and stirring adventure.

Even when police revealed the horrific scale of the crimes they had uncovered, Lake's relatives were reluctant to condemn him, though his ex-wife Cricket Balazs was a little more forthcoming. She was not surprised to hear of her ex-husband's snuff video operation. He had been making porno videos while they were married—and she had been the star. Her role had been to act out various sadomasochistic parts as she mouthed the name of the client. She had wondered at the time whether he was making other, weirder films on the side. Upon hearing the damning evidence, Lake's mother, a nurse who worked in a mental hospital, could not believe her son was capable of violence. His sister Fern, also a nurse, had always looked the other way, while his grandmother would hear no ill of her darling Leonard, insisting he was a good child who had been led astray. After all, Lake was a volunteer firefighter and he gave his time to a charitable organization that provided free equipment for old folks' homes. His cover was perfect.

It was left to a man who had lived with Lake in a commune a few years before his death to sum up the pornographer and mass-murderer behind the mask of a neighborly charity volunteer. Lake was, he said, "the pleasantest unpleasant guy you ever could meet."

During the ongoing police investigations, a fingerprint check showed that Lake was wanted under another name in Humboldt County for jumping bail on burglary charges. Following up, local sheriffs discovered that he had started to build another survivalist bolt hole, and they found maps with pointers to "hidden treasure." These too

As the hunt at Wisleyville continued, shallow graves were found as well as charred bones.

- - - - - - - - - - - - - -

turned out to be the graves of his victims. One of these was none other than his own brother, Donald. He had visited Lake to try to get some money— but his elder brother had coolly murdered him. Another grave belonged to the one man who had befriended Lake in the Marines: Charles Gunnar, whose identity Lake assumed.

Among the bodies that were dug up were those of two blacks. Ng had been seen driving two black men to the ranch, even though he was known to hate blacks and hispanics. One further mystery seemed to have been solved: that of a San Franciscan couple, Harvey and Deborah Dubs, who had disappeared along with their baby. A policeman recalled seeing a Chinese man moving furniture at their home. By coincidence, the same policeman was now working on the Lake-Ng case. Attention now focused on the escaped Ng, and police delved into his background, which was almost totally the reverse of Lake's. The son of wealthy Hong Kong parents, he was born in 1961 and was sent to an English boarding school in Yorkshire, but was expelled for stealing. For a time, he lived in Lancashire, until he was sent to San Francisco to complete his education. At 18, he was involved in a hit-and-run traffic accident and joined the Marines to escape arrest. Never in his life short of money, he was evidently a kleptomaniac and was soon arrested at Kaneoke Air Force base in Oahu, Hawaii, charged with stealing weapons worth $11,000. Sentenced to 27 months in a military jail, he managed to escape and returned to San Francisco, where he answered an advertisement for a "mercenary" in a survivalist magazine. It had been placed by Leonard Lake, and the two became partners in crime. When he and Lake were picked up on a burglary charge in Humboldt County, he was identified as a deserter and served time at Fort Leavenworth, Kansas. As soon as he got parole, he returned to Lake and the two set up their evil business.

Now Ng had become the FBI's most wanted man. The first lead to his whereabouts came a few days after the raid on the cabin, when a San Francisco gun dealer rang the police to say that Ng had phoned him about a gun he was repairing. He had asked the dealer to post it to Chicago and

> **" Ng showed he was adept at martial arts but was eventually overpowered "**

when it was explained to him that it was against the law to mail guns across state lines. Ng had cursed and rung off.

On July 6, 1985, five weeks after Lake was seized, Ng was caught stealing from a store in Calgary, Canada. When challenged, he pulled a gun and shot a security man in the hand. As more guards arrived on the scene, Ng showed he was adept at martial arts but was eventually overpowered. When FBI agents interviewed Ng in Canada, he told them he knew of the murders but played no part in them. He was, however, able to describe the murders of Paul Cosner (whose car had been found in Lake's possession) and two removal men, one of whom was burned to death.

A Canadian court sentenced Ng to four-and-a-half years for armed robbery, and he instantly made use of the excellent jail library's law section. He fought extradition to California, citing a Canadian law that prohibits the return of a murder suspect to a country with the death penalty. The case took six years to resolve and went all the way to the Canadian Supreme Court. Ng lost and in 1991 was returned to the US where he found legal loopholes to postpone his trial for a further seven years. Ng caused his case to become the longest and most expensive criminal trial in Californian history but it finally ended on May 3, 1999, when he was found guilty of 11 counts of murder. He was condemned to death row on June 30, 1999.

HENRI LANDRU

With his Toulouse-Lautrec beard and short stature, he was not an obvious magnet for women.

But somehow Henri Landru wooed and won hundreds of conquests—some said as many as 283. But what many didn't know was that they were in the company of a man who was a lady-killer in all senses of the word.

Landru, who earned himself the nickname of the French "Bluebeard," could not have timed his search for lonely women better. During World War I, his hunting ground of Paris was full of women whose menfolk were away fighting. The women were vulnerable and only too keen to seek some distraction from the conflict just to the north. The short, dapper little man they had been so at ease with killed at least 11 of them but police believed there were many more.

Born on April 12, 1869, Landru came from a poor but honest family. His father worked as a stoker in a Paris foundry and his mother was a dressmaker. Together they had a daughter but yearned for a son. When Landru came along, his parents named him Henri Désiré, meaning much desired. It was a hard-working, God-fearing close family unit. Landru's father graduated from the foundry to become a salesman in a book shop. Little Henri went to a school run by monks where he displayed a sharp mind, sang in the choir of a Paris church, and was an altar boy. In 1888 he left school to work in an architect's office and three years later fathered a baby girl by a laundry assistant. After completing his military service, Landru married her in 1893.

Landru went on to have three more children with his wife, Marie. But if she had hoped that her husband would turn out to be a respectable family man in the mold of his father, then she was to be bitterly disappointed. There were a string of short-lived jobs, most of them peppered with petty crime. His dishonesty became more ambitious down the years and landed him in court on several occasions.

Police reports at the time maintain that he was suffering from diminished responsibility. It was a

FACT FILE.

Name: Henri Désiré Landru,
  aka the "Bluebeard"
Born: April 12, 1869
Location of killings: Paris
  and Northern France
Killed: at least 11
Modus operandi: various,
  followed by burning
Justice: gas guillotined
  in 1922

kindly diagnosis. For Landru was rubbing shoulders with the city's low-life and was as pin-sharp as ever. Pimps, thieves, and bar-room brawlers were among his friends. His existence became increasingly nomadic as the threat of transportation by the courts hung over him. He appeared at home only spasmodically. His father was so distraught at the wayward behavior of his adored son that he hanged himself. Landru then went on the run to start a life that would provide him with the money he desperately craved.

> **His father was so distraught at the wayward behavior of his adored son that he hanged himself**

First he advertised for a new wife, even though he was still married. He wrote: "Widower with two children, aged 43, possessing comfortable income, affectionate, serious, and moving in good society, desires to meet widow of similar status, with a view to matrimony."

Among the many women who saw the advert was Madame Jeanne Cuchet, a widow of 39. When Mme. Cuchet met with "Monsieur Diard," as Landru was calling himself, she was greatly impressed not only by his charm as he wined and dined her but by the interest he showed in her 18-year-old son André. Despite pleas from her sister that it was too early and too dangerous to commit to a man she hardly knew, Mme. Cuchet gave up her apartment and in December 1914 moved with "Diard" to a house called The Lodge in the small town of Vernouillet, outside Paris. Mme. Cuchet and her son then disappeared without trace. Landru was now the proud owner of 15,000 Francs worth of jewels, furniture, and securities. In 1915, there were two other disappearances from The Lodge. One was Madame Thérése Laborde-Line, aged 47, from Argentina, who had no relatives to worry about her. Another was Madame Désirée Guillin, a 51-year-old former governess who had inherited 22,000 francs. Landru then moved to the Villa Ermitage at Gambais where he entertained scores of women. At least eight never returned home. These included Madame Louise Jaume, a 38-year-old devout Catholic separated from her husband, 19-year-old serving girl Andrée Babelay, divorcee Madame Anne-Marie Pascal, and Madame Marie-Therese Marchadier, aged 37.

Yet another was Madame Anna Colomb, who was so instantly smitten with the ginger-bearded man, now using the name of "Cuchet," that she dropped her real age of 44 down to 29! Mme. Colomb and "Cuchet" moved in together but Landru could not stay faithful for long and was soon using a series of aliases to carry on a string of affairs with other women. On Christmas Eve 1916, Mme. Colomb invited her sister Mme. Pelat to visit her and "Cuchet" at his villa in Gambais. It was the last time Mme. Pelat saw either of them.

Anxious that she had received no replies to letters sent to her sister, Mme. Pelat appealed to the

Henri Landru, also known as the Parisian Bluebeard, is shown here making a court appearance charged with murder in 1921.

Mayor of Gambais asking for help. It was not the first time the mayor had received such a request. A Mademoiselle Lacoste had inquired about the whereabouts of her sister Mme. Celeste Buisson who had disappeared while visiting a man called "Fremyet" at the same villa. The mayor was disturbed to learn that a man called "Dupont" also claimed to own the villa. He suggested that Mlle. Lacoste and Mme. Pelat should meet to discuss the women's disappearances. When they did, they realized that it was the same man who called himself Fremyet, Cuchet, and Diard. A call to the police revealed that a Madame Cuchet had disappeared while visiting a man called Diard. That and Landru's other criminal activities caused concern among all those whose women friends seemed to have vanished without trace.

An arrest warrant was issued on April 11, 1919, for the man who answered to all these aliases. Just a day later, by sheer chance, he was spotted in Paris by Mlle. Lacoste. The man she knew as Dupont was strolling along the Rue de Rivoli arm in arm with a smartly dressed woman. Mlle. Lacoste followed them into a store where they ordered a dinner service. She then lost them in the crowds but went straight to the police who traced the crockery order to a "Monsieur Lucien Guillet," of 76 Rue de Rochechouart. They called there the next morning to be confronted with the unmistakable figure of Landru: small, bald, and with a large red beard. As police searched his lodgings, the killer desperately tried to throw a book out of the window. It meticulously recorded all the women he had met through his advertisements, together with details of how rich they were and what he hoped to get from them.

A search of the Villa Gambais now revealed the

Landru gave evidence at his trial for murder, continuing to maintain his innocence despite the bone fragments and items of women's clothes found at his home.

sickening cause of the thick, black, oily smoke that neighbors had noticed occasionally emitting from the chimney. No fewer than 290 fragments of bones and teeth were recovered from a stove, as well as huge quantities of women's clothes and personal possessions around the house. No one knew the number of Bluebeard's victims—they still don't— and Landru did not provide an answer during lengthy police interrogations, never once admitting his guilt.

He continued to maintain his innocence at his trial at the Seine-et-Oise Assize Court in November

1921. He antagonized the court by his arrogant answers. At one stage, when asked about the missing women, Landru replied: "I am a gallant man. I cannot allow you to ask me questions concerning the ladies. If they have disappeared, it is nothing to do with me. I know nothing of what became of them. Discover proofs, bring them to me and then I will discuss them with you." His defense counsel, Moro Giafferi, one of France's top lawyers, claimed his client was a white slave trader and that the women who had vanished had been sent by him to brothels in Brazil. Why the Brazilians should relish a supply of middle-aged French ladies was never satisfactorily explained.

To hysterical scenes inside and outside the courtroom, Landru was found guilty and was sentenced to die despite the jury's extraordinary plea for clemency. On the morning of February 25, 1922, Landru was asked if he wished to make a confession to a priest. "Sir, to ask such a question at such a time is an insult," he replied. "I have nothing to say." He then turned to his lawyer, who had proclaimed his innocence to the end, and calmly comforted the distraught man, telling him: "You had a desperately difficult task, and it is not the first time an innocent man has been condemned." It was later reported, probably apocryphally, that he then handed Moro Giafferi a drawing that he had done in his cell. In 1963 the daughter of the attorney had the picture cleaned and there, on the back, appeared a confession in Landru's own hand.

Landru also did his best to upset the prosecuting counsel at his trial, France's Advocate General. He left a letter for him that thoroughly upset him when he read it:

"Maitre Godefroy, why could you not meet my gaze when I was brought back to court to hear my sentence? Why did you so indignantly rebuke the crowd for its unseemly behavior? Why today are you still searching for the vanished women if you are so certain that I killed them? It was all over. Sentence had been pronounced. I was calm. You were upset. Is there a conscience that troubles uncertain judges as it ought to trouble criminals? Farewell Monsieur. Our common history will doubtless die tomorrow. I will die with an innocent and quiet mind. I hope, respectfully, that you may do the same."

Henri Landru certainly faced his death with a quiet mind. After persuading the warders not to shave off his beard, he walked ahead of them and the snubbed priest, shivering slightly as he came outside into the cold of the execution yard. The prison gates were opened to reveal a mass of jostling spectators. Landru's shirt was ripped open and he was forced onto the block. His last words were: "I shall be brave." Then the guillotine fell.

> "After persuading the warders not to shave off his beard, he walked ahead of them and the snubbed priest, shivering slightly as he came outside into the cold of the execution yard"

ROBERT JOE LONG

Bobby Joe Long was disgusted with what he was doing but could not stop. He couldn't understand the forces that drove him to rape more than 50 women.

He certainly could not control them, he claimed later from his cell on Florida's death row. After his sexual obsession turned to murder and he had left nine women dead along the roadside, Long finally allowed himself to be caught by freeing one of his last victims. "I knew when I let her go that it would only be a matter of time," he said. "I just didn't care any more. I wanted to stop. I was sick inside."

In that self-judgment, Long was correct. The story of his life is the tale of a murderer in the making—someone almost fated to be a serial killer.

FACT FILE.

Name: Robert Joe Long, aka the "Classified Ad Rapist"

Born: October 13, 1953

Location of killings: Tampa and elsewhere in Florida, USA

Modus operandi: strangulation after rape

Killed: nine

Justice: sentenced to death in 1989

Born in Kenova, West Virginia, in 1953, Long was a lonely infant. His parents split up when he was three and from that date he and his good-looking but unqualified mother were always on the move as they wandered from town to town, job to job, and relationship to relationship. Young Bobby Joe had no stable home and was completely dominated by his mother, even sharing the same bed until he was 12.

Worse, he even appeared to be turning into a girl. At the age of 11, he was struck by a congenital disorder that he shared with other members of his family. This dysfunction of the endocrine system gave him an extra "X" chromosome, causing his glands to produce extra oestrogen and making him grow breasts. A doctor prescribed surgery and more than six pounds of tissue was removed from his chest. The physical problem was solved but throughout his life he continued to experience a proto-menstrual cycle that was said to coincide with the full moon. When he was 19, Long enlisted in the army to learn an electrician's trade, and six months later he married his childhood sweetheart, Cindy Jean Guthrie. His bride was in appearance very like his mother—it may even have been that which attracted him—but the effect of his marriage was that he moved from one woman's dominance to another's.

At the age of 20, Long was involved in a fateful motorcycle accident that fractured his skull and left him semi-conscious for weeks. He later claimed that the compulsion for sex and the lust to kill both came on after the crash, although even before the accident he had suffered four other severe injuries to his head resulting from falls from horses and bicycles. While recovering in hospital, Long discovered that sex dominated every waking thought. He fantasized about bedding every girl he met. In addition, he started to become violent at the least annoyance, and every sudden noise seemed like the explosion of a hand grenade. He worked as an X-ray technician, but lost job after job for making advances to the women patients. At one hospital it was discovered that he was making women undress before taking their X-rays. At another he was fired—and jailed for a day—for showing pornographic material to a young girl.

The compulsion for sex also ruled his home life. He had intercourse with his wife at least twice a day and masturbated a further five or six times. In 1976, by now a father of two and going through divorce procedures, he began a succession of rapes that earned him the nickname the "Classified Ad Rapist." He terrorized the Florida communities of Fort Lauderdale, Miami, and Ocala by ringing numbers listed in the classified columns of local papers and making appointments for the daytime, when he was most likely to meet unaccompanied housewives. Once inside their homes, he would pull a knife, tie the victim up, and rape her before robbing the house.

Apart from this frenzy, he lived a normal life and escaped detection for eight years, even though he was once accused of rape by a vengeful ex-girlfriend. The case went to court but the charges were dropped when he produced witnesses who testified she had specifically invited him to have sex with her. This experience appears to have

Bobby Joe Long was sentenced to death by electrocution in 1989, despite his lawyers claiming his actions were due to the effects of head injuries from an earlier accident.

triggered a bloodlust within Long's warped psyche. As the Classified Ad Rapist, he had never been excessively violent to his victims. However, he was shocked by the vindictiveness, as he saw it, of the ex-girlfriend and some part of his brain began to hate women, whom he saw as manipulative.

The first woman he killed was Ngeon Thi Long, a stripper who picked him up in a Tampa bar. He was revolted by her. "She picked me up," he said. "I didn't go after her. She was a whore. She manipulated men and she wanted to manipulate me. Once I had her in the car, I tied her up and raped her. Then I dumped her body along the highway. Next morning I couldn't believe what I had done. I was sick. Then I met another girl, a barfly, and it happened all over again."

Six more women were to pick Long up in bars, and six more bodies were to be found later along the highway. But the end of the terrifying spree of murder was in sight. As Long said in an interview from his cell on death row in Stark, Florida, he wanted to be caught. He knew he could not stop himself, so he made an unconscious decision to help the police. Long raped but did not kill victim number eight. It was to be her testimony that earned him the death sentence.

In November 1983, he saw a 17-year-old girl cycling home from her job on the night shift at a doughnut factory. She was the first of his victims who had not made the first move. Instinctively he knew this would be different. Nevertheless, he leapt out and knocked her off her bicycle, tied and blindfolded her, and put her in his car.

He drove around for a while, during which time she confided to him that she had been sexually abused by her stepfather, whom she now had to work to support as he was confined to a wheelchair. Long drove the girl around for hours, stopping at a bank machine to get cash and at his apartment. On both occasions she was able to peek from behind the blindfold and later gave police exact descriptions of where she had been. Long then raped her and finally released her at the spot

> **"He knew deep down that he would be quickly caught"**

he had kidnapped her. He knew deep down that he would be quickly caught.

Two days later, he was still free to murder his ninth and final victim. He followed a woman driving a car erratically, correctly guessing she would be drunk. She pulled over when she realized she was being followed and quickly agreed to get into his car, believing he would return her to her car when she sobered up. Kim Swann was a big-framed young woman and Long hated her instantly. He attacked her but she fought back grimly, kicking him hard on the shin with her pointed cowboy boots. She also kicked a hole in his dashboard and screamed without stopping. Long overpowered her and squeezed her windpipe until she lost consciousness. She briefly recovered, however, and began screaming again until Long again put his hands round her neck. Every time she screamed he repeated the process. At last he undressed her, but even as he looked at the sensuous figure and full breasts, the raging need for sex had dried up. She woke up again and screamed and this time he strangled her to death. He drove around for a while with the naked body beside him and dumped her body on the outskirts of Tampa. He had not bothered to rape her.

Four days later he was arrested for the kidnap and rape of the 17-year-old. Despite his lawyers claiming that the motorcycle accident was to blame for his actions, in 1985 Long was found guilty of all nine murders and sentenced to death in the electric chair.

PEDRO LOPEZ

He said he liked his girls with a "certain look of innocence." But this was no ordinary man talking.

It was Pedro Lopez and he was making a confession to the police who had been hunting him for years. Lopez has earned himself a place in criminal history as "The Monster of the Andes," the monster who killed 300 girls and who for a while won notoriety as the world's worst serial murderer.

Pedro Alonzo Lopez was born in Tolmia, Colombia, in 1949, a time when the country was ruled by riots and violence. In the midst of all this, Lopez suffered personal cruelty. The seventh son of a penniless prostitute, his life was anything but charmed. He was the seventh of the woman's 13 children and knew nothing of a mother's love or home comforts.

Witnessing her frequent sex sessions with strangers was his introduction to carnal matters and when, at the age of eight, she caught him having sex with his younger sister, she threw him out onto the streets. Kindly neighbors took Pedro in but when his mother found out, she snatched him away again and took him some distance out of town and abandoned him. It took the little boy a day to find his way back to his neighborhood.

His mother's treatment of him was to stay with Lopez forever, making him both fear and despise women. He later told police: "I lost my innocence at the age of eight so I decided to do the same to as many young girls as I could."

With Colombia's reputation as a country caring little for those who needed help most, the young Pedro was now left to fend for himself. An older, more streetwise child might have understood the motives of the first kindly stranger who offered him food and a place to stay but instead of a warm bed and hot meal, the boy's trust was rewarded by his being raped several times then cast back into the gutter. "I slept on the stairs of marketplaces and plazas," he recalled later. "I would look up and if I could see a star, I knew I was under the protection of God."

The experience taught Lopez never to trust anyone. He lived on his wits, sleeping in alleys and empty houses and his food was scraps taken from

---

FACT FILE.

Name: Pedro Armando Lopez,
aka "Monster of the Andes"

Born: 1949

Location of killings:
Colombia, Peru, and Ecuador

Killed: claimed 300 plus

Modus operandi: strangulation

Justice: life sentence

Pedro Lopez was deported to the borders of Ecuador from Peru. There he continued to kill over a hundred young girls, as he found them very trusting and innocent.

- - - - - - - - - - - - -

dustbins. It was only when he traveled to the capital Bogota, where he was taken in by a genuinely concerned American couple, that Lopez's future looked brighter. He was given his own room and enrolled in a school for orphans. But the boy was never destined to lead a normal existence. When he was 12, he was sexually abused by a male teacher and the incident drove him away from what was the nearest thing he had ever known to a secure life. Lopez stole money from the school, ran away from his adoptive parents, and became one of Colombia's street urchins once more.

He spent the next six years begging and stealing to survive. His first brush with the law was when he was 18 and stole a car, a crime at which he became adept. Lopez was arrested as he drove the vehicle across Colombia and was sentenced to seven years in prison. On his second day in jail, the teenager was raped by a gang of fellow prisoners. He got his revenge by murdering three of them with a crude knife he had fabricated. That revenge cost him another two years behind bars, which was

a lenient sentence as he pleaded that he acted only in self-defense.

The seeds of sordid and cheap sex were now planted in Lopez's mind. Although he had been the victim of several perverted attacks, he found himself aroused by pornography and with the idea of having sex with young girls. His first murder victims were innocent members of the Ayachucos Indian tribe across the border with neighboring Peru. While attempting to kidnap one of the tribe's nine-year-old girls, Lopez was caught, stripped, and tortured by the Indians. His ultimate punishment was to be buried alive and he was only saved by the chance passing of an American missionary who convinced the tribe that killing was wrong. The tribe handed Lopez over, and the missionary in turn handed him over to police in Peru for a fair hearing.

The Peruvian authorities, however, decided that the quickest way to solve what they viewed as a nuisance was to deport Lopez to the nearest border with Ecuador. Lopez had already raped and killed as many as 100 young girls in Peru, most of them from Indian tribes—and was suddenly free to hunt for more in an ideal setting. As he later told police: "I liked the girls in Ecuador. They are more gentle and trusting and more innocent. They are not as suspicious of strangers as Colombian girls."

Lopez finally made his way back to Colombia. His return saw the disappearance of many more girls, mostly snatched from market squares and street corners. He would often follow them for days, waiting until their mothers had gone off on an errand. Then he would approach his victim telling them he had a present for their mother. When the child agreed to accompany him, Lopez led her to the outskirts of town where he would rape and kill her. Lopez never worked at night, only during the day because, he later explained, he wanted his victim's face to be clear to him as they suffered in the throes of death. The killer's fantasy of watching the same effect on a fair-haired white girl was almost fulfilled but was thwarted at the last moment because her parents were too protective.

Despite his activities, Lopez was never under suspicion, the authorities instead choosing to believe that the disappearances were down to the growing South American sex slave trade. But eventually, with so many girls in the three countries vanishing off the face of the earth, police knew there was a serial killer at large and the hunt for the Monster of the Andes began in earnest.

In April 1980, a flash flood near Ambato, Ecuador, unearthed the remains of four children. Days later Carvina Poveda screamed for help after a stranger seized her 12-year-old girl daughter as they walked through a market place. Townspeople gave chase and caught up with the abductor, who was ranting incoherently, possibly realizing that his sickening killing spree was over.

Lopez calmed down as police arrived and remained silent during questioning. Finally he was tricked into a confession to his horrific crimes. A priest, Cordoba Gudino, was placed in the same cell posing as a prisoner in a bid to get him to talk. The ploy worked almost too well. Lopez revealed to the priest such revolting acts of sadistic violence that the poor man asked to be removed from the cell. The sickening tales he gleaned were so horrific that police at first suspected they were the boasts of a deranged mind. But when they confronted Lopez with their newly acquired evidence, he finally cracked.

Lopez continued to kill until the remains of four girls were unearthed during a flash flood in Amboto. Days later he was caught while trying to snatch a girl off the streets.

His interrogators listened in shocked silence as Lopez told them of his five-years as the Monster of the Andes. He gleefully recalled how he would snatch the girls, rape them, and then strangle them, all the time staring eagerly into their eyes. He said watching their life ebb away gave him heightened sexual pleasure. But there was even more to Lopez's perverted killings. Sometimes, he told the police, he would hold tea parties with the little girls and chat away with them—oblivious of the fact that the girls were already dead and Lopez was holding conversations with their propped up, lifeless bodies.

Lopez spoke of killing as many as 110 girls in Ecuador, 100 in Colombia, and "many more than 100" in Peru. His story was only fully believed when he led police to his "killing fields." At Ambato, almost two miles up in the Andes, he showed them where 53 girls, all aged between eight and 12, were buried. There were 28 other sites that horrified police visited but at many of them wild animals had got there first. Construction sites had also been used by Lopez as burial grounds, the girls' bodies entombed in concrete.

Lopez was given a life sentence but even in jail he could not stop boasting of being the most prolific killer this century. He told a newspaper reporter: "I went after my victims among the markets, searching for a girl with a certain look on her face—a look of innocence and beauty. She would be a good girl, working with her mother. I followed them sometimes for two or three days, waiting for when she was left alone. I would give her a trinket like a hand mirror and then take her to the edge of town where I would promise a trinket for her mother. I would take her to a secret hideaway where prepared graves waited. Sometimes there were bodies of earlier victims there. I cuddled them and then raped them at sunrise. At the first sign of light I would get excited. I then forced the girl into sex and put my hands around her throat. When the sun rose I would strangle her. It was only good if I could see her eyes. It would have been wasted in the dark. I had to watch them by daylight. There is a divine moment when I have my hands around a young girl's throat. I look into her eyes and see a certain light, a spark, suddenly go out. The moment of death is enthralling and exciting. Only those who actually kill will know what I mean. When I am released I will feel that moment again. It took the girls five to 15 minutes to die. I was very considerate. I would spend a long time with them making sure they were dead. I would use a mirror to check whether they were still breathing. Sometimes I had to kill them all over again. They never screamed because they didn't expect anything to happen. They were innocent. My little friends like to have company. I often put three or four into one hole. But after a while I got bored because they couldn't move so I looked for more girls."

> **I would take her to a secret hideaway where prepared graves waited**

It was no wonder that, while in custody, Lopez was segregated in the women's cell of Ambato prison, following threats to castrate him and burn him alive. Prison director Major Victor Lascano said: "We may never know how many young girls Lopez killed. His estimate of 300 may even be too low."

Lopez spent most of his time in prison cowering in the corner of his cell in Ambato Jail, high up in the Andes mountains in Ecuador. He also expected attempts at revenge from the prison guards who paraded outside cell number 14 where he was incarcerated. But Lopez still believed in his own notoriety, saying: "In prison I cannot see the sky and that is wrong for I am the Man of the Century. I will be famous in history."

HENRY LEE LUCAS

It can take arduous detective work and tough interrogation to force a confession out of a murder suspect.

But in the case of Henry Lee Lucas, it was easy— far too easy. To the embarrassment of the police, the 48-year-old vagrant made literally hundreds of confessions, many of which he supported with hard facts. He told of rapes and torture, kidnapping and mutilation, death by gunshot, knife, rope, and even crucifixion. By his own evidence, he was a serial killer without parallel, yet he had been caught only by the most random of accidents.

In October 1982 a couple of birdwatchers strolling along a riverbank at Stoneburg, Texas, came upon an empty purse. Inside was an ID card in the name of Kate Rich, an 80-year-old widow who lived 10 miles away in Ringgold. Police knew her house had recently burned down but believed that she was away staying with relatives. Upon

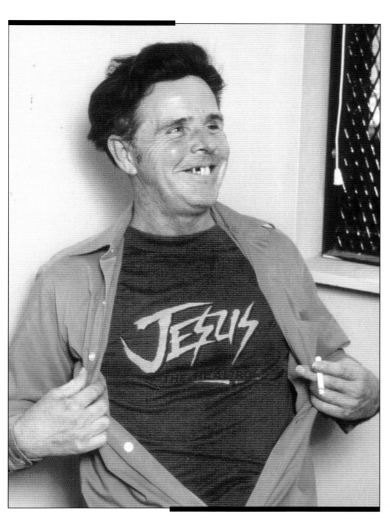

Henry Lee Lucas in Williamson County Prison, 1979.

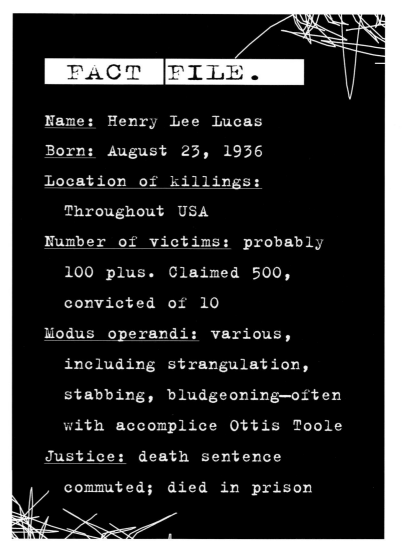

FACT FILE.

Name: Henry Lee Lucas

Born: August 23, 1936

Location of killings: Throughout USA

Number of victims: probably 100 plus. Claimed 500, convicted of 10

Modus operandi: various, including strangulation, stabbing, bludgeoning—often with accomplice Ottis Toole

Justice: death sentence commuted; died in prison

discovery of her purse, however, the local Montague County sheriff renewed his efforts to trace her. Enquiries among her relatives proved fruitless and a second careful forensic examination of the ashes of her burned-out house again yielded no trace of human remains.

The Texas Rangers were called in and house-to-house inquiries provided two interesting leads. The first was that a middle-aged vagrant and a young woman had rented a trailer-home in Ringgold that summer and that the man had done a few odd jobs for Mrs. Rich. The second lead came from a preacher in Stoneburg who told detectives that a middle-aged tramp he had employed as a campsite caretaker had been in possession of a gun. Was this the same vagrant who had stayed at Ringgold?

The police trail led to a squalid hut near Stoneburg, dubbed by locals "the Chicken Shack," where for the first time detectives came face to face with Henry Lee Lucas. With his tatty clothes, straggly hair, scruffy beard, and glass eye, he looked like the bad guy from some poorly made horror B-movie. Yet when questioned he seemed cool enough. He admitted carrying out odd jobs for Mrs. Rich. He said he had teamed up for the summer with a girl drifter named Becky but she had become homesick and had left him.

Police went away unconvinced. They checked him out further by interviewing each one of Stoneburg's 52 residents. They all had a good word for the bedraggled tramp, who had an excellent reputation as a handyman. However, a check on

> **"I was brought up like a dog. No human being should have been put through what I was"**

Lucas's background revealed a very different picture from the harmless "gentleman of the road" they had been told about.

Henry Lucas had been raised in a primitive cabin in the backwoods of Virginia where his parents ran an illegal whisky still. His father had lost both legs when a freight train had run over his drunken body. His mother, a Chippewa Indian who earned her living as a prostitute, constantly attacked her husband. She brutally beat and finally froze him to death by turning him out of their shack in the middle of winter. She also brutally beat and abused her young son. She sent young Henry to school dressed as a girl with his hair in ringlets, forcing him to suffer ridicule and beatings there too. Starved at home, he was forced to scavenge through trash cans for scraps of food. Finally, his mother beat her son so severely that he suffered with brain damage. He was later to describe his childhood thus: "I was brought up like a dog. No human being should have been put through what I was."

In 1960, at the age of 23, Lucas took revenge on his mother by raping and stabbing her to death. A judge gave him 40 years and he was admitted to a mental institution. Released briefly on parole in 1970, he served another four years for an attempted rape and kidnapping.

Armed with this disturbing background, Texas Ranger Phil Ryan returned to the Chicken Shack. He questioned Lucas about a couple of rings the vagrant had been hawking around. Again Lucas stayed cool, claiming he had been given the rings by Becky, who had been worried about getting mugged. The detective noticed a newly-packed suitcase and asked Lucas where he was going. "Dunno," he replied. "I just been in one place too long." Ryan demanded to look inside, and Lucas reluctantly agreed. Hidden beneath some clothes, Ryan found a razor-sharp two-foot dagger. "It's for self-defense," Lucas assured him. "There's a lot of mean people out there." The detective booked him for concealing an illegal weapon and marched him down to Montague County Jail for questioning.

Ryan's team were ready for a long and exhaustive interrogation session. So they were staggered when Lucas sneered: "You guys aren't interested in that dagger. What you really want to know is about Kate Rich and Becky. I'll tell you one thing. You guys are up a creek without a paddle. You ain't ever going to know what happened to them unless I tell you."

And then out it came, a catalog of sex-murders over 13 bloody years. Lucas told dozens of stories of torture, rape, and mutilation. Some were carried out by him alone, some with his bisexual lover Ottis Toole (Becky's uncle) who had a particular preference for children. He told how the killing started before the stabbing of his mother when, at the tender age of 15, he killed a 17-year-old girl because she refused to have sex.

He revealed how the orgy of death continued the day he was first released on parole, when his victim was a woman who had refused his advances. "I told them [the prison psychiatrists] not to let me loose" he said. "I told them I would do it again. They wouldn't listen."

Detectives considered the whole confession could be an act of fantasy—until Lucas got tired of

A smirking Lucas returns to Montague Jail, Texas, following a court appearance.

what he called "mind games." He took them back to the Chicken Shack and showed them the stove in which lay the charred remains of Kate Rich. In an isolated field not far away, he pointed out chunks of rotting flesh. This, he claimed, was where he had scattered the dismembered body of Becky. Why had he killed them? Lucas offered only vague ramblings. He had wanted money from Kate Rich. As for Becky, he was mad that she wanted to leave after he'd looked after her.

When Lucas appeared in court, the judge began to reprimand him for his smirking

Sheriff Bill Conway points to the spot where Kate Rich had been buried.

- - - - - - - - - - - - -

expression. "Murder," he was told, "was no laughing matter." "I know that your honor," Lucas replied. "I've done it a hundred times."

The judge paused, scarcely believing what he had heard. "What did you say?" he asked.

"I've killed about a hundred women," Lucas told him. "Maybe it's more than that if I get to counting. I know it's not normal for a person to kill a woman because she won't have sex with him but that's what I've done, lots of times."

The judge summoned the prosecutor and asked whether he really believed the defendant was mentally fit to stand trial. Lucas quickly interrupted: "Judge, if you think I'm crazy, there's a hundred or more women out there who says different. Yes, I'd say I'm mentally competent—and I'm guilty. I'd just like to get this damn thing over with once and for all."

Soon afterward, Lucas began taking detectives through the crimes he claimed were down to him, as well as incriminating Ottis Toole, who was serving a 20-year sentence in Florida for arson. One officer accused Lucas of inventing his confession in an attempt to get off with an insanity plea. Lucas turned on him: "You think I'm lying? OK, you ask them down at Plainview if they found a body without a head. And then you ask them out in Scottsdale, Arizona, if they found a head and no body." Ten months later, campers near Scottsdale, Arizona, found a skull in the desert. It was matched to a torso found outside Plainview in December 1981.

Often Lucas could produce irrefutable evidence of his involvement. He told how he had once scattered pillow feathers over the body of a 76-year-old lady he had bludgeoned to death in Jacksonville. This information had never been released to the media. It was a detail only the murderer could have known.

In this fashion, out came more than 100 names of women Lucas claimed to have killed the length and breadth of the nation. New York State, Washington State, California, Florida—all featured on his list, although his favorite killing ground seems to have been along the 500-mile I-35 interstate highway between Laredo and Gainesville, Texas. Several bodies have since been uncovered,

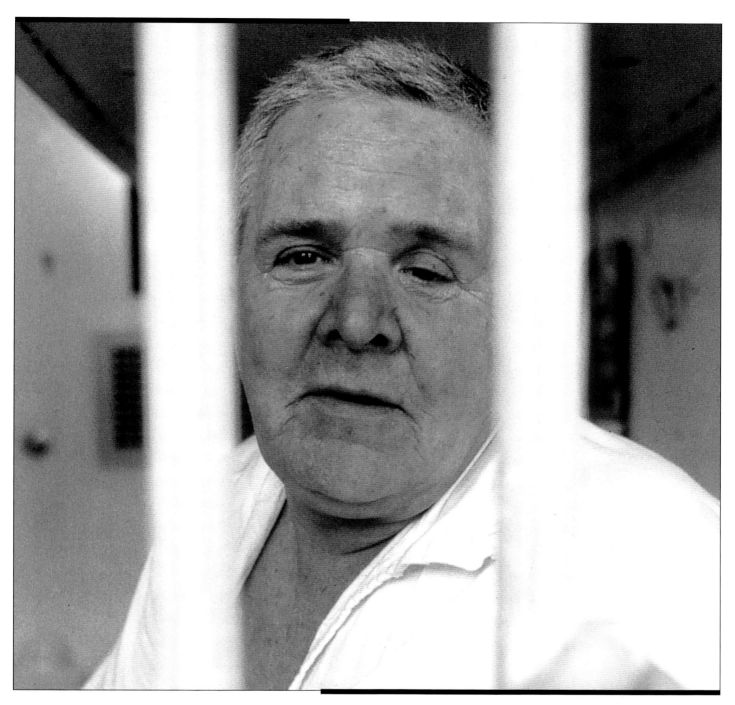

giving the road the dubious nickname the "Henry Lee Lucas Memorial Highway."

The killing spree went into overdrive in 1978 when Lucas met Ottis Elwood Toole in a soup kitchen in Jacksonville, Florida. Toole invited him to his home and Lucas was soon sleeping with both him and his niece. Toole was a car thief and arsonist who, with a string of bodies provided by his new

Lucas died on death row in Texas as attorneys from different states queued to bring him to court for other murders.

- - - - - - - - - - - - -

friend, soon turned to murder. He was equally as debauched as Lucas, though his tally of murders is reckoned to be far less. Together they raped, killed, and dismembered; Lucas enjoying sex with the body of a victim, Toole preferring to barbecue and eat his prey. "The other difference between me and Ottis," Lucas once said chillingly, "is that he just kills them when he feels like it—but I warn them first."

Eventually Toole and Lucas split up, the former returning home to Florida and later being jailed for arson, while Lucas continued on the road with Becky. The girl eventually became just another of her lover's victims, Lucas stabbing her to death during an argument, then having sex with the body before dismembering it, stuffing the remains into three pillowcases and dumping them in a field.

In his confessions to police, this was the only crime for which he appeared to show the slightest remorse. He happily implicated Toole in many other crimes, including killing a sleeping victim by pouring petrol on him and igniting it. Toole, who was already serving a 15-year sentence for arson admitted it and was sentenced to death. He died in prison of cirrhosis of the liver.

Later the total of Lucas's official murder confessions rose to 360, although he hinted that he had committed 500 or more slayings, which would have made him the worst serial killer in American history. Some of these confessions he later retracted, giving rise to further suggestions that his entire story was a sham. But while several of the murders clearly could not have been down to Lucas,

> **The total of Lucas's official murder confessions rose to 360, although he hinted that he had committed 500 or more slayings**

because eye-witness accounts placed him in other parts of the country at the crucial times, a majority undoubtedly were. In too many cases, his recollections enabled the bodies of missing persons to be recovered, most having been raped, sometimes after death.

By the time he started his first jail sentence of 75 years, Lucas had settled on a figure of 157 murders. He had been sentenced for only five of them but a further 21 murder charges were pending in Texas, Arkansas, Louisiana, Florida, and New Mexico. As attorneys from those states queued to bring him to court, Lucas languished on death row in Texas. In June 1999, as a fresh execution date neared, the then-Texas governor George W. Bush stepped in to commute the death sentence to one of life imprisonment. He died of natural causes in March 2001.

So was Lucas the worst serial killer in America's criminal history? Given the glaring inconsistencies in his confessional statements, it is impossible to judge. He claimed more than 500 murders. He might be responsible for over 100. He was convicted of just ten.

Asked to explain his actions, Henry Lee Lucas gave one of the most chilling-ever insights into the twisted mind of the serial killer. "I was bitter at the world. I had nothing but pure hatred. Killing someone is just like walking outdoors. If I wanted a victim I'd just go out and get one."

MICHAEL LUPO

When Italian hairdresser and former choirboy Michael Lupo got the deadly HIV virus, his thoughts turned only to revenge—in the deadliest form.

Lupo went on to kill four gay men in just two months. His "calling card" was to slash their naked bodies and smear them with excrement.

After serving in an elite Italian commando unit, Lupo enjoyed a promiscuous sex life. He bragged

> **❝His "calling card" was to slash their naked bodies and smear them with excrement❞**

about having sex with 4,000 gay partners and was not ashamed to admit his penchant for sado-masochism. This twisted enjoyment led to him building a torture chamber at the house he bought in London shortly after coming to Britain in 1975. One particularly sickening "game" was the slitting of his partners' scrotum so that he could massage their testicles.

As the proud owner of his own fashion and makeup shop, which he called a "styling boutique," Lupo had easy access to young men. These were said to include some of London's high society names, who were desperate to keep their gay lifestyles secret.

It was only in March 1986 when he was diag-

nosed with HIV that Lupo took his violent sexual urges a fatal step further. He picked up his four victims in gay bars, had sex with them and then killed them. It was the discovery of the last victim, 24-year-old Tony Connelly, that convinced police a serial killer was at large in London. Tony was found in a railway workman's hut in Brixton on

FACT FILE.

<u>Name:</u> Michael Lupo, aka "The Wolf Man of London"

<u>Born:</u> 1953

<u>Location of killings:</u> London, England

<u>Number of victims:</u> at least four

<u>Modus operandi:</u> trawling gay bars and strangling his victims

<u>Justice:</u> died serving a life sentence

Lupo indulged in sado-masochistic activities of the weirdest kind before killing his victims.

- - - - - - - - - - - -

April 6, 1986. He had been strangled with his own scarf. The killer became nicknamed the "Wolf Man of London" and his existence sent terror through the capital's gay community.

The statements of two terrified men who had managed to escape from 34-year-old Lupo eventually led to his arrest on May 20 of the same year.

In July he was charged with four murders and two attempted murders and pleaded guilty to them all. Although a life sentence ended Lupo's slayings, it prompted other major investigations by police in Berlin, Hamburg, Los Angeles, and New York—all popular holiday spots of Lupo's where the mutilated bodies of many gay men had been found.

CHARLES MANSON

Shortly before dawn on August 9, 1969, Susan Atkins, Susan Krenwinkel, Linda Kasabian, and Charles Watson set out on a mission ordered by their twisted cult leader.

Within a couple of hours, they had completed their grisly task—and five people lay dead in an orgy of butchery. The scene these Angels of Death left behind them was forever etched into the memories of those Los Angeles police officers who had the misfortune to stumble upon them. The slayings were the work of the infamous Charles Manson gang, a twisted Devil's Children sect which was responsible for murders that went down in American history as among the most atrocious crimes ever committed.

Right from his birth, Manson was destined to lead a life of debauchery and violence. This self-styled Messiah was born illegitimately to 16-year-old prostitute Kathleen Maddox in Cincinnati, Ohio, in 1934, his birth name being recorded as "No Name Maddox." The identity of his father is unknown and his surname derives from one of his mother's lovers at the time. Manson graduated from foster homes to detention centers when, still in his early teens, he became an established juvenile delinquent. Inevitably, his meaningless, criminal existence led to harsher penalties. He was sentenced to two years at the National Training School for Boys in Washington D.C. on March 9, 1951. Freedom would come when Manson reached his eighteenth birthday.

During one of his periods at a detention center, Manson grabbed a boy from behind and held a razor blade to his throat as he carried out a violent rape. His file was marked "Dangerous" and "Not to be trusted" and he was transferred to the Federal Reformatory in Virginia. But even then, no one could have imagined how much Manson would one day shock the world, both by the savagery he

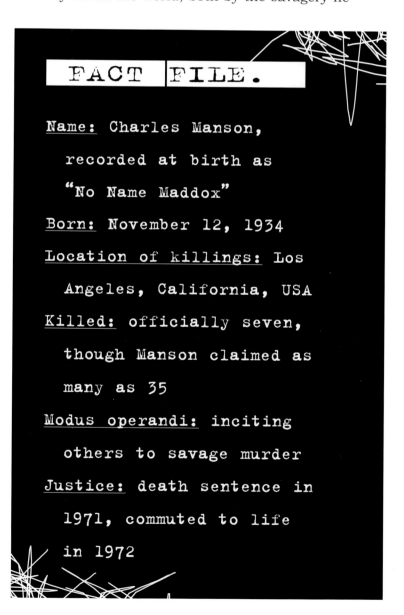

FACT FILE.

<u>Name:</u> Charles Manson, recorded at birth as "No Name Maddox"

<u>Born:</u> November 12, 1934

<u>Location of killings:</u> Los Angeles, California, USA

<u>Killed:</u> officially seven, though Manson claimed as many as 35

<u>Modus operandi:</u> inciting others to savage murder

<u>Justice:</u> death sentence in 1971, commuted to life in 1972

Manson and his so-called "Family" created shockwaves throughout California. His complete physical and spiritual control of
the group led to a series of shocking murders.

incited and by his appearance in court, his forehead bearing a slashed swastika.

In his teens, Manson's sexual preferences
veered toward other men but shortly after his
release on parole in 1954, he married Rosalie Jean
Willis, a 17-year-old waitress. Rosalie was pregnant when the two traveled to California in a stolen
car. Convicted of the theft, Manson was sentenced
to three years at the Terminal Island jail in San

Pedro. Faithful Rosalie visited him often, sometimes taking along Charles Manson Jr. but then
suddenly stopped her visits. Manson discovered
she had fallen in love with someone else and,
although he was paroled in 1958, he was never to
see Rosalie or his son again. In between jail

> **" By the time he was 32, Manson had spent most of his life in prison "**

sentences, Manson married again and had another son: a second Charles Manson Jr. That marriage
did not last either.

By the time he was 32, Manson had spent most
of his life in prison. So institutionalized was he
that, when yet another parole came up, he asked
to remain within the four walls he knew as home.
He did not feel easy being released into a society
that he felt had dealt him a bad hand. The authorities refused Manson's plea to be a voluntary
inmate and in 1967, the criminal drifter was once
more back on the road.

It was no surprise that Manson gravitated
toward the flower-power cult, with its heart in San
Francisco. With a guitar on his back and drugs
becoming a bigger part of his life, Manson felt he
had found his niche. His strange magnetism drew
drop-outs and drug addicts to him. Manson discovered he had his own strange following—and a
power over others that was to prove deadly. A

strange assembly of impressionable young women adored Manson, even giving up stable, middle-class lives to be with him.

By 1969, the Manson sect was already taking root, settling into a run-down dwelling, Spahn Ranch, outside Los Angeles. This assortment of the lost, the weak, and the potentially evil called themselves "The Family." Attracting wayward youngsters, bikers, and small-time criminals with the lure of free sex and drugs, Manson managed to gather a hard core of 25 devotees with over 60 other associates.

One day, a drug-addled Manson announced that now was the time for "Helter Skelter," his ultimate mission and named for the title of a track on the Beatles' famous *White Album.* Manson was convinced Beatle songs contained hidden messages that only had meaning for him. Songs like *Revolution 9* were especially prophetic for The Family. They believed it all led to another battle of Armageddon, Manson's term for a planned race war in which African Americans would reign supreme over the whites. Only Manson and those who chose to stay with him would be spared the mass racial slaughter. Chosen African Americans, spouted Manson, would become part of The Family—numbering no less than 144,000. They would become his "Chosen People." Manson had taken the term from the Bible, referring to the 12 Tribes of Israel, each numbering 12,000. Together, he said, they would take over the world. And The Beatles, Manson proclaimed, would be his "spokesmen." Manson told his disciples that nothing could be achieved unless he had utterly devoted followers, who alone could change the world. They would strike out at the white establishment. They would kill.

Sharon Tate, actress wife of film producer Roman Polanski, was one of the five people killed by the Manson "Family" at her home in Los Angeles.
- - - - - - - - - - - -

"Helter Skelter" got under way that fateful hot August day in 1969, when Atkins, Krenwinkel, Kasabian, and Watson entered the grounds of 10050 Cielo Drive, Benedict Canyon, Los Angeles. It was a mansion rented by film producer Roman Polanski and his beautiful actress wife Sharon Tate. Polanski, away filming, would escape the carnage that was to follow. But as the evil four stealthily made their way toward the mansion,

Sharon and the friends she had invited round for a night in, would soon die, all begging for their lives. With strange war cries, the knife-wielding killers set upon them and, in a short explosion of mind-numbing violence, five innocent people were butchered. No one will ever know what real terror and suffering the victims endured before the gang smeared the mansion walls with bizarre messages in the butchered group's blood.

One victim, Polish film director Voytek Frykowski, was battered with a club by Watson who all the while whispered: "I am the devil come to do the devil's work." He was then finished off by Atkins, who stabbed him six times with a knife. Hollywood hair stylist Jay Sebring was stabbed then finished off with a gunshot.

The most sickening sight witnessed by police called out after this orgy of violence was the pathetic body of Sharon Tate. The 26-year-old actress had begged to be spared for the sake of the child she was carrying, due in just a month's time. Her pleas for mercy had been greeted with derision and she suffered 16 stab wounds, killing both her and her unborn baby boy. A nylon rope was knotted around Sharon's neck and slung over a ceiling beam and the other end was tied around the hooded head of Sebring. The word "PIG" was scrawled in blood on the door of the mansion.

The body of Steven Parent, the 18-year-old guest of the house's caretaker, was discovered slumped in his car in the driveway. Parent had encountered the raiders as he drove from the house. They had flagged him down and then shot

him four times. Their next find was the body of Abigail Folger, heiress to a coffee fortune, lying on the lawn. She had been cut to pieces as she tried to flee.

Even after this, as America reeled in the horror of it all, Charles Manson felt he had not achieved his aim: a macabre belief that such murders would spark off a race war. There was more bloody work to be done—and this time Manson wanted to be in on the action himself. The night after the Polanski mansion slaughter, Manson, accompanied by Watson, Krenwinkel, and former college queen Leslie Van Houten, broke into the home of Leno and Rosemary LaBianca, owners of a small supermarket chain. Manson tied up the couple, then left them to his three cult slaves.

A sword, knives, and forks were used in the barbaric slaying. Police found a fork protruding from Leno LaBianca's body, with the word "War" carved in his stomach. He had been stabbed 26 times and symbolically hanged and a blood-stained pillowcase had been used as a hood. A cord around his throat was attached to a heavy lamp and his hands were tied behind his back with a leather cord. Rosemary's nightdress had been pushed over her head and her back and buttocks were covered in stab wounds. She too was hooded by a pillowcase and had been hanged by a wire attached to a lamp. On the walls, written in blood, were the words "Death to the Pigs" and "Rise." On a fridge were written the misspelled words "Healter Skelter."

❛❛She suffered 16 stab wounds, killing both her and her unborn baby boy❜❜

Charles Manson is escorted from the courtroom after being found guilty of murder.

Ludicrously, Los Angeles police did not initially connect the two raids on the Tate and LaBianca mansions. It was Susan Atkins, one of Manson's strongest devotees, who was to bring the evil group to justice. She had been picked up in connection with the slaying of drug dealer Gary Hinman, killed ten days before the mass murders.

He had been tortured to death in his hillside home in Topanga Canyon, the hippy capital of Los Angeles in the 1960s. Hinman's blood had been used to scrawl a message on a nearby wall. It read: "Political Piggy." Police also believed that another man, Donald Shea, who vanished from Spahn Ranch, a one-time movie set on the outskirts of the city, was also a victim of the Manson gang. Shea's body was never found.

Atkins, still reveling in her involvement with headline-making butchery, could not keep her mouth shut. She bragged about her role, sickening cellmates with her claims of drinking Sharon Tate's blood. "I was there," she boasted. "We did it. It felt so good the first time I stabbed her. When she screamed at me, it did something to me, sent

Patricia Krenwinkel and Susan Atkins were escorted into court in 1970 accused of murdering Sharon Tate and five others. They were part of the Manson "Family" cult.

- - - - - - - - - - - - -

a rush through me, and I stabbed her again. I just kept stabbing her until she stopped screaming. It was like a sexual release, especially when you see the blood. It's better than a climax."

Shortly before Christmas 1969, the Manson tribe were rounded up and the incredible story of this living Satan and his so-called "witchlets" was flashed around the world. Charles Manson, the

short, scraggy ex-con who had spent more than half his life behind bars, was charged with nine murders in all: the Tate and LaBianca massacres and two other slayings. But he was suspected of orchestrating as many as 25 other killings from his desert ranch. Suddenly Manson became the most talked-about and most feared criminal in the annals of Californian law enforcement. Civilization had a rare chance to look directly into the face of evil and madness.

At his trial, Manson cut a terrifying figure as he spoke of his weird band of disciples. He said: "These children who come at you with knives, they are your children. I didn't teach them. You did. I just tried to help them stand up. You eat meat and you kill things that are better than you are, and then you say how bad and evil killers your children are. You made your children what they are I am only what lives inside each and every one of you."

On March 29, 1971, guilty verdicts were returned on all counts against the Manson gang. Looking at the jury who had convicted her, Susan Atkins warned them to lock their doors and to watch their children. The hearing had taken 38 weeks and was then the longest criminal trial in American history. It cost $1.25 million and 31,176 pages of transcript were taken. Sentencing them, Judge Charles Older said: "It is my considered judgment that not only is the death penalty appropriate but it is almost compelled by the circumstances." The sentences were commuted to life imprisonment in 1972 when California's death penalty was banned by the courts as being "cruel and unusual punishment."

There was a retrial of Leslie Van Houten in 1976, ordered because her lawyer Robert Hughes vanished during the first trial. Hughes's remains were found months later in a mountain wilderness. Members of Manson's Family were heavily suspected of his death. Many years later, there were rumors that the murdered Voytek Frykowski and

> **It is my considered judgment that not only is the death penalty appropriate but it is almost compelled by the circumstances**

Charles Manson was given the death sentence which was later commuted to life imprisonment.

Jay Sebring were known drug dealers and that Manson had wanted to take over their business.

There was also talk that Manson's gang had been ordered to kill completely different victims and that Sharon Tate and her friends had simply been in the wrong place at the wrong time. The reason for this theory was that 10050 Cielo Drive had previously been rented by record company boss Terry Melcher, the son of Hollywood actress Doris Day. Melcher had once sneered at Manson's attempts to get a recording contract with him.

In 1994, all the sickening memories of the Tate massacre were rekindled when one of the butchering Angels of Death demanded her freedom. The Free Susan Atkins Campaign was launched by those who felt the one-time church choir singer turned evil killer was now rehabilitated. But while a small group of supporters were actively campaigning to get Atkins released from jail, there were many more who could not forget the horrific massacre in which she had satisfied her bloodlust and wished she had died in the electric chair.

A second appeal by Atkins was refused after Sharon Tate's sister, Patti, gave evidence. Patti, who was only 11 years old when Sharon was murdered, said: "Every year before she died, my mother would attend parole hearings of the murderers and she had to come face to face with them. That used

Five bodies, including that of Sharon Tate, were found at the Polanski home. Two of the bodies, shown here being covered in sheets, were found on the lawn.

- - - - - - - - - - - -

to make her mad because one of these people knew Sharon and they were totally indifferent to what they had done. They just destroyed their blood-soaked clothes, washed their hands with a neighbor's watering can and walked down the street to kill more people."

Atkins remains in prison. So too, of course, does Manson. Speaking from jail, he once said: "I was pretty upset for a long time. I was really mad

at a lot of people. I'm still willing to get out and kill a whole bunch of people. That's one reason I'm not too fast on getting out. Because if I got out, I'd feel obliged to get even."

Stephen Kay, who at one time ran the District Attorney's office in a Los Angeles suburb, had no doubt about the sheer evil that was Charles Manson. He said: "Manson is the greatest advertisement for the death penalty. He can cast a spell and that's how he got other people to do his killing. He had these girls from nice families willing to kill for him. He had such evil control—and he still has it today."

PETER MANUEL

He was named for one of the great saints but Peter Thomas Anthony Manuel spent his life doing the Devil's work.

Short but strong, dark and with piercing eyes, he was a liar, a thief, a thug, and a troublemaker from childhood. He spent most of his short life in approved schools, Borstal institutions, and jails, and if it could be said of anyone that he was destined to end his days on the scaffold, that man was Peter Manuel. He fulfilled that destiny at the age of just 31 when he took his final walk to the gallows.

Manuel was born on March 15, 1927, in Manhattan to Scottish parents who had emigrated to New York in search of a better life. It seems they failed to find it, for the family returned to Scotland after five years and moved to Coventry in 1937. A year later, the 11-year-old Manuel was in trouble with the law after being caught breaking into shops. A spell in an approved school helped make him a hardened little villain ready to turn to violence to obtain either money or sexual satisfaction.

In 1941, after the family home had been destroyed in a German bombing raid, the family went back to Glasgow. Manuel was unable to join them until 1946 because he was in Borstal, where he had been sent for assaulting a woman with a hammer in 1942 at the tender age of 15. Within weeks of his return to Scotland, he was arrested for housebreaking. While awaiting trial, he raped an expectant mother and indecently assaulted two other women. At his subsequent trial, in which he conducted his own defence, he was sentenced to eight years in jail. He was released in 1953.

Manuel then entered into a serious relationship with a girl and they even set the wedding date of July 30, 1955. When his fiancee discovered his criminal background, however, she dropped him. The end of the affair obviously weighed heavily on the young man's psyche because, on what would have been his wedding night, he attacked a woman in a field. Her screams alerted neighbours who called the police, but as they searched the area he managed to hide, keeping the woman quiet at knife point. Eventually the woman talked him into

FACT FILE.

<u>Name:</u> Peter Thomas Anthony
Manuel

<u>Born:</u> March 15, 1927

<u>Location of killings:</u> Glasgow
in Scotland and Newcastle
upon Tyne in England

<u>Killed:</u> at least nine

<u>Modus operandi:</u> various

<u>Justice:</u> hanged at Barlinnie
Jail in 1958

The crime scene where Isabelle Cooke's body was found in a field by police.

- - - - - - - - - - - - - -

letting her go, after which he was arrested and charged with sexual assault. Surprisingly, he was acquitted.

Six months later, the brutal young thug graduated to murder. His first victim was 17-year-old Annie Knielands whom he killed on January 2, 1956, and whose body he left on the fifth fairway of a golf course at East Kilbride, near Glasgow. She had been badly beaten around the head and, although not raped or sexually molested, semen stains on her clothing showed he had obtained sexual gratification through the act of murder. The

- - - - - - - - - - - -

Peter Manuel, a thug and a troublemaker from the age of 11, spent most of his short life in young offender's institutions and jails before his death by hanging at 31.

killing was only discovered two days later when a horrified golfer came across the corpse and ran to tell the police. On his way he met a group of people to whom he gabbled out his story.

Ironically, one of the group was Manuel who, as a result, was interviewed by detectives who were immediately suspicious of him because his face was freshly scratched. When his home was searched, items of clothing were missing that he had worn recently. However, his father gave him an alibi, swearing that he had been indoors on the evening in question.

In March that year, police received a tip-off that a burglary was to take place and Manuel was caught in the act. While still awaiting trial in September, there were burglaries on successive nights, both of which the police linked to Manuel. On the morning after the second break-in, a domestic help discovered three bodies in a neighboring house. They were Mrs. Marion Watt, her daughter Vivienne, and her sister Margaret Brown. All had been shot at close range, the older ladies dying in their beds. Manuel was the prime suspect. He was interviewed but no incriminating evidence was found.

Instead, police turned their attention to the murdered woman's husband, William Watt, who had been on a fishing trip in Argyll at the time of the slayings. Detectives nevertheless deemed it possible that he had had time to return home, kill the women, and get back to Argyll. He was charged and held in Barlinnie prison—where Manuel was also sent to serve 18 months for the first attempted burglary.

Manuel wrote to Mr. Watt's solicitor asking him to represent him in an appeal against the burglary sentence. He hinted that in return he could help disprove the case against Watt, and gave details that convinced the solicitor that Manuel must have been present at the murders. After 67 days in custody, the innocent Mr. Watt was released. Manuel did nothing to help him, merely offering the name of a known criminal who was quickly eliminated from inquiries.

Manuel came out of jail at the end of November 1957. Less than a month later, another teenage girl

> **"A shoe and a handbag belonging to 17-year-old Isabelle Cooke were discovered in a disused colliery shaft but there was no sign of the girl herself"**

was reported missing. A shoe and a handbag belonging to 17-year-old Isabelle Cooke were discovered in a disused colliery shaft but there was no sign of the girl herself. Even as police searched for Isabelle, another three bodies were found in a house just ten minutes' walk away from Manuel's home. Peter Smart, an engineering manager, had been shot through the head at close range, as had his wife Doris and their 11-year-old son Michael. They had been killed on New Year's Day 1958 and between then and their discovery on January 6, neighbors had reported that lights in their home had been switched on and off, suggesting either that the killer had stayed at the house or else had returned to the scene of the crime. On January 4, another local couple had disturbed an intruder in their bedroom but he had fled when the husband pretended he had a gun.

Peter Manuel was arrested on January 14 and charged with the murder of the Smarts and the recent, thwarted break-in. His father was charged with receiving stolen goods: a camera and gloves that had been taken from a house near Isabelle Cooke's home. In an attempt to shield his son, Manuel Sr. claimed to have bought them at a market. Now, possibly for the first time in his life, Manuel began to show remorse, but probably only because of the trouble he had got his father into. He offered a full confession in return for his

Peter Smart and his wife Doris were killed by Manuel on New Year's Day 1958.

- - - - - - - - - - - - - - - - -

Neighbors reported that the lights where still being switched on and off at the Smart's home, suggesting the killer was still in the house after the crime was committed.

- - - - - - - - - - -

Margaret Watt and her young daughter were killed by Manuel in their home. He confessed to their murder, but then retracted it later at the trial.
- - - - - - - - - - - - - -

father's release. He described in detail the murder of the Smart family and the Watts family and went on to confess to the killing of poor Anne Knielands on the golf course. He led police to the spot where he had thrown two guns into a river and showed them where he had buried Isabelle Cooke.

Although he did not include it in his confessions, police were certain that Manuel was also responsible for the murder of a taxi driver, Sydney Dunn, shot the previous December in Newcastle upon Tyne where the killer had gone for a job interview. His Scottish murders, on the other hand, were recounted in unemotional detail. When he took police to the ploughed field where he had buried poor Isabelle Cooke, he said, "This is it. This is the place. In fact, I think I'm standing on her now." He was, as police found to their horror.

The tone of Manuel's statements, made during hours of interrogation, was also eerily matter-of-fact. Describing the moments leading up to Isabelle's death, he said: "I met the girl walking... When we got near the dog track she started to scream. I tore off her clothes and tied something round her neck and choked her. I then carried her up a lane and into a field and dug a hole with a shovel. While I was digging a man passed along the lane on a bike. So I carried her again over a path beside a brickworks into another field. I dug a hole next to a part of a field that was ploughed and put her into it."

Of the Watts family murders, he said: "There were two people in the bed. I went into the other room and there was a girl in the bed. She woke up and sat up. I hit her on the chin and knocked her out. I tied her hands and went back into the other room. I shot the people in this room and then heard someone making a noise in the other room. I went back in and the girl had got loose. We struggled

> **"We struggled around for a while and then I flung her on the bed and I shot her too"**

around for a while and then I flung her on the bed and I shot her too."

These and other statements of the evil killer were read out to a shocked jury when Manuel's trial on eight counts of murder began on May 12, 1958. Ten days later he sacked his counsel and conducted his own defence. In it, he rescinded his confession and accused William Watt of murdering his own family—forcing the unfortunate man to face cross-examination by the real killer of his loved ones.

Manuel was found guilty of seven murders, as there was insufficient corroborative evidence in the case of Annie Knielands. The judge commented that "a man may be very bad without being mad" before sentencing him to death. On July 11, 1958,

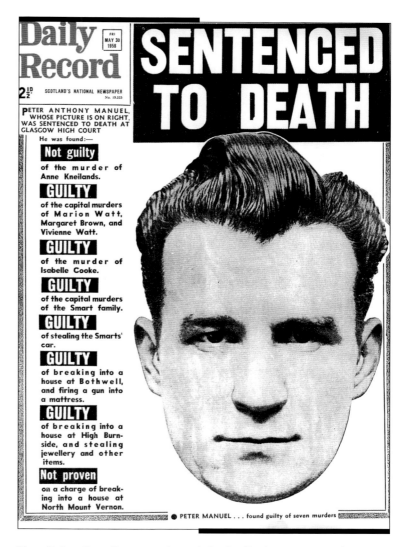

When Peter Manuel was sentenced to death for seven murders, this is how the *Daily Record* reported it.

Peter Manuel was allowed to hear Mass and take Holy Communion before making the final, short walk to keep his date with the hangman.

ROBERT MAUDSLEY

It was in jail that the killer, soon to be known as "Hannibal the Cannibal," left bodies in his wake.

Horribly mutilated, the corpses were victims of a man monster who is the most terrifying murderer to be held in an English prison. Robert Maudsley is so dangerous that he has spent more than a quarter of century locked away in a bullet-proof glass cage in a prison basement. He has been in solitary confinement all that time—unprecedented treatment for a prisoner of British justice. But then nothing about Maudsley was ever normal.

Maudsley was born in Liverpool in June 1953.

Before he was two years old, Robert, his brothers Paul and Kevin, and sister Brenda were taken away from their mother Jean and lorry driver father George. Social workers placed the children in care because of "parental neglect." Most of Maudsley's early years were spent at Nazareth House, a Roman Catholic orphanage run by nuns. By all accounts, he was a normal little boy, bonding particularly well with his two brothers and appearing relatively unscathed by his treatment as a baby.

All that was to change when his parents, who had only visited the orphanage occasionally, were allowed to take the four children back home. By this time, another eight Maudsley offspring had been born. It was the return to his dysfunctional

FACT FILE.

Name: Robert Maudsley, aka "Hannibal the Cannibal"

Born: June 1953

Location of killings: London and in custody

Killed: Four

Modus operandi: Garrotting and stabbing

Justice: Life imprisonment to be spent in solitary confinement

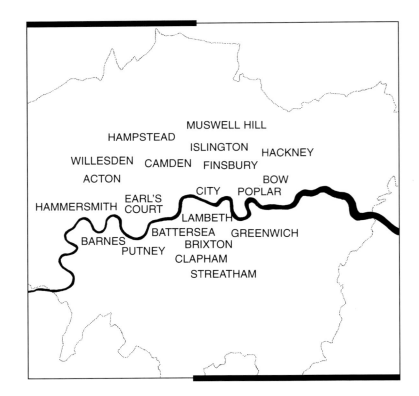

Maudsley was sent to Broadmoor Hospital for the criminally insane. While he was there, he managed to kill one of the other inmates and was sent to Wakefield Prison.

- - - - - - - - - - - - - -

family that was to sow the seeds of Maudsley's twisted character. The children were subjected to sexual and physical abuse but the worst treatment seems to have been directed at Robert. He would later state: "All I remember of my childhood is the beatings. Once I was locked in a room for six months and my father only opened the door to come in and beat me, five or six times a day. He used to hit me with sticks or rods and once he bust a .22 air rifle over my back."

Robert Maudsley was again removed from his family and placed in a series of foster homes, eventually arriving in London when he was 16. Like many young people in a friendless city, he became a drifter and drug addict. He was finally forced to

seek psychiatric help after several suicide attempts. It was during his talks with doctors that he said he heard voices in his head telling him to kill his parents.

This should have been a warning to the medical professionals. Instead, Maudsley was released back on to the London streets where he worked as a rent boy to finance his drug habit. He was 20 when he committed his first murder. The victim was a laborer, John Farrell, who had picked Maudsley up for paid sex. When Farrell showed Maudsley pictures of children he had abused, something snapped in Maudsley's head. He flew into a rage and garrotted Farrell.

Because of his previous mental problems and his state of mind when arrested, Maudsley was declared unfit to stand trial and was instead sent to Broadmoor Hospital for the criminally insane. It was here that the extent of his killing urges first became sickeningly clear. In 1977 he and another inmate took a third patient, a paedophile, hostage and barricaded themselves in a cell. They tortured their victim for nine hours before garrotting him with an electrical flex and holding up his body so that prison guards could see him through the spy door. According to one guard, the man's head was "cracked open like a boiled egg" with a spoon hanging out of it and part of the brain missing.

Despite his obviously deranged mental state, Maudsley was on this occasion found fit to stand trial. Convicted of manslaughter, he was not sent to hospital but to Wakefield Prison, known as "Monster Mansion" because of its notorious inmates. Here Maudsley's evil reputation had preceded him and he earned many nicknames such as Cannibal, Brain-eater, Spoons, and Jaws (because of his crooked teeth). Maudsley had been at Wakefield for only a few weeks before his warped mind turned again to murder. According to other inmates, Maudsley had set out to kill seven people in one bloody spree. He did not reach his target but what happened has gone down in prison history.

Maudsley's first victim that day was sex offender Salney Darwood, a man who had befriended him and given him French lessons. Maudsley invited the fellow prisoner to his cell where he garrotted him and stabbed him. He then hid Darwood's body under his bed. During the morning Maudsley tried to lure others into his cell but all refused. "We could all see the madness in his eyes," said a fellow inmate. But a second man was to die.

Bill Roberts was lying on his bunk bed when Maudsley hacked at his skull with a makeshift dagger and smashed his head against the wall. The maniac murderer then calmly walked into a prison officer's room, placed the knife on a table and told him the next roll call would be two men short.

Maudsley was convicted of double murder at Leeds Crown Court where the jury was told he was "one of the most determined and dangerous killers held in prison in this country." He was returned to Wakefield Prison, where he remained in solitary confinement, apart from a short time at Parkhurst Prison on the Isle of Wight. Here, psychiatrist Dr. Bob Johnson reported that he had almost rid Maudsley of his violent tendencies. But then, without warning, the counseling sessions were stopped and Maudsley was moved back to Wakefield.

In 1983, a two-cell unit, eerily similar to that of the fictional movie cannibal Hannibal Lecter, was constructed for Maudsley. It contained a table and chair made out of compressed cardboard and a lavatory and sink bolted to the floor. Maudsley was now classified as Britain's most dangerous prisoner, a man posing such a risk to those around him that he has spent the last quarter of a century in virtual isolation. Once a day he was allowed

> **"Bill Roberts was lying on his bunk bed when Maudsley hacked at his skull with a makeshift dagger and smashed his head against the wall"**

out of his cell for one hour's exercise in a yard 20 feet long and 12 feet wide. Every move prisoner 467637 made was under the watch of at least five guards. Maudsley described his exercise period: "I am not allowed to smoke or bring anything to drink out into the exercise yard. If another inmate attempts to speak to me from his cell window, he could be given cell confinement. The yard has CCTV cameras and is made of concrete. There are no trees, grass, or flowers. It is bare, sterile, and bleak. I find the enforced silence depressing. When the hour is up, I have to go through the search process and return to my cage. I leave my shoes outside the cage. From 9.30am to 11am I see no one."

There have been some who feel it is wrong that Maudsley should remain behind bars until he dies. One, prison visitor Jane Heaton, said: "The monster that some people call a cannibal isn't the Bob Maudsley I know. He's a caring, lovely man. When he writes to me, his letters make me laugh. He knows he did some terrible crimes; he knows he can never go free. But it just can't be right to keep any human being in solitary confinement for 25 years can it? Everyone concentrates on the crimes he committed 25 years ago. It is as if they are living in a time loop and no one is prepared to look at how he is now."

Maudsley's brother Paul, one of the few people to whom he ever felt close in his violent life, launched a campaign for what he said should be fairer treatment: "As far as I can tell, the prison authorities are trying to break him. Every time they

> **"All I have to look forward to is further mental breakdown and possible suicide"**

see him making a little progress they throw a spanner in the works. The trouble started because he got locked up as a kid. All they do when they put him back there is bring all that trauma back to him. All I want for Robert is that he be treated like other prisoners but it seems that's too much to ask."

Many others refuse to accept that 6ft 2in Maudsley has simply become a gentle giant who enjoys listening to classical music. Says a prison official: "One prison officer who was about to open his cell door with a pipe in his mouth was warned Maudsley would ram it into the back of his throat. A few days later the man was about to do the same thing when Maudsley smiled at him and said 'You just don't learn do you?' Maudsley likes to kill people and he makes no bones about it. He is the most dangerous man in the prison system."

Prison psychiatrists who have conducted numerous studies on Maudsley all say he is suffering from personality disorders but they cannot agree he is mad. Such is the interest in his mind that scientists in both Britain and America are reportedly prepared to pay huge amounts of money for his brain after he is dead.

In 2003, Maudsley spent his 50th birthday like any other day—in total isolation. He has no hopes that his existence will change. "All I have to look forward to is further mental breakdown and possible suicide," he told one visitor. "In many ways I think this is what the authorities hope for. That way, the problem of Robert John Maudsley can be easily and swiftly resolved."

IVAN MILAT

They left home to find adventure in the wild wonders of Australia: young people with packs on their backs taking time out before settling down.

But in the years between 1989 and 1992, many of those youthful adventurers were cut down, butchered, and killed—victims of Ivan Robert Marko Milat, the "Backpack Killer."

The first two bodies to be found were those of British girls 21-year-old Caroline Clarke and 22-year-old Joanne Walters. They were discovered after runners Ken Selly and Keith Caldwell were making their way through a site called Executioner's Drop, deep in the heart of Belangalo State Forest, New South Wales.

It was the stench that drew Ken to a large boulder where, below a pile of decaying leaves, he spotted bone and hair. At first dismissing the find as a dead animal, he changed his mind when he spotted a piece of black T-shirt lying close by. Ken's call to the police that day, September 19, 1992, brought fear into the hearts of parents across the world—and sparked a hunt for Australia's most notorious and evil serial killers.

Cordoning off the scene, police examined the first body. A search of the area revealed another. The next day Caroline and Joanne were positively identified. The pair had disappeared five months before, last spotted alive in Sydney on April 18 after saying they planned to hitch-hike to Adelaide. Joanne's parents Ray and Jill Walters, already in the country searching for their missing daughter, were given the terrible news by police who then telephoned Caroline's parents, Ian and Jacquie Clarke, in England. Before the girls' identities were

publicly revealed, however, the news that two bodies had been discovered caused the police to be inundated with phone calls from other parents whose student children had simply vanished on their Australian trekking holidays.

The attacks on the two girls had been frenzied

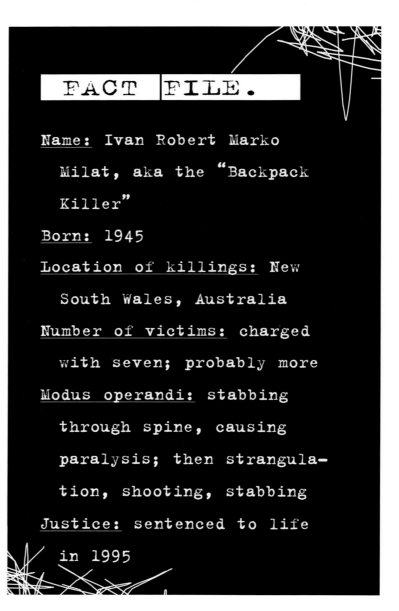

FACT FILE.

Name: Ivan Robert Marko Milat, aka the "Backpack Killer"

Born: 1945

Location of killings: New South Wales, Australia

Number of victims: charged with seven; probably more

Modus operandi: stabbing through spine, causing paralysis; then strangulation, shooting, stabbing

Justice: sentenced to life in 1995

and ferocious. Joanne had been stabbed in the heart and lungs, one cut going so deep it had penetrated her spine. Forensic pathologist Dr. Peter Bradhurst was visibly moved when he had to report that the spinal wounds could have paralyzed Joanne before the other wounds finally killed her. She may also have been strangled. Joanne had been gagged and what was left of her hands still bore the jewelry she had been wearing.

Caroline had also been stabbed and shot in the head several times. Bullet holes in a red cloth wrapped around her head showed she had been shot ten times. Disturbingly, when experts reenacted the slaughter, they realized the bullets had been fired from several angles, suggesting the killer was using the girl as some sort of sickening target practice. Examination of the murder scene in Belangalo Forest revealed six cigarette butts, spent cartridges, and a small piece of green plastic. Someone had also obviously built a fire from house bricks, an incongruous construction in a forest.

Forensic psychiatrist Dr. Rod Milton was taken to the scene to draw up a profile of the killer. After studying the scene, he came to two conclusions: that the murderer was familiar with the area and that he had carefully planned what he intended to do. The killer's treatment of his victims showed he had wanted total control and there could be an underlying sexual motive. Dr. Milton drew up a profile of the man he thought police should be hunting. He probably lived on the outskirts of a city in a semi-rural area and worked out of doors or in a semi-skilled job. He was unable to sustain a happy relationship and possibly had homosexual or bisexual tendencies. He would be in his mid-thirties and have a history of conflict with authority. But there was no reason to believe the

Artist's impression of backpackers murderer Ivan Milat during his court appearance in 1996.

man they wanted was a serial killer. That confirmation was yet to come.

Later that month, police called a public meeting in the Bowral Town Hall, hoping locals would come and offer some help in solving the murders of Joanne and Caroline. One man, Bruce Pryor, who had lived in the area all his life, was particularly alarmed to hear that other backpackers had vanished. As a father himself, he shared the anguish of those parents who were waiting to hear what had become of their children. Something made him stop one day soon afterward as he drove past the Belangalo area. His truck made its way along dirt tracks as Bruce traveled a location he knew well. Suddenly he was in a spot where he had never been before. The sight of a burned out fire filled him with foreboding. Walking into a clearing, Bruce noticed a bone and hoped it was that of a kangaroo or other wild animal. Then he saw what was unmistakably a human skull.

When police arrived on the scene, they found

a pair of sand shoes and a floppy black hat. They now knew what had happened to James Gibson, 19, and his girlfriend Deborah Everist, also 19, both from Victoria, who had disappeared while hitching a lift to a conservation festival on December 9, 1989. All that police had been able to trace of them at the time was James's camera and backpack that had been found on a roadside. Now they had his body, which, although barely recognizable as a human form, wore white canvas shoes that were still laced up. A silver crucifix was still on Deborah's body—or what was left of it.

Dr. Peter Bradhurst was again in charge of determining how the two young people died. James had suffered deep spinal stabbings, similar to those of Joanne, which would have paralyzed him before he was eventually killed. There were other stab wounds on the chest and ribs. The killer had slashed and slashed with some force. Deborah had suffered a single wound to the spine and slashes to the face and head.

Further police searches were now launched in the area in case it held the answer to the secret fears of so many anguished parents in so many different countries. At the end of October, they were ready to wind up the hunt, there being just three square miles of the allocated area left to trawl. But just as they were hoping that Belangalo State Forest was hiding no more sickening secrets, one of the search team spotted a pair of pink women's jeans. There was also a piece of rope, an empty gun cartridge packet, and tin cans shot through with bullet holes. Seeing a fireplace similar to those they had encountered previously made the police continue their search with deep feelings of misgiving. Within a short time, they found a skull with a purple headband, a piece of leg bone with a brown boot attached, and several items of women's clothing scattered nearby.

> **❝ James had suffered deep spinal stabbings, similar to those of Joanne, which would have paralyzed him before he was eventually killed ❞**

The parents of 21-year-old German girl Simone Schmidl heard the news on their radio before they were officially told by the police, who were awaiting formal identification. The remains were those of their daughter. Simone had last been seen on January 21, 1991, hitchhiking to Melbourne along the same stretch of road between Liverpool and Goulburn as James Gibson and Deborah Everist. Until then, the only trace police had of her were her glasses and camping equipment abandoned in the bush near the small town of Wangatta, in Victoria. When discovered, Simone's body was still partially dressed and her clothes were pushed up in a position that suggested she had been sexually assaulted. The trademark stabbing of the spinal column was obvious.

The pink jeans did not belong to Simone, however. They had been worn by another German girl, Anja Habschied, who with her boyfriend Gabor Neuebauer had been missing since December 1991. The last sighting of the couple was as they hitched lifts from King's Cross, Sydney, to Darwin. What was left of 20-year-old Anja and 21-year-old

Ivan Milat, who murdered backpackers in Australia, is seen here in 1996 posing with a gun.

– – – – – – – – – – – – – – –

Gabor was discovered on November 4, 1992. Anja's head was missing, together with two of her vertebrae. Dr. Peter Bradhurst wondered how he could find it in his heart to release the full details of Anja's death, for it looked very much as if she had been decapitated while alive and in a kneeling position. Gabor had been gagged and strangled. His skull showed six bullet entries.

Police now knew that the same man—or men —was responsible for the killings. The methods of murder were very similar and were carried out in a calculated, ritualistic way. The killer was getting confident, seemingly taking his time to slaughter his victims. The police had to admit they were

dealing with a serial killer who, if not captured, would strike again and again.

Photographs of the victims brought floods of calls from people who had seen them hitching their way around Australia and from hundreds of parents who did not know their children's whereabouts. But one person gave police the kind of information they so desperately needed. British student Paul Onions, 20, had been picked up by Ivan Milat—and miraculously lived to tell of his encounter.

On January 25, 1990, Paul was hitching to find fruit-picking work in the Riverina district, several hundred miles south of Sydney. He had taken a train to Liverpool and was now thumbing lifts on the highway. Milat approached Paul as he bought a cold drink, offering him a lift. As Paul clambered

Ivan Milat is led from court during his trial in 1996.
- - - - - - - - - - - - - - - -

into his four-wheel vehicle, his supposed good samaritan introduced himself as "Bill" and bombarded him with questions about where he was going and who might know of his whereabouts. As they drove on, there was something about the man that made Paul feel uneasy. His fears were confirmed when Milat launched into a tirade about "Pommies" and then said he needed to stop the vehicle to get some cassette tapes from the back. Paul noticed there was a large selection of tapes already neatly stacked in the front and decided to take the opportunity of getting out of the vehicle and as far away as possible from his weird driver.

As soon as he made to get out, Paul was ordered back into the vehicle. Despite now having a gun pointed at his head, he made the brave deci-

sion to flee for his life. He fell into lines of traffic, desperately trying to get a car to stop. Even then, Milat was determined not to let him go. He made one final dive for the young man but Paul managed to throw himself in front of a van, which stopped. The driver, Joanne Berry, was just as terrified as Paul—for she had her sister and four children with her and thought she was the one in danger from a madman. But seeing Milat running toward her van with a gun, Joanne let Paul stumble into her car and put her foot on the accelerator. At Mittagong police station, Paul told his story, giving all the details he could remember. What he did not have was the vehicle's registration number. The duty police officer told him that without it there was very little chance of tracing his attacker—which, tragically for the other victims who followed, proved to be the case.

When the hunt for the Backpack Killer got under way almost three years later following the discovery of British girls Caroline Clarke and Joanne Walters, Paul Onions' experience should have provided instant, valuable clues. But with more than 200 police officers searching the Belangalo Forest and with an avalanche of phone calls coming in, some important information was overlooked—such as Joanne Berry ringing to talk about her experience with Paul Onions and Paul himself, who on November 13, 1993, rang and begged for someone to take more seriously his report of the attack on him three years earlier. There was a third call, too, which should have made alarm bells ring. It was from a woman who said her boyfriend worked at the Readymix company with a man who lived near a forest, drove a four-wheel vehicle, owned a lot of guns, and was called Ivan Milat.

With an overload of information and a computer system that couldn't cope with it all, the manhunt for the Backpack Killer wound down on November 17, 1993. It was soon cranked up again when, later that month, a possible eighth victim was provisionally added to the list of victims. An examination of unsolved murders turned up the name of Diane Pennacchio, a 29-year-old mother whose body had been found in a wood near in 1991. She had been stabbed to death and her body had been laid face down with her hands tied behind her back. Her death was similar to the other seven forest murders because of the ferocious stab wounds and the fact Diane's body was found by a fallen tree—another trademark of the murderer's chosen killing ground—and covered with twigs and ferns.

The Backpacker task force now wisely decided it was time to streamline the information process, whittling down the files until only those considered relevant were left. One of these was yet another crucial yet previously overlooked statement. It was from a 20-year-old woman who had told police she had been backpacking in New South Wales in January 1990 when she was offered a lift. The driver's behavior gave her cause for concern and as they approached Belangalo Forest, the woman became very anxious. She managed to wrench open the vehicle's door and run into the forest—with the sound of gunshots close behind her. The woman was extremely fortunate to escape from him unharmed.

The huge stockpile of information now re-examined included Joanne Berry's report about how she had saved Paul Onions. There was a file labeled "Milat" containing a tip from a woman who said her boyfriend worked with a man who could easily be responsible for the forest murders. The woman had not given her name but two officers decided to pay the Readymix plant a visit. There they requested time sheets and found that Ivan Milat had been absent from work on every occasion that the forest murders had taken place. Milat's criminal records were investigated and revealed that, although he had served time in prison, there was nothing to suggest he was a potential serial killer. There was, however, an allegation that he had once raped a girl while armed with a knife and a length of rope.

> **"Paul identified Ivan Milat from a photograph straight away"**

Phone taps were made on Milat's house and a surveillance team kept him under constant observation. They discovered that Ivan Milat and two of his brothers owned another house just 25 miles from Belangalo Forest. Checks on vehicles Milat had owned showed that one of these was a four-wheel drive Nissan Patrol in which the new owner had found a bullet. It was only on April 13, 1994, that an officer turned up Paul Onions' statement and realized its significance. Now back home in England but still deeply disturbed by what had happened to him, Paul was telephoned and asked to return to Australia. He identified Ivan Milat from a photograph straight away.

In May 1994, police carried out seven dawn raids on properties within a 50-mile radius of

Milat stabbed and shot his young victims and buried their
mutilated bodies in the forest.

- - - - - - - - - - - -

Belangalo Forest. Two of Milat's brothers were
taken into custody but later released. Ivan Milat
was arrested after police stormed his home at 22
Cinnabar Street, Eaglevale, where he lay in bed
with girlfriend Chalinder Hughes. He was taken to
Campbeltown Police Station and charged with the
robbery and attempted murder of Paul Onions.

Milat had expressed surprise at the police
interest and denied any knowledge of the seven
brutally butchered bodies. But police discovered
items of property belonging to his victims and electrical tape, cable ties, and a bag of rope similar to
that found at the murder scenes. Gun parts were
found hidden in the garage roof, together with cartridges that matched those found near the
backpackers' bodies.

Milat was charged with the seven murders that
had so horrified the people of Australia and sent
terror into the hearts of parents whose children
had left home to experience life "down under."
Milat first appeared in court in May 1994 but the
hearing was postponed until the beginning of
February 1995 when he was further remanded in
custody until June that year. While the legal
machinery ground slowly, the public learned a

little more about the accused. Milat, born in 1945, was the son of a Croat immigrant Stijpan—who later changed his name to Stephen—and his wife Margaret. One of the couple's 14 children, Milat got into many scraps when he was a child and was obsessed with bodybuilding. But he drank and was a heavy smoker. Desperate to leave school as soon as he could, Milat went on to earn his money first at the water board and then on building sites. When not at work, he indulged his passions for four-wheel-drive vehicles, hunting, and shooting. There was some suggestion that Milat's violent nature became more terrifying and sinister after his wife Karen left him in 1987. The petite woman who had a young son could no longer take Milat's outbursts—including once smashing a glass coffee-table and ordering her to pick up the pieces.

Throughout his court appearances, Milat maintained his innocence. The court was hushed as the jury heard of the injuries inflicted on the young victims and there were gasps when the sword used to decapitate Anja Habschied was produced. Inevitably, Milat was found guilty on all counts and sentenced to life imprisonment. He was taken to a high security jail in Maitland, south west of Sydney, bragging that he would escape one day. He made one failed escape attempt in July 1995.

Even as Ivan Milat languished in jail, rumors persisted that he had been aided in his crimes by one of his brothers. One, Boris, told reporters: "All my brothers are capable of extreme violence, given the right time and place individually. The things I can tell you are much worse that what Ivan's meant to have done. Everywhere he's worked, people have disappeared. I know where he's been." When asked if he thought Ivan was guilty, Boris

Milat worked as a builder and was absent from work every time there was a murder. After a tip-off from a colleague police put him under surveillance as a potential suspect.

replied: "If Ivan's done these murders, I reckon he's done a hell of a lot more—maybe 28."

In June 2001, Ivan Milat was brought from prison to appear at an inquest into the deaths of three women in 1978 and 1979. They were 17-year-old Robyn Hickie, 14-year-old Amanda Robinson, and 20-year-old Leanne Goodall who had all disappeared in circumstances remarkably similar to those surrounding Milat's other victims. But Milat refused to cooperate with the reopened investigation. He is still suspected of being responsible for many other murders, including those of tourists from Japan and throughout Europe. He has formed a support group to lobby for his release from jail and still insists that he will one day escape—for good.

HERMAN MUDGETT

Chicago of the 1890s was fast growing into a truly great city. It had won the right to stage the coveted World's Fair in 1893 and the years leading up to that momentous event saw new trade and wealth pour in.

Prosperity, however, brought with it an army of thieves, swindlers, hoodlums, and racketeers, establishing a tradition of crime that the city has cause to regret to this day. But in all its blood-stained history, there is one man whose sheer evil secures him one of the highest positions not only in Chicago's but the world's black gallery of infamy. He justifiably earned the listing in the *Guinness Book Of Records* as "the most prolific murderer in recent criminal history."

To his neighbors, he was known as Dr. H.H. Holmes, a smart, respectable, hard-working,

A portrait of Herman Mudgett who was known as H. H. Holmes.

FACT FILE.

Name: Herman Webster Mudgett,
    aka Dr. H.H. Holmes

Born: May 1860

Location of killings:
    Chicago, Illinois, USA

Killed: admitted 27 murders
    but total could have been
    150-200

Modus operandi: women tor-
    tured or killed by
    poisonous gas, dismembered,
    sometimes had flesh removed
    with acid

Justice: hanged in 1896

As the drug store continued to prosper, Mudgett decided to build a property that became known as Holmes Castle.

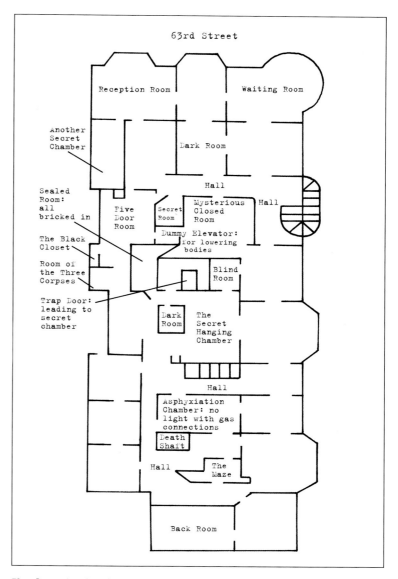

The layout of Holmes Castle contained lots of hidden chambers where his victims would be killed and never seen again.

handsome young man with a certificate proving him to be a graduate of the prestigious Ann Arbor Medical School in Michigan, Illinois. So impressive was his qualification that nobody thought to run a routine check on him. If they had once done so, they would have discovered that Dr. Holmes was an invention. In reality, he was Herman Webster Mudgett—soon to become one of history's most notorious serial killers.

Nobody knows where Herman Mudgett came from. He arrived in Chicago in the late 1880s with two wives and no money but with a mission: to get rich quick. He realized that, in this city preparing to host the World's Fair, he had found an ideal environment for his criminal ambitions. Chicago was bustling with commerce and expectation, and Mudgett discovered many eager young women keen to make their names, find fame, fortune, and fine husbands in the wake of the fair. Since he had charm, style, wit, and a way about him that women found irresistible, Mudgett was ever ready to help them—more often than not to their ultimate cost.

Mudgett also discovered the other side of Chicago: a city which attracted the downside of newly-found prosperity: ghettos beset by racketeers, gangs eking their evil way into previously respectable neighborhoods, small-time chiselers carving crafty fortunes before making a swift exit. Mudgett had found his twisted, spiritual home.

Dapper, mustached Mudgett quickly and easily found a job in the boom city as a prescription clerk at a drug store on the junction of 63rd and South Wallace Streets in a conurbation known as

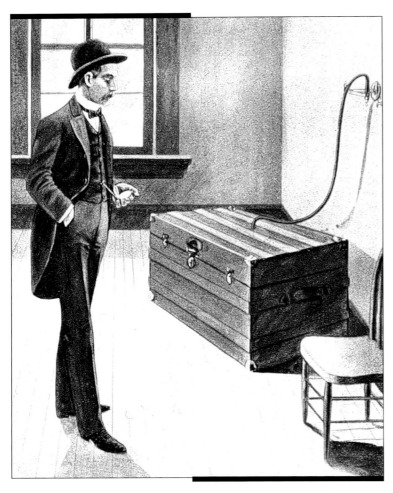

Mudgett gassed his victims by forcing them into a trunk and putting a gas pipe into a hole in the top.

- - - - - - - - - - - - - -

Englewood. His employer at the pharmacy was a widow called Mrs. E. S. Holton, who found him wise, charming, courteous, and forever helpful to her many customers. Indeed, business had never flourished so much before "Dr. Holmes" arrived. Mrs. Holton, clearly delighted with her learned employee, took a back seat in the business.

No one noticed when, after only a few months, Mrs. Holton and her young daughter were no longer seen in the drug store. Mudgett, in his guise as Holmes, told those very few customers who were interested that his former boss and her child had moved to California after selling him the

controlling interest in the shop. Mrs. Holton and her daughter were never seen again.

Mudgett had what he had wanted for a long time: a base upon which to build an empire he had decided was rightfully his. As the drug store continued to prosper, the good doctor cast his eyes on a huge, double-plot of land across the road at 701 and 703 Sixty-Third Street. It was to be the site of what later became known infamously as Holmes Castle. To finance this enormous purchase of land and the three-story property built on the site, Mudgett launched a series of daredevil scams, many of which, astoundingly, paid off. He marketed a "sure-fire cure for alcoholism" at $50 a bottle. He sold ordinary tap-water as an all-purpose "miracle cure." And, in his most audacious, money-making wheeze, he invented a device for turning water into domestic gas that almost won him a lucrative $25,000 contract from Chicago's Gas Company.

Holmes Castle was speedily erected, via a series of elaborate frauds, bogus deeds, and false promises to builders. This edifice of evil contained about 100 rooms of various sizes, with a series of false partitions, staircases leading nowhere, long, dark corridors, trap doors, and secret passageways. By 1888, Mudgett, aged 28, had completed his "command center," his empire of bent deals, from where, as Dr. Holmes, he traveled across the United States carrying out crime after crime. Then a single act of greed prefaced his downfall.

Mudgett befriended a small-time Philadelphia hoodlum, Benjamin Pitezel, and hatched a plot to fake the latter's death by murdering a vagrant, and then cash-in on a huge insurance policy in Pitezel's name. But when a body was found in Callowhill Street, Philadelphia, on September 3, 1894, it was not that of a vagrant but of Pitezel himself—murdered by his double-crossing partner-in-crime. Mudgett almost got away with it, but an eagle-eyed insurance operator cast doubt upon Pitezel's death and alerted police in Philadelphia, who in turn contacted their already-suspicious counterparts in Chicago.

Detectives raided Holmes Castle—what they found defied belief. Over the years, a string of young women had been lured to Holmes Castle with the promise of jobs, working on sundry spurious projects masterminded by their boss. Few of them, it appeared, had ever left.

In virtually all rooms, there were gas pipes with fake valves, so that guests had no way of stopping the poison fumes which eventually took their lives. In the evil doctor's huge bed-chamber was an electric bell which rang whenever a door was opened in the chilling, labyrinthian mansion. In his office was a giant, six-foot wide stove, in the grate of which lay part of a bone and a human rib.

The basement hid the grizzliest murder secrets of all. Scattered or buried everywhere were human bones, among them the ribs and pelvis of a child aged no more than 14. A hooped barrel was found containing acid, along with a surgical table on which lay a box of knives. Underneath the table were several women's skeletons; one macabre theory was that Mudgett first acid-burned off the flesh of his victims then sold the skeletons for medical research.

A nearby storeroom revealed a blood-spattered noose, beneath which were two brick vaults filled with quicklime. Also in the basement was a medieval-style torture rack on which, it was alleged, Mudgett tested his sick belief that a human body could be stretched to twice its normal length.

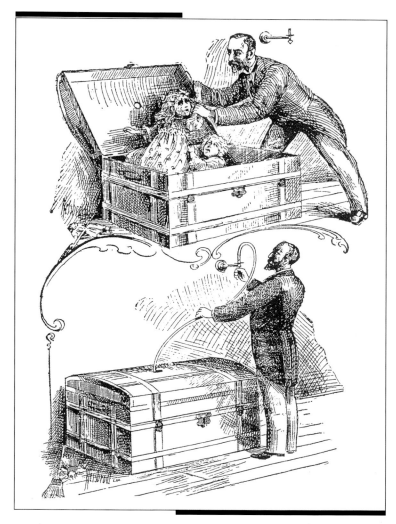

Contemporary portrayal of how Herman Mudgett put paid to his female victims deep within his Chicago "Torture Castle."

A contemporary report of the findings within Mudgett's castle reads: "The second floor contained 35 rooms. Half a dozen were fitted up as ordinary sleeping chambers and there were indications that they had been occupied by various women who worked for the monster, or to whom he had made love while awaiting an opportunity to kill them.

"Several of the other rooms were without windows and could be made airtight by closing the doors. One was completely filled by a huge safe, almost large enough for a bank vault, into which a gas pipe had been introduced. Another was lined with sheet iron covered by asbestos and showed traces of fire. Some had been sound-proofed while others had extremely low ceilings and trapdoors in the floors from which ladders led to smaller rooms beneath.

"In all of the rooms were gas pipes with cut-off valves. But the valves were fakes. The flow of gas was actually controlled by a series of cut-offs concealed in the closet of Holmes' bedroom. Apparently, one of his favorite methods of murder was to lock a victim in one of the rooms and then turn on the gas. Police believed that in the asbestos-lined chamber he had devised a means of introducing fire, so that the gas pipe became a terrible blow-torch from which there was no escape."

Although no final count could ever have been made, for much of the evidence had long since been disposed of, police estimated that Mudgett murdered no fewer than 150 people and possibly as many as 200, mainly young girls. In addition, the bogus doctor killed at least two of the three wives he bigamously led up the altar, their deaths following a torture routine the fiend took to his grave.

As the truth about Herman Webster Mudgett emerged, headlines about his foul deeds exploded across the world, at the same time as newspapers in England were writing of the horrific slayings of Jack the Ripper in the heart of London's East End.

> **❝One of his favorite methods of murder was to lock a victim in one of the rooms and then turn on the gas❞**

The Ripper was never caught but society did get its revenge on the Chicago Monster. In October 1895, he appeared before a jury in Philadelphia, after a row between police there and in Chicago over who should try him first. Still demanding to be addressed by his alias H. H. Holmes, he vehemently protested his innocence throughout the six-day trial. The 12-man jury was not fooled and on November 2, 1895 they returned a verdict of "guilty in the first degree" to the charge of murdering Benjamin Pitezel.

It was not until six months later that Mudgett signed a death-cell confession to 27 further murders and six attempted murders in Chicago, Indianapolis, and Toronto—although police firmly believed his toll of death stood much higher than this. A wheeler-dealer to the end, Mudgett actually sold his confession for $10,000 to newspaper tycoon William Randolph Hearst. But it was a bounty he would never receive.

On the morning of May 7, 1896 he was led along death row by two warders at the Philadelphia County Prison. To the very end, the liar, cheat, conman—and possibly the worst serial killer the world has ever known—refused to acknowledge his own name. "Ready, Dr. Holmes?" the hooded hangman asked him. "Yes," Mudgett replied to his executioner, adding the order: "Don't bungle." But his final instruction was not followed as he would have wished. Herman Webster Mudgett took an agonizing 15 minutes to die on the gallows.

HERBERT MULLIN

It could have been his obsessive religious background that turned high-achiever Herbert Mullin into a murdering fiend.

Or it could have been the death of his best friend. What is certain is that Mullin was a paranoid schizophrenic who chose his innocent victims at random. Born in 1947 and brought up in a strict Roman Catholic household in Fenton, California, Mullin was voted "most likely to achieve" by his fellow high school classmates. He got engaged at 17 and life looked full of promise for the sporting, all-American boy. But in 1965 his best friend, Dean Richardson, died in a road accident. Mullin set up a shrine to him in his bedroom and broke off his engagement, telling the girl he was a homosexual.

Mullin regularly experimented with hallucinogenic drugs and his increasingly disturbed mental state led to him spending a year in a mental

Herbert Mullin was sentenced to life for murder in 1973. He killed thinking he heard voices telling him to do so.
- - - - - - - - - - - - - -

hospital. After saying he could hear voices in his head, Mullin was diagnosed as a classic paranoid schizophrenic. By 1972, Mullin said Satan was urging him to kill. His first victim was tramp Lawrence White, whom he clubbed to death on October 13, 1972. On October 24, Mullin repeatedly stabbed Santa Cruz university student Mary Guilfoyle before cutting her body open and strewing her innards on the ground. He confessed these murders to a priest but later stabbed him to death. Mullin said: "Satan gets into people and makes them do things they don't want to."

The voices persisted in Mullin's head and after buying his very first gun in December that year, he fatally shot five people in one day. Four teenage boys camping in the Cowell State Park at Santa

FACT FILE.

Name: Herbert William Mullin

Born: April 18, 1947

Location of killings: Santa
    Cruz, California, USA

Modus operandi: various

Killed: 13

Justice: sentenced to life in
    1973

Cruz on February 6, 1973, were his next victims. Exactly a week later, Mullin shot dead an elderly man as he tended his garden. But the killing was witnessed by a neighbor who jotted down Mullin's car registration number and called the police.

Mullin confessed to 13 murders. His defence lawyer said he could not be guilty because he was insane. Despite Mullin's crazy claim that he was carrying out the killings to save California from an earthquake, the jury decided he was still responsible for his actions and fit to stand trial. He was eventually charged with ten murders and found guilty on two counts of first-degree murder and eight counts of second-degree murder. In July 1973, Mullin was sentenced to life imprisonment, eligible for parole in 2025.

EARLE NELSON

In just one year, Earle Nelson went on a frenzied killing spree, his victims all boarding-house landladies who were raped and strangled.

Having the face of the man called "The 'Gorilla Murderer" as their last sight on this earth must have been terrifying.

Born in Philadelphia in 1897 to a prostitute who later died of a venereal disease, Nelson was brought up by an aunt who instilled in him her devout religious beliefs. He spent much of his early years reading the Bible but, as family

FACT FILE.

Name: Earle Leonard Nelson, aka "The Gorilla Murderer," the "Dark Strangler," and the "Phantom"

Born: 1897

Location of killings: Philadelphia, Pennsylvania, and throughout USA and Canada

Modus operandi: strangulation after rape

Killed: probably 22

Justice: hanged in Winnipeg in 1928

acquaintances said, the boy was "too good to be true." When he was ten, Nelson was hit by a street-car and suffered a severe head injury which left him with mental and physical problems. He became a peeping tom and, at the age of 21, was admitted to a mental hospital for trying to rape a neighbor's daughter. Nelson absconded several times during his two years there before being finally released.

He changed his name to Roger Wilson, married a teacher, and apparently settled down. But the marriage lasted only six months and, in 1926, Nelson went on an evangelical tour through the United States and Canada, brandishing a Bible, staying in a string of boarding houses—and murdering their female owners. The first victim, 60-year-old Clara Newman, was found in the attic of her lodging house in San Francisco on February 20, 1926.

Nelson claimed 22 victims, all of whom, had fallen for his moralistic but charming approaches. He strangled and then raped his victims before moving on to the next town. As well as San Francisco, he left bodies in Portland, Seattle, Kansas City, Philadelphia, Detroit, and Chicago. Nelson became known as the "Gorilla Murderer" because of his simian jaw, dark complexion, protruding lips, and broad, throttling hands. He was also labeled the "Dark Strangler" and the "Phantom."

In 1927, Nelson crossed the border into Canada. On June 8, he broke his pattern of murdering landladies and killed his youngest victim, 14-year-old Lola Cowan. The next day he killed landlady Emily Peterson, whose body was found under a bed by her husband as he knelt to pray.

Earle Nelson was brought up by an obsessively religious aunt and spent much of his early years studying the Bible.

- - - - - - - - - - -

Nelson was arrested after a barber noticed blood on his hair following the discovery of both bodies. He was tried in Winnipeg and on June 13, 1928, went to the gallows.

Although never charged with them, the Gorilla Murderer was also an obvious suspect for the triple murder in Newark, New Jersey, of Rose Valentine, Margaret Stanton, and Laura Tidor. All, of course, were landladies.

DENNIS NILSEN

He talked to them, offered them a drink, and affectionately touched their arm. Dennis Nilsen's behavior toward his visitors sounded normal enough, even very generous—except the young men he chatted away to were dead.

Nilsen was the deranged serial killer who claimed to care more for his victims in death than anyone else did when they were alive. Sometimes tenderly powdering the corpses or propping them up in a chair to watch television with him, it was no wonder Nilsen chilled a nation as Britain's biggest mass murderer. He claimed some 15 lives—though he argued that figure was not correct—in just over four years.

Nilsen is believed to have killed for the first time in 1978 after celebrating New Year's Eve. He picked up a stranger in a pub and they slept together, although apparently without having sex. As dawn broke over Nilsen's home, 195 Melrose Road in Willesden, north London, he realized that he could not bear for his new-found bedfellow to leave. He used a tie to strangle the sleeping man, then finished him off by plunging his head into a bucket of water.

Nilsen embarked on the ritualistic behavior that went hand-in-hand with his horrible killings. He washed the victim's body in the bath, dressed it in new clothes, and kept it beside him for the rest of the day, making conversation as he busied himself in the flat. Affectionately, he snuggled up to the corpse, whispering sweet nothings. At night, he wrapped the body in a curtain and put it under the floorboards.

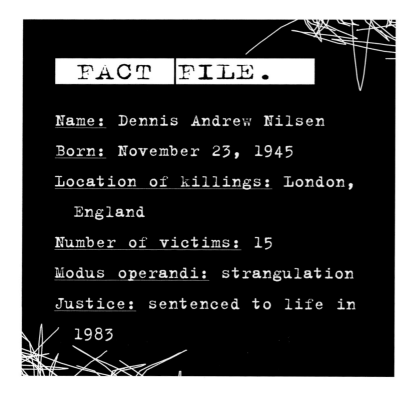

FACT FILE.

Name: Dennis Andrew Nilsen

Born: November 23, 1945

Location of killings: London, England

Number of victims: 15

Modus operandi: strangulation

Justice: sentenced to life in 1983

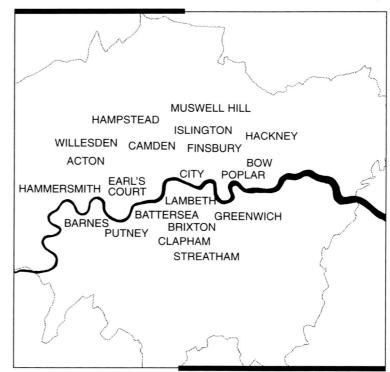

MUSWELL HILL
HAMPSTEAD
ISLINGTON   HACKNEY
WILLESDEN CAMDEN FINSBURY
ACTON   BOW
         EARL'S   CITY   POPLAR
HAMMERSMITH COURT
                        LAMBETH
         BATTERSEA   GREENWICH
BARNES   BRIXTON
     PUTNEY   CLAPHAM
                  STREATHAM

Nilsen was the killer who chilled a nation. He claimed some 15 lives—later disputed the number—in just over four years.

- - - - - - - - - - - - - - - -

This unknown victim was the first of some 15 young men to be slaughtered by Nilsen in his grim quest for companionship. The exact number has been disputed by the killer since he was put behind bars. Sadly all but one of the victims disappeared and died with no one to report them missing. They were from the depressing world of those single young men who drift along in life looking for love, or at least a bed for the night. Most were lonely homosexuals seeking companionship and never thinking about the dangers.

Only one of Nilsen's victims was missed, a Canadian tourist called Kenneth Ockendon, for whom TV and press appeals were made following his disappearance. After he failed to maintain contact with his family back home, the British

❝❝All but one of the victims disappeared and died with no one to report them missing❞❞

police were alerted and posters bearing Keith's picture appeared throughout the country. But he would never be spotted walking in the street or even staying in some insalubrious hostel. For Keith had encountered Dennis Nilsen, spent a pleasant evening talking and drinking with him, and then returned to his flat where he was strangled with the flex of his stereo headphones. Nilsen later watched impassively as the poster and TV campaign was launched.

At first, Nilsen was shocked by his own barbarity but it wasn't long before he accepted himself as a man compelled to kill. A new face, a few drinks, a short sleep, then strangulation followed by a bath usually for both men, some sexual activity, and a body lying cold and accusing the following morning. Nilsen waited until his victims were soundly sleeping or deeply distracted before he made his deadly move. Armed with a tie, he lassoed their necks and squeezed the life out of them.

When interviewed by a psychologist, Nilsen described his grisly work as "like being in a butcher's shop." It was the unsuccessful disposal of bodies that led to his capture.

- - - - - - - - - - -

Even today, not all the victims have been identified. At one stage, his compulsion to kill led to a line of bodies taking up every inch of gloomy room under his floorboards. He eventually disposed of them by chopping them up and putting them on a garden bonfire that flared into a furnace as the flesh sizzled and spat.

One of the victims was Martin Duffey, a 16-year-old from Liverpool who had a troubled childhood but a promising future in catering. No one knows why he decided to visit London when he did instead of attending the cookery course as he had planned. He slept rough for two nights before running into Nilsen.

Another was Billy Sutherland, a tattooed Scot, sometime male prostitute, and heavy drinker. But if Billy was wayward and a thorn in the flesh of his local constabulary, he had a good heart. He was devoted to his mother and close to his brothers and sisters. Sutherland asked Nilsen for a night's shelter after they had spent the evening boozing. He never woke up again.

Malcolm Barlow was unlucky enough to have an epileptic fit almost on Nilsen's doorstep. It invoked the side of the civil servant that was compelled to aid the underdog, and he tended Barlow after calling an ambulance. Barlow returned the following day to say thank you. That simple gesture from a mentally-handicapped man was a fatal act.

Graham Allen may have been dead before Nilsen struck. Halfway through eating an omelette the visitor lapsed into unconsciousness either through choking or a silent fit. It didn't stop Nilsen moving in for the kill, brave enough with this comatose victim to use his bare hands.

One nameless victim was so physically appealing to Nilsen that it was a week before the body was put underneath the floor. The killer enjoyed seven days of domestic harmony, returning from work to find a companion waiting for him and the promise of sexual contentment. Nilsen flattered himself that he was showing more care for people after death than they ever knew in life.

> to just reproduce in metal other people's ideas. I suppose I was always a maverick in a conforming conventional world. In one respect I am the eternal optimist who spent most of his life standing in the middle of the Sahara desert waiting for rain. If you do that kind of thing long enough then the pressure of a ceaseless sun will get to you one day. One day the sun

A remarkably articulate and introspective man, Nilsen offers some insight into his life and crimes through writing.

When Nilsen moved to another north London address, 23 Cranley Gardens, Muswell Hill, he no longer had access to a garden. He was forced to dissect corpses more fully, removing maggoty innards to dump on waste ground, while flushing much of the remaining skin and bone down the toilet. Nilsen lived at the top of a converted six-bedroom house that had four other occupants: a barmaid and her builder boyfriend, a dental nurse from New Zealand, and a Dutch welfare worker. They all knew little about Nilsen except that he went by the name Des and was devoted to his mongrel dog Bleep. But they thought that the neighborly thing to do was to post warning signs on his door the day the plumbing failed. The downstairs toilet had refused to flush, they said, and despite pouring acid into the pan, whatever was

causing the blockage remained stubbornly in place. Nilsen knew he had to work fast. Any full-scale probe could mean someone entering his pokey, acrid-smelling flat where flies buzzed incessantly. The odds were they would find the body of a man killed the previous week and hidden by Nilsen in his wardrobe. He got to work.

With plastic sheets protecting the floor, he painstakingly laid the body of the man out in the middle of the front room. With precision, he grasped a kitchen knife and severed the head. As soon as he had finished mopping the spurt of blood that accompanied the butchery, he reached for a sturdy cooking pot and popped in the head, which still bore all the features of the man it had once been. Filled with water, the pan went on the stove to simmer while Nilsen went off to the supermarket for some fortifying Jamaican rum. With a few drinks inside him, Nilsen was losing the appetite for his grisly task. He went to bed, leaving the

Items found by police that Nilsen used to deal with the
bodies.

- - - - - - - - - - - - - -

headless corpse spread on the floor. It was Sunday
before he finished dismembering the body. He used
the freshly sharpened kitchen knife to saw through
the waist. He put the legs and lower body in a bag
and stored it in a drawer. Then he hacked off both
arms and put them and the rib cage in black plastic sacks. He added the boiled head before closing
the door on the stomach churning remnants of 20-
year-old Scottish drug addict and drifter Stephen
Sinclair.

Whatever plans Nilsen had for subsequently
disposing of the body were to be thwarted. As he

set off for his desk job at an employment agency
in Kentish Town on Monday, his neighbors decided to resolve the difficulties with the drain once
and for all. A plumber called over the weekend
decided it was too big a problem for him to tackle
alone. The agents called in Dyno-rod, whose engineer Michael Cattran arrived on Tuesday evening.
Deep inside, Cattran had a nagging suspicion but
it sounded too ludicrous to mention. He decided to
telephone his boss for advice. The hubbub in the
house while he made the call alerted Nilsen to the
dilemma that now faced him. Cattran actually
showed him the disgusting contents of the sewer
with a flash of the torch.

It took plenty of drink before Nilsen plucked up

Nilsen escorted by police after his arrest.

- - - - - - - - - - - - -

the courage for the last filthy job he would do in his final 24 hours of freedom.

Under cover of darkness, he took a bucket, edged carefully down the manhole and collected the slabs of human flesh he himself had flushed there. He could not have known that Fiona Bridges, the barmaid who shared the house, heard his plodding feet and noted the scuffing sounds as the drain cover was removed.

Michael Cattran was astonished when he returned the next day to show his boss the extraordinary bilge and found the sewers clean. It wasn't long, however, before Fiona Bridges joined them

and described the eerie noises of the night before. Cattran then dug deeper into the sewer than Nilsen had the night before. He put his arm up a pipe and retrieved a piece of decomposing flesh. The police were called and within hours a forensic report confirmed Cattran's shocked belief that it was human.

By the time Nilsen returned home from work that evening of February 9, 1983, detectives were waiting for him. Who knows what was going through the mind of the man with a secret lust for death that was to make even the most hardened policeman blanch? He made a half-hearted attempt at innocence. He had already tried to throw people off the scent by reporting a foul smell in his drains to the landlords in the manner of an

Police search for evidence in the back garden of Nilsen's former residence.

- - - - - - - - - - -

outraged tenant. When detectives said they were there because human remains had been found in the drains, he replied: "Good grief, how awful."

At the first sign of pressure from the police, however, he caved in. He took them into his squalid flat and told them there was a body in a bag in his wardrobe. The stench of rotting flesh was confirmation enough. In the hours that followed, they heard details of one of the most appalling serial crimes from one of the most unlikely looking villains ever. It was hard to know whether he was mad or bad or perhaps both.

The spree of murdering and fascination with human corpses was spawned in Nilsen when he was very young. He was born on November 23, 1945, far north in Fraserburgh, Scotland, the second son of Olav Nilsen, a Norwegian serviceman brought to the wilds of Aberdeenshire by World War II. There he met and married local girl and former beauty queen, Betty Whyte, and the couple went on to have three children, Olav Junior, Dennis, and Sylvia. But Olav was a wayward husband and father, and Betty ended the marriage.

Dennis grew up without a father but he received enough love and attention from his grandfather, with whom they all lived, to make up for it. Fisherman Andrew Whyte and the little boy loved each other's company and had great adventures together in the harbor town. Bizarrely, through this loving, strong relationship came Nilsen's first brush with death, thought by many to be the root of his lifelong obsession.

When Andrew Whyte died of a heart attack at sea aged 62, he was brought home and laid out so that his many friends and relatives could pay their last respects. Little Dennis, just five years old, was asked if he wanted to see Grandad. Of course he did; he always wanted to see him. But when he was carried to visit the man he adored, it wasn't the lively, laughing fellow he had known. He was still and silent, yet looking like he always had. Dennis was told he had gone to sleep. The youngster's heart was thudding but he could not identify which emotion was causing his pulses to race. There was unspoken grief, the tremendous sense of occasion, and a complete ignorance of what had happened. That powerful image of death, now closely linked to a sense of thrilling excitement, loomed large in his mind for years, resulting in the macabre murders which placed him in serial-killing history.

Dennis was a shy, colorless boy who kept himself to himself. He had a small circle of friends, none of them close. But when it came to helpless animals he was inspired. He would rescue injured birds or mammals, nursing them gently back to health if he could.

When his mother got a local council apart-

> **❝❝When it came to helpless animals, he was inspired. He would rescue injured birds or mammals, nursing them gently back to health if he could❞❞**

ment, it gave him a chance to indulge his passion by keeping pigeons. A wartime air raid shelter behind the block was the ideal loft and his three handsome birds thrived. Dennis was never happier than when he was petting the cooing birds, his fond pals. But his joy was short-lived. A budding lout from the same block decided to get his revenge on Nilsen for some imagined slight and it was easy to see where the youngster was most vulnerable. One day he arrived home from school to find the treasured birds with broken necks.

Nilsen has also told a tale of being almost drowned in the sea at Fraserburgh when he was ten and being rescued by an unidentified teenage boy who masturbated over him. It is possibly true or perhaps more likely the product of his lurid imagination. His mother met a new man, Adam Scott, remarried and they moved to Strichen, where she was to have four more children. Having been a member of his local cadet force, Dennis went on to join the Army when he was 15. Soon afterward, he had a motor scooter accident while not wearing a crash helmet. He suffered head injuries which kept him in hospital for several days and his mother wondered whether these might have caused lasting damage.

In the Army, Nilsen became increasingly aware of his attraction toward men but carefully disguised his homosexual leanings in case it made him an outcast among his comrades. In fact, he had sex for the first time with an Arab boy while

This house, 23 Cranley Gardens, on an ordinary suburban street in London has since gone into the archives of horror. It was here that Nilsen flushed human remains down the toilet.

- - - - - - - - - - - - -

serving in Aden. But it was an unsatisfactory liaison, the risk of being discovered and unmasked was too great.

Nilsen experimented with mirrors. He lay a full-length mirror beside him on the bed and studied himself. For his fantasies to run riot, he discovered it was better if he excluded the head from the reflection. Then it dawned on him that the more still the body, the more exciting the experience. He took pleasure in the notion that the body beside him (in this instance, his own) was asleep—or dead. Soon he discovered that he reached a peak of excitement when his body resembled a corpse with the aid of make-up and imagination. His fantasies ran wild at the grotesque images he created with the help of white paint, blue lip coloring, and vivid red dye resembling blood trickling down his T-shirt.

When he left the Army at the age of 27, Nilsen joined the Metropolitan Police. Just a year later he quit, disillusioned with life on the thin blue line. In 1974 he found himself a job as a clerical officer for the Department of Employment at a central London branch. He joined the union and wrangled tirelessly on behalf of less eloquent workers.

After a series of one-night stands, he found a young man with whom he made a home. David Gallichan, who the bespectacled Nilsen met in a London pub, was also lonely. They lived together at the Melrose Avenue address, using cash bequeathed to Nilsen by his natural father, and their relationship lasted two years, although Gallichan pursued other affairs. When Gallichan decided to move on, Nilsen was haughty on the outside and outraged on the inside that someone so clearly inferior to himself should walk out on him. Nilsen resolved such treachery would never happen again. In a way it never did, for few visitors to Nilsen's flat actually left it alive.

One was model and dancer Carl Stotter who, during the wave of publicity following Nilsen's arrest in February 1983, told police that he had narrowly escaped death at the hands of the mass killer after meeting Nilsen in a pub and returning with him to the attic room in Cranley Gardens. Stotter had later awoken gasping for breath, with a swollen tongue and burn marks around his neck. Nilsen had not only tried to strangle him but had also thrust his head into a bucket of water. For three days, Stotter was unable to move. Nilsen nursed him, tending his injuries, after convincing him he had suffered a bad dream. Stotter sought hospital treatment but did not go to the police. Only after he read of Nilsen's arrest and crimes did he come forward, in the realization of the incredibly lucky escape he had had.

Stotter was one of at least seven young men attacked by Nilsen who lived to tell the tale. In a strange twist, Nilsen wrote to Stotter from jail and said he had spared him because "what passed between us was a thin strand of love and humanity." Police said the killer had simply run out of space in which to store another body.

In court, Nilsen's defense counsel tried to persuade the jury that the killer was mad. Thanks in part to Stotter's evidence, the panel at the Old Bailey did not believe it. He was found guilty of six murders and two attempted murders. On November 4, 1983, still showing not a shred of remorse, Dennis Nilsen was jailed for life.

Ten years later, a psychologist's interview with Nilsen was shown on television. With eerie lack of emotion, the killer said: "The most exciting part of the little conundrum was when I lifted the body and carried it. It was an expression of my power to lift and carry him and have control. The dangling elements of his limp limbs was an expression of his passivity. The more passive he could be, the more powerful I was." He spoke about the dissection of bodies and how he removed people's

> **ʻʻFew visitors to Nilsen's flat actually left it alive ʼʼ**

innards when the smell was too putrid to bear. "There isn't a lot of blood. If I stab you right now or you stab me your heart is beating. There would be blood spurting and splashing all over the place. In a dead body there is no splashing at all. The blood congeals and becomes part of the flesh. It is like a butcher's shop."

Nilsen also expounded his astonishing theory that the dead were now a part of him: "The bodies are all gone, everything's gone. But I still feel spiritual communion with these people." Nilsen was right in that there was so little left of most of his victims that police long afterward struggled to put a final figure on the death toll. Most of the bodies had been reduced to ashes and dust. There was, however, one solid relic of Nilsen's ghoulish game-play. It is an old-fashioned gas cooker that ended up in Scotland Yard's so-called Black Museum, a storage area where weapons and skulls and hangman's nooses adorn the walls. The stove remains there uncleaned since the day it was removed from the kitchen of Nilsen's home. On the hob sits a large, battered cooking pot in which Nilsen used to boil up curries before carrying them around the corner to a school hall which doubled as a day centre for local old folk. There the kindly young man would serve them up as the staple diet for charitable functions. The morbidly fascinating exhibit, unhealthily stained and still encrusted with the remnants of such meals, was also the pot in which Dennis Nilsen boiled the heads of his victims.

ANATOLY ONOPRIENKO

On April 14, 1996, acting on a tip about the owner of an unlicensed gun, Inspector Mikhail Balokh called at flat number 37, Block 70, on John the Baptist Street in the Ukraine garrison town of Yavoriv.

Balokh's hunch that the inhabitant could be the cold-blooded killer who had slaughtered 52 people across the Ukraine was doubly fortuitous. For Balokh not only ended the six-year murder spree throughout the former Soviet state but also had the foresight to handcuff Anatoly Onoprienko before he fired the gun furtively withdrawn from a cupboard.

Balokh was indeed lucky, unlike the men, women, and children who had begged for mercy but died brutally at Onoprienko's hand. In just one

20-week bloodbath, Onoprienko killed and mutilated 43 people. He hacked off fingers to get at wedding rings and pulled out his victims' gold teeth. Onoprienko's first murder was in June 1989 when he and friend Sergei Rogosin blasted a couple to death in their car. Another attack ended with a family of five, including an 11-year-old girl, being wiped out.

Onoprienko spent the next six years traveling eastern Europe where police believe he may have been responsible for other murders. In November

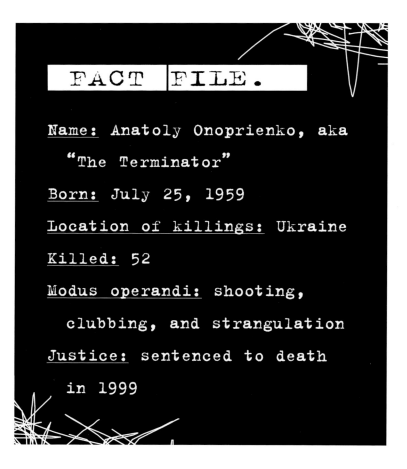

FACT FILE.

Name: Anatoly Onoprienko, aka
  "The Terminator"

Born: July 25, 1959

Location of killings: Ukraine

Killed: 52

Modus operandi: shooting,
  clubbing, and strangulation

Justice: sentenced to death
  in 1999

Onoprienko killed men, women, and children. He later commented that committing murder was like "ripping up a duvet."

1995, after stealing a shotgun from the home of local council chief, Onoprienko began another killing spree. Most of the victims were in remote villages in the Lvov region, near the border of Poland. "The Terminator" entered isolated houses at dawn, rounded up the family and shot them at close range with a 12-gauge shotgun. Victims ranged from a 70-year-old pensioner to a three-month-old baby. Onoprienko often torched the houses after stealing valuables and scattering around family photographs. Panic was so widespread in two villages that an army division was mobilized, personnel carriers patrolled the streets, and police imposed a security cordon.

After his arrest, Onoprienko confessed to the murders and appeared in court in a cage. He was declared sane enough to be responsible for his crimes and in March 1999 was sentenced to life imprisonment. He said committing the murders was "like ripping up a duvet." The brother of one of Onoprienko's victims said: "He doesn't deserve to be alive. There is no point in a trial. He should just be given to the people to see what they would do with him."

DR. WILLIAM PALMER

The classic case of systematic poisoning by a serial killer is that of Dr. William Palmer who, because of his sensational trial during the prim days of Victorian England, has gone down in history as the "Prince of Poisoners."

Palmer had one motive for murder: plain, simple greed. He had a fondness for good living and a weakness for betting heavily on horses, a costly pastime that led to a string of mysterious deaths among his family—and led the evil doctor to an appointment with the hangman.

Palmer was born in 1824 in the English Midlands, the only legitimate child among seven brothers and sisters. His father, a wood sawyer, had swindled his employer, the Marquess of Anglesey, out of £70,000 by selling the aristocrat's timber. His mother's side of the family was no more savory, an uncle having fathered an incestuous granddaughter by his own illegitimate daughter.

Miraculously, four of his siblings grew up to lead normal, honest lives, although a younger brother became an alcoholic and his eldest sister turned to prostitution.

William was destined to turn out a lot worse than any of them. He attended school in his hometown of Rugeley, Staffordshire, until he was 17, when he left to work in Liverpool. There, his first attempts to join the medical profession, by becoming a pharmacist's apprentice, were disgracefully blighted when he was dismissed for stealing money from his employer's mail—supposedly to help fund an illegal abortion service that he was running. Palmer's mother paid the pharmacist for the

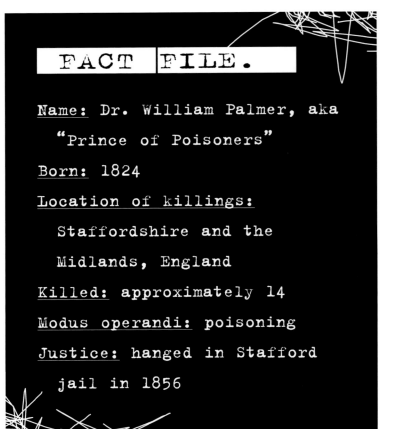

FACT FILE.

<u>Name:</u> Dr. William Palmer, aka "Prince of Poisoners"

<u>Born:</u> 1824

<u>Location of killings:</u> Staffordshire and the Midlands, England

<u>Killed:</u> approximately 14

<u>Modus operandi:</u> poisoning

<u>Justice:</u> hanged in Stafford jail in 1856

missing money and persuaded a Cheshire surgeon, Edward Tylecote, to take her son on as an apprentice to him.

For the next five years, while appearing studious and hard-working under the surgeon's tutelage, Palmer was living a secret life of profligacy. He stole from his employer and took advantage of his position to seduce his patients. He is thought to have sired 14 illegitimate children during the time he worked for Tylecote before the surgeon lost patience and returned him to his home county to work in Staffordshire Infirmary. There he learned about poisons and, it appears, committed his first murder.

A friend of his named Abley accepted Palmer's challenge to a drinking contest. After downing two glasses of brandy, Abley was violently sick, collapsed, and died within minutes. The authorities were suspicious and an inquest was held but nothing could be proved against Palmer. Only later was it learned that the medical student had been having an affair with Abley's wife. Later still, it was realized that Palmer's modus operandi was to lace the drinks of his victims with strychnine.

Palmer finally qualified as a doctor at St. Bartholomew's Hospital, London, in 1846 and returned to his hometown to start his own practice, helped by a £9,000 inheritance. The following year, at the age of 22, he married Anne Brookes, the heiress daughter of a wealthy widow. But he paid little heed to his family or to his doctor's practice, preferring to while away his time at racecourses. He even signed over his business to an assistant to give himself more time for the turf. The inveterate gambler spent hundreds of pounds and his debts mounted.

The harmony of his home life was shattered when a servant turned up with an illegitimate baby but the problem soon went away. Palmer entertained the girl and her child before sending the servant home to her mother, where she died that night. Other illegitimate babies were similarly ill fated. Several are believed to have died in infancy after licking honey from the finger of their doting parent.

It was then that a string of deaths occurred in his own family. Four of Palmer's children were killed by mysterious convulsions when only days or weeks old. Only his eldest son, Willy, survived. In 1848, Palmer invited his rich mother-in-law to visit. She detested her daughter's husband and confided to a friend before embarking on the journey to Rugeley: "I know I shall not live a fortnight." She was right; she died ten days into her visit. Throughout a painful illness, the mother had regularly been fed medicine by her daughter, who was surprised that her husband's prescriptions seemed to do the old woman no good. After mixing her final fatal dose, Palmer was distraught to find

> ❝Palmer entertained the girl and her child before sending the servant home to her mother, where she died that night❞

that the anticipated inheritance failed to match his expectations. His gambling debts now far exceeded his ability to pay.

Another relative, an uncle whom Palmer knew had allocated him a few hundred pounds in his will, was invited by the doctor to pay him a social visit. The old ploy of challenging the man to a drinking contest worked well, for the old uncle was a degenerate drunk himself. The two filled their brandy glasses and the contest seemed to be a dead heat until the uncle fell from his chair in a dead faint. Three days later, he expired.

How did Dr. Palmer get away with it? Child mortality rates were much higher in those Victorian days, of course, but so many fatalities in one family should have raised suspicions in a small country town. However, the evil physician was also a startlingly good thespian. He acted the role of an upstanding, charming, churchgoing family man, a veritable pillar of Staffordshire society. He also allayed suspicions about his

WILLIAM PALMER OF RUGELEY.

William Palmer had a fondness for gambling and bet heavily on horses. He killed to acquire money to pay for his habit.

crimes by enlisting the help of a bumbling old doctor named Bamford, retired and in his eighties, who meekly signed death certificates at Palmer's behest, attributing the untimely demise of so many people to anything from "fatal apoplexy" to "English cholera."

In 1853, Palmer insured his wife's life for £13,000 and in September of that year Annie died of what was diagnosed as cholera. Next he insured

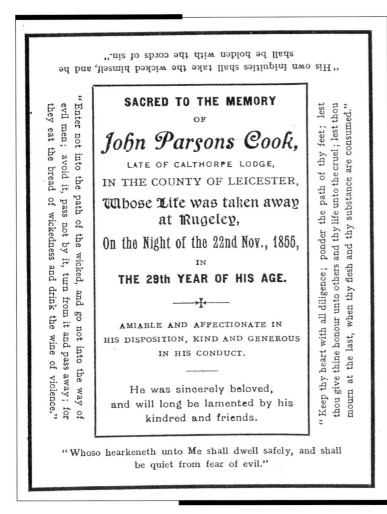

"His own iniquities shall take the wicked himself, and he shall be holden with the cords of sin."

"Enter not into the path of the wicked, and go not into the way of evil men; avoid it, pass not by it, turn from it and pass away; for they eat the bread of wickedness and drink the wine of violence."

SACRED TO THE MEMORY

OF

John Parsons Cook,

LATE OF CALTHORPE LODGE,

IN THE COUNTY OF LEICESTER,

Whose Life was taken away at Rugeley,

On the Night of the 22nd Nov., 1855,

IN

THE 29th YEAR OF HIS AGE.

———✠———

AMIABLE AND AFFECTIONATE IN HIS DISPOSITION, KIND AND GENEROUS IN HIS CONDUCT.

———

He was sincerely beloved, and will long be lamented by his kindred and friends.

"Keep thy heart with all diligence; ponder the path of thy feet; lest thou give thine honour unto others and thy life unto the cruel; lest thou mourn at the last, when thy flesh and thy substance are consumed."

"Whoso hearkeneth unto Me shall dwell safely, and shall be quiet from fear of evil."

A notice describing the death of John Parson's Cook, a gambling friend of Palmer and one of his victims.

- - - - - - - - - -

the life of his brother Walter for a massive £82,000 and he died in a drinking contest with the doctor shortly afterward. The insurance company became suspicious and refused to pay out the money. They even found a hotel employee who signed a statement saying that Palmer had been seen adding a mysterious substance to his brother's drinks but still no case was brought against him.

Dr. Palmer's wife, mother-in-law, brother Walter, four children, an uncle, and several of his more vocal creditors had met similar ends. Yet Palmer, it seemed, was regularly able to get away

with murder. He had benefited from the wills of his wife and others but it was still not enough to pay off the huge sums he owed. He became embroiled with money-lenders who pressed him for cash.

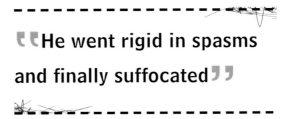

❝❝He went rigid in spasms and finally suffocated❞❞

In November 1855, at the height of his financial woes, Palmer accompanied a gambling friend, 29-year-old John Parsons Cook, to the races at Shrewsbury and saw him win more than £2,000. Afterward, Cook drained a celebratory brandy and gasped: "Good God, there's something in it—it burns my throat." Palmer himself nonchalantly knocked back the few remaining drops in the bottom of the glass. In front of a witness he declared: "Nonsense, there is nothing in it."

Cook was taken back to Rugeley, where he stayed at an inn opposite Palmer's house. The doctor prepared all kinds of food for him and was regularly at his bedside, administering broths, pills, and drinks to his violently vomiting friend. A maid who sipped some of the soup also fell ill with vomiting. Palmer claimed to other visiting medics that Cook was suffering from biliousness. In fact, he displayed not a single symptom of it.

Palmer waited until the bookmakers had paid out Cook's winnings—using the money to settle some of his own gambling debts—before finishing him off. Poor Cook suffered convulsions for several days before finally succumbing. His terrible

Palmer administered poison to one of his victims at this hotel, opposite the road where he lived.

- - - - - - - - - -

death, in which he went rigid in spasms and finally suffocated, bore all the symptoms of strychnine poisoning. Afterward, Cook's father-in-law arrived and demanded a post mortem. During analysis of his body, no trace of strychnine was found. There was evidence, however, of antimony, a lesser drug which induces sickness.

A coroner's court sat in Rugeley where the inquest jury returned a verdict of wilful murder against Palmer, who was arrested on December 15, 1855, and locked up in a cell at Stafford Gaol and House of Corrections. The townspeople were so incensed that the doctor had to be speedily moved to London to await trial. Later, the town where he had practiced his murderous trade even applied unsuccessfully to the Prime Minister to change its name.

The court case which followed at London's Old Bailey drew crowds of spectators who squeezed into the public gallery of the Central Criminal Court to witness this sensational trial. They heard the prosecution assert that only strychnine poisoning could have produced such horrible symptoms in a victim. The day before his friend's demise, Palmer had been seen buying strychnine from a local druggist. And the doctor kept a medical manual in which he had written on the first page: "Strychnine kills by causing tetanic fixing of the respiratory muscles."

William Palmer was born in 1824 in Rugeley, Staffordshire, in the English Midlands, shown here in a contemporary illustration.

- - - - - - - - - -

The jury heard how Palmer stood to benefit from Cook's death. He had been seen rifling through his friend's personal belongings soon after he died, and some cash, papers, and documents relating to his financial affairs were never found by Cook's family. Palmer was also said to have attempted to sabotage the post mortem by hampering the surgeons carrying it out. If the jury had any doubts about Palmer's guilt, the summing up by Lord Chief Justice Campbell dismissed them. He demolished every argument put forward by the defense.

It took the jury just 100 minutes to find Palmer guilty of murder. In the dock, the evil doctor was silent. His only response to the damning verdict was a twitching around his mouth which gradually turned into a sneer. Taken back to Stafford under escort, Palmer did not accept the inevitability of his fate and launched an immediate appeal. In the cells, he cheerfully declared his innocence to his brother George and solicitor John Smith. He asked about his son, saying: "Tell Willy his father has had many troubles but the least of all has been the accusation of murder against him." His confidence was sadly misplaced. His attempt to get the trial overturned on the grounds that it was unfairly heard was rejected by the Home Secretary. When Palmer heard the news, he seemed surprised. However, he showed no signs of depression as he awaited the day of his execution, without remorse and refusing to make a confession.

Palmer was due to be executed at Stafford Gaol at eight o'clock on the morning of June 14, 1856, and an estimated 25,000 people flocked to the town by road, rail, on horseback, and on foot.

❝It took the jury just 100 minutes to find Palmer guilty of murder❞

Accommodation was at a premium, with many visitors spending an uncomfortable night with their horses in the stables. They swarmed around Palmer's home in Rugeley, where white pebbles that paved the passage were sold for sixpence each and gilt-framed photographs of the interior could be purchased for up to a guinea. The tree overhanging Cook's grave was also pruned by souvenir seekers.

As the dawn of Palmer's last day broke, spectators queued to hand over a guinea a piece for seats in the quadrangle of stands that had been erected to give rich members of the public a good view of the doctor's last death throes. Police had difficulty holding the mob back as the condemned man emerged for his last walk to the gallows.

To the very end, Palmer refused to confess. He insisted he had been unjustly convicted of the murder of Cook by strychnine. Most interpreted this protestation as meaning that he had killed his

It was Palmer's addiction to gambling and greed for money that motivated his killing of friends and family.

friend by some other means. In fact, his last remark made to the priest who visited him before his execution was: "Cook did not die from strychninia." When the governor of the jail pointed out the mode of death was secondary and that the important fact was whether or not Palmer had killed him, the condemned doctor replied: "I have nothing more to say than this—that I am quite easy in my conscience and happy in my mind." During his last moments on earth, the murdering doctor uttered not another word nor even a groan, as the trap door opened.

CARL PANZRAM

Carl Panzram was an utterly remorseless killer. He once said: "I don't believe in Man, God, nor Devil. I hate the whole damned human race, including myself."

When sentenced to be executed, he said defiantly: "I wish the whole world had but a single throat and I had my hands around it." He responded to liberal do-gooders who were calling for a reprieve by telling them: "I believe the only way to reform people is to kill them." As he waited on death row, he wrote: "In my lifetime I have murdered 21 human beings, I have committed thousands of burglaries, robberies, larcenies, arsons, and last but not least I have committed sodomy on more than 1,000 male human beings. For all these things I am not in the least bit sorry."

The son of Prussian immigrant parents, Carl Panzram was born in Warren, Minnesota, in 1891 and was in trouble with police from the age of eight. He spent several terms in juvenile institutions, burning down one reform school when he was 12. He joined the army but was court-martialed for the theft of government property in 1907. After three years in prison, he

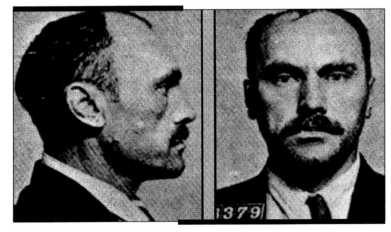

Born of Prussian immigrant parents in Warren, Minnesota, Panzram had been in trouble from the age of eight.

- - - - - - - - - - - - - - - -

returned to civilian life and embarked on a career of robbery and murder. Historians have only his word for the tally of his crimes, since he murdered indiscriminately all over the world, but his principal areas of operation were West Africa, Mexico, California, Montana, and Washington D.C.

In 1920 he bought a yacht, the *John O'Leary*

FACT FILE.

Name: Carl Panzram,
 aka John O'Leary
Born: 1891
Location of killings: West
 Africa, Mexico, California,
 Montana, and Washington
 D.C., USA
Killed: confessed to 21,
 probably more
Modus operandi: shooting,
 strangulation
Justice: hanged at
 Leavenworth in 1930

(which was also one of his aliases), and hired ten crewmen. Once aboard, the men were drugged then raped and murdered, their bodies thrown overboard. In Portuguese West Africa, he hired ten locals to accompany him on a crocodile hunt. He killed them all, sodomizing their corpses before feeding them to the crocs.

In 1928 he was jailed at Leavenworth for 20 years for one murder and a string of robberies. He told the warden: "I'll kill the first man who crosses me." He carried out his threat by battering to death a civilian employee with an iron bar. He went to the gallows on September 5, 1930, telling his executioner: "Hurry up, you bastard, I could hang a dozen men while you're fooling around."

LESZEK PEKALSKI

The school trip was in full swing, with pupils unruly and boisterous and teachers barking commands designed to deflate teenage exuberance.

No one paid any attention to the shambling figure of 16-year-old Leszek Pekalski as he lurked on the periphery. There was little to recommend him to fellow pupils or teachers, so pitiful was his appearance and attitude. When he decided to slip away, he found it surprisingly easy.

It was with remarkable ease too that he happened across a girl aged 13 and struck up a conversation. Nobody knows what was said. She probably felt sorry for him. Tragically, he did not extend the same feelings toward her. Now was the point that a misfit turned into a murderer and began a reign of terror lasting a dozen years. By the time he was 28, Pekalski had claimed the lives of at least 70 women to become Poland's most notorious mass murderer.

Pekalski had a tough start to life, abused by his mother and deserted by his father. When his mother finally abandoned him, he was brought up by nuns and, later, was cared for by Jehovah's Witnesses. The trauma of his unhappy home life left him unable to form a loving relationship with a woman, although he dearly wanted to find a wife.

On the fateful day of the school trip, he discovered that a dead girl or woman could be easily controlled. After beating, stabbing, or strangling

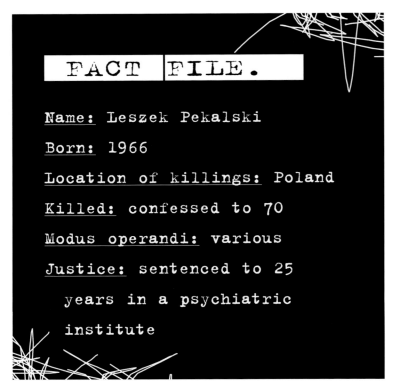

FACT FILE.

Name: Leszek Pekalski

Born: 1966

Location of killings: Poland

Killed: confessed to 70

Modus operandi: various

Justice: sentenced to 25 years in a psychiatric institute

his victims, he would have sex with them. Pekalski became a wanderer, traveling the length and breadth of his homeland and killing as he went. Frequently, those he encountered took pity on him, not realizing the grave threat that he posed. Even the police were lenient with him. In 1990 he was arrested on suspicion of rape and positively identified by the victim. The investigating officers merely ordered that he attend a psychiatric examination. He was finally given a two-year suspended sentence—and the killing spree continued.

After strangling and beating a 17-year-old girl to death with a metal post in woods near her home, Pekalski watched from a hideout as the girl's devastated father discovered the body. Eighteen months later a shop girl noticed Pekalski was still talking about the murder when the file on it was all but closed. At last the police pieced together the clues that led to him. He was arrested and talked to police freely and animatedly about his exploits.

In a handwritten confession, Pekalski admitted carrying out 70 murders. His marathon trial at the Provincial Court in the northern city of Slupsk lasted eight months. Pekalski cut a pathetic figure in the witness box and said police had forced a confession out of him. He told the court: "I'm a gullible man and I was easily persuaded by what the officers had told me. I'm mentally weak and if somebody pushes me I break down. Then I admit to things I have never done. I have never killed anyone. I'm so scared. The prosecutor threatened that the victims' families or the public would kill me if I'm acquitted or get a mild sentence. They yelled at me and told me to confess everything."

The pitiable qualities that surely lured so many women to their deaths were still apparent in Pekalski. The magistrate charged with bringing the case against him disturbed the dead women's families even more by saying he could not "help feeling vaguely sorry for him." The police hit back saying that Pekalski had confessed to crimes no one else could have known about. Argued one officer: "We couldn't find his trail for a long time. He never followed a regular pattern. There was no typical victim or a repeated killing method. He would hit with a wooden cane or would strangle his victim with a belt."

The proceedings grew near-farcical as DNA tests of hair strands which were crucial evidence against Pekalski were declared void by Doctor Ryszard from the Gdansk Medical Academy's forensic medicine institute. He said that the police had handled the hair clumsily and tainted its forensic value.

The trial dragged into 1994 when the final verdict further outraged the relatives of Pekalski's victims. For despite his earlier written confession, he was only charged with killing 17 women between 1984 and 1992—and then convicted of only one murder. He was cleared of more than a dozen others after it was felt there was insufficient evidence to convict.

Pekalski was sentenced to 25 years in a psychiatric institute. Unsurprisingly, he was diag-nosed with having an abnormal sex drive. Almost as soon as he was locked up in 1992, he asked a warden for permission to have a rubber sex doll in his cell. Pekalski appealed against the refusal and, resigned to his life away from the rest of the world, told psychiatrists that he still hoped to "find a girl" one day, either in the flesh or made of rubber.

MARCEL PETIOT

As the guillotine came crashing down onto the neck of Dr. Marcel Petiot, witnesses still wondered how such a pillar of the community, a man they revered and respected, could have lived such a murderous existence among them.

Wartime Paris thought it had seen all the wickedness the devil could bring them, with the presence of the Gestapo. But Dr. Petiot was one of their own, whose butchering betrayal would forever stay in their memories.

Dr. Petiot should never have become a doctor. Why a man with such a twisted mind should want to take up a compassionate occupation or how he was allowed to continue practicing is a mystery. Marcel Andre Felix Petiot was born in Auxerre, 100 miles south of Paris, on January 17, 1897. Many years later, after his notorious arrest, neighbors would recount how he enjoyed torturing animals

Dr. Petiot thought that the smoke of war would cover his tracks but justice finally caught up with him.

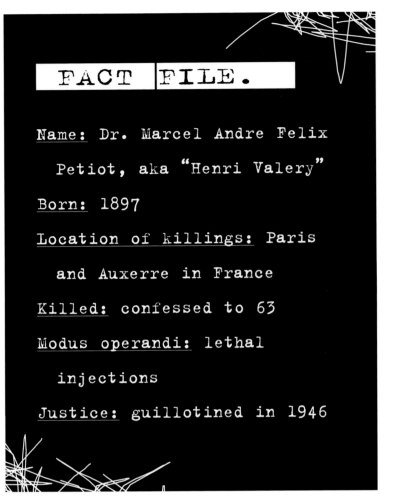

FACT FILE.

Name: Dr. Marcel Andre Felix
   Petiot, aka "Henri Valery"

Born: 1897

Location of killings: Paris
   and Auxerre in France

Killed: confessed to 63

Modus operandi: lethal
   injections

Justice: guillotined in 1946

World War I in progress, was drafted into the French infantry.

His war service was beleaguered with his mental problems, poor health in the trenches, and generally bizarre behavior. Petiot once deliberately shot himself in the foot. In 1917 he faced a court-martial accused of stealing drugs. He was discharged but was deemed so mentally unbalanced that it was recommended he enter an asylum. All this makes even more remarkable the fact that after taking advantage of an education program for war veterans, he was allowed to train as a doctor and emerged fully qualified.

Armed with his medical degree and a large amount of arrogance, Petiot moved 25 miles away from Auxerre to the village of Villeneuve-sur-Yonne. He immediately made enemies by advertising himself as a young doctor whose modern thinking and methods far outweighed anything that the village's two elderly doctors could offer. Right from the start, Petiot made sure he was paid

to death, how he was a strange loner who handed out obscene photographs to other children, and how once he fired his father's revolver in a history class.

Fiction may cross with fact in these stories but what is known with certainty is that Petiot's mother died when he was 15 and he, his father, and brother moved to Joigny, 15 miles from Auxerre. Expelled from school, Petiot soon turned to petty crime and was described by one psychiatrist as "an abnormal youth suffering from personal and hereditary problems which limit to a large degree his responsibility for his acts." In court for some of his early crimes, Petiot was said to "appear to be mentally ill." He escaped jail, was expelled from two other schools, and in January 1916, with

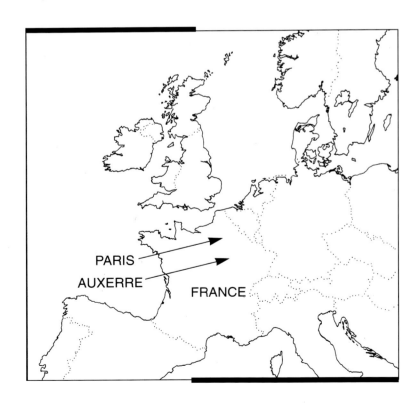

handsomely for his work in a fraud that enabled him to receive payment both from his patients and the French government.

Petiot was anything but respectable. He stole whenever he could, was callous about his patients

❝Petiot once deliberately shot himself in the foot❞

behind their backs, and then in 1926 started an affair with a young woman who later disappeared. Her dismembered body was found some weeks later in a river. Despite all this, he managed to become mayor of Villeneuve-sur-Yonne. He stole from all and sundry and even his marriage to Georgette Lablais, the 23-year-old daughter of a wealthy landowner, did not change his ways. Nor did his becoming a father to Gerhardt, the son who arrived a year later.

It was only when the home of a dairy unionist was razed to the ground and the man's wife found beaten to death that Petiot became the center of more serious suspicion. Others died in mysterious circumstances, including his housekeeper and Petiot was charged with murder. His files disappeared from police headquarters and the charges were dropped. Petiot left all this behind when he and his family moved to Paris in January 1933.

Petiot set himself up in a practice at Rue Caumartin offering various treatments for illnesses including mental health. Even when the occasional patient died from a simple ailment, even

A total of 47 suitcases were seized by police during the trial of Marcel Petiot. They contained clothes which were identified by relatives of some of his victims.

though he happily supplied drugs to addicts and carried out illegal abortions, Petiot thrived. Finally, when charged with stealing from a dead patient, Petiot pleaded insanity and was sent to a mental hospital himself.

He was released in 1937 and decided that tax fraud was an easier crime to commit on a regular basis than larceny or murder. Only a man such as Petiot could turn the 1940 invasion of Paris by German troops to his advantage. Like every period in Petiot's life, this one is a mixture of good and evil. He allegedly ascertained who among the French were collaborators with the Germans and

The Seine Assize Court, Paris, during the trial of Marcel
Petiot, who is seen between the policemen on the left.

- - - - - - - - - - - - -

secretly began helping fugitives to escape. But
many of those who gave Petiot the 25,000 francs
he demanded to help them flee France paid an even
higher price—their life. Among Petiot's first victims
were three pimps and their prostitute girlfriends
whose criminal activities meant they were wanted
by the French and German authorities alike.

Petiot's main source of income, however, was
from wealthy Jews, whom he killed and robbed.

These included pregnant newlywed Nelly Denise
Hotin who came to him for an abortion, Dr. Paul-
Leon Branbergerm an elderly Jew who wanted to
leave France with his wife, and a family of three
German Jews named Kneller whose dismembered
bodies were dragged from the Seine in August
1942. Then there was the Wolff family, six of their
friends, and another pimp and his mistress.

Petiot became a prisoner of the Gestapo after
an informer told the Germans about him. He spent
eight months in prison, during which time he was
tortured. Cynics say that it was more Petiot's ignorance about details of the local resistance

movement than his bravery that caused his inability to answer his torturers' interrogation. Petiot was released in January 1944 but in March he was a wanted man again—this time for countless murders.

On March 6, foul-smelling smoke poured from the chimney of an elegant house at 21 Rue Lesueur, in the fashionable Etoile district of Paris. Neighbors called the police and told them that the owner of the property was Dr. Marcel Petiot. Although he owned another residence two miles away, he had bought this house, a disused mansion, for half a million francs and had set about modifying it in the strangest manner. The house included a triangular room that had been sound-proofed. There was a false door, no windows but several peepholes, which Petiot had told the builders were so that he could observe his mental patients. Finally, a furnace had been installed in the cellar. The neighbors also told of some strange comings and goings at the house. These included a man arriving with a horse and cart in the dead of night, large sacks being moved, and nearly 50 suitcases being used to carry items from the house.

With the smoke from number 21 getting worse, firemen were summoned to put out the fire. Entering the property, one of the first sights they saw was a human arm dangling from a furiously burning coal stove. Close by, a heap of coal was mixed with what were obviously human bones and body parts. Around the furnace were arms and legs, some stripped of their flesh, and torsos in

"He spent eight months in prison, during which time he was tortured"

every state of dismemberment. There was also a number of scalps, with the hair still on them. In an outhouse several corpses covered with lime were discovered.

By this time, Petiot had been telephoned and he arrived on his bicycle, slightly breathless but with a glib story to tell. First he ascertained that all his listeners were French and that there were no Nazi sympathizers among their ranks. Then he whispered earnestly: "This is serious—my head could be at stake, for I am head of a Resistance group." The bodies that had been discovered, he told the gendarmes, were those of traitors to France, informers and friends of the Nazis. It had been his secret work to rid their beloved country of these people. Petiot said that he kept his files hidden in his other house in Rue Caumartin and he needed to get there to destroy them "before the enemy finds them." Though still in the control of the Germans, most Frenchmen knew that an allied invasion was imminent and liberation would surely follow, so hatred of collaborators was running high. Amazingly, the patriotic gendarmes gave Petiot the benefit of the doubt and allowed him to go to his other home to carry out the destruction of his "secret files." It would be seven months before they were to see him again.

Petiot fled Paris and laid low in the countryside. With Allied and Axis armies about to fight their way across France once again, the attention of the authorities was somewhat distracted from the goings-on at 21 Rue Lesueur. Paris police headquarters received a telegram from Germany

Judges, lawyers, and court clerks leaving the Palais de
Justice in Paris to visit the house of Marcel Petiot.

with the instruction: "Arrest Petiot. He is a
dangerous lunatic." But it arrived rather too late,
for Petiot had by now changed his name to "Henri
Valeri" and joined the new French Forces of the
Interior. At one time, Captain Valeri was even drafted in to look for the missing Petiot!

Meanwhile, with the coroner's office informed,
more and more decomposing bodies were being
dug up at 21 Rue Lesueur. It gradually sank in that
the triangular room in which the victims had been
dismembered was Petiot's personal charnel house.

With its huge sinks and soundproofing, it had
obviously been designed for draining corpses of
blood and ensuring people died with no one hearing their cries. Experts were not immediately able
to tell the cause of death but dismemberment followed a distinct pattern: the collar bone, shoulder
bone, and an arm were all removed in one piece.
It was obvious the perpetrator knew about dissecting the human body.

The initial estimate that the house contained
at least ten victims was "vastly inferior," said Chief
Coroner Albert Paul who added that he had had to
catalogue 33 pounds of charred bones, 24 pounds
of unburned fragments, eleven pounds of human
hair, and three rubbish bins of unidentifiable

human bits. From what he could ascertain, the youngest victim had been a woman in her twenties and the oldest a man in his fifties. Elsewhere in the house, police also found bags and cases containing 1,691 articles of clothing, including 28 men's suits, 79 women's dresses, and five fur coats.

When the painstaking task of trying to identify some of the bodies began, investigators were shaken to realize how utterly untrue Petiot's tale of killing traitors had been. His victims were mainly Jews who had been reported as disappearing without trace during the course of the war. German contacts revealed that Petiot had at one time been arrested on suspicion of smuggling Jews out of occupied France—but the innocents who had entered his house on Rue Lesueur had never left the triangular chamber, never mind the country. At another of Petiot's homes, police found a clue about how they might have been disposed of: a large store of poisons including digitalis and strychnine. The stock of heroin and morphine was at least 50 times that which a doctor would be expected to keep.

A full-scale manhunt was launched for Petiot. While police scoured the country for him, accomplices involved in the "escape" ring were rounded up. Some admitted sending refugees to Petiot in the knowledge they would never leave France. One said he had seen sixteen corpses stretched out in his house. Another revealed that Petiot had kept meticulous records that showed that more than 60 people had entered the triangular room never to leave it alive.

Petiot returned to Paris thinking he could keep a low profile in a city of turmoil after the war. He was reported to have celebrated with the Free French Forces when they marched into newly liberated Paris with General de Gaulle at their head. Still supremely arrogant, Petiot could not resist writing a letter to a Paris newspaper rebutting accusations that he was a Nazi sympathizer. A few weeks afterward, on October 31, 1944, Petiot was finally recognized and arrested while waiting at a metro station. He had foolishly believed that growing a long beard would be disguise enough for the most wanted murderer in France.

While awaiting trial, Petiot continued to maintain that he did not murder innocent people, only those who were "enemies of France." But no evidence could be found to support his claims that he was a key member of the resistance movement, that he assassinated Nazis single-handed, and that he developed secret weapons against the Germans. There were records, however, to show that Petiot's pre-war life had been one of fraud, theft, corruption, and murder with his scheme to enrich himself principally through the deaths of wealthy Jews. It was estimated that he stole about two million francs, plus gold and jewels, none of which was ever found.

> **"With its huge sinks and soundproofing, it had obviously been designed for draining corpses of blood and ensuring people died with no one hearing their cries"**

Petiot was charged with murdering 27 people and his trial began on March 18, 1946, at the Palais de Justice. He defended himself before the three judges and a seven-man jury. While he enjoyed the banter with witnesses and his prosecutors, he still maintained his facade of being an avenger against collaborators and inform-ers. He also tainted the memory of his victims, such as the Kneller family whom he labeled as Germans who were "getting ready for the next war." Another victim, Yvan Drefus, was called a Gestapo informer and "traitor to his people, his religion, and to his father-land."

Petiot admitted killing 19 of the 27 victims found on Rue Lesueur but denied any knowledge of the further 44 identified victims. He sneeringly told the court: "I don't have to justify myself for murders I'm not accused of committing."

The sickening facts about his crime soon became clear, however. At least 63 people had died at his hands, mostly Jews. Petiot had promised them safe passage to South America but, after receiving their money, he gave them a lethal injec-tion, telling them it was a vaccination against foreign diseases. Then he led his victims to the sound-proofed room where he told them his Resistance friends would shortly arrive to help them. By this time, the poison was doing its evil work and Petiot took perverted pleasure in peering through a peep-hole and watching his victims in their death throes. At first, Petiot had disposed of the bodies by mutilating them and then dropping them into lime. As the body count grew too high, he started incinerating them. It was this smoke, with its sickening smell, that permeated the air around the house in Rue Lesueur.

> **Petiot admitted killing 19 of the 27 victims found on Rue Lesueur but denied any knowledge of the further 44 identified victims**

Petiot explained away the presence at his home of fur coats belonging to one of his victims, furrier Joachim Guschinow, as gifts from a grateful man he had helped escape. He even said the man had written to his wife from the safety of Argentina. Investigations could not trace any of these letters.

Petiot was found guilty of all 27 murders and sentenced to death by guillotine. Asked if he had anything he wanted to say, Petiot shouted: "Nothing. You are Frenchmen. You know I have destroyed members of the Gestapo. You know what you have to do." It was only when the reality of his death sentence hit Petiot that he cried out to his wife Georgette: "You must avenge me." An appeal lodged by her failed. So too did a plea for presidential clemency.

The day before his execution was due to be car-ried out, prison guards found capsules in Petiot's cell. They thought it was cyanide but it turned out to be a sedative. It was obvious from Petiot's demeanor that sedatives had regularly been smug-gled in for him.

Petiot did not die on the scheduled day, how-ever. The execution had to be postponed when the

A group of photojournalists train their cameras on a courtyard where a murder reconstruction took place for the Marcel Petiot trial.

guillotine was found not to be working properly. He finally faced his maker on May 25, 1946, at 3.30am. Petiot only agreed to see the prison chaplain at the last minute after being begged to do so by his wife. He told the chaplain: "I am not a religious man and my conscience is clean."

Witnesses said that the condemned man was remarkably calm as he approached the guillotine; some even said he was smiling. It could have been as a result of more sedatives helpfully supplied to him. Or could it have been the knowledge that he was taking other secrets to the grave—for, after his death, even more dismembered bodies with the hallmarks of Dr. Petiot's handiwork were found buried in the leafy sanctuary of Paris's famous Bois de Boulogne.

JESSE POMEROY

Jesse Pomeroy, who grew up in the 19th-century slum streets of Boston, Massachusetts, had the least prepossessing of appearances: he was a gangling kid with one white eye, a hare lip, and obviously low intelligence.

He was shunned by other children—and his revenge for being ostracized was a terrible one.

Between December 1871 and September 1872, a number of children were abducted, sadistically tortured with whips, knives, and pins, and left unconscious in Boston's back streets. The city was shocked when the perpetrator of these foul assaults was found to be a 12-year-old boy. Sent to a reform school, he was handed back into the care of his widowed mother two years later and embarked on a youthful pursuit of fresh victims, both male and female.

When the body of four-year-old Horace Mullen was found on the beach at Horace Bay, near Boston, in April 1974, a full-scale murder hunt began. The child had been beaten, stabbed 15 times, and his throat cut. But the ensuing manhunt turned into a boyhunt when the evidence pointed toward Pomeroy, who had been released from West Borough Reform School only two months before.

It later transpired that the 14-year-old had not even waited that long before killing. Five weeks before, he had murdered nine-year-old Katie Curran, whose body he buried in the basement of a shop. When, after her son was arrested, his mother moved house, the new owners found 12 corpses buried in her rubbish tip.

Jesse Pomeroy confessed to torturing to death 27 youngsters but was tried only for the murder of little Horace Mullen. He pleaded insanity but he was found guilty and sentenced to death. There were appeals for mercy to be shown to such a young offender and a compromise was reached that he must spend the rest of his life in solitary confinement.

Still aged only 14, Pomeroy was sent to Charleston Prison where he spent the more than 40 years entirely alone in his cell before finally being allowed to mingle with other convicts. He had

---

FACT FILE.

Name: Jesse Harding Pomeroy

Born: 1860

Location of killings: Boston, Massachusetts, USA

Killed: 27

Modus operandi: torture and mutilation

Justice: sentenced to life; died in prison after 40 years' solitary confinement

used his lonely decades in solitary to study and he ended up writing a biography that chronicled his early life and terrible crimes. On September 29, 1932, he died in the same jail, aged 73.

Pomeroy's death sentence was commuted to life imprisonment and he served 58 years in solitary confinement.

HEINRICH POMMERENCKE

Heinrich Pommerencke attempted his first murder after watching the movie *The Ten Commandments* in 1959.

He was later to tell police that a scene of wanton harlots dancing around the golden calf had filled him with revulsion and fueled his certainty that women were the source of all the world's evils. They had to be taught a lesson. Immediately after leaving the theater, he attacked an 18-year-old girl, tore the clothes from her, raped her, then cut her throat with a razor. It was only the terrified girl's screams that saved her. She was heard by a passing taxi driver who went to her aid.

```
FACT FILE.

Name: Heinrich Pommerencke,
   aka "Beast of the Black
   Forest"
Born: 1937
Location of killings: Germany
   and Austria
Killed: Six
Modus operandi: stabbing
   following rape
Justice: sentenced to life in
   1960
```

Denied his first taste of killing, Pommerencke was now desperate to satisfying his twisted desires. Over the following days, he stalked several women, finally choosing Hilda Knothe, a 34-year-old waitress whom he followed as she walked home through a park at Karlsruhe, southern Germany. He raped and then stabbed her to death. This was the start of Pommerencke's killing spree—and an extension to his activities as a serial rapist that had already earned him the title the "Beast of the Black Forest."

Born in Bentwisch, near Rostock, East Germany, in 1937, Pommerencke was the product of a broken marriage and his solitary childhood was to create problems with his relationships with girls. Small for his age, he was excruciatingly shy and girls tended to ignore him. It is likely that his boast of first having sex when he was ten was untrue. This may have been just one of his fantasies, but bubbling inside him were thoughts of far more violent sexual activities. By the age of 15, Pommerencke was hanging around dance halls and trying to assault lone girls. These clumsy attempts usually ended with the girls screaming and Pommerencke running away. However, he later graduated to full-blown rape, at one time being forced to flee to Switzerland to escape prison.

Still in his early teens, Pommerencke moved to West Germany where he advertised himself as an odd-job man and took evening work waiting at tables. During this time, he was arrested for burglary and spent a short term in prison. Had police searched his rooms, they would have found piles of pornography which were to provoke his killings

> **By the age of 15, Pommerencke was hanging around dance halls and trying to assault lone girls**

during heightened sexual excitement. They were later to note that when Hilda Konthe's body was found, the clothes had been ripped off in a state of obvious sexual frenzy. This, together with the theft of his victims' money and handbags, was to become the mark of the Beast of the Black Forest.

Just a month after Hilda's death, Pommerencke followed 18-year-old beautician Karin Walde through the streets of Hornberg. He knocked her out with a large stone and raped her after tearing off her clothes. The same stone was used to bludgeon Karin to death.

Three months later, 21-year-old student teacher Dagmar Klimek was on the Italian Riviera Express train late one night when Pommerencke caught sight of her. He bought a platform ticket at Freiburg station where the train was stationary and then climbed aboard. His opportunity to attack came when Dagmar went to the toilet. While she was inside, he removed a bulb from the train corridor, plunging the area into darkness. As Dagmar came out, Pommerencke grabbed her,

Born in East Germany in 1937, Heinrich Pommerencke became known as the "Beast of the Black Forest."

pushed her out of a train door and pulled the emergency cord, causing the train to slow down. Then he jumped off to find his badly injured victim. When he did, he dragged her unconscious body into a clump of bushes, tore off her clothes and raped her. Finally, he stabbed her straight through the heart. Pommerencke started his trek home to Freiburg and when it was daylight he washed himself and the bloody knife in a village fountain.

On June 8, 1959, Pommerencke attacked 18-year-old secretary Rita Walterspacher as she walked along an isolated road leading from a railway station near Rastatt. Spotting Pommerencke, Rita's intuition told her that she was in danger and she started to run and scream. Tragically, her

Blood stains found on the gray suit Pommerencke always wore during his attacks linked him with three of the murder victims. He is shown here being escorted into the court.

- - - - - - - - - - - -

actions were not enough to save her. Pommerencke grabbed her and pulled her into woodland beside the road. Her body was later found with her clothes torn. She had been raped and strangled. This was to be Pommerencke's last murder, for the attack had been witnessed by a woman on a train. At first she thought he and Rita were a young couple playing a game but after hearing on the radio about the discovery of a woman's body, the witness contacted the police to tell them what she had seen.

The detail she gave was enough to snare Pommerencke—that and another mistake he made. He had gone into a tailor's shop in Hornberg to have a new waiter's uniform fitted. Late for work, he rushed out leaving behind a pile of old clothes and a briefcase. When an assistant opened the case he saw it contained a rifle, pornographic magazines, and a rail ticket. The assistant called police who discovered that the briefcase perfectly matched a description given by one of Pommerencke's earlier rape victims. Also, police records showed that burglaries always took place in the same locations as the rape-murders and Pommerencke had many burglary convictions.

After trying to give police the slip, Pommerencke was caught in a local fairground. Taken into custody, he was identified by one of his rape victims. At first, Pommerencke denied he was the Beast of the Black Forest but tests on bloodstains found on the gray suit he always wore during his attacks linked him with three of the murdered girls. Pommerencke had no choice but to admit to his crimes, adding two other rape-murders, 20 rapes, and a string of burglaries to his confession. "I wanted to kill seven women as seven is my lucky number," he told police, adding: "It was the films I saw. They made me so tense I had to do something to a woman." In a later interview, he began to show some remorse, telling police: "Everything I did was cruel and bestial. From the bottom of my heart, I would like to undo all this."

Police doctors said Pommerencke had something of a Jekyll and Hyde personality and his attacks were carried out as he mentally wrestled with his own inadequacies and guilt. They also believed Pommerencke's mistake of leaving his briefcase in a shop where it would surely be opened could have "fulfilled a subconscious need to be caught and punished."

At his trial, charged with four murders, 12 attempted murders, 21 rapes, and 35 other counts, Pommerencke pleaded that he had never intended to kill any of his victims but had just wanted them to be unable to put up any resistance. However, the court decided Pommerencke had "an insane lust to kill" and, on October 22, 1960, he was given six life sentences amounting to 140 years with hard labor. Aged just 23 when he was imprisoned, the Beast of the Black Forest's short but deadly reign of terror was over.

RICHARD RAMIREZ

One steamy August Saturday in 1989, a man tried to drag a woman from her car in a Los Angeles suburb.

He was attacked by her husband and the gathering crowd suddenly recognized the face they had seen in that morning's newspapers. It was of a 25-year-old man wanted as principal suspect in the hunt for a murderous maniac labeled by the media as the "Night Stalker." Now, as the crowd rained blows on him, the monster that had thrived on instilling fear into others knew how it felt. His life was saved only when a police car arrived on the scene and he was taken away bruised and bleeding.

The man who had nightly stalked the city's streets for 15 months was Richard Ramirez, a drifter, sadist, and satanist. Born in El Paso, Texas, in 1960, the youngest of eight children in a working-class family, Ramirez turned to crime at an early age. He was arrested twice for drug offenses before moving to California at the age of 22. There he slept rough and earned enough to buy drugs through petty theft. A police profile described him as "a confused, angry loner who sought refuge in thievery, drugs, the dark side of rock music, and finally murder and rape."

As the Night Stalker, he brought a unique

FACT FILE.

Name: Richard Leyva Ramirez,
   aka the "Night Stalker"

Born: February 28, 1960

Location of killings:
   California, USA

Killed: at least 16

Modus operandi: rape,
   strangulation, shooting,
   or abduction after random
   break-ins

Justice: sentenced to death
   in 1989

terror to middle-class areas of Los Angeles between June 1984 and August 1985. He would creep into a house at night, raping, mutilating, and murdering. The ways he dispensed with his victims were varied but included shooting, bludgeoning, throat cutting, or battering to death. Some men were shot or stabbed to death as they slept. Women of whatever age were beaten up, sexually abused, raped, and then killed by stabbing, strangulation, or shooting. For many of his younger victims, the terror would be heightened as he drove them miles from home before sexually assaulting or sodomizing them, then dumping them in open country to fend for themselves. Although the attacks satisfied Ramirez's sadistic sexual urges, he also stole from those he killed.

Unlike most serial killers, there appeared to be no similarities between the victims of his attacks. He picked them at random, a major factor in the delay in capturing him. His first victim was a 79-year-old woman, whom he raped and almost decapitated at her home in Glassell Park in June 1984. As far as is known, he did not kill again until February 1985 and, naturally enough, police made no links with his next two victims: a six-year-old girl snatched from a school bus stop in Montebello and a nine-year-old kidnapped from her bedroom in Monterey Park. Both were raped before being dumped and left alive. When Ramirez struck again in March, attacking two roommates in their Rosemead apartment, killing one and wounding the other, there was still no reason for police to connect the cases. The survivor of this attack, however, was able to give detectives their first firm description of the killer: he had curly black hair, dark and bulging eyes and, because of his drug addiction, foul, rotting teeth.

The pace of the killings then grew. A 30-year-old woman was dragged from her car and shot. A 64-year-old man was beaten to death and his 44-year-old wife stabbed to death in their home. Ramirez then used the blade to gouge out the woman's eyes, which he took away with him.

His next victims were a man aged 65, followed by two sisters aged 84 and 81, although the latter, an invalid, miraculously survived her beating. A 32-year-old woman had her throat slashed and within a week the same fate had befallen a 77-year-old widow. A 61-year-old woman was beaten to death in her home five days later. It was now July 1985 and police had at last linked the attacks, although they had still not made an announcement of the fact.

However, all that changed after Ramirez struck twice on the same day. He broke into a house in Sun Valley on June 20, slaughtered a 32-year-old

"For many of his younger victims, the terror would be heightened as he drove them miles from home before sexually assaulting or sodomizing them, then dumping them in open country to fend for themselves"

man, raped his wife, and battered their son before moving on to Glendale where a 68-year-old and his wife of 66 were also shot dead. Further attacks took place in swift succession, leaving a couple wounded by gunshots in their Northridge home on August 6, and a 35-year-old man was shot dead in Diamond Bar two days later. On August 17, Ramirez was in San Francisco where he shot dead a 66-year-old man. His wife was also shot but survived, providing another valuable description of the Stalker.

Panic that a particularly vicious and sadistic serial killer was at large now forced police to go public. Details of some of his earlier crimes were released; the fact that he had gouged out one woman's eyes causing the most revulsion. It was

Ramirez was arrested in after trying to drag a woman from her car and then being attacked by an angry mob who recognized him as the Night Stalker.

revealed that the Stalker sometimes left his mark as the devil's disciple—an inverted pentagram or five-pointed star—scrawled on a mirror or a wall. He also drew occult signs in lipstick on the victims' bodies. Some of the more superstitious citizens of Los Angeles began to believe that the Stalker really did have demonic powers that made him unstoppable—until the FBI got lucky.

In August 1985, Ramirez attacked a couple in the town of Mission Viejo. He shot and wounded

Richard Ramirez saw himself as the "Devil's Disciple" and drew occult signs on the bodies of his victims.

the 29-year-old man then raped his fiancée before escaping in a stolen car. When the getaway car was recovered, the only clue to the assailant was one smudged fingerprint, which was sent to a high-tech records center that had just been set up in Sacramento. The new system had been in operation for just three minutes when it matched the print from the car with one taken from Richard Ramirez when previously hauled in on a petty theft charge.

Ramirez's photograph was circulated to the media, though detectives could have had little idea of the instant reaction it would bring—as, battered and beaten, they had to rescue him from an angry mob the very next day. He was charged with 14 counts of murder, 22 of sexual assault, and 32 other felonies.

One of the murder charges was later dropped but other counts of murder, attempted murder, and rape were later added. It is reckoned that Richard Ramirez killed between 16 and 19 people, although he himself told a fellow jail inmate: "I've killed 12 people, man. I love all that blood."

During his preliminary court appearances, Ramirez shouted, "Hail Satan" and waved a hand

Ramirez was convicted of 19 murders and sentenced to death. He still awaits execution.

daubed with a pentagram on the palm. At his trial, he told the court: "You maggots make me sick. You don't understand me. I am beyond good and evil. I will be avenged. Lucifer dwells in us all."

The trial turned into a marathon. The first jury had to be dismissed when one of its members was found to be in a deep sleep. Another jury was dis-missed when a member was murdered in an unrelated attack. However, on September 20, 1989, Ramirez was duly convicted and sentenced to death. He was not impressed, snarling at the jury: "Big deal. Death comes with the territory. See you in Disneyland." In truth, he had little reason to fear the ultimate penalty. He knew he was likely to languish on San Quentin's death row for some time, as California had not carried out a death sentence since 1967.

GARY RIDGWAY

When Gary Ridgway was arrested on suspicion of being America's most prolific serial killer, there was no shortage of women prepared to provide a character assassination of him.

Like the rest of the world, they were horrified"—but probably not surprised—that Ridgway, with all his perverted inclinations, had turned into a murderer who preyed on women around Seattle, Washington.

It was in November 2001 that Ridgway was pulled in for questioning over the murders of at least 48 young women, the bodies of many of them having been found in the Green River, near Seattle.

The lorry painter and apparently normal family man was arrested after DNA tests finally linked him with the horrific crimes. That was a major breakthrough for both police and anxious relatives who had begun to believe that the murderer was either dead or in prison, because the case had remained unsolved for so long. At one point, another notorious killer, Ted Bundy, even wrote to police from death row offering help in catching their man.

Finding Ridgway guilty was not difficult, however. When he appeared in court two years later, he admitted all 48 murders, saying: "In most cases I did not know their names. I killed so many women I have a hard time keeping them straight."

The hunt for the murderer who was to be known as the Green River Killer began on July 15, 1982, after the body of 23-year-old Deborah Bonner was found on the bank of Green River in

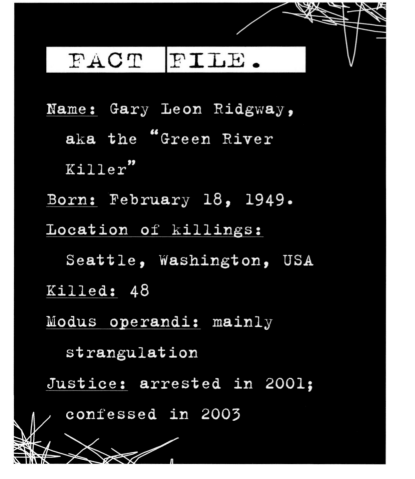

FACT FILE.

Name: Gary Leon Ridgway,
  aka the "Green River
  Killer"
Born: February 18, 1949.
Location of killings:
  Seattle, Washington, USA
Killed: 48
Modus operandi: mainly
  strangulation
Justice: arrested in 2001;
  confessed in 2003

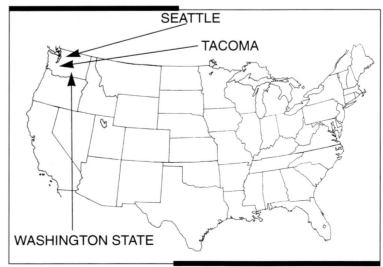

SEATTLE
TACOMA
WASHINGTON STATE

Kent, King County, Washington. It was only half a mile away from the spot where 16-year-old Wendy Coffield's body was discovered a month later.

> ❝In most cases I did not know their names. I killed so many women I have a hard time keeping them straight❞

Police began to fear that with so many young women prostitutes and runaways having simply disappeared, they were on the trail of a serial killer. They were right, of course.

Most of Ridgway's victims were picked up along the sleazy Sea-Tac Highway running from Seattle to Tacoma. They were generally strangled and their bodies hidden in woodland and ravines or dumped in the Green River. Their decomposing remains were found up until March 1984.

At first, the police had a couple of suspects in mind. One was Melvyn Wayne Foster, a 44-year-old taxi driver who seemed to possess too much information about the murders. He was arrested but cleared. The second suspect was William J. Stephens II, a 38-year-old law student. Stephens had pictures of naked women, a fascination with serial killer Ted Bundy, and a collection of police uniforms and badges. However, detectives were eventually forced to announce that Stephens was "no longer a viable suspect."

The man they really wanted was still at large.

At the time of Ridgway's arrest, he was married to his third wife Judith.

Ridgway looked more like a bank manager than a psychopath, with his neatly-trimmed mustache and dark-rimmed spectacles. At the time of his arrest, he was married to his third wife Judith. She was reluctant to talk about her husband's weird ways—but there were plenty of other women from Ridgway's past who were more than willing. Police soon learned that he met several women through "Parents without Partners" dances. His first two wives, Claudia and Marcia, together with prostitutes and girlfriends, said he liked sex outdoors.

Along Star Lake Road, victims were found of the Green River serial killer. The victims, young women, were left out in the forest and scavenged, leaving only skeletons.

- - - - - - - - - - - - -

Police were particularly interested in this aspect of the killer's secret pleasures, especially when told these sexual encounters took place at or near where the victims' remains were found.

The women also took detectives to places where Ridgway would tie them up to stakes for outdoor intercourse. Marcia and another girl, Rebecca Quay, said they were choked by Ridgway. In talking about her marriage to the killer, Marcia

said he liked to search out places that were used as dumps and then scavenge for old car parts. These spots, too, were not far from where some of the victims' bodies were discovered. Marcia also said her husband took her cycling along the Green River. She pointed out one of Ridgway's favorite places, a road where six victims were found, and showed them a state map with his favorite camping and outdoor spots marked on it. In 1991, the body of Sarah Habakangas, a 17-year-old of Virginia, had been found in one marked spot, North Bend. That same year, the body of Nicole French, 19, of Sacramento, had been found nearby. Both women had been prostitutes who hung out on the Sea-Tac Pacific Highway South strip.

In tears as she recounted the years with her

> **❝Ridgway was just 16 when he committed his first act of violence and stabbed a six-year-old boy❞**

ex-husband. Marcia, the mother of Ridgway's only child Matthew, born in 1975, told police that at one point she had taken out a restraining order against him because she was so frightened of his temper. Second wife Claudia said their brief marriage had failed because of the influence of Ridgway's mother. Ridgway was described as having been very close to his mother Mary; others said he was completely dominated by her.

Gary Leon Ridgway was born in Utah on February 18, 1949, and had an older brother Greg and a younger brother, Ed. The three boys all grew up south of Seattle in a working-class neighborhood, not far from the airport strip in what would become Sea-Tac. Ridgway was just 16 when he committed his first act of violence and stabbed a six-year-old boy. Though critically injured, the lad was not believed by police and the case was never pursued. At home, Ridgway was considered a dutiful son and though enjoying a good relationship with his mother, he did not have the same affection for his father, Tom. Mr. Ridgway worked

Ridgway's arrest was due to improved DNA testing. A sample of his DNA linked him directly with four of the Green River victims.

as a bus driver on the strip and complained about the prostitutes that gathered there. He could never have guessed what actions his son would one day take against such women.

Ridgway cared for both parents when they were ill and visited them regularly. Tom Ridgway died in 2000 and his mother died of cancer in August 2001. After his mother's death, Ridgway held a garage sale at her home. "He was always nice and polite and stayed in touch with his old neighborhood," David Malo, a neighbor, recalled.

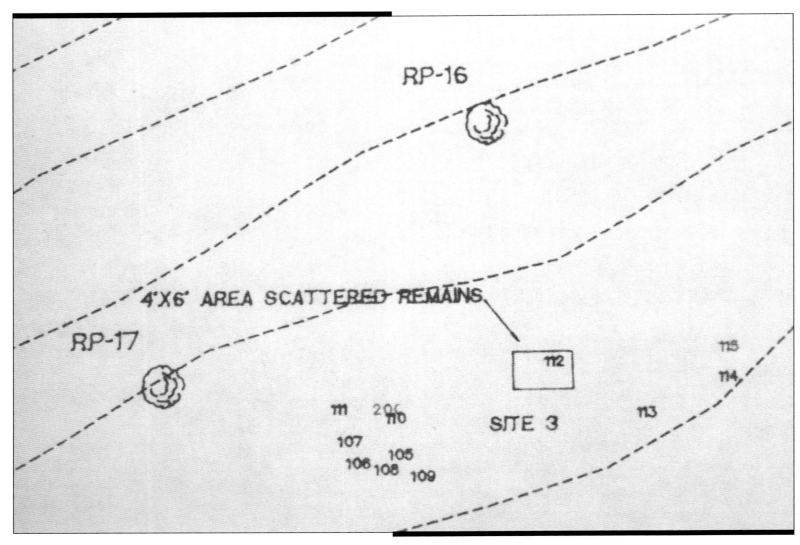

RP-16

RP-17

4'X6' AREA SCATTERED REMAINS

112

115

114

111 206
110

107

106 108 105

109

SITE 3

113

The Green River serial murders involved the death of about 50 young women around the Seattle area. Police were still finding remains up until 1990.

Another neighbor, Gino Duarte, said Ridgway seemed only interested in discussing hunting and would tell him about how he and his brothers liked to hunt in the mountains. Eventually, Ridgway and his brothers put their house up for sale for $219,000 but it came back to haunt the family after Ridgway's arrest. He had been living there when he committed some of his murders.

King County Sheriff's spokesman John Urquhart said at the time: "We are searching the house, the property, and the yard. We are interested in every square inch of every place he's lived." The searches involved the use of dogs specially trained to sniff out bodies and included four other addresses where Ridgway had lived. One of these was on a cul-de-sac near the Pacific Highway South strip where countless victims had disappeared between 1982 and 1983. Ridgway lived there with Judith until 1987 when he first came to the attention of police for soliciting prostitutes. No one seemed to make the connection between this and their deaths, but the press attention was enough to make the couple move and they found another house in the suburb of Kent. Ridgway became the self-appointed neighborhood crime informer, going around telling neighbors of break-ins or of prostitutes working in their area. He seemed obsessed with prostitutes turning tricks in cars on the dark and quiet streets. One resident, James Mattoon, recalled: "He'd go door-to-door and ask neighbors whether they knew prostitutes were having sex in cars on the street and throwing condoms out the windows. I always thought, Gosh, this guy is kind of fixated on this."

Another neighbor said that even though Ridgway "was basically a nice person he grated on our nerves and just kind of irritated a lot of us."

Meanwhile, a special Green River Task Force had been set up to track the killer down. One of the biggest expenses of an investigation that was to cost $15 million was the installation of a computer system to collate the welter of information being input. Among the basic facts of the case were that, of the 49 victims the Green River Killer was suspected of murdering, 18 were under the age of 18, 12 were between 18 and 20, 15 were 21 or older, and four sets of remains were not identified. The deaths were all violent. The victims were females of all races, and either had connections with prostitution or were hitchhiking. Most victims were last seen alive around the Sea-Tac area on Pacific Highway. On three different occasions, two victims disappeared on the very same day. Most victims were not found until their remains were only bones. Clusters of bodies were found, usually in wooded or brushy areas where trash was

❛❛Clusters of bodies were found, usually in wooded or brushy areas where trash was dumped illegally❜❜

dumped illegally, near isolated roads with clear views, or in or near the Green River. The bodies were partially or fully clothed, some of the victims being posed. The remains of one victim, Denise Bush were found in two separate dump sites, two hours apart.

An FBI profile of the killer indicated that he had a deep hatred of women, was possibly a married man who came from a broken home and probably hated his mother. It also suggested that the killer would be aged between 20 and 40, white, a heavy smoker who liked to drink, and someone with a background of sexual crime. It was an accurate portrait of Gary Ridgway who, with wife Judith, lived in Kent for ten years before moving a few miles to the middle-class neighborhood of Auburn, south of Seattle. The four-bedroom house with its acre of garden was where he was living when he was arrested on suspicion of being the Green River Killer in 2001.

His arrest was due to improved DNA testing. Ridgway had provided a DNA sample on a piece of gauze during investigation into the murders in 1984. That sample now linked him directly with four of the Green River victims: 21-year-old Marcia Chapman and teenagers Opal Mills and Cynthia Hinds, whose bodies were found in the river in 1982, and 31-year-old Carol Christensen, whose body was found in woods nearby in 1983. These were the four murders that Ridgway was initially charged with.

When the case finally came to court in

"I picked on prostitutes as my victims because they were easy to pick up without being spotted."

Having picked a girl up, Ridgway said he would then "talk to her and get her mind off anything she was nervous about." He said his aim was to make

---

❝❝He stopped to have sex with the bodies until the flies came❞❞

---

the girl think, "Oh, this guy cares—which I didn't. I just wanted to get her in the vehicle and eventually kill her." Most of the victims were killed and dumped in clusters because, Ridgway said: "I wanted to keep track of all the women I killed. I liked to drive by the clusters and think about the women I placed there." Sometimes, he added, he stopped to have sex with the bodies "until the flies came."

The court heard how Ridgway always removed clothing and jewelry to hinder identification. A particularly twisted game of his was to leave items of his victims' jewelry in the women's washroom at his place of work in the hope female colleagues might wear some of it. One witness's statement was chilling. Paige Elizabeth Miley, 21, said that in 1983 she had talked briefly with a man who asked where her "tall, blonde friend" was. Miley guessed he was the abductor of fellow prostitute Kim Nelson two days earlier.

Relatives, many wearing photograph badges of

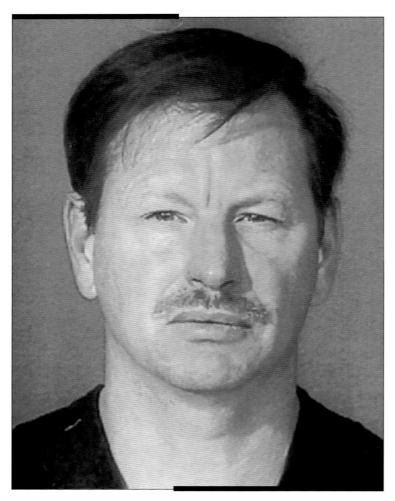

Ridgway was originally charged with four murders, but by the time his case came to court he was charged with 48.

- - - - - - - - - - -

November 2003, however, it took eight minutes to read out the names of all 48 victims with whose murders he was charged. Ridgway confessed he had "tried to kill as many women as possible." He added: "In most cases when I murdered these women, I did not know their names. Most of the time I killed them the first time I met them and I do not have a memory for faces." Relatives of the victims wept in the Seattle courtroom as they listened to Ridgway's statement on the murder spree that terrorized Washington State between 1982 and 1984. But he also confessed to the occasional murder after this time. He announced:

GREEN RIVER VICTIMS

DECEASED

Police Lieutenant Dan Nolan stands at a wall covered with the photographs of victims of the Green River killer.

the victims, often found what they heard hard to take. One, Kandice Watts, whose sister Roberta Hayes was 21 when she was last seen alive in 1987, said: "She was my sister and my brother's sister and she was very important to us." Deanna Brewer was only 13 when her sister Shirley Marie

Sheriff disappeared in 1982. She said of Ridgway: "I don't know how he can sit there so blankly." It was to these relatives' dismay that Ridgway successfully plea-bargained to escape the death penalty and instead faced a life sentence without parole. Debra York, whose 17-year-old niece Cynthia Jean Hinds was found dead on the banks of the Green River in 1982 said: "He don't deserve to live another day."

CHARLES SCHMID

Charles Schmid had everything money could buy but wanted the one thing wealth could not give him—the experience of taking another human life.

For a child whose fortunes had moved from poverty to luxury, this was the ultimate gift to himself.

Born to an unmarried mother on July 8, 1942, Charles was adopted by Charles and Katharine Schmid who owned a nursing home in Tucson, Arizona. Charles spent his childhood at the home and, although a bright child with good manners, fell out with his foster father and told friends he hated him. At school, Schmid's strange mind was already beginning to develop and he claimed to have psychic powers that helped him to win races and excel at sport. He once told friends: "I'd shut my eyes and everything would seem logical, so I'd do it."

Schmid was suspended from school shortly before he was due to graduate after he admitted stealing some tools. His teachers were willing to give him a second chance to finish his education but Schmid confided in classmates that he simply couldn't be bothered. By the time he was 16, he had set up home on his own with a very generous allowance of $300 a month from his foster parents. Most of this money went on motorcycles, cars, and girls.

Though terribly spoiled and allowed to lead his own life, Schmid was not happy. He was obsessed with his short stature—he was only 5ft 3in tall—and felt the only way to make his mark in the world was to make up stories about himself and try to buy friends for the price of a round of drinks. In a bid to stand out in a crowd, Schmid, who liked to be called Smitty, dyed his hair, created a fake mole on his cheek, wore thick make-up on his face, and put so much lip salve on his lips that they

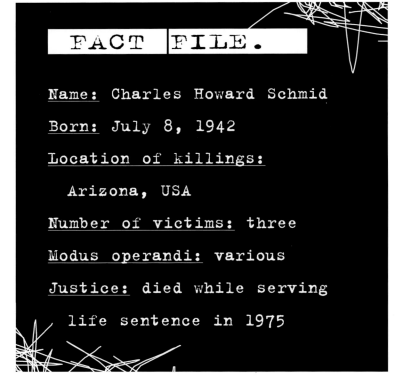

FACT FILE.

Name: Charles Howard Schmid

Born: July 8, 1942

Location of killings:

Arizona, USA

Number of victims: three

Modus operandi: various

Justice: died while serving

life sentence in 1975

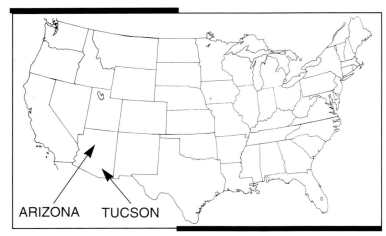

ARIZONA   TUCSON

appeared white. He thought his tough image looked complete by constantly chewing on a toothpick. He told girls he was in a rock band and tried to impress them further by stuffing his boots with newspaper to try to increase his height.

Schmid's wealthy parents thought he might settle down if they bought him a smart house of his own but it was there that Schmid became leader of a pack of drug addicts. He seduced several female hangers-on but the novelty of sex soon wore off and Schmid became bored. The spoiled little rich kid wanted to kill someone just for the hell of it.

On May 31, 1964, Schmid was chatting with his girlfriend, 19-year-old Mary Rae French, and another friend, 17-year-old John Saunders, when he suddenly announced: "I want to kill a girl tonight." His chosen victim was Alleen Rowe, who was just 15 years of age. Alleen had made the mistake of befriending Mary French who, at Schmid's suggestion, had asked her to make up a foursome and go out with John Saunders. When Alleen refused because she was swatting for her exams, the three went round to her house and, after seeing her mother leave, nagged her to get into the car with them. Alleen climbed in still wearing curlers in her hair. The group drove from Tucson out into the desert, where Schmid bound her arms and stripped her naked. As the terrified girl begged for mercy, he told her: "Mary wants us to do this because she hates you." Schmid then raped her and killed her by smashing her head with a rock. As the poor girl lay dead at their feet, Schmid kissed Mary French and told her: "Remember, I love you."

Schmid and Saunders started digging a grave and smiled at each other when Mary offered to give

Schmid was obsessed with his short stature and stuffed newspaper into his boots to increase his height.
- - - - - - - - - - - - - - - -

them a hand. Mary was more than happy to lift Alleen's body by the feet and put her in the hole. The killers buried Alleen's dress and Schmid's blood-soaked shirt with her body. After attempting to clean their car of any evidence that Alleen had been in it, they concocted a story that, although they had called round to take Alleen out, she had not been at home that evening.

It was not until a year later when Schmid got

the urge to kill again, this time on his own. He had spotted 16-year-old Gretchen Fritz at a local swimming pool and was immediately attracted by her blonde hair and lithe figure. He followed her home and was impressed by her large house in an affluent area of town. Gretchen herself was a strange girl. Though her father was an eminent heart and chest specialist, she was the family misfit and was a compulsive liar who secretly admired the life led by prostitutes. Schmid knew none of this, of course, when he called at her door saying he was a traveling salesman. They got talking and, when Schmid confessed that his story was just a ruse to get to meet her, the two shared what was to become literally a fatal attraction.

Gretchen's wild lies matched Schmid's own fabricated stories. She once lied about being pregnant by him and boasted that her brother-in-law was in the Mafia. Schmid confided in Gretchen about killing Alleen Rowe and even allowed her to read a diary full of damning evidence. So when Gretchen became jealous of his other girlfriends and looked as if she might reveal what he had done, Schmid decided she had to go too. It was a tragedy for Gretchen's younger sister, 13-year-old Wendy that the two were together when he struck. Schmid trailed the two girls and hijacked them in Gretchen's car on August 16, 1965, as they drove home from the cinema. He then strangled them.

Schmid could not resist bragging about what he had done to his new best friend, Richard Bruns. Bruns did not believe him so Schmid took him to

> **"He hijacked them as they drove home from the cinema. He then strangled them"**

where the girls' bodies lay in the desert and asked for help in burying them. Afterward he told Bruns: "Now you are in this as deep as I am." Bruns kept what he had seen to himself for nearly three months but then, tortured with guilt, walked into a police station and turned Schmid in.

The killer was arrested on November 11. At the police station, he had played to him the tapes of Bruns telling all he knew. The police then brought the two men together, hoping Schmid would be forced into a confession. He did not crack but, still protesting his innocence, was charged with the two murders. Put in a cell while these formalities took place, Schmid was ordered to remove his boots. The contents of these — a tangled mess of crushed beer cans, cardboard and rags to boost his height — filled two boxes.

Other information supplied by Richard Bruns resulted in officers rounding up Mary French and John Saunders. Getting a confession from Mary was easy, for she was still bitter that Schmid had refused to marry her when she told him she was pregnant. She volunteered a statement about being present at the killing of Alleen Rowe and how she had witnessed Schmid committing the murder. Saunders confessed too. When police were led to the murder site, they stumbled upon the sad sight of two of Alleen's rusting hair curlers. At that time, despite a lengthy search, Alleen's body was not found but police felt they had enough evidence against Schmid to take him to court for the murder of all three girls.

Schmid arrived at the Pima County Courthouse on February 15, 1966, wearing a herringbone jacket and tan trousers. His face was devoid of his trademark thick make-up and he had allowed his hair to go back to its natural color. What he couldn't do was make himself taller without access to his crumpled beer cans and bits of paper. The public could not believe just how short this alleged triple killer was but now they understood why local girls had called him the "Pied Piper of Tucson."

Legal disputes, postponements, and setbacks meant that court hearings against Schmid did not reach a conclusion until June 1967. During this time, the body of Alleen Rowe was discovered and, although in a decomposed state, it provided vital evidence that corroborated the statements given by Mary French and John Saunders. Schmid was eventually sentenced to 55 years in prison for the rape and murder of Alleen Rowe. He was sentenced to death for the murder of Gretchen and Wendy Fritz. Saunders was sentenced to life imprisonment and Mary French received five years.

Schmid still maintained his innocence and this, coupled with an appeal, saved his life, as the death sentence was abolished in the state of Arizona in 1971.

Schmid was determined to break out of the Arizona State Penitentiary and made several attempts, including hiding inside a hollowed-out exercise horse and making a fake suicide attempt. In November 1972, he and another murderer did manage to escape and hid out on a ranch where they held the owners hostage for two days before being recaptured.

John Saunders and Mary French were implicated in Schmid's first murders, helping him to dispose of the bodies.

Back in jail and facing a lifetime as just another pint-sized prisoner, Schmid decided to reinvent himself. He changed his name to Paul David Ashley and started writing music and essays to keep himself busy. He also rediscovered his arrogance —which was ultimately to kill him. He strutted around the prison as if he were superior to the other jailbirds. But one day, having told too many lies and sneered at other prisoners too often, two of them set upon him. Found lying in a pool of blood, doctors counted at least 20 separate stab wounds on his body.

Schmid died on March 30, 1975. The adoptive parents who had given him so much now no longer wanted any memory of their son and requested that he be buried in the prison cemetery.

JOHN SCRIPPS

John Scripps was a petty thief. If he had remained on home ground, his name would have been long forgotten.

But the Londoner got the travel bug and became labeled the "Tourist from Hell" because of his world-roving murder spree.

Scripps, the son of a London barmaid and a truck driver, was a childhood thief and a teenage burglar. At 19, he stole enough money to fund a trip to Canada where he met and fell in love with a 17-year-old Mexican schoolgirl. He later traced her to her home in Mexico, brought her back to Britain and married her. His bride left him when, at 23, he was jailed for three years for a string of 40 burglaries. Scripps never got over the loss. He turned to drugs and in 1988 was jailed for 13 years for heroin trafficking. He absconded in 1994 while on weekend leave from his Hertfordshire prison.

Scripps traveled to Spain, linked up with some old cellmates and obtained enough money to fly to Mexico. There he took out a new British passport in the name of John Martin and used it to travel to Singapore, Bangkok, Hong Kong, Los Angeles, San Francisco, and Miami.

In 1995 he returned to Mexico via Belize and met a 28-year-old Cambridge graduate, Timothy MacDowall, who was on a backpacking holiday. When MacDowall's family reported him missing the following month, it was found that more than £13,000 had been transferred from his British bank to various accounts opened by Scripps in America. Detectives believe Scripps had killed MacDowall and scattered parts of his body around Belize.

On March 8, Scripps arrived in Singapore and checked into the River View Hotel. At the reception desk he met chemical engineer Gerard Lowe and talked him into sharing a room to cut costs. That night he killed Lowe, cut up his body, wrapped the pieces in bin liners, and dumped them in a nearby waterway. They later resurfaced in Singapore harbor.

Scripps flew on to Bangkok and then to the Thai island of Phuket. On the plane he met Canadian Sheila Damude, 48, who was traveling with her 21-year-old son Darin. They and Scripps

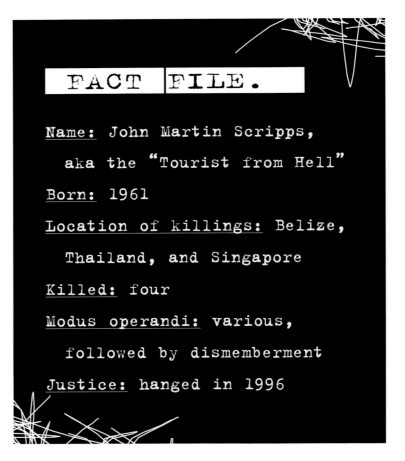

FACT FILE.

Name: John Martin Scripps, aka the "Tourist from Hell"

Born: 1961

Location of killings: Belize, Thailand, and Singapore

Killed: four

Modus operandi: various, followed by dismemberment

Justice: hanged in 1996

booked into adjoining rooms at a Phuket hotel. The Damudes were seen having breakfast there the following morning—the last time they were seen alive. Scripps murdered them later in the day, placed a "Do Not Disturb" sign outside their hotel room, and went off to dump their bodies.

He was finally arrested as he arrived back in Singapore on March 19. Police suspected him of fraud, but a search of his bags uncovered valuables belonging to the Damudes and Gerard Lowe. Also in his backpack were a hammer, two serrated knives, a mace spray, two sets of handcuffs, a set of thumb cuffs, and a 10,000 volt stun-gun. Scripps confessed to killing Lowe but would not comment about the other deaths. He was put on trial for murder and on November 11, 1995, was sentenced to death.

Scripps at first sought clemency from the Singapore government but as the prospect of a prolonged incarceration in Changi Prison dawned on him, he withdrew his plea. He languished in a windowless cell of the notorious jail for six months before being shaken awake one morning by his guards to be told that he was to be hanged in three days. To them, it was routine; 152 people had been executed at the prison in the past 20 years. But it was a milestone in one way: Scripps was to become the first Briton to be hanged for murder in more than 30 years. Still rebellious, Scripps refused to be weighed and fitted for the gallows, so the dynamics of the rope and the drop had to be estimated rather than worked out exactly.

Shortly after 5am on April 19, 1996, Scripps received a tap on the shoulder and was offered breakfast and ordered to dress himself. He refused. Having sworn that he would not go quietly and would "give them something to remember me by,"

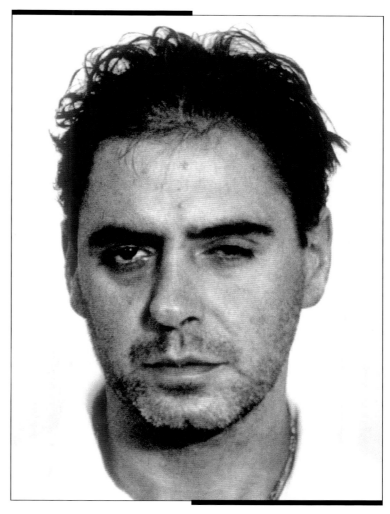

John Martin Scripps earned his nickname the Tourist from Hell through his habit of killing travelers as he toured the world.

he struggled and screamed as he was led toward the execution room. Gallingly for Scripps, his was not even to be a memorable execution for, as he discovered, he was to share his date with death with two local drug traffickers. While a Roman Catholic priest read a prayer, two prison officers bound Scripps's hands and feet. A hood was put over his head. At 6.37am precisely, the petty thief, burglar, heroin dealer, and serial killer heard the last sound of his wasted life: the metallic pull of a lever and the creak of the trap door opening beneath him.

HAROLD SHIPMAN

Even when the judge told Dr. Harold Shipman that he was going to prison for life, his wife Primrose showed no emotion.

But by then, she had developed a strong barrier against the world after discovering that her husband, a once highly-respected doctor, had murdered 150 of his patients and earned himself the reputation of being Britain's biggest serial killer. Even when a jubilant cry of "Yes!" rang out from one of the deceased's relatives after the verdict was announced, neither Primrose nor her husband revealed their feelings.

That day in court, January 31, 2000, ended a chilling chapter in the life of what used to be the very ordinary northern town of Hyde, near Manchester—normal until Shipman arrived there at the end of 1977. The year before, while he was practicing in West Yorkshire, he had pleaded guilty to forging prescriptions and stealing drugs, and asked for 74 other offences to be taken into consideration. Shipman had not been made to face the General Medical Council to be disciplined, but had simply been warned in a letter over future misconduct. He secured another job as a district physician conducting baby clinics in County Durham—a post that ensured he had no access to drugs—and he was supervised throughout because of his past misdemeanors. By the end of 1977, Shipman was considered to have sufficiently rehabilitated himself to be allowed back into general practice. Tragically for patients and doctors alike, he chose to move to Hyde.

Shipman had probably killed many, many people by the time he became chairman of the PTA committee of his children's school in the early 1990s. Prison psychiatrists who examined him after his arrest say the date of March 1, 1974, is significant simply because it was the day that Shipman became a GP and a killer. While his medical colleagues at the Donneybrook surgery, one of three in the Hyde Medical Holdings group, felt that Shipman was over-assertive and arrogant, his patients saw only the seemingly kind side of him, coupled with a confidence that defied challenge. But putting their complete trust in him was their

FACT FILE.

Name: Dr. Harold Frederick Shipman

Born: January 14, 1946

Location of killings: Manchester, England

Killed: at least 215

Modus operandi: lethal injections of morphine

Justice: sentenced to life in 2000; hanged himself in prison in 2004.

downfall, particularly for the female patients who seemed to die at an alarming rate in their own homes—and even right there in the surgery—while Shipman was in attendance.

No one liked to question their doctor as he administered the lethal heroin injections, all the while telling them he was giving them something to ease their breathing or make them feel better. Shipman signed the death certificates as "natural causes" and advised relatives not to seek a post-mortem because "it will only add to your grief." Incredibly, no one seems to have questioned these suspicious deaths.

It is thought that Shipman's first Hyde victim was 76-year-old Mary Winterbottom, retired stewardess of her local Conservative Club, on September 21, 1984. Mrs. Winterbottom went to Shipman suffering from a cold but, on his follow-up home visit, he said he found her "lying dead on her bed." Retired hairdresser Eileen Cox, 72, died at home three months later following a heart attack, according to Shipman. Jewelry was missing after engineer's widow May Brooks, aged 74, died in her chair at home in February 1985 following a routine visit by Shipman. Two weeks later, 89-year-old widow Margaret Conway died at home "from a stroke."

Events continued with an average of one suspicious death a year until Shipman left the Hyde group practice in 1992 and set up on his own. Then the number of deaths escalated. There were eight in 1993, starting with 92-year-old Hilda Couzens who was found dead within hours of a visit by Shipman on February 24. The next day, 86-year-old retired newsagent Olive Heginbotham died of "heart failure." Shipman's final victim that year was 54-year-old Eileen Robinson on December 22.

His medical colleagues described Shipman as arrogant but his patients put every faith in him as he displayed a confidence that defied challenge.
— — — — — — — — — — — —

Shipman claimed at least six victims in 1994, ten in 1995, 16 in 1996, 22 in 1997, and ten in 1998. It was only the intervention of undertaker Deborah Bamroffe in March that year that brought about an end to Doctor Death's deadly bedside manner. Deborah, at just 28 and a relative newcomer to the business, decided "there were just too many deaths for a one-doctor surgery." She voiced her suspicions to one of the doctors who had been countersigning Shipman's deaths for cremation purposes. Within days, coroner John Pollard was briefed and he called in Greater Manchester Police.

During his time at the Hyde group practice there was an average of one suspicious death a year until he left and set up on his own. Then the deaths escalated.

- - - - - - - - - -

However, Shipman still managed to kill three more patients before his arrest in September.

Charged with 15 murders, Shipman told police it was simply coincidence. He even tried to suggest that one of the victims was a heroin addict. But it was another victim, former mayor Kathleen Grundy, who helped bring about a conviction. Mrs. Grundy was a fit and active 81-year-old who worked tirelessly for charity. She was found dead at her home on June 24, 1998, by two friends. Shipman gave the cause of death as old age but Mrs. Grundy's will apparently left her entire

£386,000 estate to him. Her daughter Angela Woodruff, a solicitor and her executor, was immediately suspicious and contacted police.

Forensic tests showed the will had been typed on Shipman's portable typewriter and had his fingerprints on it. Mrs. Grundy's body was exhumed and lethal levels of morphine were found. Shipman said Mrs. Grundy was a drug addict and showed police hand-written case notes to back this up. Shipman made a big mistake when he wrote notes supporting his theory retrospectively—for they were dated on a day he was away on holiday. Shipman was charged with murder and forgery.

Among the other deaths that the police investigated was the case of 76-year-old Muriel Grimshaw who died fully-dressed, lying on her bed in her ground floor flat on July 12, 1997. Shipman had made no examination of the woman's body but said "it was a nice way to go" and had insisted there was no need for a post-mortem. Later he said she had died from a stroke and hypertension and police discovered Shipman's computer records had been falsified to back this up. Yet another victim, 57-year-old Maureen Ward, was allegedly discovered dead at her sheltered-housing flat by Shipman on February 18, 1998. The woman had successfully beaten breast cancer in 1992 but Shipman told the warden of the sheltered-housing complex that Mrs. Ward had a brain tumor. He backdated records to create a false history for his cancer diagnosis. He also altered computer records relating to Bianka Pomfret who died on December 10, 1997. Shipman gave the cause of death as a heart attack and created a bogus history of angina on her records.

Shipman's first day at Preston Crown Court was October 12, 1999, when he denied 15 charges of murder and one of forging Mrs. Grundy's will. But the prosecutor in the case, Richard Henriques, QC, said: "There is no question of euthanasia or what is sometimes called mercy killing. None of the deceased were terminally ill. The defendant killed those 15 patients because he enjoyed doing so. He was exercising the ultimate power of controlling life and death and repeated it so often that he must have found the drama of taking life to his taste." Mr. Henriques said that tests carried out on the thigh muscle of each of the deceased established a

significant presence of morphine within the bodies. He added: "All of them died most unexpectedly and all of them had seen Dr. Shipman on the day of their death."

❝ There is no question of euthanasia or what is sometimes called mercy killing. None of the deceased were terminally ill❞

Shipman was found guilty on all 15 counts of murder and one of forgery. The jury had deliberated for six days before reaching unanimous verdicts. During the preceding four months of the trial, they had heard various clues as to the character of Harold Shipman, the soft-spoken monster in the dock before them. They had been told that Shipman, one of eight children, could have been permanently traumatized and resentful of the death of his mother when she was only 43. It had been largely with her encouragement that he won a place at grammar school. When his mother died, Shipman's older sister Pauline took over running the household. She even became his date at the twice-yearly rugby dances at school because Shipman felt inadequate in the company of girls.

Fears of inadequacy also followed him to medical school but he eventually met the woman he would marry, Primrose Mary Oxtoby, the daughter of a farm worker. The couple struck up a conversation on a local bus when Shipman was 20 and Primrose was 17. She worked as a trainee window dresser for a Leeds department store. When Primrose discovered she was pregnant, the couple married on November 5, 1966. Present in court alongside their mother, and listening to their father's private fears and family secrets, were the

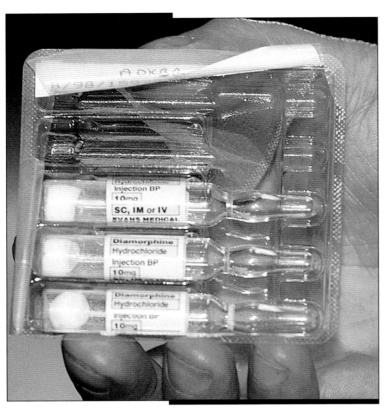

Shipman administered lethal heroin injections to his patients, while telling them he was giving them something to ease their breathing or make them feel better.

- - - - - - - - - - - - - - -

Shipmans' children: Sarah, 32, Christopher, 28, David, 20, and 17-year-old Samuel.

After the verdicts, they also heard their father addressed thus by the judge, Mr. Justice Forbes: "These were wicked, wicked, crimes. Each of your victims was your patient. You murdered each and every one of your victims by a calculating and cold-blooded perversion of your medical skills. For your own evil and wicked purpose, you took advantage and grossly abused the trust each of your victims put in you. I have little doubt each of your victims smiled and thanked you as she submitted to your deadly administrations. None of your victims realized that yours was not a healing touch."

It was not surprising that questions were asked about an extraordinary series of blunders that allowed Shipman to kill and kill again. It emerged that detectives had investigated him six months before he was finally caught, following concerns about the number of elderly women dying unexpectedly in their homes. The death rate among female patients over 65 was three times the national average but a police inquiry failed to spot anything sinister. There was not even a check that would have revealed Shipman's previous record for his dishonestly and drug addiction. While at Hyde, Shipman obtained huge amounts of heroin-based drugs by writing out prescriptions in the name of patients and telling the Co-op pharmacy next to his surgery that he would deliver them. At one stage, Shipman prescribed and obtained 12,000mg of diamorphine, enough heroin to kill around 360 people. After the death of one victim, Ivy Thomas, in Shipman's surgery in 1997, a policeman became suspicious about why there had been no effort to resuscitate her—but he did not mention his fears until an investigation into the death of Kathleen Grundy a year later.

Undertaker Deborah Bambroffe was brave enough to be the whistle-blower. She said: "My misgivings about Dr. Shipman started as a joke at first. But over a length of time, I began to feel uneasy. The scenario was always the same when you went to the houses. Usually if someone is poorly, they go to bed and you would expect them to be in their nightclothes but I can't remember one being tucked up in bed. From my experience something wasn't right at all. Dr. Shipman had either seen them that morning at the surgery or at their own home. He had always seen them within 24 hours of their dying which was strange. None of his deaths were reported to the coroner. He was always able to issue a certificate, even when families told me their mother had not been poorly."

Shipman was sent to top-security prisons in Durham, then Wakefield, Yorkshire, and was told

---

❝❝He had always seen them within 24 hours of their dying which was strange❞❞

---

he would never be released. Psychiatrists who examined him reported their belief that: "He could only get what he wanted by killing elderly women. He did it to make himself feel better. But his focus was on the act of killing and it was important to him to be in control of the process. In some ways you can view him as a necrophile because he needed bodies. But he had no interest in them after death. It was the killing—the point of death—that interested him. Dr. Shipman is a fairly extreme example of a control freak. In his mind, the killings would have been outside the normal moral framework, so he would not feel any remorse."

In January 2002, two years after his court hearing, Shipman was confirmed as Britain's biggest-ever serial killer with a horrifying official toll of 215 victims after High Court judge Dame Janet Smith compiled an official report on him. The 2,000 word, six-volume report entitled "Death Disguised" was the result of an enquiry into 887 deaths of patients in Shipman's care. Of the 215 known victims, 171 were women and 44 were men. Nearly all were elderly and living alone. Said Dame

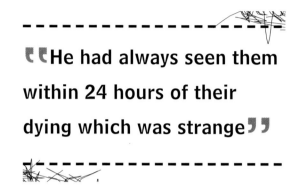

Mrs. Kathleen Grundy was found dead on June 24, 1998, after apparently leaving her entire estate to Shipman. Her daughter was immediately suspicious and contacted the police.

Janet: "Deeply shocking though it is, the bare statement that Shipman has killed over 200 patients does not fully reflect the enormity of his crimes. As a general practitioner, he was trusted implicitly by his patients and their families. He betrayed that trust in a way and to an extent that I believe is unparalleled in history. The way in which Shipman could kill, face relatives and walk away unsuspected would have been dismissed as fanciful if it had been described in a work of fiction. He disguised his character and the true

Dr. Harold Shipman killed at least 215 of his elderly female patients before he was finally arrested and convicted of murder.

- - - - - - - - - - - - - - -

nature of his victims so as to deceive, not only his victims and their families, but also his professional colleagues and those responsible for death registration and cremation certificate procedures."

Today, Primrose Shipman is trying to carry on life with her children away from the glare of publicity. But that is not easy when your husband had taken an oath to cure people but killed them instead. Primrose has only spoken once about her husband—and that was to maintain his innocence at the inquiry into the deaths. She has since refused all approaches to talk about him and, despite the fact his heinous crimes have meant that she has had to move at least four times, she stood steadfastly by him until the day he died.

Those touched by Shipman however, could not disguise their hatred. Said Dominic Henson, whose son and daughter-in-law were patients of the murdering doctor: "Maybe they should give him one of his own injections."

They didn't have to. On January 13, 2004, he took his own life in Wakefield Prison. The official announcement read: "Mr. Shipman was found hanging in his cell at 6.20am and, despite the best efforts of staff who immediately attempted resuscitation, he was pronounced dead by a doctor at 8.10am. Since arriving at Wakefield on June 18, 2003, Shipman had never been on a suicide watch." Families of many of his victims would have found it ironic that such efforts had been made to revive a doctor who had failed to keep alive at last 215 patients entrusted to his care.

GEORGE SMITH

George Smith, who went under various names during his career of murder and fraud, got rid of three bigamously wed "wives" by drowning them in the bath.

Each of these deaths was seemingly unsuspicious and in each case led to newspaper reports engendering sympathy for the bereaved and mourning widower. Unfortunately for Smith, however, the press reports jogged too many memories. The coincidence that three brides should have died in identical circumstances was noted by relatives of the deceased. And when the father of one of the victims sent a collection of the relevant newspaper clippings to Scotland Yard, the so-called "Brides in the Bath Killer" was exposed.

George Smith was born in 1872 in Bethnal Green, in Victorian London's notorious East End. The son of an insurance agent, his parents soon despaired of the boy, his mother correctly forecasting that he "would die with his boots on." An incorrigible thief, at only nine years of age he was sent to a harsh and brutalizing reformatory, which provided him with an education in crime from his fellow prisoners. Apart from three years in the army, he was in and out of prison for the rest of his life.

At the turn of the century, Smith was living under the alias "Oliver Love" and was married to Caroline Thornhill, a bootmaker's daughter who became a domestic servant to the wealthy, with impeccable references—written of course by Smith. Caroline was now in an ideal position to steal from her employers and their friends and the couple carried out a series of robberies in London and along the South Coast. In late 1899, however,

Caroline was caught trying to pawn some silver spoons from one of their thefts and she was sentenced to three months' jail. Smith abandoned his wife and when, upon her release, she spotted him by chance walking through a London street, she tipped off the police. In January 1901 he was jailed for handling stolen goods and when he was freed the following year was equally intent on revenge. He hatched a plan to waylay Caroline and kill her but she got wind of it and her family beat him up.

FACT FILE.

Name: George Joseph Smith, aka "John Lloyd," "George Oliver Love," "Henry Williams," and the "Brides In The Bath Murderer"
Born: January 11, 1872
Location of killings: London and Kent, England
Killed: three
Modus operandi: drowning
Justice: hanged in 1915

Caroline meanwhile emigrated to the safety of Canada.

While still married to Mrs. Caroline Love, George Smith had already decided to become a serial seducer, bigamist, and, if necessary, a murderer. In 1899 he had married a middle-aged boarding-house keeper whom he robbed of all her savings. He then roamed the country under various assumed names wooing lonely ladies, increasing their self esteem but reducing their bank balances. Smith hardly looked the classic Romeo but he certainly had a winning way with women. According to one of his female victims, he had a dark and mesmerizing stare that she described as "little eyes that seemed to rob you of your will."

One such weakened woman was Florence Wilson, a widow whose hand he requested in marriage the day after meeting her in the genteel seaside resort of Worthing in June 1908. She accepted and they traveled to London where Smith persuaded Mrs. Wilson to draw her entire savings of £30 from the post office and give it to him for safe keeping.

On July 3, she and her bigamous husband visited an exhibition where Smith asked her to wait for him while he nipped outside to buy a newspaper. She was still waiting anxiously as Smith

> **"He roamed the country under various assumed names wooing lonely ladies, increasing their self esteem but reducing their bank balances"**

dashed back to their honeymoon lodgings to pawn all her possessions. She never saw him again.

Smith fled to Bristol where, using his real name, he opened a second-hand furniture shop and advertised for a housekeeper. Plump 28-year-old Edith Pegler answered the invitation and became the next Mrs. Smith when they married on July 30. Edith remained loyal to him and, although he left her from time to time to seduce other likely victims, he seems to have treated her well, entrusting her with his crooked earnings.

The following year found him in Southampton where, as "George Rose," he met and wed Sarah Freeman and they set up home in London in October 1909. His plans for her were the same as for poor Florence Wilson but even more lucrative. After relieving Sarah of £300, he deserted her in one of the corridors of the National Gallery.

Returning to Bristol, Smith met Bessie Mundy and soon discovered that she had a bank balance of £2,500, a substantial sum in 1910. Using the name Henry Williams, he married her and attempted to remove the money from her bank account. This time he drew a blank. Bessie's money was a bequest from her late father and was safely tucked away in a trust fund. Unable to get at it, Smith left her after just a few weeks of marriage and returned to Edith Pegler. Bessie must have been an extremely forgiving woman because in March 1912 she bumped into him again and, after hearing his pleas

George Smith became known as the Brides in the Bath Murderer, as he killed three of his wives after his first wife left him.

Alice Burnham's life was insured by Smith before he drowned her in the bath.

for her forgiveness, took him back. They moved to Herne Bay, in Kent, where they rented a house and lived off the interest of her trust fund.

But Smith had a longer-term plan. He knew that the trust was untouchable while Bessie was alive but that if she should die leaving her worldly wealth to him, he could get his hands on the entire sum. Six days after arriving in Kent, Bessie made a new will. A day later Smith bought a £2 zinc bath. The next day, complaining that Bessie had suffered a fit, he visited a doctor who prescribed a mild sedative. Three days later, at 8am

on July 13th, the doctor was summoned by a note reading: "Can you come at once—I'm afraid my wife is dead." This time he found Bessie naked in the bath with her head below the water. He tried to revive her but in vain.

An inquest jury returned a verdict of death by misadventure and Bessie was buried on July 16. Within 48 hours, Smith had sold the contents of their house and had returned the bath to the store for a refund. Despite Bessie's relatives contesting the will, Smith received the £2,500 and returned to Edith in Bristol. He opened bank accounts in different names and bought several houses as investments.

It had all been so easy. Too easy, in fact, and by late 1913 he was on the lookout for a source of further cash, which he found in the rotund form of 25-year-old Alice Burnham. Once again he swept the unfortunate woman off her feet, and on November 4 married her under his real name, having first insured her life for £500. Smith then took his latest bigamous bride on holiday to Blackpool, where he called a doctor to provide medicine for her supposedly painful headaches.

On December 12, Smith asked their landlady to run a bath for his wife and, before retiring for the night, he made a point of appearing in the kitchen where the landlady's family were having their evening meal. As they chatted with their lodger, water began dripping from the ceiling. Smith rushed upstairs and returned shouting: "Fetch the doctor! My wife cannot speak to me." Alice's head was beneath the water and all attempts to revive her failed. Smith wept at the inquest, which again returned an accidental verdict, although he occupied the three days before her burial by playing the piano and drinking whisky. "When they are dead, they're done with," he told the landlady cheerfully.

Smith rejoined the loyal Edith Pegler while he sorted out the sale of Alice Burnham's belongings. In September 1914, he told Edith that he was going to London on business but the real reason was to

❝Alice's head was beneath the water and all attempts to revive her failed❞

pursue an affair with a domestic servant named Alice Reavil. Using the name "Charles Oliver James," he married her but within two weeks he had deserted the poor girl, abandoning her in public gardens after stealing her £78 savings.

Smith already had a third murder victim in mind: clergyman's daughter Margaret Lofty, 38, whom he had met the previous year, introducing himself as "John Lloyd." Knowing that her life was insured for £700, he married her on December 17 and rented lodgings in London where the same game was played out: a visit to a doctor to complain of headaches and a visit to a lawyer to write a fresh will. On the evening of December 18, 1914, the landlady heard splashing sounds coming from the bathroom. Shortly afterward, Smith was heard playing *Nearer My God to Thee* on a melodeon in the front parlor. Minutes later, he asked the landlady to accompany him upstairs where they found Margaret Lofty dead in the bath. She was buried

Smith persuaded Bessie Mundy to rewrite her will in his favor before he murdered her in the bath.

three days later and Smith returned to Bristol and Edith in time for Christmas.

The ease with which this latest murder was carried out was the undoing of George Smith. The modus operandi had been identical to the two earlier drownings but on this occasion, the killer's impatience had been his undoing. When she died, Margaret had been a bride for just a day and this made front-page news. The headlines read "Bride found dead in bath" and "Bride's tragic fate on day after wedding." The stories were seen by Alice Burnham's father and by the owners of the

Smith was tried at the Old Bailey and hanged at Maidstone Prison on August 13, 1915.

Blackpool boarding house where she died. Both reported their suspicions to the police, who lay in wait for "Mr. John Lloyd" when he turned up at a lawyer's office to collect Margaret Lofty's insurance payout.

The bodies of of Bessie Mundy, Alice Burnham, and Margaret Lofty were exhumed and Smith was accused of their murders (although when he came to trial at the Old Bailey, he had to answer to only one of the murders, that of Bessie, his first drowned bride). The trial was notable for three things: the amount of newspaper space given over to three murders against the backdrop of mass slaughter in World War I; the fascinating evidence of the accused's sheer ingenious evil; and the fact that the trial at times sank to a level of near farce. Smith interrupted constantly, hurling insults at witnesses, at his own defending counsel, and at the judge. At one point he screamed at Mr. Justice Scrutton: "It's a disgrace to a Christian country, this is. I'm not a murderer... though I might be a bit peculiar!"

It looked for a while as if Smith could be acquitted for lack of evidence that he had actually forced Bessie Mundy's head beneath the water, as there was no bruising on her body. Then Sir Bernard Spilsbury, a famous pathologist of the day, and Detective Inspector Arthur Neil, in charge of the murder investigation, placed a bath in an anteroom next to the court, filled it with water, and used a volunteer nurse as the victim. Spilsbury lifted the nurse's feet with his left hand while pushing her head underwater with his right. The unfortunate woman immediately passed out and it took half an hour to revive her. But the policeman and the pathologist had at least proved their point.

The jury took 20 minutes to bring in a guilty verdict. Smith was stunned into silence at last. He was taken to a condemned cell at Maidstone Prison, Kent, protesting his innocence to the end. He regularly wept in terror of his pending execution, which took place on August 13, 1915. His legs buckled as he was led to the gallows and his last words from beneath the hood over his head were: "I am in terror." The only mourner was Edith Pegler, to whom he had written the following letter from jail: "May an old age, serene and bright and as lovely as a Lapland night lead thee to thy grave. Now, my true love, goodbye until we meet again."

RICHARD SPECK

After he died, a graphic video of Richard Speck in jail became public property. It showed him with womanly breasts from hormone treatment and having sexual relations with a fellow male prisoner.

Those who had known Speck were not surprised at his strange sexual leanings. But what could explain the demons that drove him to go out one night and savagely slaughter eight innocent nurses?

❝❝He was jailed for assaulting a woman while holding a knife to her throat❞❞

Speck was born in Kirkwood, Illinois, on December 6, 1941. His family moved to Dallas when he was eight years old. Signaling how he would one day go down in the annals of criminal history, Speck had the words "Born to Raise Hell" tattooed on his arm when he was 19. A year later, while working as a garbage collector, he married Shirley Malone who was just 15 years old and the couple had a child together.

Marriage to such a young bride was destined to fail, especially when Speck lurched from one arrest to another. His crimes ranged from drunkenness to burglary and by the time he and Shirley went their separate ways in 1966, Speck had been arrested 37 times. The couple finally split after he was jailed for assaulting a woman while holding a knife to her throat.

With his wife gone, no job, an unsavory criminal record, and a pock-marked face that did not help him find long-term female companions, Speck became a drifter and a drug addict. Semi-literate, he spent his spare time reading comics or hanging out in sleazy bars. He found occasional work on cargo barges and it was his thwarted plans to

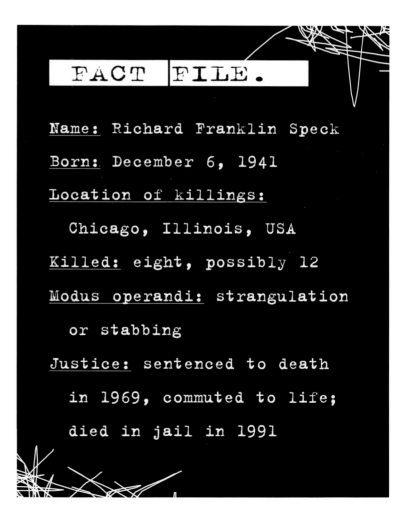

FACT FILE.

<u>Name:</u> Richard Franklin Speck

<u>Born:</u> December 6, 1941

<u>Location of killings:</u>
   Chicago, Illinois, USA

<u>Killed:</u> eight, possibly 12

<u>Modus operandi:</u> strangulation
   or stabbing

<u>Justice:</u> sentenced to death
   in 1969, commuted to life;
   died in jail in 1991

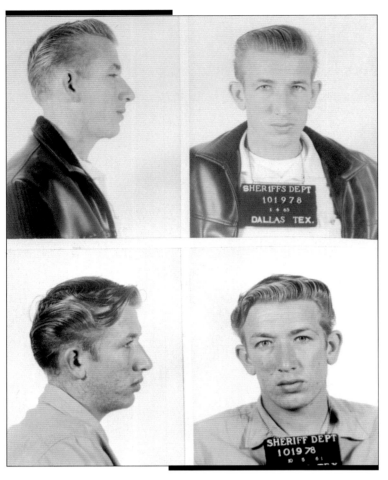

Speck had a history of robbery and burglary. Married at the age of 20, he had begun to suffer bouts of uncontrollable violence after discovering his wife was having affairs.

Orleans." Scouring the hostel, Speck found five more student nurses asleep in their beds and forced them into one room. All six girls were bound together, unable to warn three other nurses

> **" He took the two girls into another bedroom and stabbed Mary in the heart, neck, and eye before attacking Suzanne 18 times with his knife"**

returning home from seeing their boyfriends of the danger they faced. Staring down at the nine help-less and terrified girls, Speck was unsure exactly what he wanted to do next. He grabbed money and jewelry and then thought about leaving. But the mixture of drink and drugs pushed the idea of murder to the front of his mind.

The first victim was Pamela Wilkening, 20, whom he led into another room, stabbed and strangled with a strip of sheet. Apparently sexual-ly excited by this killing, he decided to continue. His next victims were 20-year-old Mary Jordan and 21-year-old Suzanne Farris.

He took the two girls into another bedroom and stabbed Mary in the heart, neck, and eye before attacking Suzanne 18 times with his knife. As her life ebbed away, Suzanne was raped by Speck. Nina Schmale, 24, died by having her throat slashed and then being strangled. Valentine

board one of these bound for New Orleans that was to finally tip him over the edge. Frustrated that there were no berths available, Speck went on a massive drinking spree, which ended with him injecting himself with an array of drugs.

Speck then became a mass murderer. On 14 July 1966, a 23-year-old nurse, Corazon Amurao, opened the door of Jeffrey Manor, a Chicago nurs-es' home on 2319 East 100th Street. There stood Speck brandishing a gun. He forced his way in, telling Corazon and two friends who had now joined her: "I'm not going to hurt you. I'm only going to tie you up. I need your money to go to New

Pasion, 23, and Nerlita Gargullo died next, both stabbed and strangled.

After calmly going to the bathroom to wash his hands, Speck returned to kill Patricia Matusek, 23, a former swimming champion. Like Valentine and Nerlita, her efforts to hide from Speck under a bed had been useless. She now begged for mercy but Speck kicked her in the stomach and then strangled her. His mind still befuddled with the drugs and alcohol, Speck felt he had time enough to rape Gloria Davy, his last victim. Left shaking and naked, Gloria's ordeal was not over yet. Speck assaulted her a second time, this time anally, before strangling her.

Speck left but, in his crazy state, had failed to check he had killed all his hostages. The girl who had first opened the door to him, Corazon Amurao, had managed to squeeze herself tightly under a bed in the darkness and listened as Speck murdered her nursing friends. Corazon was so petrified that it was several hours before she could muster up courage to drag herself out, move toward the window ledge and cry for help. When the police arrived, they were greeted by total carnage. Eight young nurses lay dead, all mutilated.

What Corazon Amurao had seen and heard led to Speck's swift arrest. She had seen the "Born to Raise Hell" tattoo on his arm. She was able to give a good description of the lanky, pockmarked killer. With this information, and the knowledge that the knots binding the nurses' wrists had almost certainly been tied by a seaman, detectives questioned officials of the Seamen's Union. They identified Speck as the man who had been trying to secure a berth on the New Orleans-bound cargo ship—and who had included a photograph of himself on his application form. Fingerprints on this

Speck was found guilty and sentenced to death. His sentence was later commuted to life imprisonment.

matched the 30 or so Speck had left at the murder scene.

Tracking Speck down was made even easier when he attempted suicide two days after the mass murders. After slashing his right wrist and left arm, he stumbled out of his cheap room at the Starr Hotel on West Madison Street and screamed for help. He was eventually taken to Cook County

Hospital where he inadvertently gave his right name.

Detectives now checked out Speck's criminal record, which included doctor's reports about his violent outbursts. In an interview with one of them, he admitted he had wanted to kill his young wife for being unfaithful to him. The police surmised that one of these storms of anger had been the trigger for his massacre of the nurses. Survivor Corazon Amurao recalled how fascinated Speck seemed to be with Gloria Davy—who bore a strong resemblance to the killer's wife.

It took a jury just 45 minutes to find Speck guilty on eight counts of murder and he was sentenced to die in the electric chair on June 6, 1969. He was saved by the Supreme Court, who waived the death penalty and sentenced him to between 400 and 1,200 years in the Stateville Penitentiary—the longest jail term that had ever been given at that time. Speck came up for parole twice, in 1977 and 1981, but on both occasions said he did not want be released, preferring to remain in prison, where he had developed a passion for oil painting.

Although he had denied the murders at his trial, Speck made a full confession to a newspaper reporter who visited him in jail. He said: "Yeah, I killed them. I stabbed them and choked them." But he refused to cooperate with police over their suspicions that he was responsible for the murders of other women in a three-month period leading up to the nurses' slaughter.

Barmaid Mary Pierce is believed to have died after rejecting Speck's advances. Her naked body was found on April 10, 1966, in a shed behind the bar where she worked. On July 2, three girls dis-

Several years after Speck died, a pornographic video of him in prison was found having sex with other inmates and bragging about his murders.

- - - - - - - - - - - - - - - -

appeared from the Dunes Park area, where Speck had been sighted. They were never seen again and no bodies were ever found.

For some reason, Speck changed his mind about snubbing the Parole Board and in August 1987 asked the Illinois Prison Review Board to consider his early release. He died of a heart attack in 1991 and when no one came to claim his body, he was cremated at the prison. It was five years later that the pornographic video of Speck emerged. In it, he bragged about the murders he had committed.

LUCIAN STANIAK

Rather than looking forward to public holidays, the people of Poland came to fear them in the mid-1960s.

A serial killer was on the loose, traveling the country in an orgy of sado-sexual carnage. Nicknamed the "Red Spider," he murdered some 20 Polish girls between 1964 and 1967, raping them before mutilating and often disemboweling them.

Police were sent a series of taunting letters, written in spidery red script, advising them where the latest body was to be found. Notes were also received by newspapers.

His first victim, a 17-year-old girl, was raped and murdered at Olsztyn on the anniversary of Poland's liberation from Nazi occupation. The Spider followed up his attack with a sinister threat to police: "I picked a juicy flower in Olsztyn and I shall do it again elsewhere, for there is no holiday without a funeral."

The slayings appeared to be random and police found no link between them until, in December 1966, the dreadfully mutilated body of a 17-year-old was found on a train in Kracow. It could be no coincidence that her 14-year-old sister had also been murdered, in Warsaw two years earlier. Both girls had been members of a painting club in Kracow and police analysis of the red ink used by the Spider showed it to be artists' paint. Among the 100 or so members of the club was 26-year-old Lucian Staniak, a translator from Katowice, whose job with a Krakow publishing firm took him to all parts of the country.

When police viewed some of his artistic endeavors, they felt sure they had found the Spider. His works were painted predominantly in blood-red, one of them depicting a disemboweled woman. One final victim, a young student, was found dead at Lodz railway station only hours before they arrested Staniak on February 1, 1967. He confessed all and said he had begun his killing spree after a court freed a woman driver who had killed his sister and parents. His first victim was chosen for her likeness to the woman. Staniak admitted 20 murders and was tried for six of them. He was sentenced to death but later judged to be insane and incarcerated for life in an asylum.

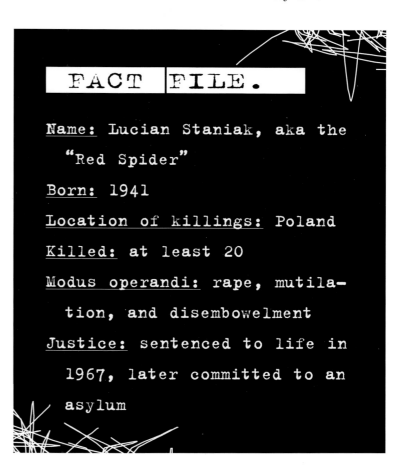

FACT FILE.

Name: Lucian Staniak, aka the "Red Spider"

Born: 1941

Location of killings: Poland

Killed: at least 20

Modus operandi: rape, mutilation, and disembowelment

Justice: sentenced to life in 1967, later committed to an asylum

JOHN STRAFFEN

Child killer John Straffen had the mind of an eight-year-old but the rage and sexual urges of an adult.

The courts simply did not know what to do with him. Born at Borden, in Hampshire, in 1930, his soldier father was posted to India before returning to England to settle in the spa town of Bath, where young John first went to school. His disturbed mental state surfaced early and he became a habitual truant and thief. At ten he was officially classified as mentally defective and sent to a school for retarded children but was allowed to leave when he reached 16. Within the year, he terrified a 13-year-old girl by placing his hand over her mouth and saying: "What would you do if I killed you? I have done it before." She escaped but a month later he had a row with another girl and he wrung the necks of her family's chickens. Now aged 17, he was again committed to a mental institution—from which his release at the age of 21 resulted in the deaths of his first two victims.

In 1951, within six months of his gaining his freedom, he strangled two small girls in the town of Bath where he lived. On Sunday, July 15, Straffen came across six-year-old Brenda Goddard playing on open land near her home. "She was picking flowers," Straffen said later, "and I told her there was plenty higher up." They walked together to a wood where he put his hands around her neck and strangled her.

A few days later, Straffen was at a movie theater in town when he struck up a conversation with nine-year-old Cicely Batstone and persuaded her to go with him to a second cinema to see another film, *She Wore A Yellow Ribbon*. After watching it together, Straffen took Cicely to a field and strangled her too.

Several witnesses saw Straffen with Cicely and when arrested he immediately asked: "Is it about the little girl I was at the pictures with last night?" He later added: "She was dead under the hedge when I left her." While in custody awaiting further interrogation, he asked an officer: "Can I speak to you? I want to show you how I did in the first girl." He then went on to blurt out the details of the death of Brenda Goddard, saying: "It only took a

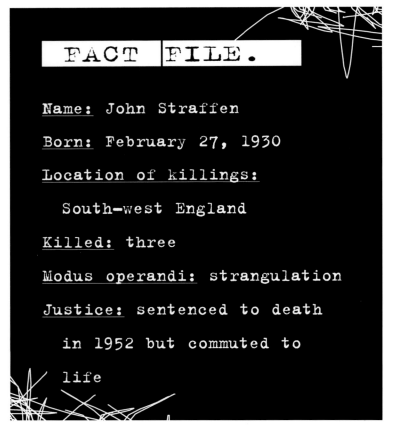

FACT FILE.

Name: John Straffen

Born: February 27, 1930

Location of killings:

South-west England

Killed: three

Modus operandi: strangulation

Justice: sentenced to death

in 1952 but commuted to

life

couple of minutes and she was dead. She never screamed at me when I squeezed her neck, so I bashed her head against the wall. I didn't feel sorry and forgot about it."

According to psychiatric records, he went on to reveal that he committed the murders simply to annoy the police and give them "something really to do" instead of arresting him for trivial offences. At his trial, the judge, Mr. Justice Oliver, addressed the growing legal debate over how to deal with the criminally insane when he told the jury: "In this country we do not try people who are insane. You might as well try a baby in arms." Straffen was found unfit to plead and no trial was held. He was committed to Broadmoor, the top-security asylum for the criminally insane, to be "detained at His Majesty's pleasure."

But less than six months later, on April 29, 1952, Straffen escaped back into the English countryside, as a result of extraordinarily lax security when he was allowed to sweep a yard beside an unlocked gate. He was at large for four hours before being recaptured. The following morning the body of five-year-old Linda Bowyer was found and Straffen was charged with her murder.

Three doctors asserted that the former mental patient was now fit to plead, partly on the basis that he understood four of the ten commandments, and his trial opened at Winchester Crown Court, where he pleaded not guilty.

The judge, Mr. Justice Cassels, halted the trial, however, when a juror was overheard to say that he thought Straffen innocent of the crime and that it had actually been committed by one of the witnesses. A fresh jury had to be sworn in and the proceedings began afresh, at the end of which Straffen was found guilty and sentenced to death.

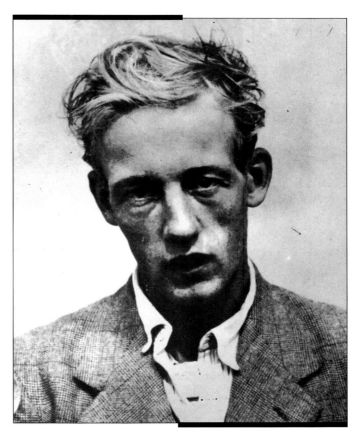

In 1952 John Straffen's death sentence was commuted to life imprisonment.

The execution was scheduled for September 9, but as public concern grew over the hanging of an obviously deranged man, the Home Secretary, Sir David Maxwell-Fyfe, ordered a reprieve, without giving any reason.

The Straffen case created a furore in Britain over the timeless dilemma of how to treat, incarcerate, and safeguard the public from dangerous mental patients. It continued to cause legal arguments over the next half century as the killer remained in jail, rather than a mental institution. By 2001, 71-year-old Straffen had notched up an infamous record as the longest-serving prisoner in Britain, having been in continuous custody since April 23, 1952.

PETER SUTCLIFFE

The half-naked body of 28-year-old prostitute Wilma McCann was found on a playing field in Leeds, Yorkshire, on the morning of October 30, 1975.

She had been stabbed to death and, judging by the extent of her numerous injuries, the killer had clearly carried out his grisly task with some relish. It could have been just another routine murder: a fatal attack upon a prostitute by one of her sick "tricks."

Nevertheless, Leeds CID put out a memo to all divisions asking for help in trapping McCann's killer, part of which read: "The motive appears to be a hatred of prostitutes." Nobody realized it, but the hunt for the Yorkshire Ripper had begun. For the stabbing of Wilma McCann was to be the start of a series of murders by a maniac with the avowed mission of sweeping prostitutes from the streets. In doing so, he had women throughout the North of England living in terror for five years. It was also a case infamous for a string of police blunders that allowed the murderer to retain his freedom to kill and kill again.

It was almost three months before the Yorkshire Ripper struck again, on January 20, 1976. This time the target was 42-year-old prostitute Emily Jackson, found dead with horrific injuries in the Chapeltown red-light area of Leeds. The post-mortem examination found more than 50 stab wounds inflicted with a heavy-duty Phillips screwdriver, which left a distinctive star shaped penetration mark. There was also the imprint of size-seven Dunlop boot on her thigh, as though the murderer had stamped on her. But the injuries that killed Emily Jackson, and presented the police with crucial clues, were the two crushing hammer blows delivered to her head.

On May 9, a prostitute who picked up a client in Roundhay, Leeds, was attacked with a hammer. Through the fog and pain of semi-consciousness, she was later able to tell police how he masturbated nearby and then slipped a £5 note into her hand, warning her not to tell anyone what had happened. She also gave what would later be recognized as an excellent description of the Ripper. But because she had been diagnosed as

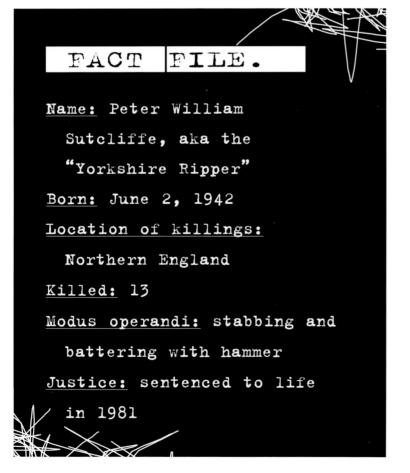

```
FACT FILE.

Name: Peter William
   Sutcliffe, aka the
   "Yorkshire Ripper"
Born: June 2, 1942
Location of killings:
   Northern England
Killed: 13
Modus operandi: stabbing and
   battering with hammer
Justice: sentenced to life
   in 1981
```

Peter Sutcliffe, who went on to become the notorious Yorkshire Ripper, is seen here on his wedding day.

Newly married Peter Sutcliffe and his wife Sonia.

- - - - - - - - - - - - - - - -

educationally sub-normal, little heed was paid to her vital evidence.

By now the police incident room was working flat out to process the hundreds of snippets of information flowing in. But as the weeks and months passed with no further attacks, detectives became puzzled. All the psychological advice they had received was that the murderer would not be able to resist the compulsion to strike again. Why was he laying low? Had he perhaps been killed or even taken his own life? This speculation ended at

7.50am on Sunday, February 6, 1977, when a jogger discovered 28-year-old Irene Richardson's body on open ground at Roundhay, Leeds. It bore the typical, sickening hallmarks of a Ripper killing: body face down, death caused by hammer blows to the skull, and stab wounds to the stomach. Bizarrely, her boots had been arranged carefully between her open thighs.

The Ripper was back and he wanted the police to know it. Within the next year, five more women would be dispatched in similarly horrific circumstances. There was Patricia Atkinson, found dead on April 23. Next was a 32-year-old Bradford prostitute who would be the only one of the 13 victims killed indoors. Her bedsheets bore the distinctive size-seven boot mark and she died from four heavy blows to the head. There were six chisel marks found on her abdomen. On June 26, the Ripper murdered his youngest victim, 16-year-old Jayne MacDonald. She was on a night out with friends but was found dead the following morning in a playground near Chapeltown. Heavy blows to the head had probably killed her but the murderer had again inflicted numerous stab wounds.

The next victim miraculously survived. The attack came on July 10 in Bradford where a 42-year-old woman was slashed from her breasts to her navel and bore four chest stab wounds. She pulled through after an emergency operation and her description of her attacker turned out to be inaccurate—hardly surprising under the circumstances.

Undercover police were by now so widespread in the Leeds and Bradford red-light districts that the Ripper struck west, in the heart of Manchester. There, on the night of October 1, he murdered 21-year-old prostitute Jean Jordan with 11 blows to the head and 28 separate stab wounds. Her body lay for more that a week in a cemetery at Moss Side but when it was at last discovered, charred from burning, it yielded a vital clue.

> **❝Her bedsheets bore the distinctive size-seven boot mark and she died from four heavy blows to the head. There were six chisel marks found on her abdomen❞**

Her murderer had foolishly paid her with a new £5 note, serial number AW 51 121565. It was one of a batch delivered to a particular bank and distributed through various employers to less than 6,000 people. One of those was a lorry driver called Peter William Sutcliffe, aged 31, the man who would one day be unmasked to the world as the Yorkshire Ripper.

Sutcliffe was among those interviewed and police dug a little into his past. After leaving school at 15, he had gone through jobs such as laboring and grave-digging with no real ambition to improve himself. But his seven-year courtship with Czech-born Sonia Szurma seemed to have concentrated his mind. In 1974 he landed a well-paid job as a long-distance lorry driver and by 1977, he and Sonia, who was working as a schoolteacher, had saved enough to buy their own home at Garden

Peter Sutcliffe worked as a lorry driver and was interviewed by police several years before he was arrested as being the Yorkshire Ripper.

Lane, Heaton, Bradford. But it was Sutcliffe's criminal past that should have alerted detectives. In 1969 he had been arrested for "going equipped for theft," officers having found him in possession of a hammer.

With hindsight, it seems incredible that this incident, taken alongside the £5 note clue, failed to ring alarm bells with detectives. Yet the inquiry, which since June 1977 had been placed in the overall charge of West Yorkshire's Assistant Chief Constable George Oldfield, had from the start been hampered by outdated processing of information. Had computers been available, it is hard to believe

When Peter Sutcliffe was finally caught, protesters and vigilantes lined the streets with signs and banners.

Yvonne Pearson, aged 22, was battered and stabbed to death on January 21 in Bradford. Her body was not found until March 26, by which time the killer had clearly returned to inflict fresh wounds. On January 31 his victim was 18-year-old Helen Rytka from Huddersfield—the only one of his victims with whom Sutcliffe actually had sex.

On March 8, police received a communication that they regarded as one of their best clues to date—the first of three letters signed "Jack the Ripper" and posted from Sunderland. Detectives took them seriously but tragically they were a cruel hoax. It was not to be the first time that the police were hoodwinked and disastrously sidetracked in their hunt for the Yorkshire Ripper.

And so the killings continued. Vera Millward, aged 41, murdered on May 16 in the car park of Manchester's Royal Infirmary, was smashed over the head and had her stomach slashed open. Josephine Whitaker, a 19-year-old building society worker, was the subject of a frenzied stabbing and died on April 4, 1979. Barbara Leach, a 20-year-old Leeds University student, was killed by a blow to her head and eight stab wounds to the stomach. Her body was found in Bradford on September 2.

It was almost a year before Sutcliffe claimed his twelfth victim, 47-year-old executive officer

that the wealth of clues spotlighting Sutcliffe would have been ignored. The Ripper himself recognized that he had made a stupid mistake in paying Jordan with a new five-pound note. Before her body was found, he had returned to Moss Side to try to recover it. He failed, and in a fury slashed the body open with a knife. In a clumsy attempt to disguise the attack as anything other than a Ripper killing, he had then burned the body on a bonfire in a nearby allotment.

The scare did little to deter Sutcliffe. In December he attacked a woman in Leeds. Amazingly, she survived and was able to tell detectives that her assailant hit her over the head, screaming: "You dirty prostitute." Soon after New Year 1978, the Ripper carried out two murders in ten days, a sign that his confidence was sky high.

West Yorkshire police launched a well-publicized campaign to track down the Ripper.

- - - - - - - -

Marguerite Walls. She was found covered with grass clippings near her home in Farsley, between Leeds and Bradford, on August 18, 1980. The Ripper had switched from his usual techniques, perhaps in a bid to confuse police, and had strangled her with a ligature. A few weeks later, a 34-year-old Singapore doctor studying at Leeds University was also attacked with a noose. But she was luckier, saved by a passing police car that scared Sutcliffe off. Jacqueline Hill was not; the 20-year-old student was killed in Leeds on November 17, 1980.

By now more than 250 officers were working full-time on the biggest manhunt in British criminal history. Nearly 200,000 people had been interviewed, over 160,000 vehicles checked, 23,000 households contacted, and £5 million spent. But now came hoax number two. A tape recording was sent to Yorkshire police purporting to come from the Ripper. The Geordie accent further convinced the squad that the man they sought

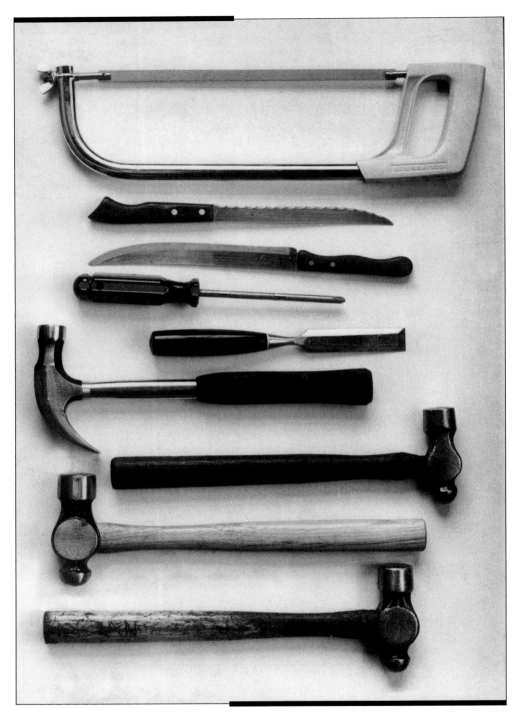

Tools found by police that Sutcliffe used to kill his victims.

- - - - - - - - - - - - -

Faced with enormous political and media interest, the pressure was bound to take its toll. In January 1980 ill health forced him off the investigation. Oldfield had told the press: "This is a personal thing between me and him." But he had, of course, been chasing the wrong man. The Ripper was, all the while, right there under the noses of the Yorkshire constabulary.

Sutcliffe was seen by police seven times and interviewed on five of those occasions, yet was never included in the list of the most serious suspects. He was interviewed twice in November 1977 about the £5 note, again in August 1978 because his car had been seen in a red-light district, again in November 1978 when his tyres were checked, and once more on July 29 about his red-light jaunts. During the July interview, the officer concerned even urged his superiors to regard Sutcliffe as a prime suspect. His report went unheeded. Sutcliffe, it was pointed out, didn't have a Geordie accent.

It was a routine police enquiry that finally ended the carnage. The Ripper was stopped with a prostitute in Sheffield, the city he had targeted as his new stalking ground. He was arrested on suspicion of theft because his car

was from the North-East. As a result, police concentrated on suspects with Geordie accents.

Over these months, Oldfield had given almost every minute of his life to hunting down the Ripper.

had false number plates but the discovery of the ball-peen hammer and Phillips screwdriver nearby rang alarm bells with the officers. Later at Dewsbury police station, Sutcliffe told his interrogators: "I am the Yorkshire Ripper." His full confession took 16 hours to dictate.

> **"Prisoners have attacked him many times since his incarceration"**

Peter Sutcliffe leaves Newport Court, Isle of Wight.

On May 22, 1981, Sutcliffe was found guilty of 13 murders and seven attempted murders. He was given a life sentence with a recommendation that he should serve at least 30 years. In 1984 he was sent to serve his time in Broadmoor hospital for the criminally insane after a panel of psychiatrists declared him mad. Other prisoners have attacked him many times since his incarceration and in 1997, prisoner Ian Kay stabbed Sutcliffe in both eyes, which left the Ripper blind in one eye.

Two earlier pointers to that fact were his self-professed view of his mission in life. One was a remark he made to his younger brother Carl by way of explanation for his crimes: "I were just cleaning up the streets, our kid. Just cleaning up the streets." The other clue to his character was a self-written poster that he kept in the cab of his truck. It read: "In this truck is a man whose latent genius, if unleashed, would rock the nation, whose dynamic energy would overpower those around him. Better let him sleep."

JOSEPH SWANGO

It was a public statement that could only hint at the private terror and shame suffered by just one of the hospitals at which Michael Swango committed his evil crimes.

FACT FILE.

Name: Joseph Michael Swango, aka the "Doughnut Poisoner," "Double-O Swango," and the "Doctor of Death"

Born: 1954

Location of killings: New York, South Dakota, Illinois, Ohio, USA and Zambia, Namibia

Killed: convicted of four; probably more than 100

Modus operandi: Lethal injections, poisoning

Justice: Two life sentences in 1999

The statement read: "If Swango is legally connected to all the suspicious deaths of patients under his care since he began his residency with Ohio State University's medical program in 1983, it would make him the most prolific serial killer in history."

It was an even more chilling fact that Swango had been able to take up doctoring positions at hospitals across two continents without anyone checking on the trail of death he had left behind him. He poisoned patients in hospitals in New York State, South Dakota, Illinois, and Ohio as well as in Zambia and Namibia in Africa. Yet one would have only needed to ask the 71 fellow medical students who trained with Swango at Southern Illinois University for a character assessment of the murdering medic: "He's nuts" was the common verdict. They had witnessed Swango's strange behavior on numerous occasions. Like how he dropped to the floor and performed punishing push-ups if he was chastised for making a mistake. Or how he would write "DIED" across patients' charts when they succumbed to a fatal illness. "Hey, death happens," he would say.

Born Joseph Michael Swango, he insisted his parents Muriel and Virgil and everyone else call him Michael. He shone at school, greatly overshadowing the efforts of his brothers Bob and John and half-brother Richard. Swango's enthusiastic membership of the Christian Brothers High School

Marching Band gave no hint of the terrifying person he would later become. But in his last year at music college, Swango became obsessed with war and violence, donning military fatigues and keeping a scrapbook of newspaper cuttings of air and car crashes, riots, and sex crimes. When challenged by his mother over his morbid interest, Swango replied: "If I'm ever accused of murder, this will prove I'm mentally unstable." After a short spell in the US Marine Corps, being honourably discharged in 1976, Swango returned to his Illinois hometown to study biology and chemistry at Quincy College. After classes, he worked as an ambulance attendant, a job he later said he enjoyed because he got to see the blood, gore, and twisted metal of car crashes. Swango graduated from Quincy in 1979 and went on to Southern Illinois University to study medicine. He would have graduated with the rest of his class in 1982 but his habit of fabricating reports on patients he had not even examined caused anxiety among his tutors and he was only allowed to stay only if he agreed to repeat his last year's training. With his bedside manner, professional ability, and general mental state all in grave doubt, Swango nevertheless, beat a number of candidates to win a place in 1983 for a year-long internship in general surgery at the Ohio State University Medical Center.

It was on January 31, 1984, that Swango was first noted as acting suspiciously. A nurse in the hospital's Rhodes Hall wing saw him apparently carrying out his rounds at mid-morning rather than the usual earlier hours. Checking on patient Ruth Barrick whom Swango had just been in to see, the nurse found the woman turning blue and suffocating. After administering emergency treatment and managing to save her, doctors were

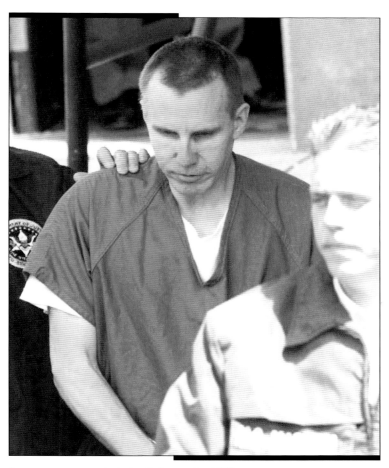

Swango was arrested in Chicago in 1997 after his return from Africa and Europe, where he had committed other murders.

baffled as to what had caused the respiratory failure. A week later, Ruth Barrick suffered exactly the same sort of breathing problems and died gasping for air. Swango had been the last person to attend to her.

Just 24 hours later, elderly patient Rena Cooper, who had been showing good signs of recovery after an operation, was found blue and shaking shortly after Swango had left her room. Mrs. Cooper was saved by the actions of other medical staff and asked for a pencil and notebook. She wrote: "Someone gave me some med in my IV (intravenous drip) and paralyzed all of me—lungs, heart, speech."

When anxious nurses compared notes, they discovered that at least six other patients, all evidently making good progress, had suddenly died. Their ages ranged from a 19-year-old to a 47-year-old. Swango had been the duty intern at the time all of them had died. Incredibly, although an investigation was carried out, none of the nurses or staff who had rushed to try to save lives were interviewed. The accusations aimed at Swango were put down to professional jealousy and he was allowed to return to his duties, this time in the center's Doan Hall. Following his return in the middle of February 1984, more woman patients were found in the throes of death. Swango told one relative: "Your mother's dead now. You can go look at her."

The high number of deaths whenever Swango was around did not, however, influence the hospital's decision to decline appointing him a resident doctor. It was simply judged that his overall performance was poor and, although Swango could have stayed on until June 1984, he walked out in March after being told the bad news. Incredibly, he was granted a license to practice medicine in Ohio despite the State Medical Board expressing misgivings about him during a routine investigation following his license application. Swango decided instead to return to his hometown of Quincy.

Swango joined the Adams County Ambulance Corps, where he shocked the crews with some of the things he had to say about his job. Once, he told them his favorite fantasy: "Picture a school bus crammed with kids smashing head-on with a trailer truck loaded down with gasoline. We're summoned. We get there in a jiffy just as another gasoline truck rams the bus. Up in flames it goes. Kids are hurled through the air, everywhere, on telephone poles, on the street, especially along an old barbed wire fence along the road. All burning."

On one occasion, an entire paramedic crew became ill after eating doughnuts bought in by Swango. Only later did they realize that Swango had eaten none himself. Then two other crew members, new to the crew and unaware of Swango's reputation, made the mistake of drinking soft drinks he had given them. Within minutes they were crippled with stomach pains. His colleagues decided to investigate Swango a little further. They found arsenic in his locker and, when tested, iced tea that only Swango had had access to was found to contain poison. When alerted, the Adams County Sheriff's Office searched Swango's apartment and discovered a hoard of phials, bottles, syringes, and a library of books on murder. There was also a selection of guns and knives.

Dubbed the "Doughnut Poisoner," Swango was arrested and charged with seven counts of aggravated battery. His trial began on April 22, 1985, ending with him being sentenced to five years' imprisonment in the Central Correctional Center. Two years later, however, Swango was released for good behavior. His application for a medical license in the state of Virginia was turned down and he instead became a job counselor at the state's Career Development before being accepted as a lab

> **❝Six other patients, all evidently making good progress, had suddenly died❞**

technician at a coal exporter's. It seems people had forgotten all about the Doughnut Poisoner and no one asked questions when several employees fell ill and some nearly died from what appeared to be food poisoning.

Applying for a job at the University of South Dakota in September 1991, Swango fabricated a glowing resume of his past appointments. He explained away his "battery" conviction by saying he was the innocent victim of a bar room brawl when he had "taken the rap" rather than get his friends into trouble.

> **The migraine headaches she now repeatedly suffered from seemed to disappear whenever she was away from Swango**

He took up the position in June 1992. By this time, Swango had a girlfriend, Kirstin Kinney, a red-haired 26-year-old nurse, who was divorced. The pair had met a year before at a hospital where Swango was taking a refresher course. When Swango moved to take up his new post, Kirstin moved with him, despite reservations expressed by her mother and stepfather. Both Kirstin and Swango made their mark in their new jobs, he being regarded as one of the best emergency doctors the hospital had ever known, and she as one of the most dedicated nurses at the local Royal C. Johnson Veterans' Memorial Hospital.

It all ended when a program about the notorious Doughnut Poisoner was shown again on television. Swango was dismissed and a party was thrown for him by a group of loyal friends. All the guests fell ill with food poisoning symptoms. Kirstin, who realized the migraine headaches she now repeatedly suffered from seemed to disappear whenever she was away from Swango, fled home

to her parents. She shot herself there after leaving a note that said: "I love you both. I just didn't want to be here anymore. Just found day-to-day living a constant struggle with my thoughts. I'd say I'm sorry but I'm not. I feel that sense of peace, the peace of mind that I've been looking for. It's nice." She added a note addressed to Swango saying: "I love you more! You're the most precious man I've ever known."

In June 1993, Swango moved to New York State and after again fudging his past employment, managed to secure himself a position at the Internal Medicine Department at the Veterans' Administration Headquarters at Northport, Long Island. His first patient, Dominic Buffalino, died within hours of Swango arriving. Other patients were to die in his care too, all suffering heart failure in the dead of night. When Elsie Harris, the wife of one of Swango's victims, sued the hospital after stating she saw Swango injecting something into her husband's neck, the case was thrown out due to lack of evidence.

Meanwhile, Kirstin Kinney's parents could not forgive Swango for driving their daughter to suicide. Neither could they believe that Swango was still practicing medicine, and it was their determination to expose him that led to his eventual sacking from the hospital. Dr. Jordan Cohen, the man who had employed Swango, was so horrified to hear the truth about him that he resigned—but not before sending a letter to every medical school in America, warning them about him.

Swango disappeared, surfacing briefly to work at a wastewater treatment plant in Atlanta. The authorities, including the FBI, were now on red alert to track him down but he managed to give them the slip, making his way to Zimbabwe in southern Africa. More forged and fabricated documents secured him jobs there in 1995, first in the operating theaters of Mpilo Hospital, Bulawayo and then at the Mnene Lutheran outpost hospital—where patients started to die with alarming regularity. Before expiring, however, some managed to cry out that they had been injected by Swango. A police investigation was launched and Swango fled to neighboring Zambia, moving onto Europe and finally back to America. He was arrested and handcuffed the moment he stepped into Chicago's O'Hare Airport on June 27, 1997.

Psychologists who examined Swango diagnosed him as a psychopath with a "preoccupation to control and manipulate." At a hearing on July 12, as he languished in the high-security Sheridan Correctional Facility in Florence, Colorado, FBI agents searched for the hard evidence that would prove Swango to be a doctor of death within the medical profession rather than any angel of mercy. Countless interviews took place with those who had lost relatives while in his care, including Elsie Harris who had tried to sue following the death of her husband. Others included all the nurses who had tried so hard to prove Swango was a killer. One said Swango had been christened "Double-O Swango" as a parody of James Bond's 007. "It was

❝Murdering is the only way I have of reminding myself I am still alive❞

as if he as acting with a license to kill," she said.

Eventually, Swango was charged with three counts of murder, one count of assault and three counts of making false statements. At this time, it could not be proved that he had murdered a fourth person, 19-year-old Cynthia McGee, at the Ohio State University Hospital but as damning evidence was produced concerning the other three murders at the New York Veterans Hospital, Swango finally pleaded guilty and was sentenced to life imprisonment without parole. He was later given another life sentence for the murder of Cynthia McGee after the discovery of a diary in which he had written about her killing: "I love the sweet, husky, close smell of indoor homicide. Murdering is the only way I have of reminding myself I am still alive."

Although only ever convicted of four murders, Swango was blamed for the suspicious deaths of many more, possibly hundreds—all poisoned. An FBI source said: "We believe that in the States alone, Swango can be linked to 100 or more mysterious deaths of patients directly in his care. It is a national scandal."

Loretta Lynch, US District Attorney for the Eastern District of New York summed up Swango's reign of murder: "Instead of using his medical license to become a healer, Swango inveigled his way into the confidence of hospital administrators and once in their trust and in their employ, he searched for victims and took their lives. He was exactly the kind of doctor you would want to avoid."

SWEENEY TODD

The tale of Sweeney Todd, the Demon Barber of Fleet Street, has been told so often that truth has often been obscured by fable.

Since early Victorian times, he has been a staple of the comic, the music hall, the theater, the movies, and even a Stephen Sondheim musical. In penning the words for Sondheim's music, playwright Christopher Bond described the tale of Sweeney Todd as "pure fiction" and that "no one has ever succeeded in finding a shred of evidence as to the existence of a Demon Barber." Most people have assumed that to be the case. But, however unlikely, most myths and legends have some faint basis in truth, and Sweeney Todd is a case in point. For the monstrous Todd is not simply a nightmare

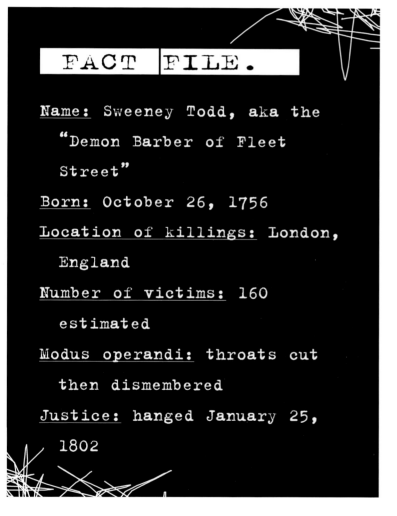

FACT FILE.

Name: Sweeney Todd, aka the
"Demon Barber of Fleet
Street"

Born: October 26, 1756

Location of killings: London,
England

Number of victims: 160
estimated

Modus operandi: throats cut
then dismembered

Justice: hanged January 25,
1802

During the Victorian period, Sweeney Todd was a legend and was
represented in illustrations, plays, and later even a musical.

SWEENEY TODD,
THE
DEMON BARBER OF FLEET STREET.

"NOT YET!" YELLED THE DEMON BARBER, SLASHING AT THE MAN WITH A RAZOR.

from folklore, an early Hannibal Lecter created to send shivers down the spine. He actually existed and carried on his trade in the squalid, festering streets of late eighteenth-century London. The true history of the barber who butchered 160 people is even more chilling. There is little doubt that at the time of his criminal spree he was Britain's most prolific serial killer.

Sweeney Todd was born on October 26, 1756, in the attic of a house in Brick Lane, Whitechapel, in the heart of London's squalid East End—later the killing ground of Jack the Ripper. Hogarth's famous 1751 engraving of Gin Lane gives a horrifying picture of the area at the time, the scene of violence, drunkenness, begging, and crime. Sweeney's gin-soaked parents, who lived on the verge of starvation, abandoned him one freezing morning in the winter of 1768 when the boy, then aged 12, awoke to find them gone, never to be heard of again.

Somehow, Sweeney survived and became apprenticed to a cutler named John Crook, whose trade included the selling of razors, but he was sacked two years later when accused of petty theft. Todd was sentenced to five years in Newgate Prison and it was from the records of this notorious jail that the true story of Sweeney Todd emerges.

In Newgate, Sweeney became "soap boy" to the prison's barber, a man named Plummer, and from him he learned the trade that he was to pursue on his release. Freed in 1775, the 19-year-old spent five years working in markets and on street corners as one of London's "flying barbers" before acquiring the lease of a shop next door to St. Dunstan's Church in Fleet Street, where he advertised himself as a barber, tooth-puller, and surgeon.

> **❝Sweeney's gin-soaked parents, who lived on the verge of starvation, abandoned him one freezing morning in the winter❞**

A surgeon is a respected profession these days but in those dark days, it was a trade commonly performed by barbers, who had access to razor-sharp tools. Apart from shaving customers and cutting hair, they pulled teeth and bled customers for minor ailments. They advertised their wares with window displays of jars filled with coagulated blood and rotten teeth.

Todd himself could have done with the services of a good barber and tooth-puller, if the description of him from *The Courier* of 1816 is anything to go by. The newspaper wrote that he was "a long loose joined, ill-shaped fellow" with large hands and feet, and reddish hair bristling with combs. He suffered from a squint and had "a huge mouth filled with black teeth."

The first murders attributed to Todd appear to have been almost random. According to a report in the *Daily Courant* of April 14, 1785, a young gentleman from the country fell into conversation with a barber by St. Dunstan's church clock when, "the two men came to an argument and all of a sudden the barber took out a razor and slit the throat of the young man, disappearing into an alleyway." An apprentice who said he was planning to visit Todd to have his hair cut was also found dead around this time. A pawnbroker and a money lender with whom Todd did business were also found in their offices with their throats cut.

After this, Todd's killings became systematic—almost a production line of murder and always carried out on his own premises. For the barber had now invented his famous revolving barber's chair. It was really two chairs in one, as a second chair was fixed to the floorboards directly underneath the first one. The floor itself under it pivoted in the middle, so that when Todd slid back a bolt, the occupant of the first chair was pitched backward into the cellar. Meanwhile, the chairs revolved, the second one surfacing before the bolt was pushed back in place. Todd could operate the bolt by remote control, for it was connected by rods to a lever behind the rear door of the shop. When he pulled the lever, the rods withdrew the bolt and the weight of the customer leaning back caused the chair to tip him head over heels onto the floor of the cellar, usually knocking him out and sometimes breaking his neck.

One of the chair's early victims was Thomas Shadwell, a beadle employed by St. Bartholomew's Hospital to keep law and order. According to a report by his son John Shadwell, a night watchman at the hospital, his father had called in for a shave on his way to work one fall night in 1798. In his pocket he had a gold timepiece given to him for 30 years' service at the hospital. He may have looked at it while Todd heated the water for his shave. That was too much temptation for Todd because, although the body was never found, the watch was—in one of Todd's upstairs cupboards after he was arrested two years later.

There may have been witnesses to murders such as that of the hospital beadle. Todd employed soap boys to heat the water, fill the soap bowls,

On the morning of January 25, 1802, the butchering barber was taken from his Newgate cell and in front of thousands was hanged on a scaffold near the main gate.

and sweep the floor, and he no doubt enforced their silence by terrorizing them—or worse. There is record of the first of his soap boys being confined to a madhouse by Todd in 1786. A bill from the Peckham Rye Asylum reads: "Paid one year's keep and burial of Thomas Simpkins, aged 15, found dead in bed after residing at the asylum ten months and four days." Other soap boys may have met a worse fate.

Todd, whose catchphrase is melodramatically recalled as "I polish 'em off!" began polishing off his clients at the rate of as many as one a month

The front cover of a "Penny Blood" that went on sale in Victorian theaters.

for the next 17 years. The only problem was how to dispose of the bodies. At first he stashed them in underground passageways beneath the adjacent church. But then a young widow named Margery Lovett arrived on the scene to solve the problem. She and Todd became lovers and the barber set her up in a pie shop in Bell Yard, just alongside the Royal Courts of Justice.

Clerks and lawyers from nearby Lincoln's Inn and Gray's Inn flocked to it at lunchtimes, queuing for the first batch of veal and pork pies to be produced from the cellar bakery at noon. They would have been horrified if they had known the origin of the secret ingredients they found so tasty. Sweeney Todd was utilizing his skills as a barber and surgeon to dismember the bodies, strip off the flesh, and package them up with heart, liver, and kidneys for Mrs. Lovett's bakery. An account of this dreadful trade was recorded for posterity in the pages of the *London Chronicle*, which reported the words of Mrs. Lovett herself upon her arrest. Although probably tainted by journalistic embellishment, it reads:

"By his own exertions he excavated an underground connection between the two (establishments), mining under St. Dunstan's Church and through the vault of that building. When he had completed all his arrangements he came to me and made his offer. The plan he proposed was that the pie-shop should be opened for the sole purpose of getting rid of the bodies of people whom he might think proper to murder in or under his shop. He said that, fearing nothing and believing nothing, he had come to the conclusion that money was the greatest thing he desired. He said that after a murder he would take the flesh from the bones and convey it to the shelves of the bakehouse in Bell Yard, the pieces to be materials for the pies."

The meat from his victims went down a treat. Todd's problem, however, was in disposing of the remaining heads, bones, and guts, which he temporarily solved by piling them in a family vault beneath St. Dunstan's belonging to the Weston family. But as the pile grew, so did the dreadful smell drifting up to street level. In October 1801 the parish constable, Mr. Otton, reported the matter to local magistrate Sir Richard Blunt, who called in the earliest version of the London police force, the so-called Bow Street Runners. The first search revealed nothing but Todd's premises nearby were put under watch. A further three unfortunate customers were observed to enter the barber's shop but not leave before Sir Richard ordered a more thorough search of the adjoining church vaults. This time they broke open a vault and found the decomposing corpses. A search of the barber's shop revealed cupboards full of clothing and a drawer packed with valuables and at the pie shop human remains were ready to be made into pies. Mrs. Lovett was sent to Newgate where, having signed a confession, she paid to have poison smuggled to her, swallowed it and died.

Sweeney Todd's arrest for murder caused a sensation. As Todd's trial approached, the *Daily Courant* reported: "Scarcely ever in London has such an amount of public excitement been produced by any criminal proceedings as by the trial of Sweeney Todd. The case of Rex v. Todd will certainly be one of the trials of the age." In January 1802 hundreds of people tried to push their way into the Old Bailey to get a sight of the Demon Barber in person.

Until his appearance in the dock, Todd had been kept in the dark over the death of Margery Lovett. When the news was broken to him at the Old Bailey, he turned pale "like some great, gaunt ghost." Todd then heard the Attorney General, in his introductory address, tell the jury that the search of the Weston vault revealed that "into old coffins, the tenants of which had moldered to dust,

❝At the pie shop human remains were ready to be made into pies❞

there had been thrust fresh bodies with scarcely any flesh remaining on them, yet sufficient to produce the stench in the church." Since almost none of these human remains could be identified, however, the case against Todd hinged on the disappearance of one victim, seaman Francis Thornhill, who had been on his way to deliver a string of pearls when he stopped for a shave at Todd's shop. The pearls were later pawned by Todd for £1,000. Todd's home, according to the Attorney General, was also found crammed with "property and clothing sufficient for 160 people."

The defense counsel claimed there was no firm evidence against Todd and he poured scorn on "stories about vaults, bad odors in churches, movable floorboards, chairs standing on their heads, secret passages, and pork pies." And of the smell in St. Dunstan's, he added: "You might as well say that my client committed felony because this court was not well ventilated."

The jury was in no doubt, however. They took only five minutes to find Todd guilty. Asked if he had any words to say before sentence was passed, Todd shouted out: "I am not guilty!" The judge replied: "You cannot expect that society can do otherwise than put out of life someone who, like yourself, has been a terror and a scourge."

At 8am on Tuesday January 25, 1802, the 46-year-old butchering barber was taken from his Newgate cell and, in front of a crowd of thousands, was hanged on a scaffold near the main gate.

JACK UNTERWEGER

Jack Unterweger, son of an Austrian prostitute and an American soldier, was always destined for a life behind bars.

Born in Styria, south-eastern Austria, he grew up in the lawless company of streetwalkers, pimps, and petty thieves. By the age of 25, he had notched up 15 convictions including burglary, rape, and pimping—having spent eight of the previous ten years in custody. When, in 1975, he was hauled back into court to face a charge of strangling 18-year-old Margaret Schaefer with her own bra, he was handed a life sentence and it was assumed

```
FACT FILE.

Name: Jack Unterweger

Born: 1951

Location of killings:

  Austria, former

  Czechoslovakia, and

  California, USA

Killed: at least 11

Modus operandi: strangulation

  with articles of clothing

Justice: sentenced to life in

  1994; hanged himself in

  prison
```

that was the last the world would hear of him. Unterweger thought differently and, in the most determined manner, set out to prove that he was anything but a common criminal. He pored over books, learning about philosophy and foreign cultures and achieving a well-crafted prose style. He acquainted himself with the great writers, absorbing every phrase and nuance. He edited a prison newspaper and literary review. He wrote a book, a semi-autobiography called *Fegefeuer* (Purgatory), which became a best-seller. There followed a play, books of poetry, and a clutch of literary awards.

Unterweger's infamy turned to fame. He became a star of the literary world that held him up as a paragon, the criminal who had reinvented himself. In his book, he had tried to explain away his violent past, writing: "I was no longer a youth. I was a beast, a devil, a child grown old before his time who enjoyed being evil." Now, he explained, he had overcome these basest of instincts and was a reformed character.

His celebrity status and a petition organized by influential Austrians helped him gain an early release from prison in October 1990 after serving 15 years. "That life is now over," he promised. "Let's get on with the new." He was feted at society parties and appeared on television chat shows. Unterweger favored white suits and red bow ties and drove expensive cars with the license plate "KACK 1." Yet while he had the facade of a celebrity writer, Unterweger still had the soul of a murderer. While a hero in public, in private he embarked on an orgy of murder.

During his first year of freedom, he is reckoned to have strangled at least six prostitutes. He was instantly under suspicion from the police as prostitute murders, normally averaging one a year in Austria, suddenly grew. The bodies of four women who had vanished from Vienna were found during April and May 1991 alone. Unterweger's killing spree spread across the Austrian countryside, where he killed six women in the spring of 1991, and into neighboring Czechoslovakia.

Then, commissioned by a magazine to write an article on crime in Southern California, he moved to Los Angeles, where three murders were committed between June and July 1991—exactly the same period Unterweger was there. The victims were prostitutes, two of them found dead in Boyle Heights and one in a Malibu canyon. All had been strangled with their own bras and their battered bodies violated with sticks and other objects.

Back in Austria, the bulging police file on murders of prostitutes was showing up stark similarities with the Californian killings. The victims were picked up in red-light districts. They were strangled with articles of their own clothing. They were naked. They had been subjected to bondage rituals. Some attempt had been made to bury them beneath branches and undergrowth. Their clothing was scattered. And although their jewelry was left, personal effects such as letters were missing. Above all, it was obvious the killer wanted to exercise power over his victims and inflict pain and humiliation.

Unterweger, whose name means "on the run," realized his license to kill was running out and again left Austria for a trip through Canada and

Unterweger's murdering infamy turned into fame as a writer and a criminal who had reinvented himself. His lust for killing did not end however, and he went on to commit other crimes.

the US. In his absence, his Vienna apartment was raided. He was arrested in February 1992 in Florida, where he was traveling with his 18-year-old girlfriend. He was extradited to Austria where he was held on remand for two years before finally standing trial in April 1994 on 11 murder charges, including the three American cases. Following a two-month hearing, he was convicted for nine of them; two of the bodies were too decomposed for the cause of death to be determined.

Sentenced to life without parole, Unterweger was taken to Graz Prison. Twelve hours later, at 3.40am on June 29, 1994, he was found dead. Unterweger had used ripped-up clothes to create the noose and hung from a curtain rod in his cell.

FRED AND ROSEMARY WEST

In privacy-obsessed Britain, it was no one else's business what went on behind the closed door and curtained windows of number 25 Cromwell Street.

Among the neighbors, there were a few mutterings about the surprising number of night-time male visitors. But the husband and wife who lived at number 25 were generally well liked. Most neighbors considered Fred West a cheery, hard-working type and his wife Rose, a busy, lively mother. There was some concern that their children were occasionally disciplined too harshly but it didn't amount to much—certainly nothing to warrant informing the police or the local social services. In fact, number 25 was just an ordinary semi-detached house in an ordinary terrace—an anonymous, grime-streaked, home of the kind found in any British town.

Yet, within number 25, an all-consuming cancer formed and flourished. In the house to which passers-by never gave a second glance, Fred and Rose West lived a secret life—one so obscene that, in a world where the word "evil" has become something of a cliché, the English language is devoid of adjectives to describe it. For more than two decades, Fred and Rose's sickening perversions went unchecked as they sadistically tortured and murdered young girls, including their own children.

In the cellar of number 25, the Wests' pathetic victims breathed their last. Only they glimpsed the depths of the Wests' depravity in those last agonizing moments. Dragged down into the darkness, they had their limbs bound tightly, their faces sheathed in sticky brown parcel tape, and had plastic breathing tubes stuffed inadequately into their nostrils. Even after the sweet release of death, the girls were denied any dignity. Mutilated and in some cases possibly cannibalized by their tormentors, the bodies would be heaved unceremoniously into pits dug in the cellar or the back garden. No one thought it odd that Fred carried out a lot of do-it-yourself work around the house. After all, he was a builder.

FACT FILE.

Name: Frederick West and Rosemary Pauline West

Born: September 29, 1941 (Fred); November 29, 1953 (Rosemary)

Location of killings: Gloucestershire, England

Killed: 12

Modus operandi: various

Justice: Fred hanged himself in jail in 1995; Rosemary sentenced to life in 1996

Rosemary West in 1995 at the time of her arrest.

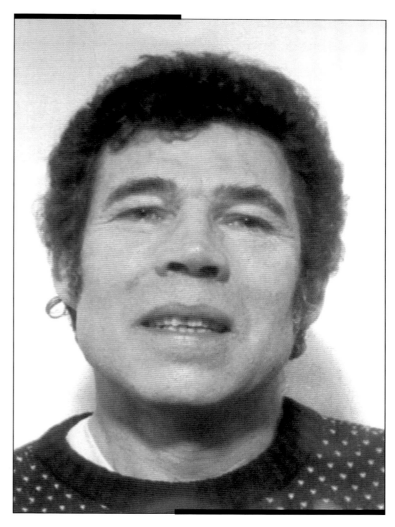

Fred West in 1995, the year he hanged himself in Winson Green Jail.

The terrible secrets of 25 Cromwell Street were unfolded to an incredulous world during Rose West's trial in November 1995. Soon everyone was asking the same questions. Why did it happen? How could fate have thrown together two of the most devilish minds in the history of crime and allowed them to feed off each other's sordid desires. Part of the answer, say the psychologists, lies in their pasts.

Rosemary Pauline Letts was born on November 29, 1953, in a maternity hospital at Barnstaple,

North Devon. She grew up in the nearby seaside village of Northam and went to infant school there. Teachers remember her as an ordinary, unremarkable little girl. As one put it: "She didn't excel at anything, neither was she a troublemaker." But at home, life for the young Rose was anything but ordinary. Her father William Letts, a steward in the Royal Navy, battered and bullied his wife Daisy and treated the seven children with appalling severity. As the third youngest, Rose escaped the worst of his attentions but her brothers lived

417

Number 25, Cromwell Street was just an ordinary house in an ordinary street. Little did the neighbors know about what went on inside the home of murderers Fred and Rosemary West.

- - - - - - - - - - - - - - - -

in fear of a man later diagnosed as a schizophrenic psychopath.

When Rose was 11, the family left Northam for Plymouth, later moving to Bishop's Cleeve near Gloucester. But by 1969 Daisy decided she could no longer hold the marriage together. She walked out, taking Rose and her two younger brothers with her. That same year, as Rose waited at a bus stop in Cheltenham, she met the man who would help shape her terrible destiny. She was chatted up by Fred West, then 27, and began to go steady

with him. At the time, police now believe, he had already committed two murders. For her part, the busty, 15-year-old Rose had begun dabbling in prostitution. It was truly a match made in hell.

Fred West's past had been equally traumatic. Born on September 29, 1941, he grew up with no guidelines to acceptable sexual behavior. His mother (coincidentally also called Daisy) regarded him as her favorite, and there were rumors that she seduced him at the age of 12. His father, Gloucestershire farm laborer Walter West, was equally fond of incestuous relationships. Fred, who had two younger brothers and three sisters, would later tell how his father regarded the children as sexual playthings, saying that it was natural for him to have sex with them and that he had a right to do so. No wonder Fred began to follow the same sick course.

In June 1961, West was hauled down to the local police station and accused of making a 13-year-old girl pregnant. To the amazement of the officers, he seemed unabashed and openly admitted molesting young girls. "Doesn't everyone do it?" he asked. It was a turning point in West's life. Before going to court, his terrified victim collapsed and refused to give evidence, so West escaped on the child-abuse charge. However, the case caused the end of his close relationship with his mother, who banished him from her house and West went to live with his Aunt Violet in nearby Much Marcle.

By the time Fred West met Rose Letts on that summer day in Cheltenham, he was already a family man. His first wife, Rena (real name Catherine) Costello, had been five months pregnant by another lover when she married Fred on November 17, 1962. He gave baby Charmaine his name and he and Rena then had a child of their own,

Police found some of the remains of the Wests' victims underneath the cellar floor.

Anne-Marie. The marriage soon ran into trouble.
Fred wanted her to enact sadistic sex games with
him, something she was not interested in. When
they split up, he took the girls with him and Rose
became their stand-in mother.

For little Charmaine, it was a tortuous childhood. The Wests abused her terribly on the
grounds she was "not one of theirs." Years later,
during Rose's trial, witnesses told of watching
Charmaine being forced to stand on a wooden
chair, her hands tied behind her with a leather

belt, while Rose raised a wooden spoon to beat her.
Police believe that at some point Fred West killed
Charmaine. When Rena came looking for her little
girl, he dispatched her in the same dispassionate
manner. Neither of them was ever reported missing and Charmaine's absence was easily explained
by Rose. "She's gone off with her mother," she told
friends.

Number 25 Cromwell Street, one of the most
notorious addresses in British criminological history, now enters the story. Rose and Fred had their
first child, Heather, on October 17, 1970, and two
years later were married and moved into their first
proper home, the anonymous, grime-streaked

The Wests' back garden is covered over as police search for bodies.

- - - - - - - - - - - - - -

semi-detached that was to be the scene of their most appalling excesses. Here they could create their own fantasy world, a world in which Rose not only freely indulged Fred's desire for sadistic sex but actively embraced it herself. The house became filled with whips and chains, manacles and bondage gear. There would be homemade pornographic films, attempts at bestiality, and a string of clients who paid for Rose's services as a prostitute.

All the time, the couple were on the lookout for young girls whom they could lure home as sexual playthings. In this, Rose played a key role. Fred later admitted that it was a lot easier to pick up girls when he had Rose in the car with him. The hapless victims felt more secure when they saw a

Police set to work at Much Marcle to look for evidence against the Wests.

- - - - - - - - - - -

woman present. Once they found out their mistake, it would be too late.

The tally of Fred West's victims had begun mounting long before he met Rose. Eighteen-year-old Anne McFall, from Sandhurst, Gloucestershire, began an affair with Fred while she was working as a nanny for him and Rena, and she was soon pregnant by him. Police believe he murdered her because she started putting pressure on him to end his relationship with Rena. She was buried in a field at Kempley, Gloucestershire, in 1967 next to the body of her unborn child. Police recovered her remains in June 1994, the year most of the victims' bodies were uncovered.

Next to die were Rena and little Charmaine, then aged eight. Police believe Fred killed his wife when she came looking for her child in 1971 and that Charmaine was strangled a few hours later. Charmaine was buried at the Wests' first home, at 25 Midland Road, Gloucester, and was found on May 4, 1994. Rena was buried next to Anne McFall at Kempley. Her body was also dug up by police in 1994.

The fourth murder was carried out on a 19-year-old Gloucester girl called Lynda Gough. She had become friendly with some of Fred and Rose's lodgers at the Cromwell Street house and in March 1973 she moved in herself. She was dead within a matter of weeks, the victim of a twisted sex game in which she was an unwilling player. Her dismembered body was found beneath the bathroom floor. Tape had been wound thickly around her head and her limbs were piled on top of each other.

Victim number five was 15-year-old Carol Cooper, the resident of a children's home in Worcester. She was last seen on the night of November 10, 1973, as she boarded a bus to visit her grandmother. West admitted killing her, although he claimed Rose wasn't involved. Carol was found under the cellar floor at 25 Cromwell Street.

Sixth to die was Lucy Partington, a devoutly religious 21-year-old from Gretton, Gloucestershire, who was studying medieval English at Exeter University. She vanished in Cheltenham on the night of December 27, 1973, as she walked to a bus stop. The Wests picked her up as they drove back from a Christmas visit to Rose's parents in Bishop's Cleeve, and over the next week they subjected her to a horrendous ordeal of torture and rape, ending with her dismemberment. On January 3, 1974, West checked into a hospital casualty department suffering from a deep cut to his hand—an injury now thought to have been caused as he hacked up his helpless victim.

Next of the known victims was Swiss-born Therese Siegenthaler, aged 21, from London. She had been hitchhiking to Ireland for a holiday when Fred West picked her up in his lorry near Chepstow. She was taken to Cromwell Street where she was imprisoned and subjected to a sado-masochistic orgy. Police eventually found her remains under a floor at Cromwell Street. Like

❝They subjected her to a horrendous ordeal of torture and rape, ending with her dismemberment❞

many of the other victims, she had limbs and bones missing—possibly hacked out by Fred West as gruesome souvenirs.

Another schoolgirl, 15-year-old Shirley Hubbard, from Droitwich, Worcestershire, was the eighth to be murdered. She vanished on November 14, 1974, as she traveled from Worcester by bus back to her foster parents' home. Fred wound one of his mummy-style masks around her face and pushed breathing tubes into her nostrils. Then he repeatedly raped her. Her body was found under the cellar floor at Cromwell Street.

Next to die in the Wests' torture chamber was 18-year-old Juanita Mott. Picked up as she hitchhiked into Gloucester from her home in Newent on April 11, 1975, Juanita was lured home by the Wests, tied with 17 feet of gray plastic clothes line and endured ligatures made from her own stockings. She was finally killed by a blow from a ball hammer, after which West decapitated her and buried her in his cellar.

The tenth victim, Shirley Robinson, was a bisexual 18-year-old who shared three-in-a-bed sex sessions with the Wests. Her fate was sealed after she became pregnant with Fred's child and fell in love with him. During the spring of 1978, Rose, who was pregnant with the child of a West-Indian visitor, began to feel jealous and put

For more than two decades, Fred and Rose's secret life flourished unchecked. To their neighbors they seemed an ordinary married couple.

pressure on her husband to get rid of Shirley. Fred later told his brother-in-law Jimmy Tyler: "Shirley is mooning about and hanging round me all the time. Rose just won't stand for it. She'll have to go." Shirley vanished on May 11, 1978. Her body was found next to that of her unborn child in the garden of 25 Cromwell Street.

A few months after Shirley's death, Fred and Rose latched on to 16-year-old Alison Chambers, exactly the kind of vulnerable girl they liked so much. She was a resident at a children's care home in Gloucester but visited Cromwell Street regularly to see a friend lodging there. The Wests asked her to become their nanny but soon after she moved in she became embroiled in their sadistic sex play. She was last seen on August 5, 1979, and was found by detectives underneath Fred's lawn.

The last known victim, Heather West, was also the one who first roused police suspicions about the Wests' family life. Fred made her life hell, administering vicious beatings when she refused to let him molest her.

She feared her parents so much that by the time she was a teenager she avoided talking in their presence. Heather disappeared on June 17, 1987, and the Wests told friends and neighbors that she had run away from home. The explanation was generally accepted—but this was one killing too far. Like many a murderer before them, over-confidence was their downfall.

In the summer of 1992, police constable Steve Burnside was walking his Gloucester beat when he was approached by a group of children who

> ❝She was found by detectives underneath Fred's lawn❞

claimed that youngsters were being abused at a house in Cromwell Street. They thought the family's name was Quest, and their warning was convincing enough to warrant further police interest. That same year, all five West children aged under 16 were taken into care and Fred and Rose were charged with a series of sexual offences, including rape and buggery.

Even now, they eluded justice. The case against them was dropped after two prosecution witnesses refused to testify. The couple hugged each other in the dock. Their ordeal, as they saw it, was over. Detective-constable Hazel Savage, of Gloucestershire Police, had other ideas. She had investigated the allegations and was convinced something terrible was going on behind the doors of number 25. In quiet chats with the West children, she first won their trust and then began to coax information from them.

The subject often came back to Heather's disappearance. Fred, said the children, would often make jokey remarks about her being "under the patio." To policewoman Savage's mind, the jokes were made a little too often to be simply the product of one man's poor taste. Early in 1994, she approached senior officers for guidance. At first they were sceptical and advised that much more evidence was needed but Savage persisted. On February 23, 1994, she obtained a search warrant and the following day police began digging in the garden. On February 25, Fred and Rose West were arrested. The secrets of the House of Horror were at last being laid bare.

Fred West never stood trial for his appalling crimes. On New Year's Day 1995 he hanged himself—a humane death by his standards. He was found shortly after midday in his cell at Winson Green jail, Birmingham. He had cheated justice but, in the eyes of many people, his final act was the only decent thing he ever did. Britain's best-selling daily newspaper, *The Sun*, summed up the nation's mood with their front-page headline: "Happy Noose Year! Joy as House of Horror killer Fred West hangs himself." His death sparked fresh revelations about the horrors of number 25 and caused a further influx of media correspondents from around the world. In Britain, however, the full story could not be published until Rose West had been brought to trial.

In October 1995 she went into the dock at Winchester Crown Court charged with ten murders in a trial that produced damning evidence—none more so that when Fred West's eldest daughter Anne-Marie took the witness box. She glared at her stepmother across the courtroom in a moment of sheer drama before summoning the courage to describe how the two of them had embarked on a systematic campaign of sexual abuse from when she was just eight. Anne-Marie's evidence on the following day was delayed after she took an overdose of pills. Finally, on November 23, 1995, the jury foreman announced that Rose West had been found guilty of all ten murders that had been linked to her. She was sentenced to life imprisonment and the judge, Mr. Justice Mantell, told her: "If attention is paid to what I think, you will never be released."

Soon afterward, police announced they were continuing investigations into the deaths of nine other girls who disappeared after visiting Cromwell

Police guarded 25 Cromwell Street from looters. It was eventually demolished and is now a landscaped footpath.
- - - - - - - - - - - - - -

Street. It has never satisfactorily been explained how there was an eight-year gap in Fred West's murderous career. The charges against him were that he killed 11 women and young girls between 1967 and 1979 before a gap until the disappearance of his daughter Heather in 1987. Experienced police officers believe that serial killers are not able to halt their murderous exploits for years at a time.

How many more died inside the House of Horrors? In October 1996, Gloucester City Council finally demolished 25 Cromwell Street. Today it is a landscaped footpath.

WAYNE WILLIAMS

The killings labeled the "Atlanta Child Murders" were a bizarre series of deaths that sparked two years of terror throughout the Georgia capital but which, even a quarter of a century later, was still causing controversy.

There are deep questions yet unanswered, not only about the police investigation into the slayings but over the conviction of the man accused of perpetrating them: Wayne B. Williams. For although the crimes were labeled "child murders," Williams was convicted of only two of the 30 homicides investigated—and those two murders were of adults.

The string of killings began in July 1979 when the bodies of two missing black children, 13-year-old Alfred Evans and 14-year-old Edward Smith, were found dumped along with a pile of garbage in undergrowth beside a suburban Atlanta roadway. They had both been strangled. Further young victims were discovered in September and November. The first female victim, a 12-year-old, was found tied to a tree with someone else's panties forced down her throat to stop her screaming. She had been sexually abused before being strangled.

Within a year of the first attacks, the number of victims notched up was seven—but that was only the start. From late 1980, corpses began to turn up in and around Atlanta, at the rate of one a month. All of them were young, not nearly strong enough to fight off an adult attacker. Their bodies were dumped in rivers or on waste ground, where they were chanced upon by passers-by. A pattern

FACT FILE.

Name: Wayne Bertram Williams, aka "Atlanta Child Murderer"

Born: May 27, 1958

Location of killings: Atlanta, Georgia, USA

Killed: convicted of two; officially blamed for 23 but still debated

Modus operandi: strangulation

Justice: sentenced to life in 1982

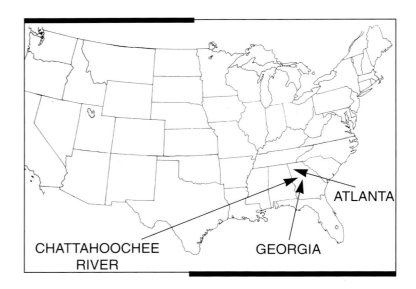

CHATTAHOOCHEE RIVER
ATLANTA
GEORGIA

emerged. The dead were aged between seven and 14, and all but two were boys. It seemed they were pounced on from behind by a man who used all his strength to squeeze the life out of them. There was evidence of sexual assault. Yet none of this helped the manhunt, one of the biggest ever launched in America.

Families began keeping their children behind bolted doors to save them from the shadowy, faceless fiend. When the number of unsolved deaths reached 26, the public were baying for justice. President Ronald Reagan was so shocked that he pledged a special grant towards the hunt for the killer. Singers Frank Sinatra and Sammy Davis Jr. and actor Burt Reynolds added their weight to the campaign. Yet months after the slaughter of the innocents started, there was hardly an iota of evidence to lead detectives toward the perpetrator. Determined officers interviewed 20,000 people in their bid to pin down the killer. A further 150,000 were quizzed on the telephone. A task force of 35 FBI officers were installed in Atlanta to flush out whoever was responsible. The investigation cost a small fortune, an estimated $250,000 a month. It was in danger of bankrupting the city. But it was all to no avail.

Bounty hunters descended on Atlanta, attracted by the bonanza of $100,000 reward money. Despite their eagerness to cash in on the string of crimes, no fresh clues turned up. Desperate parents formed vigilante groups to protect their families, arming themselves with baseball bats and patrolling the streets but failing to find a clue to the identity of the elusive killer. Police chief Lee Brown ruled out the possibility that the killer was a white man with a racist grudge against black children. A white man would be unable to mingle

The killings started in 1979 and ended in 1981 when Wayne Williams was finally caught.

with black children in playgrounds and parks without attracting attention to himself, it was said. Also, serial killers preyed on their own kind, so a white killer would target white children. It seemed a black serial killer was on the loose.

The breakthrough finally occurred in the early hours of May 22, 1981, as a team of officers kept watch on South Drive Bridge over the Chattahoochee River. Their quiet chatter was silenced by the sound of a splash only feet away from the spot under the arches of the bridge where one of them was standing. The team, comprising two policemen and two FBI officers, sprang into

Williams protested his innocence, but the killings ceased once he had been locked up.

- - - - - - - - - -

action. Two men plunged into the river but failed to find the cause of the splash. The others ran to the road and, after radioing for assistance, helped seal off the bridge. Shortly afterward, they came face to face with the man who would later be labeled the Atlanta Child Murderer—although they did not know it at the time. For one of the drivers stopped, questioned, and released that night was Wayne Williams.

Two days later, frogmen searching the muddy Chattahoochee turned up the body of Nathaniel Cater, a 27-year-old thief and ex-convict, who had been strangled. The body of 21-year-old Ray Payne, likewise black and choked to death, was hauled from the river a couple of days later. It was assumed that both had been thrown into the water from the bridge at the same time and that the Atlanta Child Murderer had broken his pattern and turned his deadly attentions to adults too. The police file labeled "Missing and Murdered Children" had to be retitled "Missing and Murdered People." The investigating team now took the obvious step of once again scrutinizing the list of drivers stopped on the bridge before dawn on May 22. Wayne Williams became the prime suspect.

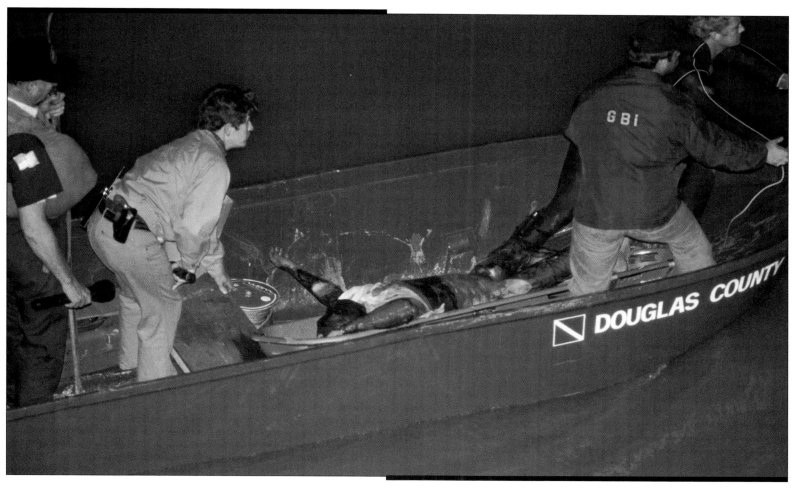

Police recover one of the bodies dumped in a river.

- - - - - - - - - - - - - -

Williams, a 23-year-old who lived with his parents in the Atlanta suburb of Dixie Hills, from where many of the victims came, was a curious figure. The only child of two schoolteachers, he dropped out of college with ambitions to become a pop music promoter. He kitted out the basement of his home as a studio but never achieved the fame and fortune to which he aspired. Instead he ran a local advertising agency while nightly manning the studio as a lonely radio ham, spending hours tuned into short-wave radio to monitor police and ambulance activity. When an incident occurred, he would speed to the scene, photograph the action, and sell the result to local newspapers and television stations. He had once been convicted of impersonating a police officer. Williams was well versed in the ways of the media for, after being pulled in for questioning, he hosted a news conference at which he declared his innocence. "One cop told me, 'You killed Nathaniel Cater. It's just a matter of time before we get you.' I never killed anybody and I never threw anything from the bridge."

Williams remained under round-the-clock surveillance while police desperately sought the evidence they needed to nail him. At this stage, they didn't even have a motive. The vital link finally came from the forensic laboratories, where scientists discovered that dog hairs taken from Cater's clothes matched those in Williams's car. It was claimed that hairs and other fibers found on vehicles owned by the Williams family further linked him with ten other victims. Williams continued to protest his innocence, however, pointing to the fact that two of the cars in question were not even in the family's possession at the time of some of the killings.

At the start of the nine-week trial, in which he was accused of murdering Cater and Payne, police became pessimistic that they would win a conviction. It didn't take long for Williams's talented lawyer, Alvin Binder, to rip the paltry evidence to pieces. However, a crucial ruling by the judge changed the complexion of the trial. He allowed the prosecution to introduce evidence which linked Williams with other victims even though he was not accused of their murders.

The prosecution, whose case had previously hung literally by a hair, were now able to paint Williams as a predatory homosexual. One witness testified that he had seen Williams holding hands with Cater a few hours before he was thrown into the river. A 15-year-old boy claimed that he had been fondled by Williams and that he had later seen his abuser with Lubie Geter, 14, a victim of the strangler. More witnesses told how they had seen Williams in the company of other victims.

In the dock, Williams denied being gay, called the FBI agents who interviewed him "goons," the prosecutor "a fool," and accused the police and witnesses of lying. He said: "I never met any of the victims. I feel just as sorry for them as anybody

> **‟I never met any of the victims. I feel just as sorry for them as anybody else in the world”**

else in the world. I am 23 years old and I could have been one of the people killed out there." It took the jury of eight blacks and four whites 12 hours to decide on a verdict. They must have also been mindful that while Williams was in custody, the string of killings had stopped. Williams, they declared, was guilty.

On February 27, 1982, Wayne Williams was led to the cells, tear-stained and still protesting his innocence, to serve a double sentence of life imprisonment. The Atlanta murder squad was disbanded after announcing that 23 of the 30 homicides investigated were now officially solved. However, it did not end the debate over whether Williams should have borne the blame for the entire string of Georgian slayings— or whether he should have been convicted of any at all. Many black citizens believed the state had manufactured much of the evidence to bring the case to a close.

So was there only one serial killer operating in Atlanta between 1979 and 1981? Or two? Or more? Many criminal historians tend to the latter theory. To confuse matters still further, evidence has since come to light that around the time of the killings the Ku Klux Klan was trying to institute a campaign of child murders in Georgia in order to provoke a race war. The debate over Wayne Williams's conviction continues to this day. But whether or not he was the Atlanta Child Murderer, all appeals for a retrial for him have failed.

RANDALL WOODFIELD

Randall Woodfield was tall, dark, and handsome. A promising student and accomplished athlete at Oregon's Portland State University, he was the leader of a Christian group of sportsmen and women and had already been given a trial with the Green Bay Packers football team.

Life held so much promise for him that it is a wonder he ever became a sex pervert and killer.

In late 1980, a string of robberies were reported along Interstate 5 through Oregon and Washington. Witnesses described a tall, strong gunman wearing a false beard who would blatantly wander into roadside stores, diners, and gas stations and demand money. At first Woodfield simply stole from his victims. As he became more unhinged, however, he turned to perversion and rape. His robberies would be accompanied by sexual assaults on staff and customers of the establishments he was raiding. He made one girl bare her breasts; another was forced to masturbate him.

Oregon was in a state of fear by January 1981 after he made his most vicious and perverted attack yet. He entered a house in the town of Corvallis and forced two girls aged eight and ten to perform oral sex on each other in their own bedroom before allowing them to go free.

One Sunday evening shortly afterward, Woodfield spotted two women cleaning a Salem office and forced them to perform various sex acts

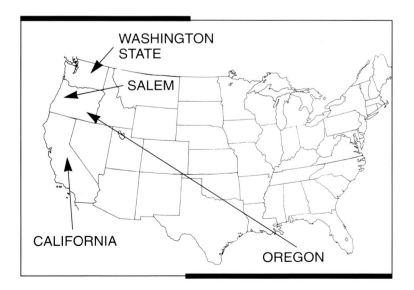

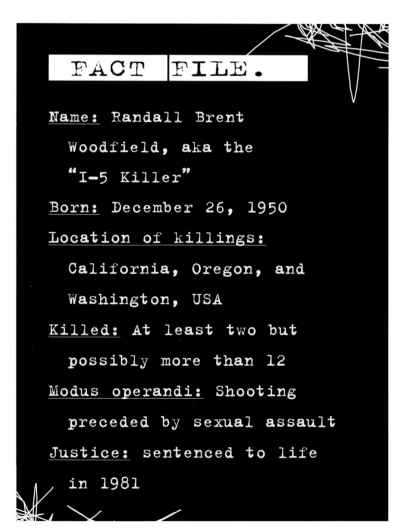

FACT FILE.

Name: Randall Brent Woodfield, aka the "I-5 Killer"

Born: December 26, 1950

Location of killings: California, Oregon, and Washington, USA

Killed: At least two but possibly more than 12

Modus operandi: Shooting preceded by sexual assault

Justice: sentenced to life in 1981

on him. Lisa Garcia and Shari Hull were themselves sexually assaulted, stripped, and finally made to lie face down on the floor. Woodfield then coolly shot Lisa twice through the head and Shari three times through the head. Neither of the girls was dead, however, and Lisa, with blood pouring from her wounds, managed to drag herself across the floor to reach a phone and call for help. Brave Lisa's description was ultimately to be instrumental in nailing her assailant. Tragically, Shari Hull died in hospital and it was then that police knew they were looking for a murderer, soon dubbed by the media as the "I-5 killer."

Woodfield next moved down I-5 to California where in Redding he concluded a robbery by sodomizing his girl victim. Later that day he sodomized both a mother and her teenage daughter before shooting them dead. Over the following weeks there were further rapes, assaults, and robberies. Californian police did not at first have the information to link the killer with any other murders outside the state.

When Woodfield moved back up the I-5 to Oregon, the attacks in California suddenly ended. Then came the murder of teenager Julie Reitz, whom he shot through the head at her home in Beaverton, a suburb of Portland. Police went through a list of local residents who might have known the victim's family—and who might have a criminal record. They quickly turned up the file on Randall Woodfield, a 30-year-old bartender.

Woodfield's records showed that he had been a bright college student who was headed toward a

> **❝Twice he was given suspended sentences for this perversion❞**

professional football career. So glittering did his future seem to be and so handsome was he that the magazine *Playgirl* chose him as a centerfold pin-up. But the picture never appeared and the signing with the Green Bay Packers never took place, because Woodfield's reputation was ruined when he was caught exposing himself in front of girls. Twice he was given suspended sentences for this perversion. Psychologists have since argued that his plunge into perversion was caused by the Packers rejecting him; his subsequent loss of status as a local sporting hero resulting in a need to dominate and rape. Woodfield was finally jailed in 1975 after robbing a woman at knifepoint and making her perform oral sex on him. He came out of prison in 1980, just before the attacks along I-5 began.

Following the murder of Julie Reitz, police knew they had their man at last. A search of Woodfield's home turned up clues that firmly linked him with the shooting of Lisa Garcia and Shari Hull, allowing charges to be brought instantly. Several victims, including Lisa, identified Woodfield and up to 20 murders up and down the Pacific coast were reinvestigated because they fitted the pattern of his sex-driven attacks. Although initially, Randall Woodfield was tried only for the murder of Shari Hull and attempted murder of Lisa Garcia, the further inquiries led to a later conviction of charges arising from his sex attacks on householders in Redding and Beaverton. He was sent to Oregon State Penitentiary with a life sentence and other penalties adding up to 155 years.

AILEEN WUORNOS

The first woman ever to fit the FBI profile of a "serial killer" was executed by lethal injection on October 9, 2002, the recipient of six death sentences.

Aileen Wuornos, aged 46, was pronounced dead from lethal injection in Florida State Prison, near Starke. Her last words from the execution chamber were: "I'd just like to say I'm sailing with the Rock (a Biblical reference to Christ) and I'll be back like Independence Day with Jesus, June 6, like the movie, big mothership and all. I'll be back." She had recently been judged sane, but she was far from sensible.

So departed "Lee" Wuornos, born in Detroit, Michigan, in 1956 as Aileen Pitman, the daughter of a psychopathic child molester who ended up in a mental institution and a mother who abandoned her at the age of four. She believed the grandparents who raised her were her real parents and only discovered the truth at the age of 13 after a childhood of physical abuse at the hands of her grandfather and of sexual abuse by young boys of the neighborhood. At 14, she became pregnant as the result, she claimed, of a rape. At 15, her

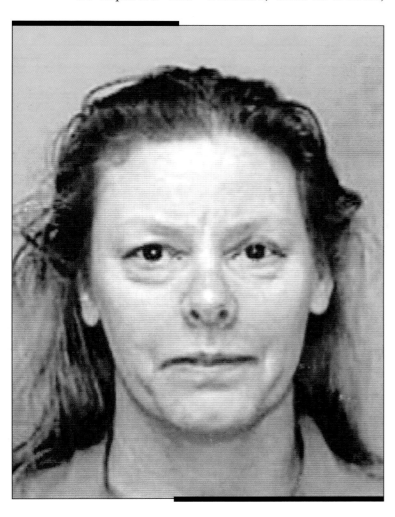

FACT FILE.

Name: Aileen "Lee" Carol Wuornos, aka the "Damsel of Death"

Born: February 29, 1956

Location of killings: Florida, USA

Killed: seven

Modus operandi: shooting

Justice: executed by lethal injection in Florida in 2002

Aileen Wuornos was sentenced to death even though it was later thought she was mentally ill.

– – – – – – – – – – – –

grandmother died and her grandfather threw her out of the house, calling her "a whore." Made a ward of court, she gave her son up for adoption immediately after birth and began a life of petty crime and prostitution.

The only close relationship she retained, with her elder brother Keith, ended in 1976 when he died of cancer. That same year, Wuornos was picked up while hitchhiking by a seemingly respectable, silver-haired Philadelphia millionaire 50 years her senior named Lewis Gratz Fell and they married soon afterward. She spent little time in his luxury condominium, however, and more time in bars and pool halls. When Gratz refused to give her money to fund her wild nights on the town, she beat him up. He successfully filed for divorce on the grounds that his new bride "has a violent and ungovernable temper and threatened to do bodily harm" to him.

At the age of 20, with a scarred face from playing with lighter fuel when she was six and a chip on her shoulder that caused her to explode into uncontrollable rages, Aileen Wuornos was back on the road: a drunk, a drifter, a petty thief and fraudster, and nurturing a hatred for men. Four years later, she walked into a gay bar in Daytona, Florida, and met 24-year-old Tyria Jolene Moore. They began a lesbian relationship that lasted four years, surviving on the proceeds of Aileen's prostitution. She was constantly in trouble with the law and on one occasion both were detained for attacking a man with a beer bottle.

On November 30, 1989, Wuornos put a

> **A drunk, a drifter, a petty thief and fraudster, nurturing a hatred for men**

.22-caliber pistol into her purse and began her brief but effective killing spree. For her first slaying, Wuornos flagged down video-repair shop owner Richard Mallory, 51, robbed him then shot him. His Cadillac was found at Ormond Beach, in Volusia County, with an empty wallet, some condoms, and a vodka bottle but no body. That turned up two weeks later in woods north-west of Daytona Beach. He had three bullet holes in his naked chest. By the time Wuornos's murder rampage was over two years later, there were at least seven dead, all middle-aged white men who had made the mistake of picking up the gun-toting hooker on the road. In each murder, Wuornos followed the same pattern of flagging down men who were driving alone on or near Interstate 75, offering them sex for money, then shooting them.

In May 1990, Sarasota construction worker David Spears stopped in his pick-up truck near Gainesville and was shot. In June the naked body of Charles Carskaddon was found north of Tampa with nine bullet holes in it. The same month, 65-year-old missionary Peter Siems drove north from his home in Jupiter, Florida, and vanished. His car was involved in an accident a month later in Orange Springs and the two women occupants abandoned it. In August a sausage deliveryman, Eugene Burress, was found in the Ocala Forest, shot twice with a .22 pistol. In September, retired police chief Richard Humphreys was shot seven times and dumped in a vacant lot in Ocala. In September 1990, truck driver Walter Antonio was

Wuornos's body is taken away after her execution.
– – – – – – – – – – – –

found blasted through the head and back in woods near Cross City. He was Wuornos's seventh and final victim.

Wuornos confessed to killing all seven men but when her trial opened at Deland, Florida, on January 12, 1992, the only charge on the indictment was the murder of Richard Mallory, her first victim. Wuornos said that she had killed in self-defense and that Mallory had been drunk and wild on marijuana when he tied her up, beat, raped,

and sodomized her. That excuse fell apart when Tyria Moore appeared as a witness for the prosecution and said that her lover had confessed to killing Mallory but had made no mention of being assaulted by him. Wuornos, distraught at her ex-girlfriend's betrayal, showed no remorse and there were several court outbursts. When the jury found her guilty, recommending the death sentence, she yelled at them: "I'm innocent. I was raped. I hope you get raped. Scumbags of America!" In the cells she added: "Everything they said about me was so full of lying. It wasn't funny. None of that stuff was true. I am totally sane. I didn't do drugs." When,

Protesters campaigned against Wuornos's execution, arguing that she was borderline "psychotic."

- - - - - - - - - - -

in later court hearings, further death sentences were meted out for five of her other murders, she screamed at a judge: "Thank you. I'll go to heaven now—and you will rot in hell."

During her ten years on death row, however, Wuornos became a different woman. A born-again Christian, she was at pains to come clean about her crimes and said she would welcome paying the ultimate penalty. In a letter to the Florida Supreme Court asking for permission to fire her lawyers and drop all appeals against execution, she said: "I'm one who seriously hates human life and would kill again."

In an interview with author Christopher Berry Deer for his book *Talking With Serial Killers* (Blake Publishing), Wuornos tried to explain her attitude to the clients she had killed: "I was really OK with those guys, that's the God's honest truth. But a few drinks and they thought I was cheap, started talking rough and dirty like I'm shit, man. I've had that all my life. Didn't need the shit; I'm a reasonable person. They wanted to fuck my ass—couldn't get that with their wives and stuff. They wanted to abuse and humiliate me. Despite what you think, I've got respect for myself. Always did have. Weird, right?"

In a 2001 TV interview, Wuornos said: "I was sentenced to death, and I need to die for the killing of those people." That was obviously her wish—but should it have been carried out? To the last, groups supporting Wuornos against her own wishes, argued she was "borderline psychotic." Her final interview, just days before her execution, was with British TV documentary maker Nick Broomfield, who said afterward: "My conclusion is that we are executing someone who is mad. Here is someone who has totally lost her mind." But Florida's Governor Jeb Bush, who had intervened pending a further mental examination, finally lifted his stay of execution after three psychiatrists concluded that she understood she would die and why she was being executed. Her wishes were carried out and Aileen Wuornos was pronounced dead from lethal injection at 9:47 am on October 9, 2002.

GRAHAM YOUNG

Graham Young had a lonely childhood, his mother having died when he was just three months old.

Initially cared for by his mother's sister, at the age of two Graham was sent to live with his father who had since remarried. After being torn from his first, happy home, the child would never trust anyone's affection again. Graham Young developed an eerie coldness toward the human race.

At school, he was different from his fellow pupils. While others his age played soccer and climbed trees, he preferred to tinker with his chemistry set. His interest was not confined to making smoke bombs or colorful explosions. He had a passion for poisons—and developed a deadly desire to try them out. Cutting himself off from the world, the lonely boy chose for his role models a number of infamous villains. He was fascinated by the activities of Victorian criminals Dr. Hawley

```
FACT FILE.

Name: Graham Frederick Young
Born: September 7, 1947
Location of killings: London
   and Hertfordshire, England
Killed: three
Modus operandi: poisoning
Justice: sentenced to life
   in 1972; died in prison
   in 1990
```

Born in 1947, Young had a troubled childhood, and he developed an eerie coldness toward the human race.

Fellow employee Jethro Batt nearly lost his life when Graham Young began working at Hadlands.

- - - - - - - - - - - - - -

Crippen, the wife killer, and Dr. William Palmer, the poisoner. Then at the age of 13, Graham Young read a book that was to change his life and seal his fate: about another Victorian medic, Dr. Edward Pritchard, who poisoned his wife and mother with antimony.

Young obtained antimony from a local pharmacist by lying about his age—and astonishing the chemist with his knowledge of poisons that he was using in his school "experiments." He began carrying a phial of the poison around with him

at all times, referring to it as "my little friend." The most obvious guinea pigs for Young's bizarre compulsion were his schoolfriends in the London suburb of Neasden. One of them became seriously ill after his sandwiches were laced with antimony over several days. When Young's stepmother discovered the bottle and confiscated it, the murderous prodigy simply switched to another supplier—at the same time turning his attention to members of his immediate family. In 1961, his sister began to suffer severe stomach cramps. Soon bouts of aches and agonizing pains afflicted the entire family. The symptoms continued to worsen throughout that year and the next. In April 1962 his stepmother died after terrible suffering. Her body was cremated, destroying all evidence of her poisoning. At 14, Young had committed the "perfect crime."

For some, that shocking event might have served as a stark reminder of the perils of playing with poison. Not for Young, however, who persisted in dosing the food and drink of his father and sister. Anxious experts finally diagnosed that they were suffering the effects of poison. Young's father had taken arsenic, they decided.

The reaction of his teenage son was breathtaking. "How ridiculous," snorted Young, "not being able to tell the difference between arsenic and antimony poisoning."

It was Young's chemistry teacher who uncovered the boy's murderous intent. Searching his desk, the teacher found drawings of people dying in agony with bottles of poison by their side. There were also charts of what doses of various poisons would kill a human being. The police were called in and, posing as careers guidance officers, interviewed Young.

He was swiftly taken into custody when police found sachets of antimony tartrate in his pockets. They were also aghast to discover that Young, although admitting affection for his family, was far more concerned with the outcome of his experiments than with their welfare. At his subsequent trial, the 15-year-old was found guilty but insane. His destination was the criminal psychiatric institution, Broadmoor.

After nine years, Graham Young, apparently now cured of his fatal fascination, was released. In June 1971, he applied for a menial job at the firm of John Hadland, makers of specialist, high-speed optical and photographic instruments in Bovingdon, Hertfordshire. While admitting to knowing something about chemicals, he did not confess his guilty past. Instead, he told how he had suffered a mental breakdown after the death of his mother. A psychiatrist's report produced on his behalf stated that Young had made "an extremely full recovery" from a "deep-going personality disorder." Young would "fit in well and not draw any attention to himself in any community," the report added. Young did slot in. His workmates made him welcome in his capacity as storeman. They shared jokes and cigarettes with him. In return, he became unofficial tea boy, happily furnishing them with hot drinks to repay their kindness.

Within weeks of Young joining the firm, staff began to be struck down with a mystery disease, which they nicknamed "the Bovingdon bug." About 70 people were affected with symptoms including diarrhoea, cramps, backache, nausea, and numbness. Head storeman Bob Egle, 59, one of Young's closest colleagues, was among the worst hit. After eight days of searing pain, he died in hospital. The doctors blamed broncho-pneumonia and polyneu-

Young gratefully accepts the job at Hadlands, where he poisoned other colleagues.

ritis. Meanwhile, other employees were still wracked with pain. By September, 60-year-old Fred Biggs was ill. His condition deteriorated over the weeks and, in November, he died.

Young seemed genuinely shocked and saddened by the death of Egle. He even went to his victim's funeral. When Biggs passed away, he apparently said: "Poor old Fred. I wonder what went wrong? He shouldn't have died. I was very fond of old Fred."

Meanwhile, many other workers were falling sick and there was a wave of panic in the company. Employees feared the chemicals they were using would cause them permanent damage. An investigation by the management included face-to-face interviews between the head of the inquiry, Dr. Arthur Anderson, and each member of the workforce. During his interview, Young could not resist revealing the impressive extent of his expert knowledge. The humble storeman asked the doctor whether he believed the illnesses were consistent with signs of thallium poisoning. Dr. Anderson was instantly suspicious. Young's knowledge of chemicals appeared too detailed for a layman. He wanted to find out more about the background of the young man who had been employed at Hadland just six months before.

Detective Chief Inspector John Kirkland, of Hemel Hempstead police, was called in and he in turn contacted Scotland Yard. Within hours, the full, sorry story of Young's past caught up with him. He was arrested on suspicion of murder. When police pounced, he was carrying a bottle of thallium—tasteless, odorless, and deadly. Young freely admitted his involvement, unable to let the opportunity to prove his skills pass. "I could have killed them all if I wished," he told detectives, "but I let them live." At his home, police found rows of bottles containing a variety of chemicals. They were stacked beneath the picture portraits of Young's heroes, Hitler and other members of the Nazi high command.

Young was accused of two murders, two attempted murders, and two cases of administering poison. Despite his confession to police, he denied the charges. His audacity was staggering. When incriminating entries in his diary were produced, he claimed they were no more than notes for the plot of a novel. A diary entry before the death of Biggs read: "I have administered a fatal dose of the special compound to F. and anticipate a report on his progress on Monday. I gave him three separate doses."

The jury at St. Albans Crown Court took less than an hour to find Graham Young guilty. He was

Graham Young as a 14-year-old fed experimental doses of belladonna and atropine to his family and schoolfriends. He became one of the youngest patients at Broadmoor.
- - - - - - - - - - -

sentenced to jail for life. Young did indeed spend the remainder of his miserable life in custody. In August 1990, at the age of 42, the arch poisoner was found dead from a heart attack on the floor of his cell at Parkhurst Prison.

ZODIAC KILLER

They are the serial murder cases that are the most difficult to solve—random and motiveless killings by a person unknown.

The classic case of this sort feature the ruthless slayer known only as "Zodiac." His brief reign of terror in the San Francisco area lasted for just a year, during which time he slew five people and wounded two more. The killings were followed by letters to newspapers, so gruesomely detailed that they could only have been written by the murder-er himself. Each letter was signed with a cross that was superimposed on to a circle: the symbol of the zodiac.

Although there is a suggestion that "Zodiac" had struck before, elsewhere in California, the first slayings attributed to him were of a teenage couple in a lovers' lane near Vallejo, 25 miles from San

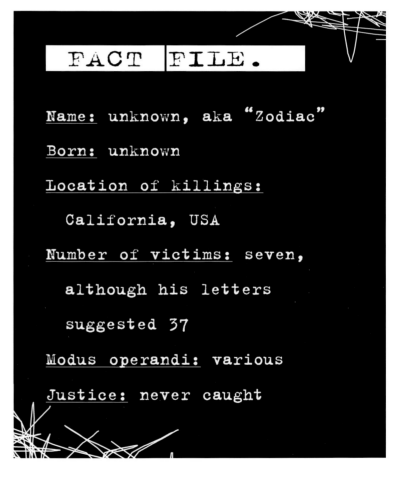

FACT FILE.

Name: unknown, aka "Zodiac"

Born: unknown

Location of killings:
California, USA

Number of victims: seven,
although his letters
suggested 37

Modus operandi: various

Justice: never caught

The brief reign of terror of the killer known as the "Zodiac" lasted for just a year, during which time he murdered five people and wounded two more.

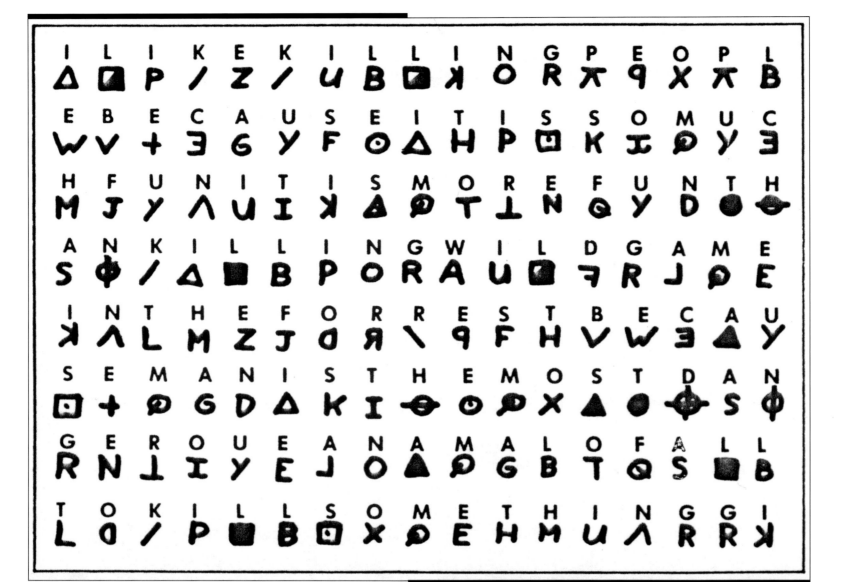

The Zodiac killer formulated a code which he sent to San Francisco newspapers.

- - - - - - - - - - - - -

Francisco, on December 20, 1968. High school students David Faraday, 17, and Betty Lou Jensen, 16, had been shot as they apparently fled from their car. They had not been molested or robbed, and there was no obvious motive for the crime. On July 5, 1969, a man with a gruff voice called police to report a double murder in the same area, adding: "I also killed those kids last year." This time police found 22-year-old waitress Darlene Ferrin dead and her 19-year-old boyfriend Mike Mageau seriously wounded. Their assailant had tailed the couple's car until it halted, and had then driven up alongside and opened fire without warning. The only clue to the gunman's identity was that Darlene had recently been pestered by a mysterious stranger whose name no one knew.

A month later, three newspapers received coded messages from the murderer, who threatened to go on a "kill rampage" if they were not published. Each paper complied, and when the three fragments were matched and decoded, Zodiac's message was found to read: "I like killing people because ... it is more fun than killing wild game in the forest, because man is the most dangerous animal of all. To kill something gives me the most thrilling experience. It is even better than getting your rocks off with a girl. The best part of it is when I die I will be reborn in paradise and they I have killed will become my slaves. I will not give you my name because you will try to slow down or stop my collecting of slaves for my afterlife." The message ended with further coded letters. Thousands of members of the public claimed to have cracked the clues and proudly sent police the results, but all leads proved fruitless.

On September 27, the gruff telephone voice of the Zodiac told police: "I want to report a murder—no, a double murder ... I'm the one who did it." The caller gave the location of the attack as the shore of Lake Berryessa, in the Napa Valley, where they found that two students had been stabbed in a frenzy of knife thrusts and were perilously close to death. Cecilia Shepard, aged 22, had been stabbed with a foot-long bayonet 24 times in her front and back and died in hospital two days later. Her boyfriend, 20-year-old Bryan Hartnell, with several bayonet wounds in his back, amazingly survived. He described the attacker as wearing a black hood with slits for his mouth and eyes. A bib extended down from the hood, onto which was a circle with an overlapping cross. He carried an automatic pistol, as well as the bayonet that hung from his belt. To further protect his identity, he wore dark glasses over the black hood. After the attack, the assailant daubed the zodiac sign on the side of the couple's white car, along with the dates of the previous slayings.

Three newspapers received coded messages from the murderer, who threatened to go on a "kill rampage" if they were not published.

Two weeks later, on October 11, Zodiac struck again, this time on the streets of San Francisco itself. Paul Stine, a 29-year-old student and part-time taxi driver, was shot through the head as he sat in a cab rank. Zodiac fled into side-streets pursued by two patrolmen and escaped in the wooded military reservation known as the Presidio. However, witnesses were able to describe a man in his forties, about 5ft 8in tall, with thick horn-rimmed glasses and crew-cut brown hair.

A shred of bloodstained shirt ripped from the cab driver's back was sent to the *San Francisco Chronicle* accusing the police of incompetence. The writer also threatened to wipe out a school bus. A man believed to be the killer rang the police four days later, offering to give himself up if he could speak with a famous lawyer on a live television show. Lawyer Melvin Belli stood by on a morning talk show as a record audience listened at home with bated breath. A man calling himself "Sam" phoned the show 15 times but the gruff voice was not apparent and police feared the caller was a hoaxer.

In November 1969 the *San Francisco Chronicle* received a further piece of bloodstained shirt, accompanied by a letter that claimed eight murders, causing detectives to search their files in vain for an eighth victim who could be attributed to the Zodiac. One of the letters complained: "I have grown rather angry with the police for their telling lies about me. So I shall change the way the collecting of slaves. [sic] I shall no longer announce to anyone when I commit my murders. They shall look like routine robberies, killings of anger, and a few fake accidents, etc. The police shall never catch me because I have been too clever for them."

At around midnight on March 22, 1970, Kathleen Johns, aged 23, was driving to her mother's home at Petaluma, north-west of San Francisco, when another driver flagged her down and told her that one of her rear wheels was wobbling. Kathleen, who had her 10-month-old baby in the car, accepted his offer to fix it but, instead of tightening the wheelnuts, he loosened them. A few yards down the road, her wheel flew off—and the driver was back at her side, this time offering

❝The police shall never catch me because I have been too clever for them❞

her a lift to a service station lit up on the horizon. She accepted but began to panic when he drove straight by the gas station and turned off into secondary roads and tracks, refusing to halt. After 30 minutes, he said: "You know you're going to die. You know I'm going to kill you."

Luckily, the kidnapper took a wrong turn and jammed on his brakes, allowing Kathleen to leap from the car and, clutching her baby, dive into a field where she lay until her thwarted attacker gave up his search. Rescued by a passer-by and taken to a police station, where she described her kidnapper as short, stocky, and in his thirties with thick rimmed glasses. Then Kathleen spotted a "Wanted" poster with a drawing of the killer of taxi driver Paul Stine. "That's him," she screamed. "Oh my God, that's him right there!"

Zodiac took credit for Kathleen John's abduction in one of his several letters to the newspapers. The letters—one claiming a total of 37 victims, another threatening that "something nasty" was about to happen—continued sporadically until April 1974. Then they stopped. So, it appeared, had the killings. Nothing further was heard from 'Zodiac and San Francisco police were left with an open file and not a single strong clue as to the identity of one of the weirdest, sickest serial killers who ever lived.

BIBLIOGRAPHY

The Butchers by Brian Lane (WH Allen) 1991

Celebrated Criminal Cases of America by Thomas Duke (Barry) 1910

A Century of Sex Killers by Brian Marriner (Forum) 1992

Chronicle of 20th Century Murder by Brian Lane (Virgin) 1993

Crimes of Horror, edited by Angus Hall (Hamlyn) 1976

Dead Ends: The Story of Aileen Wuornos by Michael Reynolds (Boxtree) 1993

The Directory of Infamy by Jonathon Green (Mills & Boon) 1980

The Encyclopedia of Serial Killers by Brian Lane and Wilfred Gregg (Berkley) 1995

The Encyclopedia of Serial Killers by Michael Newton (Checkmark) 2000

The Encyclopedia of True Crime by Allan Hall (Blitz) 1993

Encyclopedia of World Crime (six volumes) by Robert Nash (Crime Books) 1990

The Encyclopaedia of Executions by John Eddleston (Blake) 2002

A History of British Serial Killing by Martin Fido (Carlton) 2001

Hunting Humans by Elliott Leyton (Blake) 2003

Infamous Crimes That Shocked the World, editor uncredited (Macdonald) 1989

Landmarks in 20th Century Murder by Robin Odell (Headline) 1995

The Lust to Kill by Deborah Cameron and Elizabeth Frazer (NY University Press) 1987

Murder By Numbers by Anna Gekoski (Andre Deutsch) 1998

Murder Most Rare: The Female Serial Killer (Dell) 1999

Murderous Women by John Dunning (Arrow) 1986

On Trial by Frank Smyth (Blitz) 1992

Poisons and Poisoners by Michael Farrell (Hale) 1992

The Serial Killers by Colin Wilson and Donald Seaman (WH Allen) 1990

Serial Killers: the Growing Menace by Joel Norris (Doubleday) 1988

Serial Thrill Killers by Clifford Linedecker (Knightsbridge) 1990

Sex Killers by Nigel Cawthorne (Boxtree) 1994

The Sex Killers by Norman Lucas (Virgin) 1992

Sexual Homicide: Patterns and Motives by Robert Resller, Ann Burgess and John Douglas (Lexington) 1988

Talking With Serial Killers by Christopher Berry-Dee (Blake Publishing) 2003

True Crime: Serial Killers, series editor Laura Foreman (Time Life) 1993

True Crime: Unsolved Crimes, series editor Laura Foreman (Time Life) 1992

True Crimes: Lady Killers by Joyce Robins (Chancellor) 1993

True Crimes: Serial Killers by Joyce Robins and Peter Arnold (Chancellor) 1993

World Encyclopedia of 20th Century Murder by Jay Robert Nash (Headline) 1988

World Famous Gaslight Murders by Colin and Damon Wilson (Magpie) 1992

World Famous Serial Killers by Colin and Damon Wilson (Magpie) 1992

The World's Most Infamous Murders by Roger Boar and Nigel Blundell (Exeter Books) 1984

INDEX